DATE DUE

SIR JOHN BERKENHEAD
1617–1679

Sir John Berkenhead

1617—1679

A Royalist Career in Politics and Polemics

P. W. THOMAS

OXFORD
AT THE CLARENDON PRESS
1969

Oxford University Press, Ely House, London W. 1

GLASGOW NEW YORK TORONTO MELBOURNE WELLINGTON
CAPE TOWN SALISBURY IBADAN NAIROBI LUSAKA ADDIS ABABA
BOMBAY CALCUTTA MADRAS KARACHI LAHORE DACCA
KUALA LUMPUR SINGAPORE HONG KONG TOKYO

PRINTED IN GREAT BRITAIN

TO SIMONE

PREFACE

SIR JOHN BERKENHEAD is not one of those victims of time who have sunk without trace: over the centuries biographers, bibliographers, historians of the Press, literary historians, and plain historians have surfaced clutching assorted curious relics (and sometimes larger evidence) of his former fame for wit and loyalty. There may be nothing by way of tender or kind remembrance of him—perhaps he was too single-mindedly the careerist for that—but his reputation during his lifetime is plainly discernible. Contemporaries were delighted or exasperated by him, but rarely indifferent. For his was an exceptional propagandist talent in an age teeming with pamphlets and periodicals; and over a period of twenty years he exercised his skills with telling effect. Even in his other role as man of letters one discerns the publicist's knack of hitting off the consensus of opinion: that and his shrewd critical instinct won him the respect of the Cavalier literati. There is enough of Berkenhead visible to inspire a larger voyage of recovery.

Such an undertaking necessarily begins with the facts of his life and the canon of his works, so many of which were published anonymously. I have brought into view many of the formerly obscure parts of his career, and looked more narrowly at his political and psychological drives than previous biographers. And I have added very considerably to the bulk of work, particularly pamphleteering, attributable to him. This, incidentally, is especially difficult because so much material (jokes, phrases, attitudes, and so on) is shared by Royalist propagandists. I have, therefore, in most cases invoked corroborative circumstantial evidence; but I have not been afraid occasionally, and with due reservations, to speculate on the basis of stylistic resemblance and iteration of phrases used in his known works, when those parallels are sufficiently extensive and insistent.

Naturally I have taken the chronological sequence from birth to death as my scheme, though I am primarily concerned with the twenty years from 1643 to 1663, when Berkenhead was active in journalism. But my concern does not end with biography and bibliography: it has been my endeavour to raise the man complete, as it were; to observe him at work in his environment; and to present his works as points of response to a complex of circumstances. Inevitably a large part of my attention is focused on the confluence of things literary and political—a mingling which Berkenhead so fully and precisely personifies. The outcome is not only a fresh appreciation of Berkenhead's interests and qualities but also a new assessment of some of the period's major political and literary issues.

Not least, Berkenhead informs our understanding of the role of Laudianism, of Charles I's continued reliance on it in the crises of Civil War, and of its prolonged (though not, of course, unchallenged or uninhibited) vigour after the Restoration. Our knowledge of Restoration journalism, its attitudes and methods, is similarly enlivened. For the roles of editor of the official newsbook and censor of the press which he undertook for some three years after 1660 (while acquiring a variety of responsibilities, appointments, and honours) were not new to him. Twenty years before, he had made the King's Oxford newsbook, *Mercurius Aulicus*, his own, as well as his finest achievement. In every respect this was an official newsbook (the first ever published in this country), and Berkenhead made it the most sophisticated, amusing, and informative periodical of its day, stylish and entertaining beyond any of its rivals. Even his enemies confessed that he worked 'handsomly, like an Artist'. Nothing in the next twenty years, in fact, measured up to it. It was the cornerstone of Berkenhead's fame, and necessarily occupies a major part of my attention: the examination of its composition, production, distribution, and contents is, I believe, the most thoroughgoing analysis of a single newsbook of the period yet undertaken. But Berkenhead's opportunism was not confined to this periodical: in many of his pamphlets, too, he set the pace for contemporaries, continuing to intervene notably in the paper war until Cromwell's efficient supervision denied the press to Cavaliers.

Altogether, the significance of Berkenhead's closeness to the Crown and the full scope of his output and initiative are brought out for the first time. The necessary result is a revaluation of his place in journalism: his was an age when satire was used for the first time on the grand scale as an instrument of political warfare, and he looms larger than before in this corner of the battlefield. His successful example unquestionably did much to raise the status and improve the quality of journalism. He (rather than Roger L'Estrange, whom Dr. Johnson singled out for the honour) was arguably the first man in this country to make a career by putting his pen to party service. Berkenhead not unworthily personifies the coming of age of English journalism.

In such hands ephemeral work was not necessarily crude and shapeless. As an academic and friend of many men and women of fashionable accomplishment (among them William Cartwright, Katherine Philips, and Henry Lawes) Berkenhead was far from insulated from polite letters; and his propaganda discloses many of the sources of what became a great literary tradition. We see here something of the rapid evolution, in a changing environment and under extraordinary and sustained stresses, of a body of shared techniques, themes, and values—in short, of a viable satiric idiom. It provided the staple of Tory partisan writing well into the late seventeenth century and even beyond.

Berkenhead's quick repartee and smooth sophistry, for example, denote the movement towards clarity, ease, and urbane wit which culminated in Dryden. His characteristic manner is decidedly closer to 'fine raillery' than is the bludgeoning 'railing' of most of his fellow journalists, Cavaliers included. Samuel Butler is by no means disgraced by the mistaken attribution to him of pieces really composed by Berkenhead.

We see, too, how circumstances, by modifying tactics, moved Cavalier propaganda in important new directions: in the late 1640s and early 1650s the undeniable, if temporary, defeat of the Royalist cause seems to have persuaded at least some of the apologists to broaden their appeal; and out of this hope of tickling the popular ear grew a vogue for burlesque. Cavaliers' old familiarity with the Classics and their new intimacy with European letters were brought into play here. And Berkenhead was in the van as Royalist propaganda swung towards parody and the comedy of manners.

Once again we are reminded of how much the 1660s owe to the preceding decades.

The Interregnum years, in fact, far from being the waste land of frustration and inactivity that they are still often thought to have been were a time of continuing development for Cavalier literary theory and practice. With one foot in pamphleteering and the other in politer publication, Berkenhead graphically displays some of the reasons for this. He not only moved in fashionable 'circles'—I use the word with caution since it is, in my contention, a misnomer—but was also involved, as editor or composer of commendatory and other verses, in most of the major Cavalier enterprises of the 1640s and 1650s, including the Beaumont and Fletcher Folio, Cartwright's *Works*, and Denham's *Cooper's Hill*. Though manifestly no poet, he sharply focuses some of the leading tendencies of Cavalier writing. For the editorial, propagandist habit dies hard; and he seized every occasion to act as mouthpiece for the group's artistic ideals. What is more, he did so, and most emphatically, in the name of the Royal Prerogative. Advocating 'progressive' ideas of correctness, regularity, restraint, decorum, and propriety—and Dryden was later to recall his advocacy—he located their rationale in the political and social codes of the Cavalier gentleman. Because it is so explicit and insistent, his identification of literary standards with these codes explains not a little about the period's advancing Neo-Classicism.

So Berkenhead, for all his manifest limitations, is no negligible figure, no mere 'hack'. True, he had his shortcomings, some of them considerable: the group he spoke for was perhaps peculiarly exclusive, and its sense of propriety and dignity too easily lapsed into a sort of snobbery; attachment to the ideals of aristocratic culture was dangerously inclined to degenerate into cliquishness; and repressive instincts were too often flattered with the name of sense and sensibility. It is wise, too, to remember that Berkenhead wrote not for posthumous literary fame, but with precise and limited objectives which he often brilliantly attained; and one can hardly expect a propagandist at war to scrutinize his own party's failings publicly, or to temper his ridicule with much genuine sympathy. Yet Berkenhead's mockery of foes is not altogether nor always wrongheaded: there was a deal of time-serving, self-seeking, and mindless iconoclasm on the other side. He remains a caricaturist of invention and exceptional acuteness; and much that he wrote is still sharply and amusingly alive.

Because of this genuine talent, and because he so often touches the quick of Royalist life, Berkenhead deserves renewed attention. Repeatedly the inclination and achievement of his imagination make him a distinctive figure. His is a voice truly instructive and enlivening to any who are concerned to explore and define the special vigour and quality of Cavalier culture.

In order to avoid confusion the year has been taken throughout as starting on 1 January, not on 25 March as was common practice in the period. Despite their eccentricities the original spelling and capitalization have been strictly preserved in quotations from seventeenth-century sources, both printed and manuscript. Berkenhead's own spelling of his name has here been adopted: he will often be found listed in bibliographies, histories, and so on under 'Birkenhead'.

In the footnotes, page references only have been given for contemporary pamphlets and newsbooks, if they are unambiguous; when pamphlets or newsbooks are unpaged or the numbering is confused, the leaf signatures have been used.

ACKNOWLEDGEMENTS

IN its original form this book was an Oxford doctoral dissertation submitted in 1962. It has subsequently been revised, especially in matters of construction and expression, and is, I think, a little more sprightly than it was. But it is no less indebted than before to the help given me by more people and books than I can possibly mention here.

My principal sources were, of course, the pamphlets and news-books of the period, most of which are preserved in the British Museum's matchless Thomason Collection. G. K. Fortescue's *Catalogue of the Thomason Tracts* and F. Madan's *Oxford Books* were indispensable guides through the still part-unexplored territory of these ephemeral publications. I often had reason to be heartily thankful, too, for the pioneering effort of J. B. Williams' *A History of English Journalism* as well as the later, more scholarly, and comprehensive investigations of Professor J. Frank's *The Beginnings of the English Newspaper, 1620–1660.* For biographical information about Berkenhead and contemporaries I turned repeatedly to Aubrey, Wood, and of course, the *D.N.B.* My knowledge of events of the period is primarily derived from S. R. Gardiner's famous and, in matters of fact, still unsurpassed studies of the Civil War, Commonwealth, and Protectorate. In the matter of interpreting the nature and role of Laudianism I have leant most heavily on Professor H. R. Trevor-Roper's *Archbishop Laud* and R. S. Bosher's *The Making of the Restoration Settlement.* Without all these, and many others, I could not have found my way through the tangle of materials that confronted me.

I am, however, in some senses more deeply conscious of what I owe to the people who, one way or another, have had my interests and enthusiasms thrust upon them. Many libraries and librarians assisted me generously; but I want to single out the Warden and Librarian of All Souls; the Librarian of Corpus Christi; J. G. Griffith, Fellow of Jesus College; H. M. Colvin, Librarian of St. John's; and R. Drummond-Hay, Assistant Librarian of the Queen's

College, all in Oxford; and Miss H. E. Peck, Keeper of the University Archives in Cambridge. I received much help in sorting out Berkenhead's early life from the Rector of St. Helen's Church, Northwich, Mr. D. A. Iredale of Barnton, Cheshire, and, most of all, from Mrs. Marjorie Cox of Bowdon, Cheshire, formerly Lecturer in Modern History at the University of Manchester. How far I stand indebted to the staff and facilities of the British Museum and the Public Record Office scarcely needs stressing; but I should like to mention particularly my happy memories of the kindness and friendliness of the staff of the Bodleian Library.

The late Colonel C. H. Wilkinson of Worcester College, Oxford also has a warm place in my memory, much as he alarmed me at the time by his intimate and often eccentric knowledge of the history of the books and people of the seventeenth century, to say nothing of his expectation that I should quickly learn to keep up with it. His conviction that Berkenhead was worth studying first gave me my subject, and thereafter he was an unfailing source of information and ideas for new lines of investigation. Happily for me, his intuition was not found wanting by the Examiners of my thesis, Mr. Christopher Hill and Dr. John Carey. They first urged me to publish, and I have been much assisted by the advice they gave me. But I am particularly grateful to the Master of Balliol for his subsequent friendly and patient interest in the book, as I am to Professor Dame Helen Gardner, who very kindly read my text in its original and revised states. Her guidance and generous counsel have been invaluable to me. I am much indebted, too, to Emeritus Professor J. Heywood Thomas, who looked at the final draft, purging it of some of its defects, and in other ways made completion of the work possible. From a much earlier stage of things I recall the influence of Professor T. S. Clayton, now of the University of Minnesota, who was my contemporary in research at Oxford. His friendship, his fine scholarship, and his often devastating honesty have helped me more than a little. They are among the best of many good things that Oxford gave me. Finally, I want to express my profoundest gratitude to Professor H. R. Trevor-Roper, who succeeded Colonel Wilkinson as my supervisor. In large measure I owe this book to his greatly skilled and sympathetic direction of my research and to his continued advice and encouragement. My wife, parents, and friends will, I suspect, be relieved, if not surprised, that I have at last finished this project. But for all they have done to sustain me and it, I thank them most heartily.

The defects of the book are of my own making, as, I hope, are some of its virtues.

Dinas Powis
March, 1968

CONTENTS

ABBREVIATIONS

Ath. Oxon.	Anthony Wood, *Athenae Oxonienses*, ed. Philip Bliss, 4 vols. (1813–20).
Brief Lives	John Aubrey, *Brief Lives chiefly of Contemporaries*, ed. Andrew Clark, 2 vols. (1898).
B.M.	British Museum.
C.S.P. Dom.	*Calendar of State Papers, Domestic.*
C.S.P. Ven.	*Calendar of State Papers, Venetian.*
Fasti Oxon.	Anthony Wood, *Fasti Oxonienses*, ed. Philip Bliss, 2 parts (1815–20).
Harl. Misc.	*Harleian Miscellany*, 10 vols. (1808–13).
Hist. and Antiq.	Anthony Wood, *History And antiquities of the University of Oxford*, ed. John Gutch, 3 vols. (1792–6).
H.M.C.	Historical Manuscripts Commission, *Reports.*
Madan	Falconer Madan, *Oxford Books*, vol. i, 1641–50 (1912).
M. Aul.	*Mercurius Aulicus* (1643–5).
M. Bell.	*Mercurius Bellicus* (1648).
M. Brit.	*Mercurius Britanicus* (1643–6).
M. Publ.	*Mercurius Publicus* (1660–3).
P.C.C. Wills	Prerogative Court of Canterbury Wills.
S. Tracts	*Somers' Tracts*, 13 vols. (1809–15).

CHAPTER I

1617 to 1643

'*To win something of note*'

ON the day of his death, Thursday, 4 December 1679,[1] John
Berkenhead dictated his will and resigned his 'immortall soule to
the immortall God'.[2] He had been ill since early November,[3] and
John Aubrey[4] attributed his decline to the failure to hold his place
as Member of Parliament for Wilton in Wiltshire, which he had
represented for eighteen years. The electoral rebuff probably did
hurt the pride of this opinionated, confident man; and the inevitable loss of office must have threatened his pocket as well as his
self-esteem.[5] But it is unlikely that pique and depression killed him
unaided: ill health, brought on by overwork,[6] must have been the
major cause of his demise in his lodgings in Whitehall.

His will, though brief and business-like, tells something of his
manner of living prior to his unsung departure from the world. He
could afford a maid to tend him; he had a foot-boy; and he owned
property near Lincoln's Inn. No doubt he lived comfortably
out of the £3,000 that Andrew Marvell accused him of heaping up
after the Restoration.[7] Of course, he had accumulated debts too,
as even the well-to-do commonly did; and altogether he had
clearly conducted himself in a fashion befitting a knight, gentleman, and courtier in office.

He had not been born to this, however, and a more yeomanly

[1] *Ath. Oxon.* iii. 1205. [2] P.C.C. Wills, Bath, f. 15.
[3] Bodleian Library MS. Tanner letters 38, f. 97. [4] *Brief Lives*, i. 105.
[5] This and subsequent remarks on the method of advancement, style of living,
and burial of Berkenhead are based on general observations about men of such rank
by H. R. Trevor-Roper, 'The Gentry 1540–1640', *Econ. Hist. Review Supplements*,
i (1953), 16–17, and 27–9.
[6] See Andrew Browning, *Thomas Osborne Earl of Danby 1632–1712* (1944–51),
i. 311.
[7] *A Seasonal Argument* (Amsterdam, 1677), reprinted in *Hansard's Parliamentary
History*, vol. iv, 1660–88, App. III, p. xxxi.

canniness inspired his disposal of his own body: it was to be in-
terred 'without any pompe only some links to light the corps to the
Grave'. He was buried 'near to the School door' in the churchyard
of St. Martin-in-the-Fields, Westminster,[1] and though his executors intended to 'sett up an inscription for him against the church
wall'[2] no memorial survived the later demolition of the old church.
Unprofitable ostentation at the last obviously did not interest him,
but a characteristic circumspection oddly manifested itself: he
decreed that his body be laid in the churchyard to prevent its
removal from the church itself at some later date when room might
be needed for other, presumably more important cadavers.

The efficient practicality of this testament typifies the spirit in
which Berkenhead conducted much of his life. Its very omissions
are suggestive: there is no reference to the fairly substantial
library he left behind him,[3] nor is there any allusion to his own
writings. It is the will of a man who found his deepest satisfactions
in money and political success, not in literature or the life of the
intellect for their own sakes. He was no reverent contemplator of
life and death, but a hard-headed careerist. Fittingly, the friends
who drew up his will and acted as executors were lawyers; for the
administrative office which enabled him to acquire a modest estate
after the Restoration had involved him in legal practice. Yet he
was not wholly devoid of the softer virtue of gratitude, for his
largest bequests (of £40 a year) went to the master of Witton
church school which he attended as a boy and to the minister of
his home town.[4] This was tacit recognition that his career, like
that of many seventeenth-century office-holders, had advanced
through opportunities for 'rising' opened up by his education. The
other essential for advancement was a powerful patron—a factor

[1] *Ath. Oxon.* iii. 1205.   [2] *Brief Lives*, i. 105.
[3] Ibid. i. 106.
[4] Though Berkenhead's legacies are supposed to have been honoured (*Autobiography of Sir John Bramston* (Camden Soc. xxxii, 1845), p. 360) he is not mentioned
among the benefactors of Witton School by J. Weston, *Historical Notes and Records of
the Parish Church, Northwich* (1908), pp. 61 ff. Presumably the payment of debts
swallowed his estate. However, his name appears in a list of the feoffees of the school
up to 1722 (P.R.O. Chester 16, 122, p. 48). He was enfeoffed as a feoffee on 19 Dec.
1665, and again in 1669 and 1678 when new feoffments were made. This information,
for which I am much indebted to Mrs. Marjorie Cox of Bowdon, Cheshire, is conclusive proof that the bequest in Berkenhead's will was meant for Witton School.

the will does not acknowledge, unless it be in the pious concern expressed for the Church of England. For Berkenhead's great benefactor was Archbishop Laud, into whose mighty orbit he was drawn when, as a youth, he left school and home for Oxford University.

This involvement with Laud is the most important feature of the first phase of Berkenhead's life; indeed it coloured his whole career, and was not inappropriately called, by a contemporary, a conversion.[1] It had a radical effect on the direction of his growth; his mature political and religious stance was almost wholly acquired during his time at University. If he inherited from his father skill as a scribe, industriousness, and ambition, it was from the hand of Laud that he received the decisive training that fitted him out for service at the Stuart Court. Berkenhead's dying gratitude for his early education was, strictly speaking, appropriate only in so far as this had brought him under the eye of a patron who was working to revive the old system of aristocratic clientèles. From this distance in time it is plain that it was the Archbishop who turned the ambitious son of a small-town tradesman into a courtier who was to end his days in Whitehall. To see what this alliance—of longer standing and closer than has hitherto been realized—meant to Berkenhead one must begin at the beginning, in Northwich. The exercise will invigorate not only our understanding of the Laudian discipleship, but also the later investigation of Berkenhead's journalistic enterprises. For some of the talents and inclinations that flourished after 1643 did draw sustenance from roots in local and family life.

Northwich in Cheshire, where John Berkenhead was born,[2] stands about twelve miles north-east of Chester, at the spot where the River Dane runs into the River Weaver. Even in the nineteenth century it covered only about ten acres,[3] and before that in Leland's time it was simply 'a prati market toune, but fowle'.[4] In

---

[1] *M. Brit.*, no. 32 (8–15 April 1644), p. 240. The newsbook apparently based its remark on a misunderstanding of a remark of Laud's at his trial (see below, p. 18). The phrase is appropriate nevertheless.

[2] Not Nantwich, as in *Brief Lives*, i. 104.

[3] Ormerod, *History of Cheshire* (1882), iii. 154, 159.

[4] *Itinerary*, ed. L. Toulmin Smith (1907–10), iv. 4.

1621 it was a small but busy community 'crushed between Witton, Castle and Winnington', with houses, shops, market, and court-house clustered around the Weaver Bridge.[1] By then the salt industry, its chief business, had made it fairly prosperous. In this, among other things, John Berkenhead's father had a stake. Now Berkenhead was a name of antiquity and standing in Cheshire, and there were Berkenheads in Northwich from the early sixteenth century.[2] But the relationship of John's father, Randall, and his grandfather William, who married in Witton Church in 1573,[3] to their more exalted namesakes elsewhere in Cheshire is obscure. The only thing they are known to have had in common is that they were all dependants of the Earls of Derby. John's father and brother both leased property in Northwich from the Derby family;[4] and in 1652 the brother, Randall, was noted by the County Commissioners to the Committee for the Advance of Money as a former 'bailiff to the Earl of Derby'. He had apparently followed the Earl in arms to Lancashire in 1651, managed to escape in the rout at Wigan, and then taken his family to London where they were living poorly on a meagre estate of £3 or £4 a year and charity.[5] He had originally raised a foot company at his own charge—clearly the family had some substance—and served from Edgehill till the end of the Civil War, suffering many imprisonments, plunderings, and sequestrations. His loyalty, however, was seemingly unimpaired by these adversities, and he ultimately died from the effect of wounds received fighting for the Crown at Worcester.[6] His sojourn in

[1] D. A. Iredale, 'A Multitude of Interesting Anecdotes', *The Wittonian* (magazine of Sir John Deane's Grammar School, Northwich), Summer, 1960, p. 32, from material in the Lancashire Record Office.

[2] Ormerod, *History of Cheshire*, iii. 163 n.

[3] Witton Chapel Register, 1561–1678, f. 11ᵛ. No earlier Register has survived.

[4] D. A. Iredale, loc. cit.

[5] *Calendar of the Committee for Advance of Money, Domestic*, 1642–56, p. 103. Mr. David Iredale of Barnton in Cheshire kindly searched the muniments of the Earls of Derby for me, and informs me that the Berkenhead mentioned in the *Calendar* was Randall junior.

[6] *C.S.P. Dom.*, 1672–3, p. 104. This is a petition from his son, Peter Berkenhead (see below, pp. 7–8), chaplain to the King, for the place of one of his Majesty's preachers in Lancashire. Le Neve, *Pedigrees of the Knights* (Harleian Soc. viii, 1873), p. 162 states that Randall was killed at the Battle of Worcester in 1651. But Peter Berkenhead's Petition remarks, significantly, that he died 'at last' of wounds received there; and the Inventory of goods belonging to Randall was not drawn up till 1657 (see below, p. 6, n. 6.)

London is of passing interest because another brother of John Berkenhead's, baptized in Northwich in 1607, apparently took up an apprenticeship in that same city and was buried there in 1631.[1]

So, though the Northwich Berkenheads were a cadet offshoot of the county stem beneath the rank of gentry, they were not outlandish rustics with no notion of the world beyond their parish. Though plebeian they were not poor and might be expected to have inherited some capacities and some ambitions for their sons. Events proved this true of John's father, Randall Berkenhead, who was christened on 2 March 1581.[2] The next recordable event of his life, his marriage, escaped the parish registers; and the first evidence that he had taken a wife is the entry of the christening of a son, Thomas, on 25 December 1607.[3] This may not have been his first offspring: the boy who took his father's name and followed him in his trade[4] was probably the eldest son. Beyond the name Margaret[5] little is known of the identity of the mother of these and subsequent children. That name has led to the speculation that she was the daughter of Sir Thomas Middleton of Chirk Castle.[6] This, and an optimistic suggestion that she might be Middleton's sister, have been adequately disposed of by zealous investigators.[7] She appears as something more than a name in the will of Thomas Farmer, the fourth master of the free Witton Grammar School, who died in 1624. This was witnessed by her husband, described in it as an usher of the school, who was clearly a close friend of Farmer's. The latter was godfather to Thomas Berkenhead, mentioned above, to whom he left sixty shillings; but the most interesting item in the will is the bequest of £10 to 'Margaret Birchenhead',

[1] Witton Chapel Register, 1561–1678, f. 86ʳ.
[2] Ibid., f. 18ʳ. His name and status are given in the Matriculation Register, 1615–47, MS. Univ. Oxon. Arch. S.P. 2, f. 161ᵛ, and in *Registrum Orielense*, ed. C. L. Shadwell (1893–1902), i. 213.
[3] Witton Chapel Register, 1561–1678, f. 56ʳ.
[4] D. A. Iredale, 'A Multitude of Interesting Anecdotes', p. 32.
[5] Nuncupative will of 'Randle Birchenhead', proved 31 Mar. 1636, now in Cheshire Record Office. It is listed in *Wills at Chester, 1620–1650* (Lancashire and Cheshire Record Society, iv, 1881), p. 23.
[6] Le Neve, *Pedigrees of the Knights*, p. 162.
[7] See *Notes and Queries*, 8th Ser. v (1894), 288–9 and 395, and vi. 70; also *Miscellanea Genealogica et Heraldica*, 3rd Ser. ii (1896–7), 235.

'for many a dinner and supper unpaid for'.[1] For this confirms
Andrew Marvell's lofty jibe that John Berkenhead was 'a poor
Alehouse-keeper's son',[2] though the epithet 'poor' was somewhat
gratuitous. Anyhow, Theophilus Cibber hung on the fact a nice
hearsay tale[3] about the writer, to the effect that

> when an unmannerly Member of Parliament, in opposing him, took
> occasion to say that he was surprised to hear an alehouse-keeper's
> son talk so confidently in the House, he coolly replied, 'I am an
> alehouse-keeper's son, I own it, and am not ashamed of it, but had the
> gentleman who upbraided me with my birth been thus descended,
> in all probability he would have been in the same profession him-
> self'.

The boldness and sharpness of the retort are typical of Berkenhead;
unfortunately it has also been ascribed to his contemporary,
Colonel Birch,[4] who, starting life as a carrier, conveyed himself
ultimately into Parliament. Authentic or not, the story contains
the truth about Berkenhead's origin, as the will shows; and it is
appropriately confirmed by a record of a drunken episode that oc-
curred in Northwich one night in 1621. A Thomas Rogerson, the
black sheep of the district, overcome by thirst, 'raled alowd for
ale' beneath the windows of the Swan Inn, 'the howse of one
Randle Byrchenhead'. The disturbance attracted the vigilance of
the local constable, whom Rogerson challenged 'to fight yf he
durst'.[5] He was arrested. But his misdemeanour serves its turn by
identifying the house where John Berkenhead was, presumably,
born and passed his youth.

The inn was almost certainly the large house in the High Street
which Randall (father and son) leased from the Stanleys.[6] The

---

[1] For this information I am again indebted to Mrs. Marjorie Cox, who is currently working on a history of the Sir John Deane Grammar School, as Farmer's
school is now called.

[2] *A Seasonable Argument*, reprinted in *Hansard's Parliamentary History*, vol. iv,
1660–88, App. III, p. xxxi.

[3] *Lives of the Poets* (1753), ii. 180.

[4] See *Burnet's History of My Own Time*, ed. O. Airy (1897–1900), ii. 90 n.

[5] D. A. Iredale, 'A Multitude of Interesting Anecdotes', pp. 32–3.

[6] Ibid., p. 32. An Inventory drawn up in 1657 after Randall junior's death proves
he was also a publican. Exhibited 19 Mar. 1661, it is now in the Cheshire Record
Office, and is listed in *Wills at Chester, 1660–1680* (The Lancashire and Cheshire
Record Soc. xv, 1887), p. 316.

father's business interests, however, were not confined to the hostelry. He, with eighteen others, subscribed a Memorandum in 1634 confirming the local preaching minister's endowment at £10 a year;[1] and the money was derived from the local salt workings, in which the Berkenheads had an interest.[2] Apart from this, both Wood and Aubrey,[3] curiously ignoring the alehouse, describe Randall senior as a saddler. Aubrey claims as his authority for this John Berkenhead's brother (perhaps Randall junior), himself a saddler; and there was a relative, also a Randall Berkenhead of Northwich, who was a 'Sadler'.[4] It seems to have been a family trade, and one that combined naturally with that of publican.

These occupations did not, however, exhaust Randall senior's energies. He was also the Clerk to Witton Chapelry from 1630 to the end of 1633, when he fell ill.[5] The Witton Chapel Register shows that he wrote a good italic hand and was imaginative enough to adorn his records with some nicely executed Gothic lettering and ornamentation. Doubtless John Berkenhead acquired his own skill as a scribe from his father. It was to prove an important asset.

It seems, then, that Berkenhead's father was not exactly a run-of-the-mill publican; his close association with the local school best shows that. The free Grammar School, situated in the church-yard at Witton, was founded in 1557 by Sir John Deane, priest and prebendary of the parish of St. Bartholomew's in London, who endowed it with lands in the Wirral and houses in Chester, stipulating that if the revenue exceeded £12 a year the surplus should be spent on an usher or ushers.[6] It was to the building hard by the walls of St. Helen's Church, Witton, on an exposed brow of land overlooking the River Dane, that John Berkenhead went to be taught. Probably his father had him under his hand sometimes in the classroom as well as at home. The close family involvement with the school was maintained by Randall's grandson, Peter Berkenhead, who also acted as usher there from 1653 to 1656,

---

[1] J. Weston, *Historical Notes and Records of the Parish Church, Northwich*, p. 28.

[2] Ormerod, *History of Cheshire*, iii. 156.

[3] *Ath. Oxon.* iii. 1203 and *Brief Lives*, i. 104 respectively.

[4] Will, proved 11 Feb. 1678, now in Cheshire Record Office. It is listed in *Wills at Chester, 1660–1680*, p. 29.

[5] Witton Chapel Register, 1561–1678, ff. 89ᵛ and 96ʳ.

[6] *Notitia Cestriensis*, vol. i (Chetham Soc. viii, 1845), pp. 328–9 and note.

before proceeding to Christ Church in Oxford.[1] He was granted a
Lambeth M.A. on 23 February 1662,[2] having apparently been
appointed schoolmaster of Berkhamstead, Hertfordshire on 17
February.[3] Subsequently he seems to have been made Rector of
Stambourne, Essex on 4 December 1662,[4] and granted the living of
Somercotes St. Peter, Lincolnshire by the Crown on 11 June 1663[5]
—gifts in which his uncle, John Berkenhead, by then Master of the
Faculties, may have had a hand. Peter Berkenhead was later, in
1672, made one of the King's preachers for Lancashire, though the
appointment was apparently cancelled.[6] His career reflects the
influence his uncle had acquired. As one of a family which owed
Witton School so much, that uncle had good reason to support it
and remember it in his will.

If Berkenhead's manner of leaving the world was revealing, his
entrance into it has been more obscured by dispute. He was born,
his parents' sixth child, in 1617; but this is not the date usually
given by biographers. For some reason his birth was not at the
time recorded in the Parish Register; but later, possibly in 1869
when the old school building was demolished,[7] someone inserted
the date of his christening under 24 March 1616, attempting to
forge an old hand.[8] This date may have been extracted from
papers discovered at the time, but is incorrect. For Berkenhead
matriculated at Oxford on 13 June 1634, when his age was recorded
as 17.[9] The forger's mistake, repeated in the 'Life' in the *D.N.B.*,

[1] Information supplied by Mrs. Marjorie Cox; see p. 6, n. 1 above.

[2] J. Foster, *Alumni Oxonienses, 1500–1714*, i, p. lv (Mathews's 'Addenda', inter-
leaved in Bodleian copy).

[3] *C.S.P. Dom.*, *1661–2*, pp. 275 and 562.

[4] *46th Annual Report of the Deputy Keeper of the P.R.O. (1885)* (1886), p. 26, App. I,
Presentations on Patent Polls, 1660–85.

[5] P.R.O., E331, Lincoln 10 (Bishops' Certificates of Institutions to Benefices,
First Fruits and Tenths Office), and Institution Books. Sec. B. 1660–1721, i. 174ᵛ.
It is, of course, possible that there are two Peter Berkenheads involved here.

[6] *C.S.P. Dom.*, *1672–3*, p. 104, and E. Axon, 'The King's Preachers', *Trans. Lancs.
and Cheshire Antiq. Soc.* lvi (1938), 94–5. Mrs. Marjorie Cox kindly drew my attention
to these items.

[7] J. Weston, *Historical Notes and Records of the Parish Church, Northwich*, p. 51.

[8] A marginal note in the register, f. 65ʳ, reads, somewhat ambiguously, 'Fictitious
1869'.

[9] Matriculation Register, 1615–47, MS. Univ. Oxon. Arch. S.P. 2, f. 161ᵛ, and
Subscription Book, 1615–38, MS. Univ. Oxon. Arch. S.P. 39, f. 183ᵛ. The correct
date is also given in *Registrum Orielense*, ed. C. L. Shadwell, i. 213. Wood (*Ath. Oxon.*

was probably due to a misunderstanding of some note that he was born on 24 March 1616. This, ignoring the seventeenth-century habit of reckoning the New Year from 25 March, was misinterpreted. 24 March 1617 is the correct date of birth. So Berkenhead was seven in 1624 when Farmer died, and the master under whom he received his early education was Richard Pigott.[1]

Pigott was a friend of Richard Baxter, the zealous Presbyterian; and another of that persuasion, Edmund Calamy, approved of the schoolmaster as an 'able, prudent and religious man'.[2] Significantly, several of Pigott's pupils went on to his old university, Cambridge, and became Presbyterian ministers; and he himself, when headmaster of Shrewsbury School in 1647, was pronounced fit to be a member of one of the Shropshire 'classes'.[3] Because of his 'Puritan' sympathies he was ejected from that headmastership in 1662. So, though perhaps not violently anti-Anglican—three of his sons were ordained in the Church of England[4]—Pigott's sympathies were clearly never with the right wing in Church or State. And as he was very close to Richard Mather, curate and preacher at Witton from 1628 to 1640,[5] it seems that local churchmanship leaned towards what a Laudian would have dubbed 'Puritanical'. With a father who was acceptable to such men in the capacity of usher and Parish Clerk, it is unlikely that Berkenhead encountered pressures at home to upset this tendency in church and school; and, not surprisingly, there is no Berkenhead in the list of Papists and Delinquents in Northwich Hundred in May 1648.[6] Yet John's brother Randall fought for the King from the first. Probably the explanation of this devotion lies in local loyalties, in this case personal loyalty to the Stanleys; though it is not impossible that Randall was converted to Laudianism by his brother's influence.

Not all the family were as tenacious as these two; and John

iii. 1203) wrongly stated that Berkenhead matriculated in 1632 at the age of 17; and his error is repeated in *The Register of the Visitors of the University of Oxford from 1647 to 1658*, ed. M. Burrows (The Camden Soc. N.S. xxix, 1881), p. 473.

[1] Information supplied by Mrs. Marjorie Cox, see p. 6, n. 1 above.

[2] J. B. Oldham, *A History of Shrewsbury School, 1582–1952* (1952), p.53.

[3] W. A. Shaw, *A History of the English Church during the Civil Wars and under the Commonwealth, 1640–1661*, ii. 407.

[4] A. G. Matthews, *Calamy Revised* (1934), p. 389.

[5] Information supplied by Mrs. Marjorie Cox.

[6] *Calendar of the Committee for Compounding, Domestic*, 1643–1660, pp. 119–22.

Berkenhead's loyalty is best put into perspective by the behaviour of his brother Isaac. He first comes into view in March 1651, when Colonel Robert Lilburne, acting on Cromwell's orders, pounced on 'a knot of Royalists as they were embarking at Greenock for the Isle of Man'[1] to concert measures with the Earl of Derby for a rising in Lancashire. One of the prisoners was a Berkenhead, and, as Royalist leaders anticipated, terror loosened his tongue. His disclosures, together with those of one Thomas Cook, were a disaster to current Stuart ambitions.[2] For his kind confession Berkenhead was clothed at the State's expense and dispatched at the end of September to assist the authorities against the Earl.[3] Among other things he was to be a prosecution witness at the latter's trial. A loftier Berkenhead, Henry of Backford (the family seat in Cheshire) sat on this 'Black Tribunal'. He had joined the King in Shropshire in 1642, but like many of the country gentry he subsequently decided that his interests were better served by Parliament. Anyhow, 1651 found two very different Berkenheads united in hounding a former 'patron' of the family. The episode is not flattering to either of them, but on the face of it the humbler man played the more dishonourable part—though he had a hard choice between execution and confession and no one seems to have been outrageously surprised when he turned his back on martyrdom. Subsequently, S. R. Gardiner, the historian, laid this betrayal —for such it certainly was—at John Berkenhead's door.[4] It is a formidable charge and runs clean contrary to the latter's name for loyalty. But an anonymous letter of March 1651 in fact referred to the turncoat as 'brother to Aulicus',[5] and William (later Sir William) Dugdale in 1655 similarly identified the informer as John's brother.[6] Contemporary newsbooks[7] and State Papers[8] confirm

[1] S. R. Gardiner, *History of the Commonwealth and Protectorate, 1649–1660* (1894–1901), i. 406.
[2] See *The Nicholas Papers*, vol. i, 1641–52 (Camden Soc. N.S. xl, 1886), pp. 234–5, 237–8, and 290; also *C.S.P. Ven.*, 1647–52, p. 177.
[3] *C.S.P. Dom.*, 1651, pp. 417 and 447–8.
[4] *History of the Commonwealth and Protectorate, 1649–1660*, i. 406.
[5] H.M.C., Ormonde, N.S. 1 (1902), p. 166.
[6] H.M.C., 5th *Report* (1876), p. 176b.
[7] *Mercurius Politicus*, no. 70 (2–9 Oct. 1651), p. 1121 and no. 75 (6–13 Nov.), p. 1194; also *A Perfect Diurnall*, no. 96 (6–13 Oct. 1651), p. 1358.
[8] See above, n. 2.

that Isaac was the traitor. Gardiner was not often astray in matters of fact, but in this case other and lesser historians have been sounder than he was.[1]

Nevertheless, one editor of the Clarendon Papers accepted the tale that John Berkenhead was the backslider,[2] and identified him with a similarly treacherous Berkenhead mentioned by one of Clarendon's correspondents in 1653. This Berkenhead, 'sent to Denmark', had there done Parliament 'great service' by pretending to be a servant of Charles II.[3] The Danish King entrusted him with letters for Charles, but he carried them instead to Cromwell's Council of State. He followed this up by ensnaring some credulous Cavaliers who swallowed his tale that 'he would bring them to a parcell of his master Tho: Scots money, and share with them . . .'. Having lured them into a room in Lambeth, he locked them in, and 'fetcht a guard of red-coates to hurry them to prison . . .' Clarendon's informer lamented[4] that Berkenhead had

turned so exquisite a property to the present power, that his late masters do now themselves stand in awe of him; fearing (least to ingratiate himself the more) he bring some of them under the lash for their malignant whispers.

This double-dealing was, if anything, more deplorable than his 1651 about-turn; and it makes one suspect that that too was premeditated. It certainly blots John Berkenhead's copybook if he is the culprit. However, Thomas Scot, Cromwell's spy-master, mentions in his diary sending 'one Isaack Birkenhead' to Denmark where he 'ran some hazard, and gave some Intelligence'.[5] The stratagem was indeed daring, and it suggests that Isaac had been able to convince some Royalists at least that he had been an

[1] G. Ormerod, *Tracts Relating to the Military Proceedings in Lancashire during the Great Civil War* (Chetham Soc. ii, 1844), p. 313, n. 1; G. F. Warner, *The Nicholas Papers*, vol. i, 1641–52, pp. 234–5, 237–8, and 290, referred to in his index under Isaac Birkenhead; and W. C. Abbot, *The Writings and Speeches of Oliver Cromwell* (Cambridge, Mass., 1937–47), ii. 399, 479.

[2] *Calendar of the Clarendon State Papers*, 1649–54, ed. W. D. Macray (1869), pp. 206 and 218, referred to in his index under 'Sir John Birkenhead'.

[3] Bodleian Library, MS. Clarendon 45, f. 283ᵛ. The letter is dated 13 May 1653.

[4] Ibid., f. 487ʳ.

[5] C. E. Firth, 'Thomas Scot's Account of his Actions as Intelligencer during the Commonwealth', *Eng. Hist. Review* xii (1897), 121–2.

unwilling informer in 1651. That he was unusually persuasive is
apparent from the Lambeth episode, but that is also more sordidly
unscrupulous than his Danish enterprise. Double agents—and he
seems to have been one—need to be good liars and are certainly
mercenary. Their careers are also inclined to be short and not so
sweet; and in 1654 Isaac, his usefulness expended, was packed off
on his last journey, as Adjutant-General to General Venables,
commander of the English expeditionary force to the West
Indies.[1] Despite appearances, this was not much of a reward; for
dispatch to those parts was then often little better than a sentence
of death, as the high mortality rate among the troops shows.
Sure enough, Isaac succumbed to the climate and died on 29
September 1655,[2] leaving a trail of confusion behind him. It has led
to his brother John being unjustly accused of trimming his sails
during the Commonwealth.[3] That idea must now be abandoned;
and John Berkenhead's contemporary reputation for fidelity to the
Crown stands intact. Yet it will be seen that his character was not
unakin to his younger brother's:[4] at crucial moments in his career
he too knew how to be self-seeking, ruthless, and less than precisely honest; and a cool nerve was to serve him well.

The initial alignment of these three Berkenhead brothers behind
the Crown is, then, probably to be accounted for in terms of
special local ties, since it appears that doctrinally their home,
church, and school background must have inclined altogether
another way. Certainly there was nothing to shape a Laudian; and
the motivation of John Berkenhead's deep and prolonged attachment to that wing of the Stuart cause has to be searched out not in
Northwich but at Oxford. It was there that he really set his foot on
the path to favour, fame, and ultimately, some sort of fortune.
There Archbishop Laud dangled before him an unexpected prospect of advancement. It was unprecedented in that even the

---

[1] *The Narrative of General Venables* (Camden Soc. N.S. lxi, 1900), pp. 66, 122–3, and
125. It appears that Isaac typifies the rather low character found in many members
of Venable's army. (See S. R. Gardiner, *History of the Commonwealth and Protectorate,
1649–1660*, iii. 365.)

[2] P.C.C. Wills, Aylett, f. 196.

[3] C. S. Emden, *Oriel Papers* (1948), p. 62. He refers to the *Calendar of the Clarendon
State Papers* alluded to above.

[4] Isaac was born in 1622: Witton Chapel Register, 1561–1678, f. 73[r].

well-to-do Berkenheads had made their mark in the country, not at Court. Not surprisingly the ambitious young man seized his opportunities with alacrity.

It was apparently in October 1632, at the start of the academic year, that John Berkenhead entered Oriel College, for towards the end of that year he paid his fifty shillings caution money.[1] Many scholars from Witton School, including his nephew Peter, were financially assisted at University under the terms of a fund bequeathed by Thomas Farmer,[2] but there is no evidence that John benefited from it. Presumably his father could afford the caution money and provide sufficient for his subsistence. As a servitor, the lowest rank in College, consisting of 'students whose parents were below the then well-defined class of gentlemen',[3] he would live frugally and be expected to perform what would now be considered menial duties, like waiting on tutors and wealthier fellow-students. Servitors did not have their own rooms, but usually slept in tutors' apartments. In return they paid lower University and College fees than the more privileged undergraduates. This does not mean that Berkenhead was exceptionally poor or a social outcast; for between 1630 and 1640 sixty-eight such students, many of them children of parish clergy, entered Oriel College, against fifty-eight sons of more exalted parentage. Nor was there any question of them being intellectually inferior, as most College Fellowships were filled from their ranks. The rise of Berkenhead's friend, Thomas Barlow, to the Presidency of The Queen's College, Oxford, and the See of Lincoln, indicates that servitors were not barred from high academic and clerical honours. They have, in fact, been described as a relic of the great Church system, whereby men of humble birth were commonly elevated to important office.[4] On their way up, however, even successful servitors had to tolerate

---

[1] *Registrum Orielense*, i. 213. Perhaps this was the date Wood (*Ath. Oxon.* iii. 1203) meant to indicate by stating that Berkenhead entered Oxford at the beginning of 1632.

[2] *Notitia Cestriensis*: vol. i (Chetham Soc. viii, 1845), p. 329. Mrs. Cox informs me that Peter was a beneficiary.

[3] This quotation and the subsequent observations on the servitor's lot are taken from *Registrum Orielense*, i, p. vi.

[4] J. R. Green and Geo. Roberson, *Studies in Oxford History*, ed. C. L. Stainer (Oxford Hist. Soc. xli, 1901), p. 37.

minor hardships, and it seems that Berkenhead felt the need to augment his income by (as an opponent later put it) blowing 'the Organ bellows of Christ Colledge' for a fee.[1] Apart from this and the fact that his tutor was Humphrey Lloyd, later Bishop of Bangor,[2] little is known of Berkenhead's first few years at Oxford. He duly matriculated, though not until some time after entering the University: such a delay was not unusual in the period, and in his case was convenient, for when he did sign the books he was over sixteen and able to subscribe to the Thirty-nine Articles and the Prayer Book and take an oath to observe the Royal Supremacy. All this he did on payment of the usual modest fee of fourpence.[3]

As for his studies, the course at Oxford was still dominated by the old disciplines of Grammar, Rhetoric, and Dialectic. His later writings show that he acquired from it at least a competency of Greek and Latin, an admiration for Homer and Virgil, and no mean skill as a sophist. One of his journalistic enemies subsequently described him as 'being of his profession a Student in the Law, and very apt Scholler; hath learned very well, and is become as good a Scholler as his Tutors, & Professours, not onely in the Theorie, but also in the Practicall part', so that he had risen to be a 'learned Lier, and Master in that art . . .'.[4] Sarcasm aside, that evidence is confirmed by some of Berkenhead's pamphlets and his Parliamentary speeches after the Restoration, which reveal a particular knowledge of historical and legal precedent. Perhaps he originally set his sights on the legal profession, though he neither proceeded to the degree of B.C.L. after taking his M.A., nor entered one of the Inns of Court; if this was his original idea, his inclination was sensible, since education in the Law was the surest guarantee of promotion for men who had no hereditary claim to recognition. Anyhow, the Civil War interrupted Berkenhead's academic career; but he did eventually acquire professional qualifications of some sort when, at the King's request, Oxford granted him an honorary

---

[1] *Newes from Smith*, 5 Feb. 1645, p. 8. Presumably with the same thing in mind, *An Answer to Mercurius Aulicus* (of about 9 Dec. 1643), p. 4, referred to Berkenhead's 'Organist at Oxford'.   [2] *Ath. Oxon.* iii. 1203.

[3] For the facts about matriculation and the studies followed at this period see C. E. Mallet, *A History of the University of Oxford* (1924), ii. 320–5.

[4] *The True Character of Mercurius Aulicus* (1645), pp. 2–3.

D.C.L. on 9 April 1661.[1] It is a sounder compliment to him than the backhander just quoted, that he was judged to be a 'man wittie and well learned' by Sir John Bramston,[2] himself a successful barrister and brother to one of Berkenhead's executors.

Of course, Bramston may not have been thinking specifically of the Law, but his words serve as a reminder that Berkenhead had two talents especially useful to an advocate—quickness in argument (which many antagonists granted him) and a good memory.[3] One riled opponent suggested that Berkenhead could 'challenge one of the first places; if not the very first of all' among Oxford sophisters.[4] That was a way of saying he was the deepest-dyed in duplicity; but it was also half admiring; and it is true that, though Berkenhead's intellect was not deep, his wit was sharp and his manner coolly assured. He may never have had to exercise those gifts in a court of law, but they served him well in journalism and politics.

No doubt he tuned his wits before hostilities began in disputations with fellow-students. Under the Laudian Statutes[5] every candidate for the Bachelor's degree, after two years at University, had to respond and oppose at debates held in the Arts Schools three times a week in full-term. It was also a formality of admission to the degree that the new graduate should 'determine'—that is discuss and resolve—a disputed question, or maintain a thesis against an opponent. These 'determinations' were held in Lent, after the formal presentation for the degree; and Berkenhead's name appears in a list of 'determiners' for 1637.[6]

By then he had already found favour with his patron; and Laud's influence was to dominate his career. Ironically, it was not, it seems, debating prowess nor any intellectual feat that first attracted the Archbishop's attention; nor, as has been seen, was Berkenhead ready grounded in Laudian churchmanship, though he may have been drawn to it from the time he set foot in Oxford. It is

---

[1] *Fasti Oxon.* ii. 254, and *Ath. Oxon.* iii. 1203.
[2] *The Autobiography of Sir John Bramston,* p. 360.
[3] *Brief Lives,* i. 106.
[4] *The True Character of Mercurius Aulicus,* p. 8.
[5] For this see Mallet, *A History of the University of Oxford* ii. 323–4.
[6] Congregation Register, 1634–47, MS. Univ. Oxon. Arch. Q16, f. 122ᵛ.

well, therefore, to contemplate the capacities that may have won Laud's approbation, First, Berkenhead was temperamentally and financially indisposed to indulge in the debaucheries, common in Oxford at the time, that Laud was keen to stamp out. He had inherited his father's capacity for hard work; even his plebeian status had its advantages, for Laud's henchmen were often plucked from society's lower reaches.[1] Having no traditional privileges to rely on or to defend, they were commonly amenable to the Archbishop's discipline, not least because it opened their way to otherwise unattainable powers. Berkenhead had nothing to lose and all to gain from answering the call of his new master. But none of these considerations explains why Laud singled him out. The answer seems to be that he happened to have one talent that distinguished him from the run of aspiring youth—he could write a good hand. It was this that first engaged him to Laud: according to Aubrey,[2] when the Archbishop visited the University for the last time in late August 1636 he

had occasion to have some things well transcribed, and this Berkenhead was recommended to him, who performed his businesse so well, that the archbishop recommended him to All Soules' College to be a fellow.

This telescopes the actual sequence of events but is otherwise acceptable. It was, though the incident has previously been overlooked, very soon after that month of August that Berkenhead received his first favour. On 14 January 1637, he supplicated Congregation for admission to his B.A. degree;[3] the next day he was admitted;[4] and on 16 January Dr. Richard Baylie, Vice-Chancellor of the University, wrote to inform Laud, then Chancellor, that 'They got Birkenhead his grace for bachelor; this morning he is to be presented and has promised to deliver these letters'.[5] Berkenhead did not, however, complete the formalities for taking his degree in the normal way: on 28 February he appealed for permission to receive it *in absentia*, on the grounds that he was

[1] J. E. C. Hill, *The Century of Revolution 1603–1714* (1961), p. 69.
[2] *Brief Lives*, i. 104.
[3] Congregation Register, 1634–47, MS. Univ. Oxon. Arch. Q16, f. 14.
[4] Ibid., f. 212ʳ; and *Fasti Oxon.* i. 488.   [5] *C.S.P. Dom.*, 1636–7, p. 368.

residing elsewhere.[1] This supplication was accompanied by letters
from the Chancellor, so presumably the latter was responsible for
Berkenhead's absence and 'elsewhere' was Lambeth. This is not
mentioned by Wood or Aubrey, but a mere eight years after the
event Berkenhead's foe, Marchamont Nedham, then editing the
Parliamentary newsbook *Mercurius Britanicus*, was better informed.
As a former chorister of All Souls College, who took his B.A. in
October 1637,[2] he might have known personally of Berkenhead's
departure from Oxford in that year; and later, as a journalist on the
other side, he had reason to make Berkenhead's movements his
business. Altogether his evidence rings true when he reproaches
Berkenhead[3] with having been

once (to my knowledge) an amanuensis, that is, a Scribe, to one of
Canterburies Pharisaicall Chaplains. And swaggered some years in
Lambeth with an Italian Inkehorne at his girdle, such a one as the
Pope's own Secretary wears; and never transcribed anything but
what Mr. Lombard, and Mr. Leyfield first dictated unto him.

Lombard is untraceable; Leyfield was Edward Leyfield—his father
married Laud's half-sister[4]—who obtained a D.D. by Laud's
diploma some time around 1638 and was remembered in the
Archbishop's will.[5] It seems that Berkenhead was reasonably close
to the centre of power at Lambeth; and he was granted his M.A. by
Laud's diploma, doubtless a payment for services rendered. Anyhow, the Archbishop wrote to Oxford on 5 October 1639, requesting
that his protégé be admitted to the degree;[6] and the 'grace' was
granted on 14 January 1640.[7] College as well as University honours
were now coming Berkenhead's way: he had become a commoner of
Oriel, by paying another fifty shillings caution money, at about the
time he received his B.A.;[8] and on 14 January 1640, he became a

[1] Congregation Register, 1634–47, MS. Univ. Oxon. Arch. Q16, f. 15ʳ.
[2] See the 'Life' in the *D.N.B.*
[3] *M. Brit.*, no. 67 (20–27 Jan. 1645), p. 527; cf. *The Scotch Mercury*, no. 1 (5 Oct.
1643), p. 3. [4] *Fasti Oxon.* i. 427.
[5] Ibid., i. 513, and a copy of Laud's testament, Bodleian Library, MS. Add.
c. 304b, ff. 25ʳ and 27ᵛ.
[6] Congregation Register, 1634–47, MS. Univ. Oxon. Arch. Q16, f. 173ʳ⁻ᵛ.
[7] Ibid., f. 173ᵛ. In Wood (*Fasti Oxon.* i. 513) the date is misprinted as 'Jun. 14';
and the slip is copied in the *Registrum Orielense*, i. 213.
[8] *Registrum Orielense*, i. 227.

full Fellow of All Souls, having been elected probationer-Fellow in the previous year.[1] Again his sponsor was Laud.

To win such steady promotion Berkenhead must have pleased the omnipotent Chancellor. Nedham had no doubt that it was diligent boot-licking that won those 'laurels'; he mocked the years at Oxford and Lambeth as a time when Berkenhead learned 'to lappe the rudiments of Logicke and Popery . . .'.[2] This is manifestly partial, but it not inaccurately suggests the sort of devotion demanded by Laud, who found the habit of independent thought in others distasteful. *Britanicus* was also right to regard Berkenhead as one of Laud's converts,[3] though the remark was based on a misunderstanding of Laud's claim at his trial that he had won Berkenhead back from Popery.[4] He meant Henry Berkenhead, founder of the Professorship of Poetry at Oxford; but the onlookers, thinking he meant John, broke into uncontrollable laughter. Clearly Berkenhead's closeness to the Archbishop was notorious, and the feeling in London was that they were Papists together. The notion was tendentious, but 'conversion' was an apt word to describe Berkenhead's 'enlightenment'. Laud did reveal to him a vision—of an England transfigured, an Ecclesiastical State where, as a loyal proselyte, he would have a place in the sun.

This is the drift of many attacks on Berkenhead when he was editing the Royalist newsbook, *Mercurius Aulicus*. One opponent jeered at his 'university ambition wherein is included every mans hope of aspiring';[5] another better understood that academic recognition was only a means to an end—which was 'a Cassock, for hee does nothing but dreame of a Benefice, which the folly of the Court intend to conferre upon him'.[6] This was inexact, for Berkenhead

---

[1] Information supplied by Professor E. F. Jacob, from All Souls College Archives, Admission Book. Wood (*Ath. Oxon.* iii. 1203) states wrongly that Berkenhead was made a probationer-Fellow in 1640.

[2] *M. Brit.*, no. 70 (10–17 Feb. 1645), p. 549.

[3] No. 31 (9–15 Apr. 1644). At this time the editor was Thomas Audley. (See B. Williams, *A History of English Journalism* (1908), p. 224.)

[4] Henry Wharton, *The History of the Troubles and Tryal of William Laud* (1695), p. 226.

[5] *The Recantation of Mercurius Aulicus, or Berkinheads Complaint* (14 Mar. 1644), p. 5.

[6] *The Court Mercurie*, no. 10 (7–14 Sept. 1644), K1ᵛ; the same sort of accusation was made by *Certaine Informations*, no. 39 (9–16 Oct. 1643), p. 300; and *The Spie*, no. 7 (7–15 Mar. 1644), p. 49.

was never ordained,[1] but it aptly underlines ecclesiastical allegiance as a fundamental inspiration. A third foe, spreading his fire, landed nearer the mark of Berkenhead's true aim, which was to win 'a Lordship, a living, a Clerkeship, a Knighthood, or something of note'.[2] Something, anything—that was probably Berkenhead's ambition as he set about winning 'the itching ears of those who were entrusted with great honors in the Court . . . so to come to great preferment'.[3]

Cleaving to Laud in 1637, Berkenhead cannot have forseen how marketable his talents would become in the Civil War, with its thirst for propaganda pamphlets. To have imagined himself famous editor of a newsbook would have been impossible. But he must have realized that his stock might rise at Lambeth and even bring him to 'something of note' in political life. He was content, therefore, to detach himself from the centre of academic life, in order to drudge for a patron whose word was law at Court and University. His later success as propagandist confirmed his judgement; he never lost the eye for an opening nor his sense of where to strike.

The opinions, activities, and people he identified himself with at Lambeth can be deduced from a manuscript[4] which he later gave to his friend, Thomas Barlow. It was a holograph copy of Anthony Stafford's tract, *A Just Apology, or A Vindication of a Booke Entituled 'The Femall Glory'*, written in 1637 or 1638, but not published until the nineteenth century.[5] Stafford's ruthless disdain for Puritan feelings, his hysterical advice on how they should be handled, and his refusal to acknowledge the mounting opposition to the King and Laud reveal the uncompromising tenour of the ideas Berkenhead was imbibing. Because it shows that he forgot nothing of his lessons and remained inflexibly true to their spirit and letter, even in adversity, it is interesting to observe that he echoed Stafford's

[1] See below, p. 114.
[2] *Ruperts Sumpter* (20 July 1644), A1ᵛ.
[3] *Newes from Smith* (5 Feb. 1645), p. 8; compare *Anti-Aulicus*, (6 Feb. 1644), p. 2.
[4] For a description of it and details of Barlow's inscription proving that the author gave it to Berkenhead, see H. O. Coxe, *Catalogue of Oxford College MSS.* (1852), under MS. Queen's College 227.
[5] The best account of Stafford and of the two works mentioned here is by G. C. Moore Smith, 'Anthony Stafford', *Notes and Queries* clii (1927), 219–21, 239–43, and 431.

tract in his 1647 pamphlet, *The Assembly Man*. Indeed, the general
assumptions common to these works indicate the ethos of all
Berkenhead's satire.

Stafford's *A Just Apology* was hopefully dedicated to Laud and
Bishop Juxon of London, whose patronage he wanted. *The Femall
Glory*, extolling the virtues of the Virgin, had been furiously
attacked in a famous sermon of 1636 by Henry Burton, the
Presbyterian minister, for which Star Chamber punished him in
February 1637. Stafford's was not the last word on *The Femall Glory*,
for William Prynne, whose memory was long and, in this case, male-
volent, quoted from it extensively at Laud's trial in 1645.[1] To him
it was typical of the 'scandalous' books which Laud, 'with his
Chaplaines Agents, by his instigation or command, compiled,
authorised, imprinted, published . . . in defence of Popish Errors'.[2]
So Berkenhead's possession of the manuscript of *A Just Apology*
demonstrates his solidarity with the ultra-Laudians. But it tells
more than that too, if one asks how it may have come into his hands.
Prynne did not identify the 'Chaplaines Agents' who ran Laud's
propaganda machine, but Berkenhead was one of them. Evidence of
this appeared in London newsbooks in the 1640s where he is
identified[3] as scribe to Dr. William Bray, licenser and censor of
books to the Archbishop.[4] According to one editor he 'was brought
up' at Lambeth under Bray and did himself 'license bookes there'.[5]
In fact, Berkenhead did not issue licenses in his own name;[6] but
there is no reason to doubt that he assisted Bray in making works
fit for publication. This almost certainly explains how he came by
Stafford's manuscript. It also means that when he later licensed
Oxford pamphlets[7] he was in a sense continuing his Lambeth work.
Laud himself never succeeded in getting a grip on the Oxford
Press; and it is a nice, if neglected irony that his design was finally
fulfilled, albeit sketchily, by one of his protégés. It may seem a

---

[1] *Canterburies Doom* (1646), pp. 215–17.

[2] Ibid., pp. 185–6.

[3] *Mercurius Civicus*, no. 6 (8–16 June 1643), p. 46.

[4] See the *D.N.B.*, and the various references given in the index to Prynne's
Canterburies Doom.

[5] *Britaines Remembrancer*, no. 1 (1–19 Mar. 1644), p. 4.

[6] See F. B. Williams, 'The Laudian Imprimatur', *The Library*, 5th Ser. xv (1960), 101.

[7] Bodleian Library, MS. Add. c. 209, f. 4ᵛ.

small matter, but it is important because it demonstrates that during the period of the Court's enforced domicile at Oxford from 1643 to 1646, when it was fighting for its life, the Royalist propaganda machine was still linked with the policies of the prelate whose power had seemingly been destroyed.

At Lambeth, Berkenhead's position was humble enough, for though acquiring valuable experience of propaganda techniques he was still apparently only an amanuensis. Most of his scribing has perished, but a lead on some of it survives in a memorandum, once owned by Archbishop Sancroft.[1] It concerns various papers connected with Laud, formerly in the possession of his secretary William Dell. This memorandum is not in Sancroft's writing, but is endorsed by him 'A note of papers in the hand of Mrs. Hatton; given unto mee by Mr. Berkenhead'. A later endorsement identifies the latter as 'Sir John Birkenhead'. The natural assumption that the papers listed were in Mrs. Hatton's possession in Sancroft's time (the singular 'hand' frequently bore this meaning in the seventeenth century) is coincidentally supported by the fact that a copy of the first item in the memorandum (with notes transcribed from the original) turned up in the nineteenth century in the Manchester area, where the Hatton family once had considerable estates.[2] The memorandum, as well as being given by Berkenhead, seems to have been written out by him. He must have met Dell at Lambeth and might well have maintained the sort of connection and interest that would have furnished him with the information Sancroft wanted. And he was certainly in contact with Lord Hatton around 1649.[3] Moreover, the handwriting and method of compilation look like those of a trained scribe. Most surviving examples of Berkenhead's writing date from after 1660 and are in a hasty current script less tidy than that of the list; but there are some suggestive points of resemblance, to be found also in a 1645 specimen of his signature.[4]

[1] Bodleian Library, MS. Tanner 61, f. 243. It is reprinted in *Laud's Works*, ed. James Bliss (1847–60), iii. 259–60.
[2] *Laud's Works*, iii. 260.   [3] See below, p. 174.
[4] For a post-1660 specimen see B.M., MS. Harl. 7001, f. 289[r]; the 1645 signature is in the Bodleian Library, MS. Add. c. 209, f. 4[v]; the memorandum is Bodleian Library, MS. Tanner 61, f. 243[r].

Other problems raised by the memorandum are less resolvable. The identity of Mrs. Hatton is unknown, as is her connection with Dell; the most likely hypothesis is that she and 'Mr. Dells Lady' (mentioned in the memorandum as the probable possessor of the documents) are the same. A reference to Dell's death proves that his wife was a widow when the memorandum was compiled; and she could have remarried between then and the time of Sancroft's endorsement. The date of Dell's decease is unknown:[1] he was alive in 1645 when he fixed an inscribed plate on Laud's coffin,[2] after the execution on 10 January; but he seems to have been dead by the summer of 1648. For the memorandum refers to him dying while the compiler was in France, and there is no record of Berkenhead being abroad before that time, when he was in Amiens.[3] But as Berkenhead was in France subsequently this would only give an early limit. Unfortunately, the timing of Sancroft's endorsement is equally doubtful: all that can be said is that, as he refers to Berkenhead as 'Mr.', he must have received the paper from him before 14 November 1662, when the latter was granted a Knighthood. The list was, therefore, made some time between 1648 and 1662, possibly soon after Dell's death. At least one can be certain that the purpose of the compiler was to track down papers containing evidence of how William Prynne had blackened Laud's name by distortion and misrepresentation. It is, in this respect, of a piece with Berkenhead's observations on Laud's death in 1645[4] and with that enthusiastic loyalty to his patron's memory shown in speeches in Parliament after the Restoration,[5] when he frequently clashed with Prynne.[6]

Admittedly, there is no absolute proof that Berkenhead wrote the memorandum, but the accumulation of evidence pointing to him is too formidable to ignore. In turn it suggests a solution to

[1] For clarification of the confusions which have arisen concerning Dell's identity see H. R. Trevor-Roper, 'William Dell', *Eng. Hist. Review* lxii (1947), 377–9.

[2] W. H. Hutton. *S. John Baptist College*, University of Oxford College Histories (1898), pp. 172–3, implies that Dell fixed the plate on the coffin when Laud's body was translated to that College in 1663. It is more probable that it was nailed on when the Archbishop was first buried in London: for an argument to this effect see Bodleian Library, MS. Rawlinson D. 912, f. 541.

[3] See below, p. 164.   [4] *M. Aul.*, no. 101 (5–12 Jan. 1645), p. 1332.

[5] See below, p. 230.   [6] *Brief Lives*, ii. 173.

problems raised by some other manuscripts associated with Laud. The first is a copy of a Latin poem celebrating the latter's elevation to the See of Canterbury on 6 August 1633.[1] The author, it seems, was Greville Gibbes, eldest son of Sir Ralph Gibbes of Honington in Warwickshire. This manuscript, handsomely written and bound in vellum gilt, has been described as 'having all the appearance of an autograph'.[2] But it could equally well be a copy made by a trained scribe with a taste for coloured ink and exuberant ornamentation; and there are interesting resemblances to the hand in the Sancroft memorandum.[3] Possibly Berkenhead, who had recently gone up to Oxford, was employed by Gibbes to prepare a presentation copy of his flattering effusion. Perhaps this was how Berkenhead's scribal talent was first remarked by Laud. Anyhow, by 1636 his penmanship was known in the University, presumably because he had already practised it for profit.

Another coincidence points towards the suggestion that he produced the Gibbes manuscript: it has been observed[4] that the Gibbes hand is very like that of the unidentified amanuensis who wrote the inscription found in many of the manuscripts sent by Laud from Lambeth to Oxford at various times. This hand does not seem to occur in books of the first or second donations of 1635 and 1636 respectively; but it is found frequently in those of the two donations of 1639 and 1640.[5] The timing of this tallies with Berkenhead's removal to Lambeth, and it is reasonable to propose that he was the previously unidentified amanuensis.

Finally, in this round-up of manuscripts comes Wood's description[6] of a document 'written by the hand of John Birkenhead'. It contained

all the passages which concern the University of Oxon, since the said Archbishop's first Nomination and Election to the Chancellorship of the said University. It commenceth 12 Apr. 1630, and ends

[1] Bodleian Library, MS. Lat. Misc. e. 102.

[2] *Bodleian Library Record* vi (Jan. 1959), 516.

[3] See Bodleian Library, MS. Lat. Misc. e. 102, ff. 6ᵛ–7ʳ.

[4] *Bodleian Library Record*, loc. cit.

[5] See, for example, in Bodleian Library, MS. Laud Misc. 365. For the timing of the gifts see *A Summary Catalogue of Western Manuscripts in the Bodleian Library at Oxford*, vol. i, ed. R. W. Hunt, 1953, p. 128.

[6] *Ath. Oxon.* iii. 141.

on the 14 of Dec. 1640, and bound up in a Vellom Cover in fol. and endorsed by the Archb. thus, *Gesta sub Cancellariatu meo Oxon.*

Wood was shown this by Dr. Peter Mews, President of St. John's College, Oxford, and used it extensively when preparing his *History and Antiquities of the University of Oxford.* It almost certainly came to St. John's through a previous President, Dr. Richard Baylie: as Laud's kinsman and executor he was able to save a number of the Archbishop's papers from Prynne's clutches;[1] but this one could have been given him by Berkenhead, whose connection with him is known.[2] From St. John's it passed into Sancroft's possession —the 'triangle' of Laud, Berkenhead, Sancroft again—and thence to Henry Wharton, his chaplain, who was editing Laud's 'Remains'.[3] Wharton died before publishing the *Gesta,* which was printed in 1700 by his father Edward, Rector of Saxlingham in Norfolk.[4] It consists largely of letters to and from Laud, and shows that Berkenhead was involved in recording the Archbishop's history in order to justify his actions, well before the Sancroft memorandum was drawn up. Though untraceable beyond Saxlingham, this manuscript is substantial evidence of Berkenhead's work for Laud and buttresses the suggested identifications of his hand.

Above all, it indicates that he was close to the Archbishop and entrusted by him with substantial tasks as an amanuensis; and his promotion up to 1640 suggests that he may have been playing an even more active part as one of Laud's agents. Perhaps his delivering letters in 1637 was but one instance of a regular employment as go-between with the University. In 1640 he was certainly moving freely between Oxford and Lambeth: on 14 July he was in Oxford, presenting Thomas Stanley, the translator of Anacreon and editor of Aeschylus, for incorporation in the University;[5] in December he was presumably back in Lambeth at work compiling

---

[1] See the 'Life' in the *D.N.B.*   [2] See above, p. 16.

[3] Wharton's own account of how he got his manuscripts can be seen in *The History of the Troubles and Tryal of William Laud,* a2^{r-v} and b1^r.

[4] *The Second Volume of the Remains of William Laud,* where it is titled 'An Historical Account of all Material Transactions' and occupies 217 pages. It is reprinted from there in *Laud's Works,* vol. v, part 1. In this form the last date in the narrative proper is 4 Dec., for which Wood's '14' seems to be a mistake.

[5] G. M. Crump, 'Thorn Drury's Notes on Thomas Stanley', *Notes and Queries,* N.S. v (1958), 101–3, gives the presenters' names; *Fasti Oxon.* i. 516 gives the date.

the *Gesta*. But his days there were numbered. On 18 December Laud was at last pulled down by his pursuers and on 1 March 1641 was thrust into the Tower. Even then Berkenhead may not have left him: some servants accompanied the Archbishop into detention, and an opponent later mentioned Berkenhead's having been 'made Register to the Prelates of Oxford' after breaking out of 'the Gaole at London'.[1] Rival propagandists had by then good reason to regret the escape, if such it was. At most it can only have been a short incarceration, for Berkenhead was back in Oxford in 1641, when he gave two books to All Souls Library. The inscription in one of these shows that it had been given to him by Laud himself.[2] Clearly Berkenhead had been no anonymous underling in the Archbishop's household. For this and other 'gifts' he was soon to demonstrate his gratitude in devotion to the cause—a devotion that, however misplaced, was unmistakably sincere and courageous.

Meanwhile, 1642 found Berkenhead still in Oxford, presumably making the most of his All Souls Fellowship: on 24 February he subscribed to the Protestation imposed on the University by the Commons.[3] During this time he inevitably moved among the ardent Laudians clustering round Dr. Brian Duppa, the Archbishop's devotee and a former Vice-Chancellor of the University. Most scintillating of these young 'satellites' was William Cartwright, preacher and poet, praised of Ben Jonson and soon to be lamented by the King himself. Into his company and that of others in the 'knot of the choicest Oxford Wits always together'[4] Berkenhead fell. It is not really clear just how choice his wit was in 1642: true, twenty years later the editor of a work by one of the group praised Berkenhead lavishly,[5] but that cannot be taken too seriously, as it was by then politic to flatter the sole survivor of the 'knot', especially as he had influence at Court. The fact that Berkenhead

---

[1] *An Answer to Mercurius Aulicus* (about 9 Dec. 1643), p. 2. *The Scotch Mercury*, no. 1 (5 Oct. 1643), p. 1, similarly refers to a gaol-break.

[2] The inscription on the fly-leaf of *A Relation of the Conference betweene William Lawd . . . and the Jesuite Fisher* shows this. It does not mention Berkenhead, but the Benefactors' Register of All Souls proves it was his book. The other volume, now lost, was a copy of John Fletcher's *Plays*.

[3] *Oxford Protestation Returns, 1641–2* (Oxfordshire Record Soc. xvi, 1955), p. 114.

[4] David Lloyd, *Memoires* (1668), p. 425, note *b*.

[5] Robert Waring's *Amoris Effigies*, ed. William Griffith (1661); see further p. 176. below.

did not contribute to any volume of academic verse before 1643[1]
suggests that even if he sparkled privately he was not very interested in winning public laurels. Indeed, it seems that up to 1642,
when he was forced to come to rest in the University, he had not
involved himself in the 'normal' activities of a Fellow; and there is
no evidence that he had any inkling of his talent as a writer, soon
to be tested.

But now the Civil War was upon the country: with his patron
incarcerated and the Stuart regime fighting for survival on its own
terms, Berkenhead's prospects cannot have seemed altogether
bright. It must have been hard for him to know where to turn for
security at such a juncture; for the University was not in a position
to bestow favours on him as Laud had done. Yet even then circumstances were actually moving his way: soon the Court would
arrive in Oxford, transforming it into a political headquarters and
garrison. This was to prove a congenial environment in which
Berkenhead's scribal and publishing experience and his opportunism would win him his unexpected chance. Political struggle,
which raised and felled so many, was to bring out his best abilities
as a public defender of an embattled regime: it lifted him out of
obscurity into nation-wide renown.

When Laud fell, most of his henchmen scuttled away. Had
Berkenhead been the natural turncoat some sources hold him to be,
he must surely have followed suit. But just as he was one of the few
laymen in the Laudian group, so, too, his staunchness marks him
out. He was to prove the most tenacious of all the Archbishop's
bright young men. Arguably such devotion was in 1643 Berkenhead's
only hope, but subsequent events were to prove it far more than
merely expedient. And even in 1643 his eagerness to serve publicly
contrasts with the marked reluctance of Peter Heylin, another
Laudian who was offered identical opportunities as editor of the
Royalist newsbook. This is not to say that Berkenhead was a
paragon of virtue: his fanatical Laudianism issued ultimately in
inflexibility and an addiction to political cliché—though in that he
was not alone in the Cavalier camp, nor is it hard to find men who

---

[1] For the various volumes and names of contributors see Madan, nos. 726, 728,
731, 816, 840, 871, 931, 964, and 965.

match him on the other side. It does argue, however, the injustice of Wood's and Aubrey's accusations that Berkenhead was ungrateful to benefactors.[1] True, there are minor incidents in his private life which make some sort of sense of this; but his public conduct was, from a Stuart point of view, exemplary throughout. His loyalty, whatever else it may have been, was not dishonourable.

This, however, is not the moment to examine his conscience in venial matters. It is Berkenhead's attachment to the Laudian ethos that holds the stage at the close of the first act of his career. In the next he was to fulfil the promise that Laud had, presumably, detected in him: by the end of 1643 he was to be an established leading publicist for the Crown; and as acknowledged spokesman of the King and his close advisers he unflaggingly advocated Laudian doctrines. He was, however, no mere mouthpiece: the character and strategy of Cavalier propaganda owed much, as will be seen, to his shaping hand. His journalism is a notable feature of the political scene during the first Civil War.

[1] In, respectively, *Ath. Oxon.* iii. 1204 and *Brief Lives*, i. 105.

CHAPTER II

1643 to 1646
'Much applauded by great persons'

THE Battle of Edgehill and the fruitless chase by the King's army to Brentford in 1642 showed that the military struggle would not be resolved overnight. In August, with the Civil War gaining momentum, the members of Oxford University were called from their studies to drill. The flow of freshmen shrank to a trickle, the studious atmosphere was shattered,[1] and the energy of many of the Fellows was channelled towards the writing of prose and verse proclaiming confident Stuart defiance. Within the walls of Oxford there was shelter for troops and courtiers, there was plate for the melting to finance the military effort, and there were talented and devoted champions of Royal claims. Here, too, were printers well-equipped to publish manifestos to order, and good lines of communication with London already established. For Charles I, Oxford was in every way a happy choice of garrison not least perhaps because dignity and ceremony and tradition, as he understood them, were at home there.

The King believed actively in the power of propaganda: [2]after he fled from London he carried printing presses with him into the north Midlands and the Welsh Borders, and kept them busy presenting his case to the nation.[3] It has been suggested that there was even a Royalist press at Edgehill.[4] Be that as it may, Charles

[1] C. E. Mallet, *A History of the University of Oxford*, ii. 350–60.

[2] *Burnet's History of My Own Time*, i. 80–1; and *The Life of Edward Earl of Clarendon* (1817), i. 104–5 and 116.

[3] See J. H. Hinde, 'On Early Printing in Newcastle', *Archaeologia Aeliana*, N.S. vi (1865), 225–6; and L. Hanson, 'The King's Printer at York and Shrewsbury, 1642–3', *The Library*, 4th Ser. xxiii (1943), 129–31. The latter refers to important earlier studies of this topic.

[4] Percy Simpson, *Proof Reading in the Sixteenth, Seventeenth and Eighteenth Centuries* (1935), p. 232.

certainly brought the press to the provinces for the first time in some fifty years.[1] In 1643 this determination to fight with pen as well as the sword, which was shared by the King's advisers,[2] inspired a major new phase in the history of English journalism.

The spearhead of Royalist propaganda was the newsbook, *Mercurius Aulicus*, a small quarto publication of either four, six, or eight leaves. It appeared normally once a week, being composed on Sunday and published, probably, on Monday. Each number contained military and political intelligence received at Court during the preceding seven days, with reports arranged according to the date of their arrival in Oxford. *Aulicus* ran from 1–7 January 1643, until 31 August–7 September 1645;[3] but there were gaps in the sequence in late 1644 and in 1645, so that in all 118 numbers were produced. These lapses, and the decline in the newsbook's general efficiency, must be examined later, for they were more extensive than has been realized, and the measures taken to overcome them are striking proof of the Court's determination to keep *Aulicus* running.[4] A high value was placed on its effect on public opinion and loyalist morale. *Aulicus* was emphatically not a printer's private enterprise, as all newsbooks in England before its time had been; nor was the editor solely dependent on his own resources. Material was contributed by many in academic and Court circles; views and information were supplied by the ruling junto, which also directly sponsored the newsbook's publication and distribution. Its circulation was more extensive and its standing in public esteem was far higher than has been commonly imagined; for it was authoritative and thorough to a degree not approached by earlier English periodicals, and rivalled by few, if any, of its contemporaries. It is a worthy claimant to the place it must now be granted as England's first official newsbook.[5]

---

[1] E. G. Duff, 'The Printers, Stationers, and Bookbinders of York up to 1600', *Transactions of the Bibliographical Soc.*, v (1898–1900), 106.

[2] Donald Nicholas, *Mr. Secretary Nicholas (1593–1649)* (1955), p. 176.

[3] Corpus Christi College, Oxford and the British Museum possess complete sets of the newsbook. A volume of summarized extracts was published by F. J. Varley in 1948 under the title *Mercurius Aulicus*.

[4] See App. I.

[5] J. B. Williams, *History of English Journalism*, pp. 10 and 157, wrongly grants this title to newsbooks written by Marchamont Nedham for Oliver Cromwell.

This, then, was the most influential work on which John Berkenhead was ever engaged: it made his name and set the pace for
English journalism for some twenty years. It is important, therefore, to discover the extent of his responsibility for the character of
Aulicus. That he won Royal favour and national repute as its
editor is not surprising; but how and why he came to be chosen for
that duty has never been explained. As will be seen, he was not,
contrary to accepted belief, the first editor; and he was not so much
chosen as allowed (in the best Tory tradition) to emerge from the
ranks. He proved himself well worthy of the chance he was offered;
and as variations in *Aulicus*'s quality show, he rapidly became its
most resourceful and effective composer. Its characteristic excel-
lences and its greatest successes, its best wit and its shrewdest
attacks, were inspired primarily by him.

Aulicus's first editor

That Berkenhead edited *Aulicus* was widely recognized by
contemporaries, including Aubrey[1] and Wood: the latter vehemently asserted that 'all that were then in Oxford knew that John
Berkenhead began, and carried them on'.[2] This is confirmed in the
description of Berkenhead by a personal acquaintance as the man
who 'writ the Mercurius Aulicus'.[3] All these statements date from
some years after the event; but as early as June 1643 a rival journa-
listi dentified *Aulicus*'s editor as a Fellow of All Souls College, and in
July named him as 'Master Berkenhead'.[4] These facts were subsequently repeated in at least five other London newsbooks and
one pamphlet.[5] In most eyes 'Berkenhead' was virtually synony-
mous with *Mercurius Aulicus.*

---

[1] *Brief Lives,* i. 104.   [2] *Ath. Oxon.* iii. 1204.
[3] *Autobiography of Sir John Bramston,* p. 359.
[4] *Mercurius Civicus,* no. 5 (1–8 June 1643), p. 34, and no. 6 (8–15 June 1643),
p. 46 respectively. In the first of these the writer assumed wrongly that Berkenhead
had been a chaplain to Laud.
[5] *Certaine Informations,* no. 37 (25 Sept.–2 Oct. 1643), p. 287 names him and gives
a brief outline of his career to date. See also *M. Brit.,* no. 6 (26 Sept.–3 Oct. 1643),
p. 46; no. 11 (2–9 Nov.), p. 85; no. 13 (16–23 Nov.), p. 100; no. 31 (8–15 Apr.
1644), p. 240; no. 67 (20–27 Jan. 1645), p. 527; and no. 99 (22–29 Sept.), p. 881; *The
Welch Mercurie,* no. 1 (21–28 Oct. 1643), p. 7; *The Spie,* no. 4 (13–20 Feb. 1644), p.
27; and no. 17 (15–22 May), p. 131; and *The Kingdomes Weekly Post,* (28 Oct. 1645),
p. 17. The pamphlet is *The Devills White Boyes,* (26 Oct. 1644), p. 8.

Yet, although associated with academics to whom the King would naturally have turned for 'vocal' support, Berkenhead had given no sign of possessing literary capacities fitting him for this important job. His rise to fame—so rapid that it affected Wood's memory of the sequence of events—was actually facilitated by two less spectacular factors: his scribal skill and his Lambeth apprenticeship. These led the actual first editor of *Aulicus* to employ him as an assistant. That first editor was another Laudian, a proven writer and controversialist, Dr. Peter Heylin.

Oddly enough, with the possible exception of one pamphlet in July 1644,[1] none of the Londoners ever alluded to Heylin's association with the newsbook. Even that pamphleteer may have been thinking of one of the occasions on which Heylin had to edit *Aulicus* without Berkenhead's assistance. This, according to Wood, happened twice: first in August and September 1643, and later in June 'and so forward, 1644 (when Birkenhead went with the King to Worcester)'.[2] Stylistic changes around these dates confirm that Heylin alone composed numbers 30 to 38, ranging from 23–29 July until 17–23 September 1643, and numbers 74 to 77, running from 26 May–1 June until 16–22 June 1644. Heylin himself admitted that he wrote the last four,[3] so Wood was probably right also about the first group. He did not suggest why Berkenhead stopped writing during August and September 1643, but that may also have been because he was out of Oxford.[4]

It is strange that Wood, knowing so much, should have insisted that Berkenhead began *Aulicus* and that Heylin merely took over from him on those two occasions.[5] Maybe it was a belated riposte to *Britanicus*'s accusation that, by the end of September 1643, the task of producing *Aulicus* had proved too great for one man. Wood must have had a vested interest, in fact, in simplifying the picture of its origins: for Heylin, in a brief account of his own life which Wood had read, indicates that, up to the end of

---

[1] *Ruperts Sumpter* (20 July 1644), A1ᵛ. Even this might refer to Duppa, whose name was frequently associated with *Aulicus* by London journalists.

[2] *Hist. and Antiq.* ii. 461.

[3] See his diary, printed as a preface to his *Memorial of Bishop Waynflete*, (Caxton Soc. 1851), p. xxiii.

[4] For more on this absence see p. 109 below.

[5] *Ath. Oxon.* iii. 556.

September 1643, he was principal editor. Under the 27th of that month he wrote in his diary:[1]

> I cleared myself of my employment under Secretary (in writing Merc. Aulic.) which was committed to Mr. Berkenhead, who had of late so interlaced his expressions and intelligences that I could hardly call it mine.

This cannot refer to the August and September numbers, and it must be concluded that Heylin was really chosen as editor in the first place. His biographer, George Vernon, confirms this in his statement[2] that Heylin was summoned to Oxford to speak with Secretary of State Edward Nicholas,

> from whom he was to take directions for some special and important Service; which was at last signified to Dr. Heylyn under the Kings own hand, viz. to write the Weekly Occurrences which befel his Majesties Government and Armies.

Vernon described him as very unwilling to undertake this task—a notion certainly borne out by the tone of Heylin's own remark. But he acquiesced and persevered until 'he had made it facile by his own diligence and example'.[3] Vernon obviously used as his source the diary that Wood saw; so the latter either blundered or deliberately suppressed the truth, as he can hardly have overlooked the relevant entries. A motive for suppression is suggested by Heylin's other biographer, John Barnard: describing Vernon's facts as 'unworthy to be mentioned', he tried to brush aside the whole idea that Heylin edited a newsbook.[4] But things 'unworthy' are not necessarily untrue, and Barnard does not actually deny Vernon's accuracy. The conflicting statements of Wood, Vernon, and Barnard have created confusion: some writers have simply accepted the idea that Berkenhead began *Aulicus*,[5] while the bibliographer, Madan, seems to have been uncertain which version of

---

[1] *Memorial of Bishop Waynflete*, pp. xxiii–xxiv. The diary is there printed from Wood's copy, which is to be found in the Bodleian Library, MS. Wood E. 4.

[2] *The Life of . . . Dr. Peter Heylyn* (1682), p. 123.

[3] Ibid., p. 124.

[4] *Theologo-Historicus, or the True Life of . . . Peter Heylin* (1683), pp. 16–17 and 22.

[5] See, for example, H. R. Fox-Bourne, *English Newspapers* (1887), i. 11. J. B. Williams, *A History of English Journalism*, does not state who was the first editor, but only goes so far as to suggest that more than one man had a hand in *Aulicus* (p. 41).

the facts to rely on.[1] The truth is that in this matter Thomas Pope-Blount, Eliot Warburton,[2] and the writer of Heylin's 'Life' in the *Dictionary of National Biography*, who all follow Vernon, are right, against Wood, Aubrey, and all later biographers of Berkenhead.

Any lingering doubts aroused by the lack of explicit details in Heylin's own statements are dispelled by an examination of the newsbook itself. It is accepted that Heylin wrote a 'supplement' to the third week, published about 27 January 1643; and several other pamphlets by him in that year, though not supplements in the strict bibliographical sense, had the same function. In some of them Heylin identified himself with *Aulicus*'s interests by attacking various of its opponents; and in all there are marked resemblances to the language of corresponding passages in the newsbook.[3] Indeed, in style and argumentative technique they are closely identifiable with the opening numbers of *Aulicus*. The mannered writing, with its Latinistic phrasing, its pedantic turns of thought, and its occasional heavy-handed humour, is quite unlike Berkenhead's characteristic manner. In the first three weeks, in fact, there is no trace of his more racy phrasing and spicy humour. In the fourth the pattern changes: on Tuesday 27 January *Aulicus* reports on the Battle of Bodmin, which is the subject of Heylin's supplement; and here there appears for the first time some of that unforced wit in which Berkenhead excelled. Most likely, at this point the pressure of having to write simultaneously the supplement and the fourth week of the newsbook forced Heylin to enlist for the first time the aid of the young man whose abilities as a scribe were presumably known to him from Lambeth days. Of course, Berkenhead may have been transcribing Heylin's copy from the start; but in either case it was the special situation of the fourth week that gave him the chance to begin 'interlacing' expressions of his own. For all concerned this was a happy chance: Heylin, with his copious style, was undoubtedly more at home in spacious controversy and leisurely narration than in the restricted space of a weekly periodical: Berkenhead might have been made for the job

---

[1] Compare his statements under nos. 1204, 1328, and 2043.
[2] *Censura Celebriorum Authorum* (1690), p. 707, and *Memoirs of Prince Rupert* (1849), ii. 89 respectively.　　　　　　[3] See App. II for these and other supplements.

and seized his chance to shine in public. Heylin did not at once
sever his connection with *Aulicus*; but Berkenhead made his
presence felt and indispensable very swiftly. By June 1643 his name
was on opponents' lips, and it was at his request that Heylin, at
the end of September 1643, gave up all editorial responsibility.[1]
Even before that final take-over Berkenhead had been rewarded in
April with the appointment of Reader in Moral Philosophy.
Aulicus was 'much applauded by great persons'[2] in Oxford and
Berkenhead recommended for the Readership by a letter from the
King, dated 31 March, praising his 'Discretion and Abilities' and
his many 'acceptable Services'.[3] This duly secured his unanimous
election on 3 April 1643.[4] The normal duties of the position —to read
in the Schools of Ethics, Politics, and Economics[5]—cannot have
been exacted in the circumstances. Nor is it likely that he drew the
usual stipend of £100 a year,[6] as the King was inclined to distribute
honours that cost nothing to give. It was nevertheless a token of
Royal favour, marking another step in Berkenhead's advancement.
This reward—for political not academic services[7]—also measures
the Court's estimate of the newsbook's importance. Berkenhead,
happily, did not have to content himself solely with intangible
recompense: according to one London source of 1644, the King
allowed the editor a stipend of £30 a year 'for writing his weekly
pamphlets',[8] and this presumably went Berkenhead's way once
Heylin had resigned.

    These two men were not the only composers of *Aulicus*: a third,
who proves the official interest in journalism, was George Digby,
one of Charles's Secretaries of State. Like Heylin, he wrote a
supplement to the newsbook; this was a long account of the first
Battle of Newbury, published about 25 September 1643 and used

---

[1] *Memorial of Bishop Waynflete*, p. xxiv.
[2] *Mercurius Civicus*, no. 4 (25 May–1 June 1643), p. 32.
[3] Convocation Register, 1641–1647, MS. Univ. Oxon. Arch. Sb 25, f. 24ʳ.
[4] Ibid., f. 24ᵛ.
[5] C. E. Mallet, *A History of the University of Oxford*, ii. 322.
[6] *Hist. and Antiq.* ii. 872.
[7] Mallet, op. cit., ii. 183 suggests Berkenhead's claims to the post were,
academically speaking, rather frail.
[8] *The Kingdomes Weekly Intelligencer*, no. 83 (26 Nov.–3 Dec. 1644), p. 666, quoted
by J. Frank, *The Beginnings of the English Newspaper, 1620–1660* (Cambridge, Mass.,
1961), pp. 75–6.

as the basis of *Aulicus*'s own narrative of the fight.[1] In December Digby became further involved in journalism when Berkenhead fell ill. On the 22nd of that month, a scout belonging to the Parliamentary commander, Sir Samuel Luke, reported that 'Mercurius Aulicus came not out this weeke till Wednesday late at night, and that Aulicus lyes a dyeing'.[2] The number in question was the fiftieth, for 10–16 December; and *Britanicus* spotted the deterioration in style.[3] It also observed, truly, that the previous issue had shown some falling off, and ironically enquired what had become of Berkenhead. Though *Britanicus* put no name to the substitute editor, his description of his writing as 'lies in Parenthesis, and Comma's [*sic*], and full Points'[4] is a fair characterization of Digby's style at its worst.

The Editor's function

Berkenhead, then, was not sole editor of *Aulicus*; but the numbers by Heylin and Digby show that his inspiration was a vital factor in its success. As he exercised increasing control through 1643, London unease at *Aulicus*'s effect on public opinion mounted. His propagandist skill shows in his use of what have come to be regarded as standard techniques of political journalism—the planted idea, the inadequately denied rumour, and the inside story. He had no monopoly of these devices among contemporary journalists but, as has been observed, he used them 'in a more fully developed way'.[5] In nothing is his superiority more marked than in the use of innuendo and smear; and one result of his take-over of *Aulicus* was a growth in the proportion of this sort of banter as 1643 and 1644 passed. Eventually it predominated over more sober material. Other factors, it is true, assisted the process, and they will be examined later; but the bent of Berkenhead's imagination was a main cause of the change. Heylin's laborious presentation of news

---

[1] See App. II.
[2] *Journal of Sir Samuel Luke* (Oxon. Record Soc., xxix, xxxi, xxxiii, 1947–53), pp. 221–2.
[3] No. 18 (21–28 Dec. 1643), p. 137.
[4] No. 17 (14–21 Dec. 1643), p. 131.
[5] J. Frank, *The Beginnings of the English Newspaper, 1620–1660*, p. 48.

was much less popular than Berkenhead's vivacity[1] and deservedly so, as the former's four numbers in 1644 show. These were composed when things were not too rosy for the Royalists; and with the King away in the field, information was slow to reach Oxford.[2] That granted, they still compare unfavourably with later numbers written by Berkenhead when fortunes were even dimmer. Heylin was less cunning at concealing defects: he openly admitted the perplexity in which shortage of intelligence had placed him,[3] whereas Berkenhead habitually reacted to such trouble by jollying the reader along with matter more entertaining. Heylin was tentative when in doubt,[4] where Berkenhead outfaced the hazards with a sublimely confident air. Contemporaries noticed these differences, and one remarked in 1644, that the 'new upstart Scribe' had none of the old one's vigour, spirit, and liveliness, and altogether lacked his knack of tacking stories together smoothly.[5] Heylin must have sighed with relief when Berkenhead resumed his duties; and the return of the latter is still unmistakable and welcome. It was his buoyant wit and considerable ingenuity in manipulating facts and dates to conceal setbacks that kept *Aulicus* afloat so long.[6]

His propagandist sleight of hand deserves closer scrutiny. Madan noticed that attempts were made to conceal lapses in publication in 1644 and 1645 by faking pagination and signatures to give the impression that the missing numbers had been printed.[7] He did not observe that the decline in *Aulicus*'s efficiency was even greater than this suggests: internal evidence and allusions in London newsbooks prove that there were serious discrepancies between the apparent and actual dates of publication in many instances. Sometimes the appearance of lateness may have been due

---

[1] *Ath. Oxon.* iii. 556.

[2] The timing of *Aulicus*'s publication (see App. I) shows this. Heylin himself remarked on the difficulties created by the King's absence in no. 35 (27 Aug.– 2 Sept. 1643), p. 475.

[3] No. 74 (26 May–1 June 1644), p. 1004, and no. 77 (16–22 June), p. 1048.

[4] No. 75 (2–8 June), pp. 1016 and 1018.

[5] *The Spie*, no. 21 (13–20 June 1644), pp. 161 and 162 respectively.

[6] See App. I.

[7] No. 2044, where he gives a full collation of the newsbook. The new analysis of the dislocations in its publication is fully documented in App. I of the present study.

to delays in transporting *Aulicus* from Oxford to London, but most often other factors were involved. *Aulicus* began to lag behind events very early in 1644, and from then on appeared anything from a week to a month later than the dates on the title-pages suggest. At least once, several numbers were published simultaneously, in a desperate effort to save face. The major causes of this deterioration were military setbacks and a disintegrating intelligence network. The efforts made to cover up help us to gauge the importance that the Court attached to its newsbook; and their partial success—witnessed by London rivals' anxiety to undeceive readers—is a tribute to Berkenhead's resourcefulness and initiative.

The editor's skill was, then, important; but he was not wholly dependent on personal resources. London newsbooks and pamphlets were agreed that he had help; and *Britanicus* enviously contrasted Berkenhead's position with his own private status.[1] They all knew full well the advantages of official backing, and lacking it themselves, jeered not very convincingly at an editor who had the aid of a horde of 'tributary Wits'[2] and could 'summon all Poets and Schollers of any comptency [sic] of wit, from the age of sixteene to sixty, to be aiding and assisting to the next Diurnall'.[3] *Britanicus* even published lists of alleged contributors,[4] mentioning among others Barton Holliday, Jaspar Mayne, Brian Duppa, and Phineas Williams from the academic world and Digby, Jermyn, Cottington, and Stewart from the Court.[5] These specifications should not always be taken literally, though the general drift of the accusations is sound.[6] Sometimes, however, *Britanicus*'s analysis is substantially accurate: in March 1644, his suggestion that Berkenhead had been given time off[7] does coincide with a disturbance in the publication of *Aulicus*,[8] and some unevenness in the wit and style hereabouts might well be due to the direct intervention of Digby and Jermyn,

---

[1] No. 85 (26 May–2 June 1645), p. 771.
[2] No. 2 (30 Jan.–5 Feb. 1644), p. 9.
[3] No. 6 (26 Sept.–3 Oct. 1643), p. 41.
[4] No. 23 (12–19 Feb. 1644), p. 177.
[5] No. 25 (26 Feb.–6 Mar. 1644), pp. 191 and 194.
[6] They make no sense if, for example, applied to the relevant number here, no. 59 (11–17 Feb. 1644).
[7] No. 25, p. 191.
[8] See App. I.

as *Britanicus* guessed.[1] What is certain is that *Britanicus* and others commonly equated a decline in the quality of *Aulicus* with Berkenhead's absence or reduced initiative. But, of course, this was not their only nor their most important point concerning assistance rendered Berkenhead. A counterfeit *Britanicus* weighed in interestingly on this topic, attributing the political and religious commentary to Digby, Jermyn, and Duppa, leaving Berkenhead with only 'an honourable reference for the managing of the Wormatick remnant at the close . . .'.[2] This 'remnant' was the running commentary, found at the end of many numbers, on the errors and contradictions of London newsbooks. It was, perhaps, the most effective of Berkenhead's methods of undermining confidence and solidarity in London, and was duly copied by opponents. The arguments of the counterfeit *Britanicus* are echoed suspiciously in a pamphlet published just before it on 14 March. This, too, saw *Aulicus* as the wicked contrivance of flippant scholars, ambitious clerics, and a host of Court favourites and Papists; and it even described how contributions to the newsbook were taken to Berkenhead's office—probably in Oriel College where the junto met—by 'that State-Crittick, George Digby' and the 'wormatick wits' of the University.[3]

The theory subscribed to by the Londoners was best expressed by the counterfeit *Britanicus*'s statement that the task of 'framing' *Aulicus* belonged to Digby and Jermyn, who were supplied with information by the junto, while Berkenhead was 'but the pen-man and composer'.[4] The true *Britanicus* repeated this in 1645, exulting that the Oxonians were 'glad ever and anon to shift their Authours'.[5] In weighing such evidence it must be remembered that the witnesses were anything but impartial: by boasting that it took a 'nonsense Corporation of Humourists'[6] to combat him, *Britanicus*

[1] No. 27 (11–18 Mar. 1644), p. 207.

[2] No. 28 (18–25 Mar. 1644), pp. 215–16. Its previous number, no. 27 (12–18 Mar.), p. 208, also attributed the first sheet to the statesmen. The genuine issues were printed by R. White, and the counterfeit by G. Bishop, who had collaborated with White up to no. 24 (19–26 Feb.).

[3] *The Recantation of Mercurius Aulicus*, pp. 1 and 3 respectively.

[4] No. 29 (25 Mar.–1 Apr. 1644), p. 224.

[5] No. 68 (27 Jan.–3 Feb. 1645), p. 533, This portrays Berkenhead as merely a transcriber.

[6] No. 91 (21–28 July 1645), p. 817.

hoped to inflate his own reputation; and by associating with *Aulicus* prominent Royalists of extremist views the Londoners undoubtedly aimed to discredit both it and the Oxford regime. Yet, as will be seen, *Aulicus* did derive material and opinions from the junto, and the Secretary of State did take a personal interest in its success. So the Londoners rightly portrayed Berkenhead as the servant of these masters. It is probable, too, that he consulted with other Oxford propagandists, perhaps, as was suggested in 1644, meeting the Royalist astrologer George Wharton, and John Taylor the Water Poet once a week at 'the signe of the Maremaid Taverne at Cairfaix'.[1] There is evidence of an association between Berkenhead and Wharton, though not one of an entirely amicable nature. A ballad of 1666, sneering at Berkenhead's alleged cowardice, tells of a quarrel between the two men, in which the astrologer overcame the journalist and 'bang'd him from Baudycouts unto Allsoule'.[2] Nothing is known beyond this tantalizing glimpse of discord; and whatever personal grievances arose, the Royalist apologists presented a remarkably united front to the world. They shared many views and often exploited a common stock of arguments and jokes. So some of *Aulicus*'s material may have been concocted at those meetings of Laudian academics previously mentioned: one of the men listed by the Londoners as a contributor— Jaspar Mayne—was a member of the Duppa circle. Another Laudian whom Berkenhead must have known at All Souls was Jeremy Taylor, and it is interesting that *Britanicus* attributes what it calls *Aulicus*'s policy of duplicity to advice given to Berkenhead by him.[3] Another newsbook, *The Spie*, similarly and convincingly attributed to Taylor *Aulicus*'s defamatory stories about the minister who had succeeded him in his parish.[4] Undoubtedly Berkenhead culled material from his special acquaintances in University and at Court.

It would be wrong, nevertheless, to conclude that he was just a

[1] *No Mercurius Aquaticus* (19 July 1644), p. 3. *The Spie*, no. 10 (28 Mar.–3 Apr. 1644), pp. 83–4 similarly located some of *Aulicus*'s 'Newes-mongers' in an Oxford alehouse.
[2] Bodleian Library, MS. Don. b. 8, p. 344; 'Baudycouts' is possibly Bodicote near Banbury.
[3] No. 54 (14–21 Oct. 1644), p. 423.
[4] No. 17 (15–22 May 1644), p. 133.

hack transcriber. Heylin found how liberally he interpreted his
duties as copyist; and an opponent sarcastically suggested that
Berkenhead's duty was to copy down lies in his table-book and
then stretch them further to fill the newsbook.[1] No one could deny
him the exercise of that sort of initiative. Nor are the contradictions of some of his critics reassuring: at one moment Digby is
'the only man that can tell the supreamest lies' in Oxford;[2] at
another all *Aulicus*'s iniquities are laid at Berkenhead's door as
'a knowne notorious odious forger'.[3] The treatment of Digby
exposes the limitations of their evidence. As early as 26 September
1643, they detected his influence;[4] and rightly, for it was about
then that he was appointed Secretary of State in succession to
Lord Falkland, killed at the first Battle of Newbury, and necessarily gained some control over the Oxford propaganda machine.
Digby had recently advocated using more guile in news presentation,[5] and there is a noticeable decline in the amount of straight
information retailed by *Aulicus* around this time. Nor is there any
doubt that he wrote some copy for the newsbook. So in general
terms it was right to emphasize his close connection with *Aulicus*.[6]
But observers often overstated their case: *The Spie* attributed the
change in *Aulicus*'s manner in June 1644 to Digby's absence from
Oxford;[7] and this was a contributory factor since Heylin (then
editing) could not obtain swift and sound intelligence. But even
more important, was the absence of Berkenhead.

The truth concerning the editor's duties seems to be that his
superiors supplied him with information, documents, and lines of
argument; but, with the exception of the first month or so of its

---

[1] *The Court Mercurie*, no. 9 (31 Aug.–8 Sept. 1644), J1r.

[2] *M. Brit.*, no. 23 (12–19 Feb. 1644), p. 179.

[3] Ibid., no. 69 (3–10 Feb. 1645), p. 547.

[4] No. 5 (19–26 Sept. 1643), p. 35.

[5] *A True and Impartiall Relation of the Battaile . . . neare Newbury* (about 25 Sept.
1643), p. 1.

[6] *M. Brit.*, no. 11 (2–9 Nov. 1643), p. 85; no. 27, counterfeit (12–18 Mar. 1644),
p. 210; no. 50 (2–9 Sept.), p. 397; no. 52 (30 Sept.–7 Oct.), p. 409; no. 54 (4–21
Oct.), p. 423; no. 62 (16–23 Dec.), pp. 487–8; no. 64 (30 Dec.–6 Jan. 1645), p. 503;
no. 65 (6–13 Jan.), p. 511; no. 67 (20–27 Jan.), p. 530; no. 70 (10–17 Feb.), p. 552:
The Spie, no. 6 (27 Feb.–6 Mar. 1644), p. 45; no. 17 (15–22 May), p. 129: *Mercurius
Civicus*, no. 45 (28 Mar.–4 Apr. 1644), p. 460: *Newes from Smith* (5 Feb. 1645),
pp. 4–5.

[7] No. 20 (6–13 June 1644), p. 153.

run, and of weeks when he was ill or absent from Oxford, Berkenhead was effectively responsible for the final form of *Aulicus*. Far
from being a mere transcriber he had a hand, and an increasingly
strong one, in framing the newsbook. His dexterity must be
accounted a major factor in its success, and its importance was
acknowledged by his opponents in August 1644, when they
formally deprived him of his Readership as a penalty for writing
Aulicus.[1]

The Editor's sources

The quality of Berkenhead's journalism will be examined later;
for the moment it is important to re-emphasize that there was ample
contemporary recognition that *Aulicus* was an official periodical
sponsored by men close to the King. While it remained fashionable
to attribute Charles's intransigence to his evil counsellors, critics
contented themselves with admonishing the editor for making
'bold with his Majesties Royall-Reproaches'.[2] So they passed over
its practice of anticipating Royal Proclamations, like those against
Acts and Ordinances of Parliament and the Assembly of Divines in
May and June of 1643.[3] This anticipation actually showed the
closeness of *Aulicus* to the King; and by July 1644 the diplomatic
pretence was dropped and *Britanicus* boldly traced the progress of
lies from the King, down through the Court and its newsbook to
the cobbler in the street.[4] By then *Aulicus* could safely be represented as boasting about some piece of news, 'I have the Kings

[1] In an eighteenth-century manuscript history of the Fellows of All Souls College
(Warden of All Souls College MS. 51), the entry about Berkenhead contains a
quotation, apparently extracted from the minute-book of the Committee for
Plundered Ministers, to the effect that he was deposed from the Readership on
15 Aug. 1644 for writing *Aulicus*. This may mean that the source of income for the
post was cut off at that date. Unfortunately, the source of the note cannot be found:
there are minute-books of the Committee extant in the Bodleian Library (MSS.
Bodl. 322–9) and in the British Museum (MSS. Add. 15669–71) but they do not
cover 1644, and contain nothing about Berkenhead. The quotation was copied by
Philip Bliss and inserted in the Bodleian Library copy of the 1644 sermon formerly
attributed to Berkenhead (Bliss B. 53). I am grateful to the Warden of All Souls
College for confirming that Bliss copied the entry accurately.

[2] *M. Brit.*, no. 6 (26 Sept.–3 Oct.), p. 42.

[3] See *M. Aul.*, no. 20 (14–20 May 1643), p. 259, and no. 24 (11–17 June 1643),
p. 313. The Proclamations were dated 20 and 22 June 1643, respectively.

[4] No. 44 (15–22 July 1644), p. 344.

hand for it, and he hath Prince Ruperts hand for it'.[1] Soon its
habit of insisting that things were going badly for Parliament, and
of contradicting itself, were attributed to the monarch's example.[2]
Momentarily in 1645 the fiction that the King and *Aulicus* were at
cross purposes was revived.[3] But the truth all the while was, as
another observer suspected,[4] that *Aulicus* represented accurately
the King's real opinions. This was vividly recognized when, in a
moment of exasperation, *Britanicus* threw restraint to the winds
and demanded, 'Who do you think now wrote Aulicus, the King or
Berkenhead?'[5] This outburst was occasioned by the discovery that
expression and arguments in the newsbook were identical with
those in one of Charles's letters recently captured by Parliament.
That was and is proof of how closely *Aulicus* identified itself with
the views not of moderates at Court, but of an intransigent King.

More commonly the Londoners protested that *Aulicus* was informed by the King's Secretaries. Many phrases, all uncomplimentary, were used to express this: the newsbook was the 'licenst
liar',[6] railing by authority of the Crown,[7] it had a 'patent' under
the Great Seal to retail fictions;[8] it was the 'Register, or Scribe to
the Junto',[9] it offered 'coined intelligence and slander out of the
Secretaries mint',[10] stamped 'Carol. d. gratia'.[11] In short, it was
'none of the least plots against the State' concocted by the Oxford junto.[12] A leader of that junto, Secretary Edward Nicholas,
was accused of habitually supplying *Aulicus* with stories[13] and of

[1] *Ruperts Sumpter*, (20 July 1644), A1ᵛ.
[2] No. 52 (30 Sept.–7 Oct. 1644), p. 408; and no. 59 (18–25 Nov. 1644), p. 464.
[3] No. 67 (20–27 Jan. 1645), pp. 527–8; and no. 81 (28 Apr.–5 May 1645), p. 739.
[4] *The Question Disputed* (1645), A3ᵛ and p. 6.
[5] No. 92 (28 July–4 Aug.), p. 826. This reprints the letter of the King, dated
8 June, and there are certainly echoes of it in *Aulicus*, no. 115 (25 May–8 June),
p. 1617.
[6] *M. Brit.*, no. 11 (2–9 Nov. 1643), p. 88.
[7] Ibid., no. 10 (26 Oct.–2 Nov.), p. 79.
[8] *The Scotish Dove*, no. 1 (13–20 Oct. 1643), p. 7; the same editor had made this
point in *The Scotch Mercury*, no. 1 (5 Oct. 1643), p. 1. *M. Brit.*, no. 84 (19–26 May
1644), p. 761, uses the same metaphor.
[9] *M. Brit.*, no. 22 (5–12 Feb. 1644), p. 169.
[10] Ibid., no. 70 (10–17 Feb. 1645), p. 550.
[11] *An Antidote against the Malignant influence of Mercurius (surnamed) Aulicus*, no. 1
(2 Sept. 1643), p. 1.
[12] *The Spie*, no. 16 (8–15 May 1644), p. 121.
[13] *M. Brit.*, no. 50 (2–9 Sept. 1644), p. 397.

collaborating closely with Berkenhead in its production.[1] Evidence sustaining the allegations was printed in *The Kingdomes Weekly Intelligencer*: it compared a report in *Aulicus* with letters from Nicholas intercepted by Parliamentary troops, concluding justifiably that 'you may now know from whom *Aulicus* hath his Intelligence weekly'.[2] Not only opponents believed this: in July 1643 the Venetian Resident in England described *Aulicus* as being 'printed at Oxford with the King's consent and information from the Secretary of State'.[3] And it was because they knew this was true that Royalists so readily believed what it published.[4]

Their trust was not born of blind faith: they had good reason, in 1643 at least, to find *Aulicus* more satisfactory and authoritative than any other newsbook. Because of its official standing it could draw on the information then flowing into the junto; and intelligence carried from London by spies quickly found its way into print. At the very first *Britanicus* complained enviously that *Aulicus* had 'hithertoo had as exact intelligence from some of the close committee, and both Houses as can be wished'.[5] This punctuality so embarrassed the Parliamentarians that in October 1643 the Lords instigated an enquiry into the question of how *Aulicus* came to know even 'some Things privately passed in this House'.[6] The answer, of course, was that there were informers sitting in Parliament: in 1644 one of them, Lord Rochford, was publicly accused of providing the Court with information in return for the King's pardon,[7] and in June 1645 a member of the Commons, Mr. Holles, was suspected of sending intelligence to Lord Digby.[8] He was cleared, but there must have been guilty men, as throughout its run *Aulicus* printed quite detailed accounts of transactions that the Londoners would have preferred to conceal. Often information came speedily and accurately: on 22 August 1643 *Aulicus*

---

[1] *M. Brit.* no. 73 (3–10 Mar. 1645), p. 587, and no. 83 (12–19 May 1645), p. 757.
[2] No. 47 (6–13 Mar. 1644), p. 383.
[3] *C.S.P. Ven.*, 1642–3, pp. 306–7.
[4] *The True Character of Mercurius Aulicus* (1645), p. 3.
[5] No. 1 (23–29 Aug. 1643), p. 7.
[6] *Lords' Journals*, vi. 254.
[7] *Ruperts Sumpter* (20 July 1644), A4ᵛ. *M. Brit.*, no. 44 (15–22 July 1644), p. 347 also accuses Lord Rochford.
[8] *Commons' Journals*, iv. 172 and 213.

received details of speeches delivered in the Commons on the previous day;[1] in March 1644 it reported accurately on the impeachment of Sir Francis Willoughby;[2] and best of all, it summarized correctly a speech by St. John delivered in a voice so quiet that only six people had been able to hear it.[3] *Britanicus* itself indignantly drew attention to all these cases; and though it occasionally rejoiced that *Aulicus* was no longer getting good intelligence[4] the truth was that even the setting up of the Council of State[5] and the imposition of an Oath of Secrecy did not prevent news travelling to Oxford. *Aulicus's* arch enemy could only go on resenting word-for-word reports of speeches in the Commons.[6] The members were continually exhorted to look about themselves to discover the informers and eventually this had some effect. In 1645 *Aulicus*, previously so sensitive to every whisper on London, was labouring with sluggish and inaccurate intelligence.[7] Even so, news occasionally got through to Oxford to the very end: as late as June 1645 there were in the capital 'sure Intelligencers which lie Sculking about in every Corner to supply *Aulicus*: Not a Mouse stirres but he hears of it'.[8] As long as there were Royalist sympathizers in London—and at the end of June there was still talk of the good friends the King until very recently had had at Westminster[9]—there were ways of getting information to Court. Not only news of Parliament travelled this course: in October 1643 Dr. Daniel Featley, the Anglican divine, was accused of being *Aulicus's* intelligencer at the Assembly of Divines.[10] The newsbook denied it,[11] as Featley did later;[12] but the cleric was excluded from meetings of

---

[1] This was noted by *M. Brit.*, no. 3 (5–12 Sept.), p. 18.

[2] No. 26 (5–12 Mar.), p. 201 (misnumbered 291).

[3] No. 33 (22–29 Apr. 1644), p. 256.

[4] No. 52 (30 Sept.–7 Oct.), p. 409.

[5] *M. Brit.*, no. 24 (19–26 Feb. 1645), p. 188, expected this to inhibit *Aulicus*, as did *The True Informer*, no. 23 (17–24 Feb.), p. 167. *The Spie*, no. 7 (5–13 Mar.), p. 51, was similarly hopeful, but had changed its tune again in no. 17 (15–22 May), p. 131.

[6] *M. Brit.*, no. 54 (14–21 Oct. 1644), p. 429 and no. 58 (11–18 Nov.), p. 459.

[7] No. 84 (19–26 May), p. 762, and no. 85 (26 May–2 June), p. 776.

[8] *M. Brit.*, no. 88 (23–30 June), p. 794.

[9] *The Scotish Dove*, no. 88 (20–27 June), p. 691.

[10] *M. Brit.*, no. 6 (26 Sept.–3 Oct.), p. 43.

[11] No. 41 (8–14 Oct. 1643), pp. 569–70.

[12] *Sacra Nemesis* (1 Aug. 1644), pp. 8–11.

the synod and imprisoned. *Aulicus* continued to receive 'inside' information about the Assembly's deliberations, at least until April 1645.[1] Altogether opponents, whatever they wrote about *Aulicus*'s fraudulence, really found it an all too authoritative and dangerously well-informed enemy.

The carriage of intelligence

Aulicus's coverage was not uniformly thorough, of course; and as methods of conveying information to Oxford have a bearing on these fluctuations, as well as on the whole question of circulation of news in the period, it is worth considering them in some detail. During most of *Aulicus*'s run, movement of goods and people between Oxford and London was subject to restrictions. These, however, were not fully effective and right up to 1646 the Royalists contrived, with much ingenuity, to circumvent them. One Royalist agent in London, John Barwick, had letters concealed in pedlars' merchandise and inside the covers of books being smuggled to Oxford.[2] The smugglers were usually women, like the one denounced in 1643 for taking to Court each week, by river and on horseback, 'the most materiall Letters that goe'.[3] Another, arrested in 1644, was charged with being 'a constant conveyor of dangerous Intelligence betwixt Oxford and London'.[4] Aware from scrutiny of *Aulicus* that valuable information was slipping through, London journalists occasionally unmasked the go-betweens. *Mercurius Civicus* complained of the 'shee Informers' the Oxford newsbook sent to London,[5] and denounced two of them—Mrs. Penyall, daughter of a man living near Nettlebed on the Oxford to London road, and 'Mistris Guy, a Proctors wife', both of whom had passes to travel the route.[6] It threatened to print more names, but either this was bluff or the people concerned bought its silence. There must, after all, have been a deal of such collusion for the traffic in pamphlets and letters to flourish as it did.

[1] *M. Brit.*, no. 80 (21–28 Apr. 1645), p. 731, ruefully suggested that Featley's ghost was the culprit.
[2] Peter Barwick, *The Life of Dr. John Barwick*, ed. G. F. Barwick (1903), pp. 26–8.
[3] *The Parliament Scout*, no. 5 (20–27 July 1643), p. 40.
[4] *A Diary, or an Exact Journall*, no. 20 (19–26 Sept. 1644), p. 139.
[5] No. 4 (25 May–1 June 1643), p. 32.
[6] No. 79 (21–28 Nov. 1644), p. 729.

In any case, with everybody a potential spy it was extremely
difficult for the authorities to identify the culprits. This is obvious
from the movement of military scouts about the country: one—a
Royalist—managed to ride for half a day in the company of a
troop of Parliamentary soldiers before he was discovered.[1] In 1643
and much of 1644 such agents were out and about in many parts of
the country: the Royalist Governor of Reading every day sent
spies into the enemy lines,[2] and the information they gleaned was
carried daily to Oxford by scouts pretending to be 'sorry contry
fellowes'.[3] They were known to use The Beard Inn at Newbury as
a rendezvous from which news was passed along the line to the
Court.[4] Others were 'constantly upon the roade betwixt Cambridge
and Oxford, and upon all occasions give intelligence . . .'.[5] Similarly, spies were sent into London 'from the King's Army onely of
purpose to heare newes to carry to the King'.[6] Two of them,
Motte and Hungerford, were seized in late 1643, after tricking
their way into the City through the Court of Guards.[7] Even in
October 1645 Royalist scouts were about the roads; so, though not
so well served as formerly, the Court was still receiving some
useful intelligence from this source.

Much of this information was militarily unsatisfactory and the
intelligence branches of both armies throughout the war have been
adjudged inefficient.[8] But the scouts did collect much information
of one sort and another that was extremely useful to a newsbook
editor. *Aulicus*'s remarkably detailed accounts of major battles,
minor skirmishes, and plundering raids could not have been
written without the material sent to Court by the scouts. It is no
coincidence that the newsbook ran into severe difficulties when
their activities were curtailed. Before that, particularly in 1643, its
reporting of troop movements was so full that the Parliamentary

---

[1] *C.S.P. Dom.*, 1645–7, p. 201. This was in Oct. 1645.
[2] *Journal of Sir Samuel Luke*, pp. 64–5.
[3] Ibid, p. 66.
[4] Ibid., p. 70.
[5] Ibid., p. 43.
[6] *A Continuation of Certain Special and Remarkable Passages*, no. 22 (3–8 Dec. 1642),
p. 6.
[7] *The Weekly Account*, no. 5 (27 Sept.–4 Oct. 1643), p. 6.
[8] F. J. Varley, *The Siege of Oxford* (1932), p. 125 n.

scouts of Sir Samuel Luke often had little or nothing to add to the news it published:[1] and Luke himself habitually received copies and sent them on to friends.[2] It is also noticeable that Heylin, editing *Aulicus* during the King's absences from Oxford, admitted that he was getting 'but little newes' from some areas,[3] and had to rely largely on intercepted letters and material filched from London newsbooks. As he explained 'where the Court is, thither the newes is sooner certified'.[4]

Normally *Aulicus*'s accuracy and fullness were the envy of opponents.[5] Of course, Parliament had its own system of scouts and spies on which it expended much care and money;[6] and local commanders like Sir William Brereton, Sir John Gell, and Colonel Hutchinson also set up efficient intelligence networks of their own.[7] But these efforts did not necessarily benefit London journalists in any way, as those of the Royalists automatically assisted Berkenhead. True, the London newsbooks sometimes reported details from Luke's letters read out in Parliament;[8] and John Cleaveland accused *Britanicus* of currying favour with Gell and Brereton by giving them good write-ups.[9] As a Cavalier he might be a suspect witness, but on the other side Colonel Hutchinson's wife repeated the accusations;[10] and William Prynne charged *Britanicus* with accepting bribes to give 'puffs'.[11] It seems that some editors had private arrangements with people who were in a position to feed them information and finance. John Dillingham, for example, made *The Parliament Scout* something of a mouthpiece of the Earl of

[1] *Journal of Sir Samuel Luke*, pp. xi and xv.

[2] *The Letter Books, 1644–45, of Sir Samuel Luke*, H. G. Tibbutt, for H.M.C. (1963).

[3] No. 72 (26 May–1 June 1644), p. 1004.

[4] No. 35 (27 Aug.–2 Sept. 1643), p. 475.

[5] See, for example, *The Parliament Scout*, no. 33 (2–9 Feb. 1644), p. 278.

[6] See, for example, *Commons' Journals*, iii. 423 and 443; *C.S.P. Dom.*, 1644–5, pp. 583–4.

[7] For Brereton see J. R. Phillips, *Civil War in Wales and the Marches, 1642–1649* (1874), i. 290. For Gell and Hutchinson see Lucy Hutchinson, *Memoirs of the Life of Colonel Hutchinson*, revised edn. by C. H. Firth (1906), pp. 101–2.

[8] *The Weekly Account*, in 1644, frequently quotes such letters.

[9] *The Character of a London Diurnall* (Jan. 1645), reprinted in *Character Writings of the Seventeenth Century*, ed. H. Morley (1891), p. 312. *M. Brit.*, no. 75 (17–24 Mar. 1645), p. 606 does praise Brereton lavishly, as it did Luke in no. 28 (18–25 Mar. 1644), p. 218.

[10] *Memoirs of the Life of Colonel Hutchinson*, pp. 101–2.

[11] *A Checke to Brittanicus* (14 Feb. 1644), p. 3.

Manchester. It was only as a special concession, however, that London editors were allowed to see official newsletters;[1] and though it has been suggested that Thomas Audley, one of *Britanicus*'s editors, attended Close Committee meetings to take notes, this is not certain.[2] It does not tally with Audley's earlier statement in 1643 that he was 'neither of the Court nor Councell'.[3] Perhaps it was a later development; but even in the summer of 1645 *Britanicus* could still step far enough out of line by publishing a 'Hue and Cry' after the King to bring down punishment on the heads of Audley and his collaborator, Nedham.[4] In short, none of the London newsbooks of this period was organized or sponsored as *Aulicus* was.

Parliament did not disregard the value of newsbook propaganda; but, partly because it was not sure if it could control the London press,[5] it left the defence of its actions to the private enterprise of individual journalists, instead of sponsoring a periodical itself. So editors and publishers had a considerable strain, financial and otherwise, imposed on them if they aimed to compete with *Aulicus*. The latter could well afford to jeer at *The Parliament Scout* for asking Parliament for £500 for itself and its fellows 'to bring intelligence'.[6] The fact that the Oxford printer, Henry Hall, after the Restoration petitioned the University for repayment of £90 he had spent out of his own pocket on *Aulicus*[7] shows that it simply was not run on a normal commercial basis. Not that it was unprofitable to everyone involved, for in London, where it was reprinted by a loyal stationer, it was in great demand and sold at inflated prices. So it enjoyed the best of both worlds.

Printing and distribution also felt the benefit of the Court's determination to boost *Aulicus*. It is impossible to estimate accurately the number of copies printed each week, which probably

[1] J. B. Williams, *History of English Journalism*, pp. 9–10.
[2] W. M. Clyde, 'Parliament and the Press, 1643–7', *The Library*, 4th Ser. xiii (1932), 418.
[3] *M. Brit.*, no. 12 (9–16 Nov. 1643), p. 96.
[4] W. M. Clyde, op. cit., p. 416 and n.
[5] *C.S.P. Dom.*, 1644–5, p. 24.
[6] No. 76 (9–15 June 1644), p. 1034.
[7] Madan, no. 2043. The widow of the other Oxford printer, Leonard Lichfield, also petitioned the King for repayment of £1,000 spent by her husband on printing during the Civil War (*Oxford Books*, iii, p. xxxi). Some of this was almost certainly spent on *Aulicus* (see below, p. 49).

varied with the availability of paper at Oxford. It has been suggested[1] that, in the case of the earlier Corantos, 400 was the size of an issue and that in the 1640s 500 was the average total for a weekly newsbook. Of course, this figure is variable: new weeklies probably rated 250 copies, established ones 500, and the best, such as *Britanicus*, between 750 and 1,000.[2] The limitations of the seventeenth-century handpress set a ceiling on production: if a weekly periodical was to be effective the printer had to complete his work in about one day, in which space he could not have perfected more than 1,500 copies of a one-sheet pamphlet on one press, even assuming that he worked round the clock.[3] The size of *Aulicus* varied between one and two sheets, but a simple calculation is ruled out by the existence of more than one press in Oxford at this time, combined with the survival of two versions of the title-page of the second number.[4] Both were printed in Oxford and suggest that more than one setting of type, and probably more than one press, was used by Henry Hall. There was, moreover, another Oxford press, belonging to Leonard Lichfield; and he, too, seems to have assisted in the work.[5] These extra presses could have been used to increase either output or speed of production. *Aulicus* was also regularly reprinted in London from as early as the second week to as late as no. 103, for 26 January–2 February 1645.[6] This reprinting scandalized Milton, who made political capital of it in *Areopagitica*, blaming the government too much and the Stationers' Company too little. *A Perfect Diurnall* had a truer view of the problem when

[1] Folke Dahl, *A Bibliography of English Corantos* (Bibliographical Soc., 1952), p. 22.
[2] Figures suggested by J. Frank, *The Beginnings of the English Newspaper, 1620–1660*, p. 57.
[3] R. C. Bald, 'Bibliographical Studies in the Beaumont and Fletcher Folio of 1647', *Trans. Bibl. Soc.*, *Supplement* 13 (1938), p. 23. 1,000 is the number of copies of a declaration that Cromwell's travelling press was able to produce in twenty-four hours, J. D. Ogilvie, 'Papers from an Army Press, 1650', *Edinburgh Bibl. Soc. Trans.* ii (1938–45), 421. Frank, op. cit., p. 314 notes that two men working eight hours apiece could perfect 1,000 sheets on one press.
[4] The two versions can be seen in the B.M. copies, Burney 13 (1)—this is identical with the Bodleian Library copy, Art. 4 M. 68, and the Corpus Christi copy—and Burney 15 (1). Burney 14 (2) is a London reprint with a third version of the title-page.
[5] *M. Brit.*, no. 48 (19–26 Aug. 1644), p. 379.
[6] Madan, no. 2044, lists nineteen London reprints: there are another fifteen extant in the B.M. Burney and Thomason collections.

in January 1645 it acclaimed Parliament's latest measures against the Company's laxness. He hoped that these would stifle the printing of malignant pamphlets in London, especially 'the Oxford Aulicusses'.[1] But it was not easy to control the Stationers, and until they were tamed 'secret' presses could flourish with their connivance. According to John Lilburne, the Company even sent printing materials to the King and acquiesced in the 'weekly printing, divulging, and dispersing of "Oxford Aulicus" ' in London.[2] The man who probably reprinted it there was Richard Royston, described as 'the constant factor for all other scandalous books and papers against the proceedings of Parliament', and 'friend' of *Aulicus*.[3] He was eventually arrested at the end of July 1645,[4] but the newsbook's run was then practically over.

His work may have doubled the output of *Aulicus*; but even that was probably not the end of Royalist efforts to multiply copies. For they had presses working at Shrewsbury until about August 1643, and the Court certainly wanted to reprint *Aulicus* there. Parliamentary newsbooks had been circulating too well in that part of the country and in July it was suggested to the Governor of Shrewsbury, Sir Francis Ottley, that he should 'have an Eye upon the Press, and . . . see our Diurnals reprinted there'. This, he was assured, would 'do the King, and his Cause good Service, and Secretary Nicholas shall thank you'.[5] The contemporary catalogue of Shrewsbury publications[6] shows that another Oxford periodical, *Mercurius Rusticus*, was duplicated there in 1643; it does not list *Aulicus* (and no Shrewsbury copies have been discovered),

---

[1] *A Perfect Diurnall*, no. 77 (13–20 Jan. 1645), p. 612.

[2] *Englands Birthright* (10 Oct. 1645), quoted by W. M. Clyde, 'Parliament and the Press. II', *The Library*, 4th Ser. xiv (1933–4), 43–4. Lilburne asserts that this was proved to the faces of the Masters and Warden of the Stationers' Company in their own hall. Clyde points out ('Parliament and the Press, 1643–7', *The Library*, 4th Ser. xiii (1932–3), 399–400) how divisions in Parliament and the attitude of the Stationers' Company made control difficult.

[3] H.M.C., 6th *Report* (1877), pp. 71–2. Royston is referred to as the 'friend' of *Aulicus* in *Aulicus His Hue and Cry* (13 Aug. 1645), quoted by W. M. Clyde, 'Parliament and the Press, 1643–7', *The Library*, xiii. 418.   [4] *Lords' Journals*, vii. 518.

[5] L. C. Lloyd, 'The Book Trade in Shropshire', *Trans. Shropshire Arch. and Nat. Hist. Soc.* xlviii (1934–5), 83.

[6] This is described by L. Hanson, 'The King's Printer at York and Shrewsbury, 1642–3', *The Library*, 4th Ser. xxiii (1943), 129–31; and there is a photographed copy of it in the British Museum.

but since it is incomplete it is just conceivable that the Governor acted on the advice given, just before the presses left town. This is admittedly an outside chance; for despite exhortations from Oxford[1] these presses had not functioned satisfactorily at Shrewsbury,[2] partly because of a paper shortage.[3]

In the autumn of 1643 the printers removed to Bristol, which had fallen to the Royalists on 26 July and was more strategically placed and more easily supplied than Shrewsbury. Comparatively little is known of the printing done there, but the presses were busy by November 1643,[4] and continued production until 1645.[5] Contemporary comments indicate that they were far more active than the scarcity of surviving imprints suggests. *Mercurius Civicus* described them as the source 'from which they do divulge many most false and fictitious relations';[6] and another complained that the Bristol printer, supplied with paper from Exeter, was infesting all the West Country and South Wales with 'most dangerous Books'.[7] Duplication at Bristol would certainly have been the most effective way of promoting *Aulicus*'s distribution there; and it apparently did circulate well, for the stubborn loyalty of Western people was, by one enemy, largely attributed to its influence.[8] *Britanicus*, who was fond of puns, may have had Bristol reprints in mind when in December 1643 it accused *Aulicus* of 'oppressing' in Bristol, Oxford, and York.[9] Anyhow, the possibility that it was reprinted in Bristol cannot be neglected.

[1] 'The Ottley Papers' (Part I), *Trans. Shropshire Arch., and Nat. Hist. Soc.*, 2nd Ser. vi (1894), 56 and 57.   [2] L. C. Lloyd, op. cit., p. 82.

[3] H. Beaumont, 'Arthur, Lord Capel, The King's Lieutenant-General for Shropshire, 1643', *Trans. Shropshire Arch. and Nat. Hist. Soc.* i (1939–40), 80.

[4] J. E. Pritchard, 'The Earliest Bristol Printed Books', *Trans. Bristol and Gloucestershire Arch. Soc.* lvi (1934), 197–9.

[5] F. A. Hyett, 'Notes on the First Bristol and Gloucestershire Printers', *Trans. Bristol and Gloucestershire Arch. Soc.* xx (1895–7), 43. Bristol fell to Parliament on 11 Sept. but some time before that the presses moved to Exeter: on 15 Aug. 1645 Thomason received a copy of *Certain Prayers to be used in his Majesties Armies and Garrisons* printed there.

[6] No. 40 (22–29 Feb. 1644), p. 417.

[7] *The True Informer*, no. 59 (16–23 Nov. 1644), quoted by W. M. Clyde, 'Parliament and the Press, 1643–7', *The Library*, xiii. 406 n.

[8] *Newes from Smith* (5 Feb. 1645), pp. 4–5.

[9] No. 17 (14–21 Dec. 1643), p. 132. No. 55 (21–28 Oct. 1644), p. 434, insisted that *Aulicus* was obviously designed to impress Western readers. No. 83 (12–19 May 1645), p. 760, referred explicitly to a press in Bristol.

In the circumstances, dogmatism about the size of an issue would be inappropriate; but probably the figure of 1,500 mentioned is too low. When John Hall of Durham started editing a new *Mercurius Britanicus* in 1648 he printed 200 copies at his own expense for distribution among the Members of Parliament alone.[1] Even 3,000 copies would have fallen well short of what the market could absorb,[2] as the printing of 9,000 copies of several publications in 1642[3] and of 10,000 of a pamphlet in the mid-1640s shows.[4] The time factor was vital of course, but with everything running smoothly it is not beyond the bounds of possibility that 5,000 copies of *Aulicus* could have been published in some weeks.

There was unquestionably a great demand for it: newsbooks normally cost a penny, but *Britanicus* (and others) often grumbled about the inflated price fetched by *Aulicus*. They followed its rise from 3d. in November 1643[5] to '18 pence a peece' in 1645,[6] when scarcity and the danger to the sellers had become more acute. As virtually the only Royalist 'product' on the market it was from the first in a strong selling position; but this inflation was quite extraordinary. Enthusiastic demand undoubtedly contributed to it.

The Court, which so zealously sponsored the printing of the newsbook, naturally attended to its distribution also. There were various methods of circulation available and they used most of them. While the Crown retained some control over the Posts, copies were probably dispatched direct from Oxford by that means; but Parliament, despite all efforts, was getting a firm grip on the system before the end of 1643.[7] Special King's messengers could, however, still distribute *Aulicus*:[8] it would almost certainly have come under the heading of 'Books Sent Forth by His Maiesties Command'; and the King issued an order in March 1644 concerning

---

[1] *Mercurius Elencticus*, no. 29 (7–14 June 1648), p. 224 (misnumbered 222).

[2] J. Frank, *The Beginnings of the English Newspaper, 1620–1660*, p. 57.

[3] *Commons' Journals*, ii. 616.

[4] J. Frank, op. cit., p. 314 n., and *The Levellers* (Harvard Univ. Press, 1955), p. 95.

[5] *M. Brit.*, no. 12 (9–16 Nov. 1643), p. 92. It grumbled about *Aulicus*'s sales fairly frequently, e.g. no. 21 (29 Jan.–5 Feb. 1644), p. 162; no. 47 (12–19 Aug.), p. 267; and no. 51 (23–30 Sept.), p. 399.

[6] *The True Character of Mercurius Aulicus*, p. 3.

[7] *C.S.P. Dom.*, 1641–3, pp. 82 and 501.

[8] *Commons' Journals*, ii. 720.

the publication of these books by Sheriffs, Constables, and other local officials.[1] Orders of the Commons in 1641 and 1642 show that pamphlets as well as Declarations and other official documents were normally circulated by these officers in the Shires, Cities, and Boroughs of England.[2] The clergy, too, were accustomed in the 1640s to making their pulpits sounding-boards for news. Royalists frequently complained of this abuse of preaching, but in truth put pressure on clerics to take an interest in *Aulicus*;[3] one got into trouble with Parliament for showing copies to friends[4] and some, apparently, used it instead of the Bible as a text for their sermons.[5]

Even after the Court lost control of the Posts, Parliament's supervision of the system was not rigorous enough to stop Royalist pamphlets being enclosed in letters from London. After being read in Town, each copy by as many as four or five readers,[6] pamphlets and newsbooks were commonly dispatched into the country,[7] multiplying further the readership. So *Aulicus* travelled from Oxford to the capital and out again. In the autumn of 1643 it was passing freely into London because, ironically, it was not covered by the ban on the entry of Royal Proclamations and packets for the King's Bench and Common Pleas.[8] So, by reprinting or rephrasing Proclamations, the editor was able cheerfully to circumvent that prohibition. He was not so fortunate later: in May 1644 Parliament set a 'strict watch upon all the Court of Guards to search all Passingers, men & weomen, to the Quicke'.[9] This produced results: in March 1645 an attendant of the French ambassador was caught carrying hidden about his person '16 Aulicusses, besides divers Letters'.[10] The same month, the guards searched an 'outlandish man', a weekly traveller from Oxford, and discovered in his doublet a 'store of *Aulicus* Pamphlets, and in his drawers under his breeches

[1] Madan, no. 1585.
[2] *Commons' Journals*, ii. 135, 389, and 611.
[3] *M. Brit.*, no. 21 (29 Jan.–5 Feb. 1644), p. 162.
[4] *Walker Revised*, ed. A. G. Matthews (1948), p. 247.
[5] *M. Brit.*, no. 70 (10–17 Feb. 1645), p. 551.
[6] J. Frank, *The Beginnings of the English Newspaper, 1620–1660*, p. 67.
[7] Richard Brathwaite, *Whimzies* (1631), ed. J. O. Halliwell (1859), pp. 20 and 22.
[8] *M. Brit.*, no. 14 (23–30 Nov. 1643), p. 107.
[9] *The Knyvett Letters, 1620–1644*, ed. Bertram Schofield (1949), p. 148.
[10] *The Kingdomes Weekly Intelligencer*, no. 91 (11–18 Mar. 1645), p. 732.

were found about 150 Letters and papers'.[1] Manifestly, any traveller to London might smuggle illicit books,[2] and some seem to have been regularly employed in the work. Possibly the second, well-furnished smuggler was one of Richard Royston's creatures (admittedly usually women) who journeyed from house to house between Oxford and London disguised as beggars and picked up books left at pre-arranged points by watermen in Royston's pay.[3]

The watermen, notorious gossips, played an important part in the circulation of news and books in the Civil War. As late as 1646 they contrived to convey goods and intelligence to Oxford despite attempts to stop the traffic.[4] Getting round regulations was not too difficult: supplies for the Court were often shipped up the Thames by barge, ostensibly destined for Henley; but there carriers picked them up and took them on to Oxford overland.[5] Naturally the watermen did not go down river empty-handed, and in March 1644 guards near Westminster ferreted out 250 copies of *Aulicus* on a barge from Henley.[6]

By repute, carriers were even busier tittle-tattlers than bargemen, and, like them, put profit before politics. They moved slowly, but they could go where the Posts never called and would often disregard prohibitions. Private citizens used them as readily as the Posts to deliver letters and pamphlets,[7] and the Oxford regime inevitably enlisted their impartial industry. In December 1643 'all commodityes which the Cavileers want' were brought by carriers 'from London to Wickham under Wickham mens names, and soe sent in the night to Oxford by waggon loads at a tyme'.[8] The carriers of Long Compton, Witney, and Woodstock, too,

---

[1] *The London Post*, no. 28 (11–17 Mar. 1645), p. 8.
[2] Sir Frederick Cornwallis was used in this way in April 1643 (*Commons' Journals*, iii. 40).
[3] Peter Barwick, *The Life of Dr. John Barwick*, pp. 27–8.
[4] F. J. Varley, *The Siege of Oxford*, p. 144.
[5] I. G. Philip, 'River Navigation at Oxford during the Civil War and Commonwealth', *Oxoniensia*, ii (1937), 157.
[6] *Mercurius Veridicus*, no. 9 (19–26 Mar. 1644), A2^{r-v}.
[7] *Letters of Lady Brilliana Harley* (Camden Soc. lviii, 1854), pp. 18 and 27; *Conway Letters*, ed. M. H. Nicolson (Yale Univ. Press, 1930), p. 67; *Memoirs of the Verney Family*, ed. F. P. and M. M. Verney (1904), ii. 276; and *Nicholas Papers*, vol. i, 1641–1652, p. 158.
[8] *Journal of Sir Samuel Luke*, p. xiv.

helped supply the Court with necessities,[1] among them 'divers
Packs with Paper (for Mercurius Aulicus to vent his falsities and
querks in)'.[2] Doubtless they also carried the finished product back
to London. So by one means or another, every number of *Aulicus*
managed to get through to the City, though after 1643 there were
considerable delays.[3]

Once in London, distribution was no problem. *Britanicus* piously
suggested that conscientious Stationers would not sell *Aulicus*,[4]
but Stationers were after all business men, and there were plenty
willing to purvey it openly in Paul's Churchyard and Westminster
Hall where they had their stalls.[5] They paid no heed to purists'
complaints and continued to send for copies from Oxford.[6] *Aulicus*
may even have been delivered to the door, but it was commonly
vended on the streets by 'the Hawkers and Mercury-Women'[7]
who played a great part in circulating subversive literature
throughout the 1640s and 1650s.[8] Henry Walker, that most
enterprising of newsmen, employed 500 of them, according to
John Taylor to scatter his books throughout England, Wales, and
Ireland.[9] That was in 1642, but soon after that Royalists like
Taylor had reason themselves to be glad of the hawkers, who ran
considerable risks for them.[10] They proved particularly useful to
newsbook editors—the title 'Mercury-woman' was a result of this
association—and by 1659 hawkers and 'Mercuries' were recognized
as the normal distributors of the official periodical.[11] Meanwhile,
they advertised *Aulicus* with a discreet cry: 'Will you buy a new

[1] *Mercurius Civicus*, no. 6 (8–16 June 1643), p. 47.
[2] Ibid., p. 41.
[3] *The Welch Mercurie*, no. 3 (3–11 Nov. 1643), p. 8, commented on its weekly
arrival; and *Britanicus* was able to review every copy of *Aulicus* published during its
own lifetime. For the delays see App. I.
[4] *M. Brit.*, no. 8 (10–17 Oct. 1643), p. 62.
[5] *M. Brit.*, no. 10 (26 Oct.–2 Nov.), p. 78, and no. 40 (17–24 June 1644), p. 317.
For the long association of these two places with news, see Wheatley and Cunning-
ham, *London Past and Present* (1891), iii. 53–4 and 484.
[6] *Mercurius Civicus*, no. 79 (21–28 Nov. 1644), p. 729.
[7] *M. Brit.*, no. 14 (23–30 Nov. 1643), p. 107.
[8] Roger L'Estrange in *The Intelligencer*, no. 1 (31 Aug. 1663), p. 3. The Mercury-
women sold pamphlets wholesale from the presses to the hawkers who retailed
them on the streets. See H. R. Fox-Bourne, *English Newspapers* (1887), i. 11 n.
[9] *The Whole Life and Progress of Henry Walker* (12 July 1642), A2ʳ.
[10] J. B. Williams, *History of English Journalism*, pp. 47–8, 92–3, 112, and 121.
[11] W. Kilburne, *A New-Years-Gift for Mercurius Politicus* (29 Dec. 1659).

merry booke, that Tom Thumbe and Galagantea never sold better'.[1] They were probably its main 'outlet' in London.

These, then, were the principal means, a mixture of casual and organized, whereby *Aulicus* was dispersed. More than idle curiosity prompts enquiry into the effectiveness of these methods and the composition of the newsbook's readership. For these matters are sometimes obscured by misunderstanding or misinformation; and the answers provide one measure of *Aulicus*'s influence and importance. As for the readership, it was virtually a convention of 'character' writers and academic observers to dismiss it as a nosy and gullible mob; and plenty of contemporaries were eager to believe this. No one would deny that every newspaper has readers whose motives and intelligence are questionable; but the 're-actionaries' protested too much and too late, and their image of periodicals as universally vulgar and mendacious is a distortion. Comparison of observations by men like Richard Brathwaite and Donald Lupton on the Corantos of the 1630s[2] with the conclusions of modern investigators[3] proves this.

The demand for news was, in fact, an important manifestation of the desire of the literate population outside London to assert itself in the life and government of the nation. This is one reason why the Court—the bastion of conservatism and privilege—refused to countenance the publication of anything but foreign and the most harmless home news before the Civil War forced its hand. The hostile attitude of most published comment on newsbooks was, at least in part, a pandering to such reactionary sentiments. It was the somewhat sterile reflex of an exclusive tradition feeling itself threatened by new and encroaching social forces. Ironically, in 1643 the regime which had relied so heavily on suppression of news itself set about capturing a nation-wide audience with an enthusiasm and skill unprecedented in English journalism. The rapidity with which Berkenhead and others mastered newsbook

---

[1] *The Court Mercurie*, no. 10 (7–14 Sept. 1644), K1ᵛ.

[2] In *Whimzies* (1631), ed. J. O. Halliwell (1859), and *London and the Country Carbonadoed* (1632), reprinted in *Harl. Misc.* ix. 330–1, respectively.

[3] See Folke Dahl, *On Quoting Newspapers. A problem and a Solution* (1948), reprinted from *The Journalism Quarterly*, and *A Bibliography of English Corantos and Periodical Newsbooks, 1620–1642* (Bibliographical Soc., 1952), and D. C. Collins, *A Handlist of News Pamphlets, 1590–1610* (1943).

techniques is quite remarkable; and they were to stand their exponents and the Court in good stead over the ensuing decades.

Conventional criticisms of the press were, nevertheless, echoed well into the second half of the century. They were, of course, increasingly applied in a partisan spirit: it was the enemy's newsbooks which were cheap and nasty. Even major journalists like Berkenhead and Roger L'Estrange themselves wrote nostalgically of happy, secure days when there was no need for newsbooks.[1] They were paying lip-service to old formulas, and in practice applied themselves to the business in hand. Partisan politics, and the propaganda that goes with them, had come to stay.

Aulicus, anyhow, was not aimed at the mob, of which it often wrote with the utmost disdain, but at men of capacity and consequence. During the Civil War several priests and ministers actually edited newsbooks;[2] and before, during, and after hostilities clergymen great and small followed the printed news closely.[3] Among the readers of *Aulicus* one finds the Rector of Ducklington, near Oxford,[4] and the Puritan minister, Thomas Edwards.[5] Like the clerics, the aristocracy and gentry and their wives were, over the years, regular purchasers of periodicals and pamphlets;[6] and among them Sir Humphrey Mildmay and Edmund Ludlow took

---

[1] In a letter prefaced to the *Itinerary* of John Raymond (1648), and in *The Intelligencer*, no. 1 (31 Aug. 1663), quoted in the 'Life' of L'Estrange in the *D.N.B.*, respectively.

[2] See under Peter Heylin, Bruno Ryves, Richard Little, and John Hackluyt in J. B. Williams, *History of English Journalism*.

[3] *The Diary of John Rous* (Camden Soc. lxvi, 1856), p. 121; *Trevelyan Papers*, Part III (Camden Soc. cv, 1872), p. 222; *The Diary of the Rev. Ralph Josselin, 1616–1683* (Camden Soc., 3rd Ser. xv, 1908), pp. 165 and 173; Henry Wharton, *History of the Troubles and Tryal of William Laud*, p. 337; John Cleaveland, *The Character of a London Diurnall* (1645), reprinted in *Character Writings of the Seventeenth Century*, ed. H. Morley (1891), p. 307, and L. Hanson, 'English Newsbooks, 1620–1641', *The Library*, 4th Ser. xviii (1938), 382.

[4] See his diary in the Bodleian Library, MS. Top. Oxon. c. 378, pp. 366, 374, and 382.

[5] *Gangraena*, Part I (1646), p. 54.

[6] For examples see *Letters of Lady Brilliana Harley*, pp. 19, 32, 69, 252, and 254. *Savile Correspondence* (Camden Soc. lxxxi, 1858), pp. 55 and 61; *Hamilton Papers Relating to 1638–50* (Camden Soc. N.S. xxvii, 1880), pp. 187–8; *Duppa–Isham Correspondence, 1650–1680* (Northants Record Soc. xvii, 1955), pp. 8, 77, and 93; *Letters from Roundhead Officers* (Bannatyne Club, 1856), p. 33; *Memoirs of the Verney Family*, ii. 82; *Chirk Castle Accounts, 1605–1666*, ed. W. M. Myddleton (1908), pp. 100 and 145; *Conway Letters*, p. 261; and *The Knyvett Letters, 1620–1644*, pp. 109 and 110.

Aulicus.[1] Academics, too, were avid news-readers:[2] in January 1644 one Richard Watkins, a B.C.L. at Oxford, was asked by a friend in Wales to send him '2 or 3 Mercuries for the 2 or 3 last weekes'.[3] A more famous scholar, Brian Twyne, one of the great antiquaries of his day, even did *Aulicus* the honour of quoting it as a source in one of his compilations.[4] Clearly it was not just what an opponent scornfully called 'the giddy youth of the University'[5] who bought and trusted the Oxford newsbook. Even those who did not trust it purchased it, for Prynne was well acquainted with its pages,[6] as were the Earl of Essex and Sir Samuel Luke,[7] who incidentally does not once refer to *Britanicus*.

At the same time, the circle of a newsbook's influence extended beyond the ranks of the privileged and literate: *Britanicus* boasted in 1644 that the very ploughboy had, through its efforts, come to distrust *Aulicus*.[8] It is unlikely that ploughboys or other labourers could read; but there is ample evidence that news pamphlets and political tracts were read aloud in public.[9] High and low alike were agape for news and open to propagandist suggestion. Still, perhaps most interesting of all *Aulicus*'s readers are the statesmen. For though there had been isolated instances of pamphlets published at the instigation of officialdom before the Civil War,[10] *Aulicus* was the first manifestation in England of a prolonged and constructive interest in journalism on their part. The pains taken by the Oxford junto with its composition and publication have been remarked upon; they also directly promoted its circulation. The Earl of

[1] See, respectively, P. L. Ralph, *Sir Humphrey Mildmay*, Rutgers Studies in History, no. 3 (New Brunswick, U.S.A., 1947), p. 212, and *Memoirs*, ed. C. H. Firth (1894), i. 72.

[2] For examples see *The Genuine Remains of . . . Thomas Barlow* (1693), p. 328; *Memoirs of the Verney Family*, ii. 249; and *Conway Letters*, p. 190.

[3] *C.S.P. Dom.*, 1644, p. 9.

[4] 'An Account of the Musterings of the University of Oxford', printed as an Appendix to *Chronicon . . . De Dunstaple*, ed. Thomas Hearne (1733), ii. 783 and 785.

[5] *The Court Mercurie*, no. 10 (7–14 Sept. 1644), K1ᵛ.

[6] *A Fresh Discovery* (24 July 1645), p. 17.

[7] See in *The Letter Book 1644–45 of Sir Samuel Luke*, ed. H. G. Tibbutt, for H.M.C. (1963); for example, letters no. 88 and 503.

[8] No. 51 (23–30 Sept.), p. 399.

[9] *Letters of Lady Brilliana Harley*, p. 12; *The Clarke Papers*, vol. iv (Camden Soc. lxii, 1901), pp. 229 and 231.

[10] See D. C. Collins, *A Handlist of News Pamphlets, 1590–1610*, nos. xlviii and cxliv.

Forth received copies of *Aulicus* direct from Sir Edward Nicholas,[1] who also dispatched it in his letters to the Court's Ambassador in Spain and to the Residents in Paris and Vienna.[2] Arthur Trevor, Royalist Governor of Shrewsbury, forwarded at least one number of 'the Mercury, the lawful issue of this week' to the Marquis of Ormond in Ireland.[3] Not only loyal servants of the Crown made the newsbook known outside England; for in July 1643 the Venetian Resident in London sent a copy of one of its reports to the Doge and Senate in Venice.[4] There were not many places of importance—if any—to which *Aulicus* could not penetrate: it reached out through 'the greatest part of England',[5] and overseas. Nor was its circulation abroad ineffective: Stephen Marshall, the forceful Presbyterian divine, complained bitterly of aspersions on his character being printed in *Aulicus* and 'sent . . . into other Kingdoms' by a 'great Officer of State'.[6] His apprehensions were not baseless, for it was to counteract such influence on the Continent that a periodical in French, *Le Mercure Anglois*, was started in June 1644.[7]

All the evidence points to one conclusion: the composition, production, and circulation of *Aulicus* benefited enormously from Court sponsorship. In all these respects it set a standard of efficiency and thoroughness previously unknown in English journalism. One may reasonably inquire whether that outlay of effort and expense was rewarded. It is not easy to measure the effect that propaganda has on the course of events. The newsbook was 'an important force in moulding public opinion';[8] but the relationship between opinion and action is rarely simple and direct. Many men, when it comes to the push, will act according to expediency of some sort even where that clashes with principle or prejudice.

---

[1] *C.S.P. Dom.*, 1644, p. 64.

[2] *Commons' Journals*, ii. 1003. This notes the interception of Nicholas's letters; a similar occurrence was referred to by *M. Brit.*, no. 6 (26 Sept.–3 Oct. 1643), pp. 45–6.

[3] Thomas Carte, *A Collection of Original Letters and Papers* (1739), i. 27.

[4] *C.S.P. Ven.*, 1642–3, pp. 304–7.

[5] *The Flying Post*, no. 1 (3–10 May 1644), A1^r. *The Scotch Mercury*, no. 1 (5 Oct. 1643), p. 1, refers to *Aulicus* being in Edinburgh.

[6] *A Copy of a Letter Written by Mr. Stephen Marshall* (about 17 May 1643), p. 1.

[7] See App. III.

[8] J. Frank, *The Beginnings of the English Newspaper, 1620–1660*, p. 57.

Still, while the active force of belief is variable and hard to assess, it is a factor that has to be reckoned with. The rallying cry of faction does fulfil a real function, even if men's motives for heeding and echoing it are intricate. Thus *Aulicus* must have had some impact on the course of the Civil War. Its London opponents did not doubt that its effects were great: they lamented the 'winged speed' with which it was sent into all quarters of the nation,[1] and the eagerness with which the kingdom attended its arrival each week.[2] These numerous and persistent rivals claimed that before their challenge all its statements passed 'for current truths',[3] and that it insinuated its 'Venimous influences into many English hearts'.[4] They feared its potency as the 'sole object' of Malignant faith[5] and 'the common source and spring of all their fictions'.[6] The way in which London Royalists seem to have taken their cue from *Aulicus* to denounce as forgeries letters from the King to the Queen published in 1645, suggests that this was no overstatement.[7] Some even put a figure to its effects: *Britanicus* estimated the seizure of 500 copies as a setback comparable with the King's failure to take Gloucester.[8] *Aulicus*, it reckoned, had done Charles 'Prodigious service',[9]—better than Rupert's, it hazarded in a moment of euphoric sarcasm.[10] Another more cautiously suggested that it had done Parliament more damage than '2000 of the King's Souldiers'.[11] This is all very flattering, and questionable; yet by representing the enemy forces as perpetually on the verge of collapse, the newsbook may have encouraged recruitment to the King's standard and discouraged defection. Opponents certainly believed it had a material influence on political and military morale;[12] and their assertion that many Royalists 'never began to

[1] *Newes from Smith* (5 Feb. 1645), p. 4.
[2] *The Recantation of Mercurius Aulicus* (14 Mar. 1644), p. 3.   [3] Ibid.
[4] *The True Character of Mercurius Aulicus*, p. 4.
[5] *A Continuation of Certain Speciall and Remarkable Passages*, no. 3 (17–24 July 1644), p. 7.
[6] *Mercurius Civicus*, no. 37 (1–7 Feb. 1644), p. 392.
[7] *M. Brit.*, no. 94 (18–25 Aug. 1645), p. 841.
[8] No. 4 (12–19 Sept. 1643), p. 25.
[9] No. 39 (10–17 June 1644), p. 303.
[10] No. 101 (13–20 Oct. 1645), p. 897.
[11] *The True Character of Mercurius Aulicus*, p. 4.
[12] Ibid., p. 7.

distrust their Cause' until *Aulicus* faltered, and only despaired when it failed to appear, is not unreasonable.[1] The efforts made to keep it going suggest that the junto's estimate of its value was not lower than that of their enemies, whose bold attempts to define the incalculable at least convey the contemporary sense of *Aulicus*'s power.

The best evidence of *Aulicus*'s strength is, nevertheless, the legion of pamphlets and periodicals marshalled against it. Altogether during its run some twenty-two periodicals appeared in London, devoted, in various degrees, to discrediting it.[2] Of these the most dedicated were the newsbooks, *Mercurius Civicus*, *Mercurius Britanicus*, *The Scotish Dove*, and *The Spie*; and the last three expressly set themselves to fight *Aulicus* with its own weapon—a blend of factual reporting and satirical commentary. Their efforts to copy its manner excited the superior Royalist sneer that it was unbecoming for Puritans to be witty.[3] These 'Puritans' needed no reminding that *Aulicus* was a byword for wit, or that its eloquence had captured the public imagination. Ruefully they confessed that it knew how to 'mix folly and knavery, and Roguery too, and do it handsomly, like an Artist'.[4] This was backhanded, but the Londoners were not joking when they complained that its 'fine reasonable posture', its 'smooth language', and its 'alluring tongue'[5] had made too deep an impression for their peace of mind.

Besides these newsbooks London also produced some seventeen pamphlets attacking *Aulicus*'s position; and passing references to it in tracts primarily concerned with other business are too numerous to list. Altogether this was formidable opposition to what was virtually 'the onely Paper Engineer' the Court had,[6] and nearly a dozen pamphlets rallied to help it to repel onslaughts. Through it all, though towards the end showing the strain, *Aulicus* did as

[1] *M. Brit.*, no. 60 (2–9 Dec. 1644), p. 471 and no. 98 (15–22 Sept. 1645), p. 873, respectively.

[2] For these and the other pamphlets and periodicals referred to, see App. III.

[3] *Britanicus Vapulans* (4 Nov. 1643), p. 3.

[4] *Good Newes from All Quarters of the Kingdome* (13 Sept. 1643), A3ᵛ.

[5] In, respectively, *M. Brit.*, no. 10 (26 Oct.–2 Nov. 1643), p. 80, no. 59 (18–25 Nov. 1644), p. 464, and *An Answer to Mercurius Aulicus* (about 15 Dec. 1642), p. 1.

[6] *M. Brit.*, no. 39 (10–17 June 1644), p. 304.

much as could be done to 'hold up all with the pen and the press'.[1]
It is no exaggeration to state that in the process it transformed the
constitution and character of contemporary journalism; and its
effect is apparent not only in its immediate rivals, whose number
and vehemence are witness to its importance, but also in the later
Royalist newsbooks of the second Civil War.

Perhaps its most far-reaching achievement was the establishment
of official journalism in this country. For above all else *Aulicus*
demonstrated the superiority in all departments of a newsbook
backed by a powerful and extensive organization. The quality of
its printing, the extent of its circulation, and the excellence of its
intelligence were a spur to rivals. Moreover it drew attention to
the need to employ talented writers as editors, as the subsequent
career of its arch enemy, Marchamont Nedham shows. Periodical
journalism became for individuals and regimes a way to favour. If
Thomas Audley really was admitted to meetings of the Close
Committee in 1645, it was because Parliament recognized, however
tentatively and belatedly, the need to combat Royalist propaganda
with something more authoritative than it had previously relied on.
This may even have been one motive—though obviously not the
chief one—behind the progressive improvements of the postal
system in the 1640s and 1650s.[2] When new stages were set up
between London and Preston in late 1644, among the postmasters
and intelligencers appointed was Sir John Gell. As *The Perfect Occurrences* had a correspondent in Derby[3] and was full of notices of Gell's
exploits in that year, it is reasonable to suggest that the latter fed
information to the editor. So the postal organization, though not
primarily devised for the benefit of newsbooks, served their turn.

It was, however, left to the increasingly more powerful army to
rationalize the structure of London journalism. In September 1647
Fairfax made representations to Parliament about the licence of the
press, as a result of which an official weekly news bulletin was
issued.[4] At about the same time a rash of illicit Royalist periodicals

[1] *M. Brit.*, no. 23 (12–19 Feb. 1644), p. 179.
[2] *C.S.P. Dom.*, 1644–5, p. 170.
[3] C. H. Firth in *Memoirs of the Life of Colonel Hutchinson*, p. 397.
[4] W. M. Clyde, 'Parliament and the Press. II', *The Library*, 4th Ser. xiv (1933–4),
57–8.

began to appear, offensive to Parliament and the troops. This irritated the authorities, who set about purging the body journalistic: distasteful newsbooks were cast out and new, palatable periodicals served up by the Council of State.[1] Meanwhile, the work of perfecting the Posts went ahead, and about 1648 they were increased to two a week. Later Cromwell and his lieutenants bent their energies to improving communications and controlling public opinion by censoring the mails. To strengthen his hold Cromwell sponsored *Mercurius Politicus*, the most important of all the official newsbooks published in London. It ran from 13 June 1650 until April 1660; and between October 1655 and April 1659, together with its companion-piece, *The Publick Intelligencer*, it enjoyed a total monopoly of printed news. Able and even eminent men were associated with it: John Thurloe, Cromwell's spymaster, was close to it; John Milton acted in some sort of supervisory capacity, as, it seems, did John Hall of Durham; though the bulk of the work from 1655 on was done by Nedham. It was as much concerned with the suppression of undesirable news as with the publication of authoritative information, but such a newsbook must have had access to official sources of intelligence.[2] It is to Cromwell's credit that, realizing the importance of a periodical, he employed able men to produce it for him. He further demonstrated his willingness to learn from enemies by taking a travelling press with him on some of his campaigns:[3] this led to the production in 1651 of *Mercurius Scoticus*, the first newsbook written and printed in Scotland. If, as may be, its editor was William Clarke, General Monke's secretary, it too had access to official sources of information.[4] Monke certainly used the press later to condition and instruct his troops politically while they were in Scotland; and when

[1] These were *A Brief Relation* and *Severall Proceedings in Parliament* begun in Oct. 1649, and *A Perfect Diurnall*, edited by John Rushworth, which commenced in December of the same year. For these and the other newsbooks mentioned hereabout see J. B. Williams, *History of English Journalism*.

[2] This is confirmed by C. H. Firth in his preface to the *Clarke Papers*, vol. iii, p. vii.

[3] See J. D. Ogilvie, 'Papers from an Army Press, 1650', *Edinburgh Bibl. Soc. Trans.* ii (1938–45), 420–3, and *A View of Part of the Many Traiterous . . . Actions of H. H. Senior, Sometime Printer to Cromwell* (1684).

[4] W. J. Couper, *The Edinburgh Periodical Press* (1908), i. 57–8 and 166–9. He doubts whether Clarke was editor, but on false grounds.

he came south in 1659 he employed a journalist, Henry Muddiman, to feel his way into public opinion; and it was he who as editor launched the *Mercurius Publicus* and *The Parliamentary Intelligencer* which in 1660 toppled Nedham's newsbooks.

With the Restoration of Charles II the wheel came full circle: the Court took over the newsbooks, which were henceforth issued from the office of the Secretary of State. Until 1663 Edward Nicholas held that post, and though Muddiman was still employed as official journalist the periodicals were supervised during these three years by Nicholas's old ally John Berkenhead. Journalism had virtually 'arrived' as an auxiliary of government, and the journalist's status had risen with it. In the long run *Aulicus* played a signal part in this process, not least because in Berkenhead it had a gifted editor who commanded attention. Like his contemporaries we can only conclude (from examining the composition and publication of *Aulicus*) that he admirably exploited his talents and his closeness to the centre of power at Oxford. To learn more of that skill and the Court's policies one must look now more narrowly at the newsbook's contents.

CHAPTER III

1643 to 1646

'Exceedingly bold, confident, witty'

As the first official newsbook published in England *Aulicus* pre-sented the reader with a quantity of news and a quality of writing to which he was quite unaccustomed in periodicals. It stirred the enemy into assuring the public that it was full of false reports and 'satyricke stuffe'.[1] Their story was that it 'always play'd the Court bouffon, and, . . . put off every thing either with a jest or a jeere',[2] and was 'so accustomed to publish notorious untruths that with the common lyar he is justly suspected even when he stumbles upon a truth'.[3] This was wishful thinking, but it is roughly what has been thought of *Aulicus* ever since, at least until quite recently.

The examination in the last chapter showed that in fact no simple formula properly accounts for variations in its efficiency and manner. Analysis of its military, political, and religious intelligence confirms that this holds too for its handling of facts. Its thorough-ness can be gauged by comparing it with the many 'supplements' published at Oxford during its run:[4] several of these have been acknowledged as the best contemporary sources for the events they describe, and though, naturally, they are often more expansive than the weekly their accounts equally often add few essentials to its narratives. *Aulicus*'s accuracy was at its zenith in 1643, when its punctilious method of citing sources, giving dates and statistics, and its full descriptions of important events at once and deser-vedly established it as England's premier newsbook. For too long it has suffered from the stigma which S. R. Gardiner fixed upon

[1] *The Recantation of Mercurius Aulicus* (14 Mar. 1644), p. 7.
[2] *The True Character of Mercurius Aulicus* (1645), p. 8.
[3] *A True Relation of the Great and Glorious Victory . . . Obtained by Sir William Waller* (14 July 1643), p. 2.
[4] See App. II for a list of supplements.

F

it,[1] but the more favourable conclusions of some recent historians[2] will
be amply supported and reinforced by the present investigation.
The truth is that it was not in 1645 what it had been in 1643, yet
even towards the end, when most evasive and bluffingly strident,
it occasionally published useful material. Taken over all, *Aulicus*'s
military and political reporting reflects much credit on Berkenhead;
and it remains a valuable source of information. But history, in any
case, is not just 'facts', and measurement of *Aulicus*'s accuracy
does not exhaust its possible claims as an historical document.
Its opinions are equally if not more important. The two chief
editors, as has been seen, were thorough-paced Laudians, working
hand in glove with Charles's intimate advisers. Through their
endeavour *Aulicus* consistently represented one political outlook at
Oxford, which was that of the King, and not of Hyde or Falkland.
This is important, for it shows that whatever tactical professions
were made, Charles and his immediate circle relied on continuing
political and religious Laudianism.

In Berkenhead they had a fitting and reliable spokesman; he was
not the man to indulge deviationism. On the other hand, he did go
his own way in repartee and ingenious caricature. This talent won
Aulicus the title of 'Court bouffon'; and its blossoming, along with
declining Royalist fortunes, accounts for the gradual conversion of
the newsbook from a comparatively 'objective' chronicle to something more like a 'running-comedy' of Rebellion (often informative
in a different way of course). The constant throughout Berkenhead's 'reign' is his stylish though unaffected and unornate prose;
and at his best he is both informative and entertaining. Free agent
he was not, but he did stamp his personality on Cavalier journalism
and, through it, on the whole world of contemporary news-writing.
In particular his work has a bearing on the development of political
satire in this period; it will be the final function of this chapter to
examine this, for by and large it is the accuracy of Berkenhead's
information and the special slant of his views—both to be assessed
first—that give his journalism its sting.

---

[1] *History of the Great Civil War, 1642–1649* (1886–91), vol. i, p. ix.
[2] J. H. Hexter, *The Reign of King Pym* (Harvard Univ. Press, 1941), p. 213;
D. R. Guttery, *The Great Civil War in Midland Parishes* (1951), p. 1; and M. R.
Toynbee in *Oxoniensia*, xvi (1951), 101–2.

Military Coverage

The lion's share of space in *Aulicus* was naturally devoted to military intelligence in the shape of accounts of marches, skirmishes, and battles. These were usually reported with punctilious regard for detail; and London newsbooks, simply not in a position to be so precise, could often only retaliate with rather desperate raillery. *Britanicus* jeered at *Aulicus* for being 'Register . . . to all his Maiesties battells' and for chronicling 'every stroake and discharge'.[1] It laughed at scrupulous dating of events[2] and suggested mockingly that casualty figures were faked.[3] The Oxford newsbook very properly replied that it gave 'all the particulars' as necessary disproof of enemy exaggerations and inaccuracies;[4] and criticized pamphlets that omitted casualty figures, wryly calling them 'a particular that deserves mention in a battaile'.[5] It scorned journalists who did not know the proper 'termes of Art to describe a Siege'.[6] The editor was trying genuinely to establish a viable technique of war-reporting. Not only did it date each event carefully, but also, in the relevant cases, it noted the day, sometimes the time of day, when dispatches had reached Oxford. Even in 1644 and 1645, when it did try to deceive by delaying the publication of its reports, there is no evidence that it ever lied about the actual timing of events. In such cases it can still be a useful source for modern investigators. *Britanicus*'s sneers about its precision are certainly irrelevant.

Of the offence of fiddling casualty figures—the common weakness of wartime regimes—it is sometimes guilty. Describing the defeat of the Fairfaxes by the Earl of Newcastle in July 1643, it adjusted the numbers of slain and captured.[7] Yet it seems to have

---

[1] No. 32 (15–22 Apr. 1644), p. 250. It makes a similar criticism in no. 37 (20–27 May), p. 289.

[2] No. 36 (13–20 May), p. 280. See also no. 70 (10–17 Feb. 1645), p. 550, which mocks *Aulicus*'s division into weeks and days.

[3] No. 59 (18–25 Nov. 1644), p. 464. Compare no. 38 (27 May–3 June 1644), p. 295.   [4] No. 13 (26 Mar.–1 Apr. 1643), p. 158.

[5] No. 58 (4–10 Feb. 1644), p. 824.

[6] No. 75 (2–8 June 1644), p. 1018.

[7] No. 27 (2–8 July 1643), p. 350. The measure of its accuracy throughout this chapter has been taken from S. R. Gardiner, *History of the Great Civil War, 1642–1649*.

been accurate about Prince Rupert's capture of Cirencester in the same year;[1] and though glibly passing it off as the first truth told by *Aulicus*, *Britanicus* actually copied its list of dead for the first Battle of Newbury.[2] Indeed, that London newsbook frequently and intriguingly cadged details and documents from *Aulicus*, often without questioning their dependability. Clearly, no generalization about *Aulicus*'s handling of figures is satisfactory: wariness is needed, but it was not nearly as bad as opponents wanted people to believe.

It was also accused of inventing letters and dispatches.[3] This, too, is untrue. A comparison of its narratives of major battles with those of the fullest and most reliable modern chronicler, S. R. Gardiner,[4] shows how genuine its intelligences usually were. Exposition of the manœuvres of both armies is surprisingly accurate, and is executed with commendable clarity and fluency. To savour the excellence of *Aulicus*'s best war-reporting one should refer to the account of the Royalist victory at Cropredy Bridge in July 1644. Even Berkenhead's characteristic jibe at the strategy of the Parliamentary general Sir William Waller, the best chooser of ground of the day—'you know his condition of old, hils, boggs, hedges, ditches, these you must grant him, hee'll not fight else'[5]— was to the point; and his claim that the Parliament's army had been smashed cannot be faulted.

A little less inaccurate was the accusation that *Aulicus* never conceded victory to the enemy:[6] defeats of the King's forces could hardly be denied; but it is true that everything was done to soften their blow. In October 1643 *Aulicus* confessed a setback in Lincolnshire, but took some sting out of it by being vague about details, on the grounds that the beaten soldiers would not say what had

---

[1] No. 5 (29 Jan.–4 Feb. 1643), pp. 62–3.

[2] *M. Brit.*, no. 6 (26 Sept.–3 Oct. 1643), pp. 44–5.

[3] *The True Character of Mercurius Aulicus*, p. 6.

[4] *History of the Great Civil War, 1642–1649.*

[5] No. 78 (23–29 June 1644), pp. 1054–60. This could be an eyewitness account by Berkenhead, who had been with the King on his marches of the previous four weeks. The quotation is from p. 1055. The report is, incidentally, much finer than the one from the first number of *Aulicus* (written, I consider, by Heylin) which Professor James Sutherland quotes (*On English Prose*, Univ. of Toronto Press, 1965 (1957), pp. 59–61) as an example of Berkenhead's brisk and easy narrative technique.

[6] *M. Brit.*, no. 59 (18–25 Nov. 1644), p. 465.

happened.[1] Similarly in the summer and autumn of 1643, when things were not going well in Cheshire and the north Midlands, *Aulicus* published practically nothing about that area; and it referred to defeats there only when better tidings had come in.[2] Yet in this it shows no more guile than the Londoners, who, as it emphasized,[3] reacted in the same way to events in Wales in 1645.

As it toned down poor news, so *Aulicus* emphasized the cheering: a clash at Cheriton in Devon in June 1643 is puffed up into a Royalist success of 'importance and consequence'.[4] The Battle of Lansdown in the same year was claimed as 'an absolute victory';[5] and the first and second Battles of Newbury were trumpeted as triumphs for the King.[6] In each case the narrative is excellent and full of interesting details, but the conclusions drawn are highly optimistic. Another evasive tactic was to delay the full reporting of bad news: *Aulicus* employed it when Weymouth was lost in March 1645.[7] But such circumspection did not always indicate evasion: in 1643, for example, the captures of Exeter and Bristol by the Royalists were first reported as rumours only, and readers warned that the news was not fully authoritative.[8] Discretion of this sort has been hailed as a virtue in the London newsbooks,[9] but overlooked in *Aulicus*, which in fact relied on it less frequently, partly because it was better and more speedily informed.

In late 1643 and early 1644, of course, Royalist fortunes were prospering, and *Aulicus*, in confident mood, felt it could afford to be open in its observations. Its coverage of the Battle of Alresford in March 1644 best illustrates this:[10] it is acknowledged as a limited defeat for the Crown, and the editor describes, quite correctly, how Waller's troops were allowed to occupy high ground the night

---

[1] No. 42 (15–21 Oct.), p. 586. The next week (22–28 Oct., pp. 600–1) did give more facts, but minimized the defeat.

[2] No. 47 (19–25 Nov.), pp. 676–7.

[3] No. 114 (4–11 May 1645), p. 1580.

[4] No. 24 (11–17 June 1643), p. 318.

[5] No. 27 (2–8 July), p. 361.

[6] See, respectively, no. 38 (17–24 Sept.), pp. 527–31 and no. 95 (20–26 Oct. 1644), pp. 1232–40.

[7] No. 107 (2–9 Mar.), p. 1398.

[8] See, respectively, no. 22 (28 May–3 June), p. 290 and no. 30 (23–29 July), p. 403.

[9] S. R. Gardiner, *History of the Great Civil War, 1642–1649*, vol. i, p. x.

[10] No. 65 (24–30 Mar.), pp. 910–12. The quotation is from p. 910.

before the fight. Victory, he admits, was thrown away by some Royalist soldiers who 'engaged themselves and others too farre, to seek out an enemy even within the Rebel ambuscadoes'. *Britanicus* inevitably accused *Aulicus* of trying to minimize defeat by pleading that the details were too 'various and intricate' to gather at once.[1] In fact, the Royalist account contains some of the best contemporary evidence about the battle. On this occasion*Aulicus* certainly respected truth more than the Londoners, who claimed a fantastic victory.

In sharp contrast to this good reporting is *Aulicus*'s feeble account of the decisive overthrow at Marston Moor. Initially, with wild inaccuracy, it claimed a Royalist victory.[2] This is too brazen to have been simply a lie, and it is probably true, as the editor claimed when conceding victory the next week,[3] that he was misled by rumours spread by Parliamentary troops driven from the field by Rupert's first impetuous charge. Still, the loss was deliberately minimized: contradictions in London accounts were paraded, attention was switched to the relief of Latham House, and it was claimed that the real object of Rupert's campaign—the relief of York—had been accomplished.[4] This was *Aulicus*'s lamest account of a major battle to date, as it was the first irreparable setback in the field for the King's armies.

Greater evasions and downright distortions were to come. The boast of March and April 1645[5] that General Goring was doing nicely in the western campaign was somewhat at odds with the series of disasters he had run into. Though *Aulicus* confessed that it could not get speedy information from Goring,[6] there is no reason to think that false rumours circulated at Oxford as they had after Marston Moor. By this date there was something in *Britanicus*'s assertions that *Aulicus*'s reports were palpably unreliable. Yet it still published authoritative information about the abortive siege of Oxford in May 1645[7]—the reports on this make especially good reading, about the King's desperate marches,[8] and about the

[1] The phrase appears on p. 910 of *Aulicus*. *Britanicus*'s comment is in no. 31 (8–15 Apr.), p. 240.

[2] No. 79 (30 June–6 July 1644), p. 1072.

[3] No. 80 (7–13 July), p. 1082.   [4] Ibid., pp. 1085–6.

[5] No. 109 (23–30 Mar.), p. 1526 and no. 110 (6–13 Apr.), p. 1540.

[6] No. 116 (13–20 July 1645), pp. 1620–1.

[7] No. 115 (25 May–8 June), pp. 1615–17.   [8] Ibid., pp. 1604–11.

triumphs of Montrose in Scotland.[1] Gallant as Montrose's achievements were, however, he could hardly be expected to save the day for the King. In asserting that he would do so, as in its insistence that the New Model Army was foundering, *Aulicus* was but faithfully voicing the incurable Micawberism of George Digby. None the less, the dispatches about Montrose's heroic campaign compare favourably with the London newsbooks' denials.[2]

The later numbers of *Aulicus* also contain useful accounts of sieges and minor skirmishes: those of the daring relief of Basing, for example, are interesting.[3] *Britanicus* criticized the detailed fullness of such reports as mere camouflage—a distraction from Royalist failure in open battle.[4] There was something in this; but in one respect it is an unfair accusation: though *Aulicus* had an ulterior motive, the sieges marked an important stage of the war and were legitimate copy. In its reckoning of what *Britanicus* disdainfully termed 'victories over foure, and grand conquests of valiant Buffe-coates and warlike apparell, in stead of men',[5] *Aulicus* again provides valuable and often unique witness to some of the minor exploits of the war.[6] Nor was this just a refuge in hard times, since the very first week contained a precise account of a clash in Burford.[7] The only element of dishonesty in the later examples is that their importance is sometimes exaggerated: the facts appear to be sound.

On two points *Britanicus*'s criticisms were fully merited—the increasingly late reporting of news, and the gaps in publication. Complete silence was *Aulicus*'s nearest approach to admission that conditions were hopeless: never was it more at a loss for words than after the disastrous Battle of Naseby on 14 June 1645, when

[1] No. 108 (16–23 Mar.), pp. 1516–18; no. 114 (4–11 May), pp. 1583–5; no. 115 (25 May–8 June), pp. 1611–12; and no. 118 (31 Aug.–6 Sept.), pp. 1729–32.

[2] See, for example, *M. Brit.*, no. 75 (17–24 Mar. 1645), p. 605 and no. 85 (26 May–2 June), p. 773.

[3] The account of the relief is in no. 89 (8–14 Sept. 1644), pp. 1160–6. Earlier and subsequent events are chronicled in no. 41 (8–14 Oct. 1643), pp. 641–2; no. 80 (7–13 July 1644), p. 1076; no. 88 (1–7 Sept.), pp. 1147–8; no. 96 (27 Oct.–2 Nov. 1644), p. 1242; no. 118 (31 Aug.–7 Sept. 1645), p. 1727.

[4] No. 22 (5–12 Feb. 1644), p. 173; no. 35 (6–13 May), p. 273; no. 56 (28 Oct.–4 Nov.), p. 444; and no. 64 (30 Dec.–6 Jan. 1645), p. 507.

[5] No. 64 (30 Dec.–6 Jan. 1645), p. 507.

[6] See, for example, its description of a skirmish at Canons Ashby in Northamptonshire, no. 68 (14–20 Apr. 1644), pp. 948–9.

[7] No. 1 (1–7 Jan. 1643), pp. 1–3.

publication ceased for nine weeks.[1] Attempts to disguise such gaps did not deceive *Britanicus*, nor did it go unnoticed when *Aulicus* spun out old material by looking back 'over his shoulder at the week that is past',[2] once even stretching to an event six months away.[3] He did, however, pull some wool over enemy eyes; for they never realized just how far publication was trailing behind events. *Britanicus* could not help noticing when three numbers were published at once, but it apparently did not notice, to take one example, that the number for 13–20 July 1645, was not really compiled until about 12 August.[4] Berkenhead's ingenuity was not entirely in vain.

There is then no way of summing up *Aulicus* in a simple formula. As a purveyor of accurate information with a minimum of misinterpretation it was most impressive in 1643 and early 1644, when it could fairly claim that the King's position was good and getting better. Some small deterioration set in in the autumn of 1643 when it stopped giving full details of occurrences in Oxford itself. This was a matter of policy, not ignorance, of course; and the substantial deficiencies date from the defeat at Marston Moor, after which the newsbook suffered from slow and bad news. Even then it occasionally commands attention.

Political Coverage

This basic pattern of early pertinency and fullness, fading as time passed but never failing completely, holds in *Aulicus*'s coverage of the London political scene. Its principal aim was to exert pressure so as to 'hasten the disintegration' of the Parliamentary coalition;[5] The basic premise of its commentary was that Parliament was but a pretended Parliament. To this end it emphasized differences in and between Lords and Commons,[6] arguing that no institution so divided against itself could be regarded as genuinely representative of anything but faction.[7] Parliamentarians certainly were not of one accord; determined men were still

[1] See App. I.   [2] *M. Brit.*, no. 45 (22–29 July 1644), p. 354.
[3] Ibid., no. 73 (3–10 Mar. 1645), p. 585.   [4] See App. I.
[5] See J. Frank, *The Beginnings of the English Newspaper*, p. 37.
[6] For example in no. 62 (3–9 Mar. 1644), p. 864.
[7] No. 79 (30 June–6 July 1644), p. 1063.

in the process of assuming control, eliminating the half-hearted, and bringing the Upper House to the Lower's heel. This progressive concentration of power alarmed Royalists, and *Aulicus*, in 1644, attacked Parliament as a forced assembly bent on rule by committee.[1] To some extent, however, the closing of ranks in London deprived the editor of one means of making scandal; so he switched attention to disagreements between Parliament and the City, Parliament and the Army, and within the Army itself. Friction between, for example, Waller and the Earl of Essex, Major-General Browne and Essex, and Cromwell and the Earl of Manchester, was relished.[2] In some cases, like the last, the Londoners had to concede that the stigma on the Good Cause was a very real one.[3]

As for the citizens, they were repeatedly told that Parliament was exploiting them. *Aulicus*, meticulously reporting the many excises and taxes imposed on them, asserted that Parliament had never passed an Ordinance 'but in one part or other, 'twas to fetch in money',[4] which, though pretended for public use, always found its way into 'the pockets of private Rebells'.[5] This indignation was all very pious but, to say the least, doubt was cast on its sincerity when it contradictorily complained that the same poor citizens had themselves pushed fifty-four such Ordinances through Parliament.[6] But mostly *Aulicus* wanted to stress that the Londoners were unwitting and unwilling dupes; it also hoped to convince them that their sacrifices were in vain. Like the King, it apparently believed that the way to a man's heart was through his pocket; and even towards the end it argued that, because of the ringleaders' peculation, cash for the war effort was in short supply in London.[7] Of course, this was also meant to discourage the Scots, in whose coyness on the brink of war *Aulicus* discerned a doubt about Parliament's capacity to satisfy their monetary needs.[8] When they

---

[1] No. 58 (4–10 Feb.), pp. 825–6.

[2] See, respectively, no. 79 (30 June–6 July 1644), p. 1063; no. 86 (18–24 Aug. 1644), p. 1127; and no. 103 (26 Jan.–2 Feb. 1645), pp. 1361–2.

[3] *M. Brit.*, no. 71 (17–24 Feb. 1645), p. 567.

[4] No. 72 (12–18 May 1644), p. 981.   [5] No. 71 (5–11 May), p. 977.

[6] No. 73 (19–25 May 1644), pp. 992–3.   [7] No. 110 (6–13 Apr. 1645), p. 1539.

[8] No. 71 (5–11 May 1644), p. 975. *M. Brit.*, no. 82 (5–12 May 1645), p. 750 (misnumbered 450), stated that the purpose of *Aulicus*'s policy that year had been to make men believe the Scots would not advance.

did finally succumb to temptation readers were assured that what they really wanted to get their hands on was 'the fattest earth for their new plantations'.[1] *Aulicus*'s policy may seem cynical, but it was shrewdly aimed at real, and not entirely groundless, fears in London[2] that the dowry meant more than the bride to the Scots.

Its remarks on the New Model Army were directed at the same point of weakness; people were reminded that it must be paid for by higher taxes. To the last *Aulicus* consoled itself that as these were not forthcoming, the army was on the point of collapse.[3] This was fanciful, but it was true that recruitment was not altogether satisfactory.[4] There may be something in *Aulicus*'s engaging story[5] that young men were decoyed to the Bear Garden in search of entertainment, only to find themselves press-ganged. Even profane pastimes might in an emergency succour the Good Cause.

These few instances display the newsbook's technique well enough: undeniably well-informed of stresses and strains in the enemy camp, it so highlighted them as to draw the 'Rebels' in the image of hypocritical inconsistency. Its treatment of leading Parliamentary personalities sustains this. Henry Martin, the most prominent proto-Republican of the time, and as notorious for his loose living as his free-thinking, quickly attracted *Aulicus*'s attentions. It was reasonable to suggest that he had 'introduced some new principles of State',[6] but it was simply untrue that these were embraced by the leading Parliamentary faction. Sarcasm, not factual accuracy, was served by the argument that the Commons unjustly sent Martin to the Tower (for threatening the person of the King) since 'his language was but the Sense of the House'.[7] Later this may have looked shrewdly prophetic, but at the time Martin was still far to the left of his leaders. *Aulicus*'s policy of treating 'Rebels' as more extreme than they were made it difficult if not impossible for genuine moderates to negotiate. Extremism is

[1] No. 116 (13–20 July 1645), p. 1668.
[2] See *M. Brit.*, no. 85 (26 May–2 June 1645), p. 774.
[3] No. 115 (25 May–8 June 1645), p. 1603.
[4] See *M. Brit.*, no. 57 (4–11 Nov. 1644), p. 448.
[5] No. 116 (13–20 July), p. 1665. There is another notice about pressing in no. 94 (13–19 Oct. 1644), p. 1203.
[6] No. 24 (11–17 June 1643), p. 313.
[7] No. 34 (20–26 Aug. 1643), p. 455.

self-propagating and self-perpetuating. It is also self-defeating; and *Aulicus*'s right-wing Royalism did something to aid and abet the rise to power in London of more uncompromising opponents.

An interesting feature of *Aulicus*'s handling of Martin is its attempt to link Pym with him—a characteristic use of the device of guilt by association.[1] The editor's motive was, of course, a recognition of the skill and drive of Pym's leadership,[2] which he also attempted to undermine through assaults on the Earl of Essex. In direct attack Pym was represented as a juggling politician primarily playing for personal aggrandisement. He was even accused of gross sensuality,[3] and at his death *Aulicus* savagely triumphed over his diseased corpse.[4] In fact, though the Londoners, not to be outdone in superstition, staunchly denied this post-mortem corruption, that much was true. Propagandists on both sides were, regrettably, not loath to wring a moral, however savage, from such misfortunes. Fortunately the best were equally ready with more witty scurrility.

After Pym's death other prominent Parliamentarians, like St. John, Say, Lenthall, and Strode, were subjected to *Aulicus*'s resourceful denigratory tactics. Its assessment of their motives reveals the same 'twisting' of facts natural in propaganda; but it kept close enough to part of the truth to worry and incense London apologists. Their indignant counter-attacks were commonly cruder than *Aulicus*'s slick unruffled sniping at individuals, which Berkenhead defended with a typically suave statement of principle:[5]

Nor should we touch any of their persons, but onely to let you see, that the principall worthy Members in this great Reformation . . . are themselves the most notorious scandalous Delinquents, this Rebellion can afford.

This was no mere tongue-in-cheek defence of scurrility: there may be some mock reluctance here, but primarily it bespeaks the

---

[1] J. Frank, *The Beginnings of the English Newspaper, 1620–1660*, p. 38.
[2] For example see no. 49 (3–9 Dec. 1643), p. 703.
[3] No. 33 (13–19 Aug. 1643), p. 452.
[4] No. 49, loc. cit. This was, on both sides, a common propaganda tactic.
[5] No. 104 (2–9 Feb. 1645), p. 1365.

genuine conviction of extreme Royalists. *Aulicus*'s tactics were not just a propaganda 'front', behind which more realistic calculations were going on; it was the authentic voice of the King and his most favoured advisers. As spokesman for the diehards of the junto, it could not admit, for it could not understand, that Parliament's leaders were responding to and defining profound movements within the body politic. So it nestled in the delusion that the wickedness of individuals had perverted men from total allegiance to the Crown. They would, it believed, gladly return to it on the King's terms once their eyes were opened to their masters' evil intent. Without wishing for a moment to suggest that those masters were all white as the driven snow, it must be admitted that the purist intransigence of *Aulicus* manifests a temper (and that not confined to the Court) which drove the nation ever deeper into war with itself. For it was a temper that made a virtue—as the embattled often do—of inflexibility. *Aulicus*'s brand of insistence upon the enormities of influential Parliamentarians might have been calculated to produce the very thing it feared. It studiously, even brilliantly, avoided conceding to the foe even a misguided idealism and common human feeling. It is that sort of blindness, so damaging to human politics, that seems to distinguish the stance of men like Berkenhead and Digby from that of Clarendon and Falkland. Of course, even Clarendon (by no means a diehard) could not escape from the orthodox 'theological' explanation of rebellion. He was, however, a man of sufficiently flexible mind and broad sympathy to go beyond such as *Aulicus* in recognizing the greatness of some of his foes and the fallibility of many of his friends. Nor was he adamant against all concession. True, one would hardly expect propagandists to put the opposite case well or to be openly large in sympathy; but the fact remains (and it is significant) that there was not even a show of giving moderate Royalist voices a public hearing. The tone and temper of *Aulicus*'s handling of political enemies and problems was more unyieldingly and wittily dismissive than it would have been if control of the Oxford press had rested in some other hands.

Under the general guidance of Digby and Nicholas, the editors Heylin and Berkenhead relentlessly advocated the highest claims made for the King and his Prerogative.[1] To them Parliament was the sole enemy of 'the Property and Liberty of the English Subject, so much pretended by this faction to befoole the people'.[2] They felt sure that 'all Nobles and Gentry'[3] were for the King; and for the rest, they were 'such cattle as were never thought fit to die by the Sword'.[4] Inevitably all responsibility for bloodshed was laid at Parliament's door; and while detecting a progressive hardening of 'Rebel' opinion towards the monarch,[5] *Aulicus* could only account for this in terms of individual malice. One of its last observations on political issues was that if the Parliamentary Ordinance of 12 August 1643 was compared with the King's Declaration of 12 August 1642 'no other History for this matchlesse Rebellion' was needed.[6] This was putting things in a nutshell with a vengeance.

The prospect of negotiations naturally stirred this stalwart 'fundamentalism': *Aulicus* portrayed the King as eager for peace but thwarted by Parliament's determination to settle all by the sword, 'as long as any man will hazard his life and soule in their cause'.[7] It even had the nerve to represent the abortive Waller plot of 1643 as a triviality, inflated by Parliament to encourage the continuance of hostilities.[8] Unfortunately the pious image of pacific monarchy was contradicted by Charles's own sentiments expressed in a private letter to Rupert on August 3, 1645.[9] Nor did it square with editorial reaction to the Uxbridge negotiations earlier in the same year. Perhaps as a concession to moderates, publication of *Aulicus* was twice suspended before formal talks began on 29 January. On the first occasion *Britanicus* suggested that

---

[1] *M. Brit.*, no. 28 (counterfeit) (18–25 Mar. 1644), p. 217 counted on this fact.

[2] No. 31 (30 July–5 Aug. 1643), p. 415.

[3] No. 38 (17–23 Sept.), p. 529. Similar sentiments were expressed in no. 106 (23 Feb.–2 Mar. 1645), p. 1387.

[4] No. 38, loc. cit.

[5] See no. 61 (25 Feb.–2 Mar. 1644), p. 851; no. 74 (26 May–1 June), p. 1006; and no. 111 (13–20 Apr. 1645), p. 1543.

[6] No. 117 (10–17 Aug. 1645), p. 1702.

[7] No. 90 (15–21 Sept. 1644), p. 1171. Earlier, in no. 54 (7–13 Jan. 1644), p. 773, it ascribed London's hostility to the French ambassador to his wish to 'be a Peacemaker'.

[8] No. 26 (25 June–1 July), p. 331.

[9] See S. R. Gardiner, *History of the Great Civil War, 1642–1649*, ii. 157–8.

the pause was a stratagem to make people believe that accommodation was genuinely desired by the Cavaliers.[1] It greeted the
reappearance of *Aulicus* as an affront and proof that there was no
serious intention to treat.[2] At the second pause it rejoiced that,
as the King had at last recognized Parliament, *Aulicus* must now
accept that it had been wasting its time and paper.[3] That was
premature; and when it appeared yet again, still calling Parliament 'Rebels', the exasperated Londoner blankly concluded that
Charles must be dead for his newsbook to contradict him so.[4] In
fact, as men well knew, *Aulicus* throughout represented the King's
real 'harsh thoughts of Anger'.[5] A peaceful outcome to Uxbridge
had never been likely; and though the Court was not alone in pre-
varication, *Aulicus*'s unconciliatory language before and during
negotiations made their futility plain before treating actually broke
down on 22 February. It could well be that Berkenhead deliberately
used the newsbook to undermine any moderate platform.

    In nothing is *Aulicus*'s antipathy towards the Oxford moderates
more apparent than in its sparse coverage of the Oxford Parliament:
the Proclamation summoning it on 22 December 1643 was dutifully
printed in *Aulicus*, but with very little flourish; and subsequent
notices about it conveyed only the barest of facts. There was no
flicker of enthusiasm nor even real interest, except when the
editor was roused to deny vehemently that these moderates
predominated in the Oxford assembly.[6]

    This characteristically stiff-necked attitude makes one doubt
contemporary suggestions[7] that Lord Falkland had a hand in

---

    [1] No. 60 (2–9 Dec.), p. 471. The pause came between *M. Aul.* no. 96 (27 Oct.–
2 Nov.), and no. 99 (17–23 Nov.), with which no. 97 (3–9 Nov.) and no 98 (10–16
Nov.) appeared. For further details see App. I.

    [2] No. 62 (16–23 Dec.), p. 487.

    [3] No. 64 (30 Dec.–6 Jan.), p. 503. Berkenhead explained away the King's momen-
tary acknowledgement of Parliament as a mere expediency in *Mercurius Anti-
Britanicus*, part 2 (11 Aug. 1645), p. 1.

    [4] No. 67 (20–27 Jan.), pp. 527–8. The *Aulicus* in question was no. 100 (29 Dec.–
5 Jan.).

    [5] *The Question Disputed* (26 July 1645), p. 5.

    [6] No. 62 (3–9 Mar. 1644), p. 873.

    [7] *M. Brit.*, no. 6 (26 Sept.–3 Oct. 1643), p. 41 and no. 11 (2–9 Nov.), p. 85,
B.M., E. 375 (1), pp. 4–5 (a poem by Robert Bostock, dated by Thomason to
10 Feb. 1647). The suggestions were probably a result of the habit of lumping all
enemies together, regardless of their differences.

Aulicus before his death in September 1643. There is certainly no
trace of his conciliatory temper there; and his death was but
offhandedly 'lamented',[1] in true keeping with Heylin's private
opinion that 'the church lost no great friend. I am sure I did not'.[2]
His ideas of toleration were anathema to the Laudians who ran the
propaganda machine.[3]

Religious coverage

Political controversies were, of course, largely expressed in
terms of doctrinal allegiance, and the overwhelming weight of
emphasis in *Aulicus* falls here. In terms of coverage the pattern is as
before. Its interpretation of events, too, is familiar: denial of the
existence at Court of any theology but its own.[4] Consistency,
sincerity, and conviction are not despicable; but they can be
misplaced, and even dangerous. In its handling of some of the major
religious issues the newsbook mirrored the King's fatal compromising as fearlessly as it did his more noble rigour.

Dedication to the ideal of the Ecclesiastical State inspired *Aulicus*'s lofty indifference to the beliefs and fears of Parliament's
supporters. This was the stubborn spirit that was to carry Charles
resolutely to the scaffold, believing himself a martyr for his Church,
whatever others said about bigotry and obstructionism. It was a
zealot's faith, that with brave dignity withstood the touch of the
severest trials. But it was also obdurate and sometimes blind.

Like the King, *Aulicus* was optimistic in its calculations of the
political probabilities, and defended the use of Catholic troops and
the Queen's allegiance to Rome as though oblivious that they
were terrible liabilities. As for Henrietta Maria, the newsbook
flatly denied that she aimed at undermining the religion of the land[5]
and that Mass was openly said for her at Oxford.[6] But its anger at
interference with her Capuchin priests in London[7] must have
made many, however wrongly, doubt those protestations. The

---

[1] No. 38 (17–23 Sept. 1643), p. 529.

[2] *Memorial of Bishop Waynflete* (Caxton Soc. 1851), p. xxiv.

[3] Nothing by Falkland was published in Oxford between 1643 and 1646.

[4] No. 57 (28 Jan.–3 Feb. 1644), p. 813, for example.

[5] No. 28 (9–15 July 1643), p. 369.

[6] No. 34 (20–26 Aug.), p. 468.

[7] No. 14 (2–8 Apr.), p. 172.

vacillations of Charles's policy over the use of Catholic troops
landed it in its most indefensible compromises: their presence was
repeatedly defended,[1] although the King's offer of 12 April 1643 to
throw them aside had been duly reported.[2] Similarly, legitimate
anxieties aroused by Charles's efforts to contrive an Irish cessation
(which would have released soldiers to fight in England) were
unheeded. *Aulicus* complacently offered, as strongest proof that the
King was a devoted Protestant, the argument that the Irish
Catholics complained of were defending the Church of England
against Anabaptists and Brownists.[3]

Even in such ambiguities the editor could not be accused of
diplomatic evasion. It was partly because of his open avowals that
enemy propagandists were able to canvass with such success the
theory that Prelacy was 'but a cloak for Popery in its most dangerous form, a standing conspiracy to deliver England to Rome', with
Laud as conspirator-in-chief.[4]

That was unquestionably fanciful: *Aulicus*'s ground was the
conviction that Bishops, orthodox clergy, and the Prayer Book
were essential to salvation and national stability. From this position, which it unflinchingly held, it argued that only what it
derisively called 'tender consciences'[5] could possibly object to
Episcopacy. Complaints against Anglican clergy it regarded as
mere sedition—'clerics in all Rebellion are the first that are undone'.[6]
Taking its cue from the Proclamation against the Oppression of the
Clergy, it reported prominently the most glaring cases of persecution,[7] making the most of these 'atrocities' to rouse sympathy
and horror. Its decree concerning the much-derided Prayer Book
was equally absolute: 'those who do so wretchedly prophane and
abuse Gods service are no lesse mischievously bent against their

---

[1] For example, see no. 30 (23–29 July), p. 394 and no. 35 (27 Aug.–2 Sept.),
p. 474.

[2] No. 15 (9–15 Apr.), pp. 189–90.

[3] No. 48 (26 Nov.–2 Dec.), p. 686.

[4] M. D. George, *English Political Caricature to 1792* (1959), p. 18.

[5] No. 39 (24–30 Sept. 1643), p. 539.

[6] No. 56 (21–27 Jan. 1644), p. 794.

[7] For examples see no. 21 (21–27 May 1643), p. 275; no. 33 (13–19 Aug.), p. 448;
and no. 41 (8–14 Oct.), pp. 569–70. The Proclamation was printed in no. 20 (14–20
May), pp. 257–9.

Soveraigne'.[1] That book was revered as 'the formall legall difference betwixt a Protestant and a Papist . . . the sure and only badge
of a Protestant'.[2] This cannot have reassured uneasy souls, for it was
expressed with a confidence verging on arrogance. It suggested
that the minds behind *Aulicus* were so wedded to the outward
forms of religion that they could never consider modifying them.
Thus did piety and politics become ever more hopelessly inter-
twined.

Aulicus traced the course of iconoclasm throughout the land,[3]
and its sense of outrage was an understandable reaction to tragic
excesses. But it is indicative of its own fanaticism that vandalism
was presented as the hallmark of every reformer. It tackled the
Assembly of Divines and the Covenant in this fundamentalist
spirit. While denouncing both as political contrivances, designed
to trap men into committing themselves to Parliament's side in
the struggle, the editor urged that Anglican shibboleths be used
in just the same way, to test each person's loyalty to the cause.
Propaganda like this, from a source known to be close to the
King, must only have helped deepen the gulf of mistrust between
Charles and Parliament. The reader could only conclude that his
choice lay between supporting the Revolution and obtaining no
reform at all.

Naturally *Aulicus* felt no impulse to suppress information about
the progress of reform at London: seeing every attempt to adjust
the interdependence of King and Anglican Church as sedition it
took care, in fact, to keep the public fully informed; and the
Assembly's deliberations and the progress of the Covenant were
covered with remarkable precision. Nor was it always wrong in its
analysis of motives: there was some substance in its principal
objection that the Assembly was Parliament's creature, conceived
so that the Houses might 'better comply with the Kirk in Scotland,

[1] No. 24 (11–17 June), p. 313. This defence of the Prayer Book actually anticipated Royal Proclamations against the Acts and Ordinances of Parliament (20 June)
and the Assembly of Divines (22 June).
[2] No. 48 (26 Nov.–2 Dec.), p. 686. Neglect or desecration of the Prayer Book
were frequently condemned, as in no. 50 (10–16 Dec. 1643), pp. 712 and 715, and
no. 52 (24–30 Dec.), pp. 735–6.
[3] For examples see no. 11 (12–18 Mar. 1643), p. 130; no. 16 (16–22 Apr.), p. 199;
no. 26 (25 June–1 July), p. 339; and no. 40 (1–7 Oct.), p. 560.

and (having found the King so difficult in yielding to a change of
the present Government) set up a face of Ruling Elders by their
owne authority'.[1] The threat of a foreign religion being imposed
from above may have gone home to many readers; but the pride in
the King's intransigence was equally daunting to the moderate.

Aulicus refused to respect the Assembly's intentions or abilities,
and represented it as a body of ignorant men who 'by their factious
and seditious preaching'[2] had deliberately fomented war against
the monarchy. They knew little Latin, Greek, or Hebrew,[3] but
were all too familiar with simony, sacrilege, and adultery.[4] This
was largely unfounded slander, and *Aulicus* was sounder in handling disagreements among the Divines, and the wild growth of
heresies. Tensions between Presbyterians and Independents[5]
certainly existed, and the entry of Holmes and Goodwin into the
Assembly was significant for the reason *Aulicus* suggested: they
were 'knowne Independents, and hated the Presbytery as much as
the Episcopacy'.[6] This was shrewd; and vituperation aside, *Aulicus*
clearly was a very capable observer, sufficiently well-informed to
judge which way the wind was blowing. Even in late 1644 and
1645 'inside' intelligence about the Assembly's debates occasionally got through.[7]

But pride of place in *Aulicus*'s catalogue of religious disasters was
held by the Covenant. It was denounced as illegal and treasonable,
but recognized, sarcastically, for what it was—the ultimate sanction for all 'Blasphemies and Treasons so usuall now in pulpits'.
This the editor rightly saw was the prime threat to the established
government of Church and State and of 'near consequence for the
maintenance of this Rebellion'.[8] Adopting his usual tactic of playing
on real fears, he sought to discredit the Covenant's sponsors as

---

[1] No. 24 (11–17 June 1643), p. 316.
[2] The phrase is from the King's Proclamation of 22 June, printed in *M. Aul.*,
no. 26 (25 June–1 July).   [3] No. 94 (13–19 Oct. 1644), p. 1205.
[4] No. 41 (8–14 Oct. 1643), p. 576.
[5] No. 35 (27 Aug.–2 Sept.), p. 481.   [6] No. 47 (19–25 Nov.), p. 676.
[7] See for examples no. 112 (20–27 Apr. 1645), p. 1560 and no. 113 (27 Apr.–4 May),
p. 1567.
[8] The two quotations are from no. 42 (15–21 Oct. 1643), pp. 595 and 593 respectively. For further examples of its treatment of the Covenant as treasonable, see
no. 26 (25 June–1 July), pp. 335–6 and no. 27 (2–8 July), p. 349.

insincere men grasping at control of men's 'goods and consciences'.[1] This was uncomfortably close to the truth, in that the Covenant was essential to bring the Scots into the war because they would not budge without money and a firm prospect of Presbyterianism being erected in England.[2] Many Royalists felt that if the Scots could be kept out of things they might beat Parliament; and *Aulicus* clutched hopefully at every straw of disagreement between Parliament and the northerners. In September 1643 it even went so far as to assert unashamedly that letters to London from Edinburgh announcing the success of negotiations were forged.[3] That did not get the Royalists far; and *Aulicus* fell back on the old arguments that money was elusive and people generally reluctant to take the Covenant, so that the Scots would not intervene. The reassurance was first cousin to the blind optimism with which Charles conducted his relationship with them.

Meanwhile a close watch was kept on dissensions among the Dissenters[4] stirred up by the Covenant, even in the Commons itself.[5] But the argument that it was 'by most neglected'[6] was increasingly futile, for all that *Aulicus* clung to it even after the discovery of the Waller plot had enormously advanced the progress of the Solemn League.[7] The futility can be gauged by the eagerness with which the newsbook grasped the Lords' refusal to take the Covenant with the Commons and the Assembly at St. Margaret's Westminster in September 1643.[8] For by then there were only three Peers left in the Upper Chamber. So *Aulicus*'s point was purely academic, and can have cut little ice in London. Yet even this was directed at an important 'target'; and *Aulicus* did generally get its priorities right. It understood which developments were central and fastened its squibs on the most influential clerics. One of them, Stephen Marshall, was stung into making a public defence of his reputation against its scurrilous insinuations;[9] but

---

[1] No. 29 (16–22 July), p. 390.
[2] No. 39 (24–30 Sept.), p. 538.
[3] No. 35 (27 Aug.–2 Sept.), p. 481
[4] No. 33 (13–19 Aug.), p. 439.
[5] No. 15 (9–15 Apr.), p. 185.
[6] No. 28 (9–15 July), p. 374.
[7] No. 24 (11–17 June), p. 314.
[8] No. 39 (24–30 Sept.), p. 543.
[9] The insinuations were made in no. 7 (12–18 Feb. 1643), p. 88 and in no. 8 (19–25 Feb.), p. 92. For Marshall's reaction see above, p. 59.

the habit of mockery did not prevent the editor from recognizing his decisive part in negotiations with the Scots.[1] While very properly concentrating on the powerful Presbyterian leaders,[2] *Aulicus* kept a wary eye on emergent Independents; and, as early as spring 1643, spotted Hugh Peter one of 'their best Divines'.[3] As he became more influential his name cropped up more frequently:[4] he was a good butt for the satirist and *Aulicus* understood early on the growing menace of Independent views among Parliament's soldiers.[5] Political foresight, as much as random scare-mongering, inspired the prophecy early in 1644 that the 'Rebels' would eventually 'square their Church according to the Army'.[6] This explains its attacks on Cromwell in 1644 and 1645, and on lesser figures like Lady Waller, whose husband's troops were characterized as 'a rabble of such keene rebellious Brownists, that they usually call his Excellencies followers Malignants and Cavaliers'.[7] Such observations are doubly worth notice because their timing often contradicts the fairly recent contention that before 1644 the Royalist attack on sectaries was voiced chiefly by lightweights like John Taylor.[8] In fact, *Aulicus* began its campaign against women and tradesmen in the pulpit early in 1643.[9] The offensive had the weight of authority behind it from the start.

Tracing the rise of Independent power, *Aulicus* before the end of 1644 suggested that orthodox Presbyterianism was on the way out. It detected deviations from pure Scottish discipline in the Ordinance for the Ordination of Ministers,[10] and saw Laud's execution

[1] No. 31 (30 July–5 Aug.). p. 410.
[2] See no. 40 (1–7 Oct.), p. 558, which attacks Henderson most spitefully.
[3] No. 14 (2–8 Apr.), pp. 170–1.
[4] See for examples no. 52 (24–30 Dec. 1643), pp. 738–9 and no. 79 (30 June–6 July 1644), p. 1066.
[5] See for examples no. 81 (14–20 July), p. 1087; no. 98 (10–16 Nov.), p. 1251; and no. 113 (27 Apr.–4 May 1645), pp. 1568–9.
[6] No. 60 (18–24 Feb. 1644), p. 839.
[7] No. 78 (23–29 June 1644), p. 1054. His Excellency is, of course, the Presbyterian leader, the Earl of Essex. Lady Waller was attacked in no. 33 (13–19 Aug. 1643), pp. 445 and 449; no. 37 (10–16 Sept.), p. 518; no. 52 (24–30 Dec.), p. 746; no. 82 (21–27 July 1644), p. 1102; no. 83 (28 July–3 Aug.), p. 1110; no. 84 (4–10 Aug.), pp. 1115 and 1118; and no. 87 (25–31 Aug.), p. 1142. This list is not exhaustive.
[8] M. D. George, *English Political Caricature to 1792*, p. 24.
[9] See for examples no. 8 (19–25 Feb.), p. 97, and the appropriate references in n. 7 above.
[10] No. 94 (13–19 Oct. 1644), pp. 1204–5.

as, in part, a submission to Brownist pressure.[1] Parliament's vote, in spring 1645, against unordained ministers rather disturbed *Aulicus*'s interpretation of the political scene, so the newsbook highlighted Independent anger at the measure.[2] The editor seems to have become a little unsteady as he tried to trace the rapid movement of events and policies in London. He decided to depict the 'Kirk' triumphant and, diverging from his former line, presented the collapse of the Uxbridge Treaty as a victory for Scots Presbyters.[3] Uxbridge was indeed virtually a Scottish negotiation: what *Aulicus* apparently did not realize was that Parliament's leaders used the Treaty to entice the northerners into the war. Anyhow, by July 1645 *Aulicus* had resumed its old tack and discovered that the Scots, being intent upon 'conformity' and 'uniformity in religion', were feeling outflanked by the founding of the New Model Army under Fairfax.[4]

Aulicus's vacillations interestingly suggest some reasons why Oxford extremists were incapable of viewing Parliament's actions whole and steadily. The inclination to see in them only 'horrible contradictions',[5] inevitable among Rebels fighting for personal gain, could be misleading. Good information about London developments was used principally to discredit Parliament and confuse public opinion; and contradictions occasionally appear in which the propagandist and political analyst seem to be at loggerheads. The careful tracing of serious disagreements between Presbyterians and Independents opposes the assurance that it was really 'not materiall to their Reformed Religion' whether a preacher was in Holy Orders or not.[6] *Aulicus* wrote perceptively enough of 'the Reformation of Religion being a chiefe incentive of the present Warre',[7] and realised that people 'deepe in the Reformation, must needes be also great sharers in the Rebellion';[8] but it carried analysis no further towards formulating a constructive policy. As it refused the logical solution—agreement to a measure of reform to disarm the foe—it fell back on the cliché that

[1] No. 101 (5–12 Jan. 1645), pp. 1332–3.
[2] No. 113 (27 Apr.–4 May), pp. 1568–9.
[3] No. 114 (4–11 May), p. 1585. [4] No. 116 (13–20 July), p. 1670.
[5] No. 104 (2–9 Feb.), p. 1366. [6] No. 42 (15–21 Oct. 1643), p. 595.
[7] No. 11 (12–18 Mar.), p. 130. [8] No. 52 (24–30 Dec.), p. 736.

Parliament's religion was nothing but a mask for sedition[1] and that 'the great Rulers'' aims were identical with those of minor fanatics.[2] Logical and minute analysis was used only to reach such predetermined conclusions; and if satirical observations were facilitated by this, constructive thinking in Royalist circles was impeded by the authoritative utterances of the King's own mouthpiece. For example, *Aulicus* responded to complaints against idle priests and pluralists by returning the compliment in the shape of a grotesquely amusing image of the ranting preacher. The ripost was undoubtedly a great success and was a motif of Royalist and Tory propaganda for several generations. But such a triumph of laughter rang a little hollow for the nation as a whole, since it could only drive opposing propagandists, their readers, and their masters into more embattled attitudes. Without wishing to be loftily wise after the event, and without expecting propagandists to be fairminded, one cannot but remark the effect of this verbal warfare. English politics were, partly on its account, blighted for years to come by intemperate prejudices, and much intolerance had to be endured before an equitable settlement was finally achieved. Obviously, propaganda did not create civil discord, but it exacerbated it. If it is only to be expected that *Aulicus* should have been unconstructive, it is equally not to be imagined that its intransigence and that of many of its opponents had no consequences. Indeed, as a source known to be close to the King and his intimates, its contribution to the war of words had an especially sinister aspect. It was frequently and rightly assumed that they thought as *Aulicus* thought, and so it did much to enforce existing differences and misunderstandings. It is not only from the vantage-point of three hundred years' perspective that this can be seen; for one of the few contemporary pamphlets to advocate moderate views directs us to the same conclusion:[3]

But the London Pamphlets querie, whether Papists are likely to settle the Protestant Religion? And *Aulicus* seeming no lesse scrupulous, askes whether Brownists or Anabaptists will? But if a third

[1] No. 104 (2–9 Feb. 1645), p. 1366.
[2] No. 43 (22–28 Oct. 1643), p. 604.
[3] *Liberty of Conscience, or the Sole Means* (24 Mar. 1644), A1ᵛ.

should resolve them both, and say, that the Protestant Religion hath not been in England these eighty years, he might run the hazard to be thought a libeller, and yet it may chance be found so.

Unfortunately, it was becoming increasingly impossible to hold to such a middle course. At the opposite pole from *Aulicus* the commonly expressed view of the King as the tool of Laudian Popish conspiracy sought and found its confirmation in the Royalist newsbook. *Britanicus*, the most influential of London periodicals, often accusingly alluded to Bishop Duppa's connection with it;[1] and *Civicus* hailed its shrewdly executed policy of *divide et impera* as the hallmark of 'the Canterburian faction' and proof of its Machiavellian and Jesuitical affiliation.[2] Its advisers were a band of priests and friars,[3] and its editor one of the 'pragmaticall Popish–Arminian frie'.[4] Such alarmism was inordinate, but there was no denying that *Aulicus*, insisting on submission to the King on his own terms, seemed to regard the monarch as tyrant rather than father of his people, to believe in might as the measure of right, and to wish to 'outlaw the Common Law by the Canon Law'.[5] Significantly, it gave not the slightest hint of sympathy for the idea of a mixed monarchy which *Britanicus* advocated and which Hyde himself regarded with some favour.

Britanicus lamented that *Aulicus* proved Digby and the Laudians to be still in control at Court, and concluded that as long as they were, nothing could break the deadlock and bring a peaceful settlement.[6] That was a sound argument. *Aulicus*'s editors gave full scope to the King's contentment with reassuring formulas and to his fundamental intransigence. This tactical and temperamental accord is nowhere more apparent than in Charles's reliance, in most crises, on an identical policy of 'divide and rule'.

Politically, the most remarkable thing about *Aulicus* is this continued and open advocacy through the years of armed conflict

---

[1] For examples see no. 9 (17–26 Oct. 1643), p. 66; no. 13 (16–23 Nov.), p. 97; no. 20 (4–11 Jan. 1644), pp. 154–5; and no. 25 (26 Feb.–6 Mar.), p. 194.

[2] *Mercurius Civicus*, no. 132 (27 Nov.–4 Dec. 1645), pp. 1151–2.

[3] *An Answer to Mercurius Aulicus* (about 15 Dec. 1643), p. 2.

[4] *The Spie*, no. 2 (30 Jan.–5 Feb. 1644), p. 11.

[5] *The True Character of Mercurius Aulicus*, p. 6.

[6] No. 62 (16–23 Dec. 1644), pp. 487–8.

of those Laudian policies which led the King to war in the first
place. But if it shows us some of the reasons for Charles's fate, the
future career of its major editor will remind us that in some senses
the King did not lose. In victory and defeat *Aulicus* held spiritedly
and defiantly to a course that, having brought Charles to the scaffold, was to guide the faithful remnant through to some sort of
triumph under his son.

Certainly it would be grossly inappropriate to think of *Aulicus* in
terms of failure if one is measuring its impact on public opinion or
its technical quality as an intelligencer and propagandist. In all
these respects it was phenomenally successful, and the comparison
with Heylin shows how much was owed to Berkenhead's skill.
Heylin admitted Berkenhead's responsibility for many of the expressions and news items employed, even before he gained full
control; and the noticeable increase in satirical material as 1643
progressed was due to this intervention. Analysis of later numbers
—for example, the last dozen of 1643—when Heylin had given up
the work altogether, confirms this. That, however, was not the
only change wrought by Berkenhead; in the same period *Aulicus*
achieved an increasingly fluent presentation of news items. The
most obvious sign of this is the dropping of rigid introductory
formulas like 'This day it was reported'. Berkenhead had a knack of
so knitting his reports together that each flowed easily and logi-
cally into the next; and his narratives have a compelling onward
movement and an immediacy that Heylin's lacked. He also presented reports in such a way that the reader could be left 'to make
his inferences . . . from these Relations'.[1] The way of telling the
story made its own point. Heylin, on the other hand, usually tacked
sententious comment on to the end of each item.

Berkenhead's superiority is equally manifest in his flexible and
vivacious prose, so different from Heylin's characteristically
ornate, elaborate opening address to the reader in the first number:

And that the world may see that the Court is neither so barren of
intelligence, as it is conceived; nor the affaires thereof in so unpros-
perous a condition, as these Pamphlets make them, it is thought

---

[1] No. 51 (17–23 Dec. 1643), p. 720.

fit to let them truly understand the estate of things that so they may no longer pretend ignorance, or be deceived with untruthes; which being premised once for all, we now go on into the businesse; wherein we shall proceed with all truth and candour.

The stately Ciceronianism of this was much less answerable to the needs of journalism than Berkenhead's almost racy conversationalism. His intimate, sometimes buttonholing manner, is nicely illustrated by his piece about the flight of John Fiennes from Banbury in October 1644:[1] The 'Rebels', he observed

were routed in earnest, and Master John Fines made to run (for the running part was his) to Compton house, from thence to Warwick, where (through a fals alarme) he slept not an houre, but ran to Killingworth Castle, and thence suddenly (stop him some body!) to the blew Brethren of Coventry, & all these stages in one night.

There is a real and distinctive 'voice' here, which devastatingly assumes a mocking breathlessness. The passage is an enactment of what it describes; and Berkenhead, capturing gesture successfully, gives to an abstraction (in this case the cowardice of which 'Rebels' were repeatedly accused by Cavaliers) the tangibility of things felt and seen. The writing has panache; and Berkenhead brilliantly exploits the mimetic potential of his medium. The result is an excellent caricature. A similar graphic capacity is found in his more 'sober' narratives of the battles at Alresford and Cropredy,[2] and in his sketches of minor affrays like those at Holme Bridge, near Wareham in Dorset,[3] and at Sir Alexander Denton's house at Hillesden.[4] But since it was as a satirical writer that Berkenhead really made a mark, his comic pieces claim fullest attention here; in any case they best focus those qualities which made him a distinguished propagandist.

He had particular freedom of manœuvre in the running commentary on the London newsbooks, printed at the end of many numbers of *Aulicus*, and regarded in London as the special province of Berkenhead and the University wits.[5] This commentary first appeared in the fifteenth week, for 9–15 April, not, as Madan

---

[1] No. 95 (20–26 Oct. 1644), pp. 1226–7.   [2] For these see below, p. 91.
[3] No. 61 (25 Feb.–2 Mar. 1644), pp. 853–4.   [4] No. 62 (3–9 Mar.), pp. 866–8.
[5] *M. Brit.*, no. 27 (counterfeit) (11–18 Mar. 1644), p. 208.

stated, in the thirtieth number.[1] It did not become a regular item immediately, but at the start of May the editor ominously remarked that 'More of this stuffe might be produced, had I list and Leisure'.[2] The appearance of more formidable opponents[3] made him find time and by the twenty-ninth week it was a regular enough feature for him to apologize for omitting it.[4] Even then, and again contrary to Madan's impression, it was not always published, and after the eightieth number, for 7–13 July 1644, *Aulicus* dropped it altogether. So it occurs in fewer than half of the issues. The chief target of the commentary, which varies from half a side to four and a half sides, was not, as Madan supposed, *Mercurius Britanicus*.[5] As *Aulicus*'s most relentless foe the latter devoted at least half of its weekly space to a point-by-point refutation of Royalist intelligence. But the Oxford newsbook usually responded to this pestering by suavely ignoring the Londoner's existence—so much so that in August 1645 *Britanicus* erupted irritably: '*Aulicus* what say you, you may say little, there are so many speakes for you'.[6] This was true enough: Royalist writers, including John Taylor, Daniel Featley, and John Cleaveland, produced pamphlets[7] which show that *Britanicus* was really considered a dangerous rival to *Aulicus*, whose lofty disdain was a stroke of propaganda, not a mark of actual unconcern. When Berkenhead occasionally dropped his pose of indifference, *Britanicus* pounced; and in February 1645 it gleefully rejoiced that he had spent much energy 'in rage and fury against *Britanicus*; which (you know) is more than ever he durst do before'.[8]

A true view of *Aulicus*'s dealings with *Britanicus* is doubly desirable since a historian of the press, J. B. Williams, implied that the decline of the former from September 1644 was due to getting entangled in an undignified squabble with the Londoner.[9] Certainly in the later numbers, when there was no appended running commentary, Berkenhead padded out his reports with criticisms of opponents; but it is naïve to suppose that he forgot his proper

---

[1] No. 2043.

[2] No. 18 (30 Apr.–6 May 1643), p. 134.

[3] See App. III.

[4] No. 29 (16–22 July 1643), p. 391.

[5] No. 2043.

[6] No. 47 (12–19 Aug.), p. 368.

[7] See App. III.

[8] No. 73 (3–10 Mar. 1645), p. 586.

[9] *A History of English Journalism*, pp. 60–1.

purpose in a fit of pique. Royalist disasters in the field, not a bad 'press', forced *Aulicus* from its former course; only by this man-œuvre could it stay in existence and cover up, as far as possible, the disintegration of Royalist resistance.

One must also insist on the distinction to be made between the castigation of rivals at the end of an *Aulicus* and the same thing in the body of the news. In the latter case it is obvious that reporting events has taken second place to smearing other editors: normally, however, Berkenhead's motives were more complex and there is no direct correlation between space devoted to criticism of London newsbooks and the quality or quantity of news reaching Oxford. In 1644, for example, the number which reports very fully on Cropredy Bridge also prints two sides of sarcasms against other newsmen.[1] Earlier in that year *Aulicus*'s volubility against rivals was meant to draw attention to London exaggerations of Waller's victory at Alresford.[2] So the running commentary was used to temper extravagant enemy claims, to compensate for bad news, or to underline a Royalist victory. The criticism that Berkenhead was 'glad to dresse himself up with odd remnants out of our London-Pamphlets and buttons them together with learned Commen-taries'[3] is relevant only to his later numbers.

One need hardly labour the lesson that any rule-of-thumb definition of a newsbook as substantial as *Aulicus* is liable to mislead, and that there is no satisfactory substitute for a careful analysis of each number, made in the light of all the circumstances of its composition. Anyhow, in principle, Berkenhead's attention to other newsbooks was a legitimate part of the editorial function. Indeed, if *Britanicus* was right, Berkenhead regarded it as so im-portant that he employed agents to search out contradictions in London publications for him.[4] His policy certainly enjoyed some success: *Britanicus* admitted that the 'variety of our misreporting Pamphlets' was the greatest possible slur on Parliament's good name.[5] Fundamentally, therefore, *Aulicus*'s attempts to discredit and confuse Parliament's supporters through their newsbooks

[1] No. 78 (23–29 June 1644).   [2] No. 66 (31 Mar.–6 Apr. 1644).
[3] *M. Brit.*, no. 98 (15–22 Sept. 1645), p. 873.
[4] Ibid., no. 32 (15–22 Apr. 1644), pp. 252–3.   [5] Ibid.

were more purposeful than has commonly been imagined. Its success here can be gauged from the periodicals that imitated its example. The most extreme reaction is found in *Britanicus*, which, during the height of its campaign against Oxford, virtually gave up reporting news to concentrate on the piecemeal dismemberment of each number of its rival. Even so, it rarely, if ever, equalled Berkenhead's demoralizing mockery and spicy repartee. Undeterred or perhaps inspired by this, others attempted the feat: most dangerous of these satirical 'parasites' were *The Scotish Dove* and *The Spie*, of which the latter got nearest to *Aulicus*'s standard of wit. For all their jeers at Oxford's 'Satyricke stuffe', the Londoners testify eloquently to its hold on popular imagination.

The business of detraction, at which Berkenhead excelled, was undoubtedly facilitated by the simplification of motives apparent in *Aulicus*'s political analyses. The conviction of being staunch for truth against the oncoming hordes of Evil not only stiffened the will to resist, but also strengthened the satiric nerve. On both sides good and ill were, with increasing precision, measured in partisan terms. Propagandists like Berkenhead, untrammelled by the need to accommodate complex views of human right and wrong, jubilantly flung sarcasm at foes great and small. He ranged from light-hearted flippancy, through stern mockery, to downright indecency. Any exploitable factor—political, circumstantial, or physical—was a fair target. Thus in April 1643 Sir William Brereton's tenacity as a commander was sarcastically interpreted as a sign that he, 'being well beaten at the first onset . . . had no minde to go away till he had perfected the Earles victorie, and his owne overthrow'.[1] Later Sir William Waller, known not only as a soldier but also as the husband of a famous preaching wife, was pictured leading 'his pretty portable Armie' to Basing siege; there the soldiers ran from the trenches, not to hail him, but to pay homage to his spouse.[2] The other Parliamentary general, Essex, was awkwardly free from compromising weaknesses, but even he gave *Aulicus* an opening by slipping away in a cockboat after his defeat at Lostwithiel.[3] Berkenhead contrived to sidestep the

---

[1] No. 14 (2–8 Apr.), p. 179.   [2] No. 88 (1–7 Sept. 1644), p. 1147.
[3] Ibid., p. 1154.

deplorable fact that the Royalist army had let too many of the enemy slip out of its grasp after the battle by playing up the indignity of this exit. Errors and setbacks were usually passed off like this, with a laugh: having mistakenly reported that Lord Kirkcudbright had been captured, the editor jovially admitted that it was really his Sergeant-Major who had been taken, and added cheekily that 'the mistake (they say) is not great'.[1] No circumstance, not even a man's name, was too slight to serve its turn: Berkenhead got in a dig at Lord Say and Sele and the depleted House of Peers simultaneously by writing of 'this House of Three Lords (whereof my Lord Say was two)'.[2]

In Royalist mythology 'Rebels' were men and women steeped in avarice, ignorance, blasphemy, and lechery—as Berkenhead reminded readers in numerous vignettes. He laughed over Lady Mildmay mistakenly putting a gold sovereign into the collection plate one Sunday, and then demanding it back from the minister, much to the delight of her husband, who as Keeper of the Crown Jewels had neglected no opportunity to enrich himself.[3] He tried to muffle London celebrations of the Marston Moor victory with a variation on the second theme, capping his equivocal account of the battle with a scoffing description of the Earl of Pembroke as he swaggered into St. Martin-in-the-Fields, and swore—as he always did in Royalist lampoons—that Rupert was routed. At Pembroke's heels was 'his Genius (Michael Oldsworth)', his secretary, and commonly reputed to be the writer of all his speeches. Striding ahead, the Earl 'smiled severall wayes and vexed his formall Beard, to make it yeild one look like a man of understanding'.[4] Cutting sarcasm such as this was often deployed by Berkenhead; and the Earl, as will be seen, was to feel it again at a later date. As for blasphemy, the war years spawned many tales of sacrilege, and Berkenhead made much of one of these—the alleged baptizing of a horse (christened 'Charles') in a Lostwithiel church in 1644.[5] He also chronicled a minister in Rutland, who, one morning at Holy Communion, turned, chalice in hand, and saluted an outraged

[1] No. 64 (17–23 Mar. 1644), p. 887.   [2] No. 72 (12–18 May 1644), p. 982.
[3] No. 44 (5–11 Nov. 1643), pp. 615–16.   [4] No. 80 (7–13 July), p. 1086.
[5] No. 95 (20–26 Oct. 1644), p. 1219.

congregation with the words: 'as I am a faithful sinner, Neighbours, this is my mornings draught'.[1] True or not, these tales are lent apparent authenticity by adept use of circumstantial detail, an expert sense of timing, and a flair for reproducing the timbre of actual speech. This flair gives redeeming spice to indecent stories like that of the 'holy Rebell', a prisoner at Shrewsbury, who was accused of committing buggery with 'the Keepers own Mare'.[2] This scandal went down well, for *Aulicus* used it twice; and later Berkenhead wrote two political ballads on similar misdeeds. The strain of crude sensationalism ran through Royalist satire down to the Restoration and after. It is amusing, in the circumstances, to find Berkenhead protesting in *Aulicus* that something Sir Humphrey Mildmay had done was too improper to be published.[3]

As these instances suggest, the chief target was not vice concealed by a goodly front, but manifest falsehood and deformity open and apparent. Berkenhead was a caricaturist, seeking out the distinguishing tell-tale detail, preferably physical, which could be so exaggerated as to make the victim ridiculous or repulsive. So, after his abortive siege of Faringdon House in 1645, Oliver Cromwell was mocked: Royalist defiance, Berkenhead claimed, had heated his face 'seven times more red then ordinary'.[4] These attacks on Cromwell as a greedy, bloody, and appropriately red-faced boor, who delights in defacing churches, are an interesting feature of *Aulicus* in 1644 and 1645. For they reveal a certain foresight behind the talent for denigration. Another butt was Sir Samuel Luke, more famously satirized in Butler's *Hudibras*.[5] Luke was a hunchback and Berkenhead described him with cruel irony as one 'who abhors anything that's comely' because in its presence he could 'scarce disguise himselfe'.[6] Happier because more suggestively allusive was his earlier notion that Luke had 'made Chalgrove field like Bosworth . . .'.[7] Lenthall, Speaker of the Commons, was

[1] No. 71 (5–11 May 1644), p. 972.
[2] No. 51 (17–23 Dec. 1643), pp. 719 and 734, and no. 57 (28 Jan.–3 Feb.), p. 807.
[3] No. 104 (2–9 Feb. 1645), p. 1365.   [4] No. 112 (27 Apr.–4 May), p. 1571.
[5] This is not to say that Hudibras was Luke: Hudibras is a creation of Butler's comic imagination. But doubtless those who argue that the poet was drawing on his knowledge of Luke are right.
[6] No. 62 (3–9 Mar. 1644), pp. 866 and 867.
[7] No. 26 (25 June–1 July 1643), p. 345.

similarly jeered at for being able to write 'his minde handsomely; though he hath an impediment in his speech'.[1] John Sedgewick, the Presbyterian divine, appeared repeatedly as the preacher with a missing thumb;[2] and Stephen Marshall, that energetic orator, was belittled (if that is the right word) as 'the fat man' sweating in the pulpit.[3] Among the best of these thumb-nail sketches is that of Hugh Peter, portrayed in July 1644, as he returned to Westminster to report on the campaign of the Earl of Essex, 'with such a stocke of newes, that on Thursday last it cost the Lower members two full houres to heare it over once, though his fingers, eyes and nosthrils help'd his tongue to dispatch'.[4]

As in many of Berkenhead's descriptions we glimpse the subject in action—here an animated and dramatic speaker. The man alive in his characteristic gestures comes across with a freshness and authenticity that more formal portraits often sadly lack. At the time this was periodical journalism of a new and high order; one can understand how the inventiveness and spontaneity of Berkenhead's wit won even bitter opponents' grudging admiration.[5]

His humour, it has been observed, at least matches up to good modern platform repartee.[6] One might, perhaps, expect at least that much, or even hope that the comparison could be reversed. 1643 affords a characteristic sample of Berkenhead's best: when the Assembly of Divines asked the House of Commons for another scribe because one clerk could not dispatch all their business, Berkenhead remarked that the Divines could 'buy no Inck or Paper without asking the Members leave'.[7] The implicit political perception (of the Assembly's dependence on the Commons) was sound; and by sarcastically reducing it to a mundane subservience he makes it at once credible (because a tangible and strictly logical extension of the actual relationship) and absurd (because incongruously petty

---

[1] No. 62 (3–9 Mar. 1544), p. 872.
[2] For examples see no. 43 (22–28 Oct. 1643), p. 599, and no. 45 (5–11 Nov.), p. 640.   [3] No. 57 (28 Jan.–3 Feb. 1644), p. 806.
[4] No. 79 (30 June–6 July 1644), p. 1066.
[5] *The True Character of Mercurius Aulicus*, pp. 3 and 6; *M. Brit.*, no. 7 (3–10 Oct. 1643), p. 49; no. 10 (26 Oct.–2 Nov.), p. 80; and no. 25 (26 Feb.–6 Mar. 1644), p. 196.
[6] C. S. Emden, *Oriel Papers* (1948), p. 60.
[7] No. 51 (17–23 Dec. 1643), p. 720.

and unreasonable). The comedy here both observes and interprets an important political fact. And as before, the caricaturist makes his point largely by emphasizing disproportion—here a discrepancy between the Assembly's pretensions and its actual domination by Parliament. He also assumes (and the reader who laughs tacitly assents to the assumption, however unwittingly) that the discreditable triviality measures the importance of the relationship being discussed. Little wonder that *Aulicus* was repeatedly accused of excelling in sophistry. No doubt Berkenhead's training in rhetoric as an undergraduate helped him perfect the techniques of propaganda; while Laudian indoctrination gave him not only the motivation for writing caricature but also conviction of the righteousness of the cause in which he deployed his skills so uninhibitedly.

Comedy, it has been argued, is concerned with deviations from normal human behaviour. Without wishing to suggest that this generalization comes near to being a satisfactory analysis of the complex structure and functions of laughter,[1] one may say that it does serve as a description of one characteristic concern of many satirists, not least those of Berkenhead's period. He certainly displays, and assumes in the reader, a clear sense of what is proper conduct and a keen eye for physical and mental foibles—that is, for every sort of departure from what he accepts as normative. It is this sensibility together, of course, with his verbal adroitness, that makes him a political satirist of some distinction. At best his 'norm' has some inclusive breadth of human reference so that even enemies like Luke found him amusing. But it must be admitted that the commitment which inspired him also, because in him it often took an exclusive and narrow form, shortened his reach. Though extremely sensitive to disproportionate behaviour in others, he was ignorant of similar excesses in himself and his fellow Cavaliers. He did not, in other words, always take care to disguise or mitigate his own extremism.

Partly because of this there is a qualitative difference between his partisan satire and that of, say, Dryden, with whom he later

---

[1] Among other things, it begs the question of 'normality', and suggests a view of comedy as essentially a cautionary, authoritarian thing. Its actual function is more imaginatively liberating than that definition suggests.

became friendly. Their political views are certainly not unrelated, and the portraits of Shimei and Corah in *Absalom and Achitophel* show, in method and substance, their debt to the tradition of Cavalier satire which Berkenhead helped create. But there is a difference in the quality of the commitment to party that one finds in the two men. Dryden, one feels, had reservations that never entered Berkenhead's mind. It is not sufficient explanation of this difference to talk of the heat of battle, nor to say that Berkenhead was no poet (though he wrote verse). It is not because of some purely aesthetic defect (if there were such a thing) that he could never have imagined an Achitophel or an Absalom, but because he was unwilling even to countenance, as Dryden could, the existence of potential human greatness in the enemy.

One cannot really separate political views from the power of sympathetic imagination; and Berkenhead's unreadiness, or inability, to communicate a sense of fair-mindedness and moderation in his satire of opponents marks not just a tactical difference between himself and Dryden, but a basically less perceptive experience of man's political nature. The poetic excellence of *Absalom and Achitophel*, its metaphorical and structural coherence and conviction, establishes the maturity and validity of Dryden's understanding of political man and his desire, in the making of political choices, to lose as little as possible of what is humanly valuable. Berkenhead seems rarely, if at all, to have felt the need for that sort of reservation. Yet Dryden would not have totally disapproved of his satire: his caricatures are sharp-witted, readable, and amusing, and do lay bare something of the nature of political vice. They are always closer to inspired raillery than to mere railing, as Berkenhead usually assumes the tone not of angry indignation, but of amused superiority; and it has been well observed of *Aulicus*'s Oxford contemporary, *Mercurius Rusticus*, that 'it did with a bludgeon what Berkenhead was doing with a rapier'.[1] And whatever else it did, Berkenhead's conviction of rightness and superiority did lend his satire an air of dignity and confident poise. So by introducing political satire and stylish writing of this calibre into newsbooks, *Aulicus* both lifted journalistic standards

[1] J. Frank, *The Beginnings of the English Newspaper, 1620–1660*, p. 41.

and helped spread a vogue for witty repartee through the nation. It fostered a climate in which greater writers like Butler and Dryden could flourish. For some three years it broadcast the message that change meant anarchy, and that Dissent was sedition. Persistently and eloquently it canvassed the image of the Nonconformist that has bulked so large in English politics and literature. To complement this stereotype of fanaticism *Aulicus* publicized and was itself the perfect expression of the notion of the laughing Cavalier—a being compounded of heroic loyalty and devil-may-care wit—which has endured to the present day. Of course the newsbook was not the sole source of these metaphors; but its wide circulation and contemporary acclaim justify the conclusion that it did as much as any and more than most to fix them in the popular imagination.

For this, too, Dryden may have respected Berkenhead. It would be improper to suggest that *Aulicus*'s current literary and historical value was a result solely of the editor's efforts, as he was so variously supported by other men and resources. But his peculiar talent and enterprise undoubtedly were crucial to the newsbook's character. Through his intervention and direction *Aulicus* became more than merely competent: it acquired style. If not a great writer, Berkenhead occupies a major place in the history of journalism and a far from negligible one in that of political satire. *Aulicus* proved that talented men could profitably be employed in writing newsbooks; and out of that realization grew a more direct relationship between the daily shifting pattern of events and the serious literary pursuits of cultivated men and women, so that literary traditions and techniques became more deeply involved in partisan debate. More remains to be seen of this process at work in those warring decades. For now, the narrative can pause, with Berkenhead brought by three years' work on *Aulicus* into the public eye and the favour of Charles I. His newsbook was not the least achievement of the Court, great patron of the Arts. It was, too, the foundation of his whole career, setting a pattern for his future. That pattern, however, is not quite complete yet: while editing *Aulicus* Berkenhead also penned other substantial propaganda pieces, and to place them in the picture we must run back a little in time.

CHAPTER IV

1643 to 1646
'Things halfe made up ...?'

BERKENHEAD's considerable weekly stint as editor of the main
organ of Cavalier propaganda from 1643 to 1646 was not the sum
of his efforts. Three additional pieces have long been associated
with his name: they are two poems contributed to University
'anthologies' of 1643, and a sermon, published in 1644, which
raises a curious biographical problem. Together these illuminate
his association with the Cartwright circle and the royal family.
But to these pieces must be added (for the first time) three substantial pamphlets (one published in three parts), a preface to
one of *Aulicus*'s 'supplements', and some marginal notes printed in
a pamphlet by John Taylor. The last, incidentally, bears on
Berkenhead's work as licenser of the press. Altogether these additional writings show that he was more prominent and active at
Oxford than has been realized.

They also help to clarify two important features of Royalist
propaganda: first, its developing relationship with 'serious'
literary conventions; and second, its success in defining a body of
viable satirical themes and images. Both these factors were fundamental to the evolution of a mature satirical idiom. Herein lies
the purpose of observing Berkenhead's habitual mannerisms (his
insertion of up-to-the-minute satirical reference in celebratory
and elegiac verse, and his reiteration of arguments and illustrations)
and of noting the range and character of his imagery and the
occurrence of parallel motifs in other Cavalier writings. He well
represents certain important developments. But he was more than
merely representative: he had some influence, and one of his
pamphlets is among the best published at Oxford in the period.

So before examining his work in detail it is well to take some measure of the Court culture he was defending. It has been quite recently pointed out that in one sense even the paintings of Van Dyck and the architecture of Inigo Jones were propaganda for the King's ideal of an absolute monarchy.[1] The use the Court made of Jones's talent is indeed interesting. His genius was employed to embellish those elaborate masks enthusiastically patronized by the Queen; and one reason so much ingenuity and money was lavished on these entertainments was that often they projected fantasies of greatness and power and pandered to precious delusions. Even when, in passing, the masks alluded to current political discontent, magical peace and concord were contrived for the close. To Charles and Henrietta Maria, who sometimes performed in them, and to their admiring courtiers, there was here some escape from the unpleasant pressures of a reality in which there were hard-headed Scotsmen and intractable Parliamentarians to contend with.

This pattern is marked out too in the more weighty Cavalier drama,[2] whose heroes are inspired by a mystical *esprit de corps*, and move, undaunted by the inscrutable changes of fortune, to their inevitable triumph. Of course, adulation of aristocratic virtues and scorn for the mob had already found expression in John Fletcher's much-admired plays. And Court writers found another sympathetic model in Greek romances which exalted the same sort of heroism, compounded of self-sacrifice and devotion to noble causes. But the Cavalier dramatists flattered the Court with an even more exalted image of aristocratic honour. As the closest-knit and most powerfully organized caucus within Royalist ranks, the Laudians zealously contributed to this literary mythology, and stimulated that desire for insulation from society at large already strong in the Stuart regime. One such protégé of Laud was James Shirley; another, less distinguished as a dramatist, was William Cartwright, who wrote *The Royall Slave*, a play with which the Court was regaled when it visited Oxford in 1636. The piece was received with a rapturous applause that was certainly not merited on artistic grounds alone: but it had reassured the audience in their belief that all right-thinking men gave unquestioning

[1] J. E. C. Hill, *The Century of Revolution* (1961), pp. 99–100.
[2] For the character of this see A. Harbage, *Cavalier Drama* (New York, 1936).

obedience to the Crown. This was an image of society the Court could live with, and was nearly to die with; but there were elements in it that were not just wishful thinking. For men did prove willing to sacrifice their lives for the monarch; and life seemingly imitated art in a man like Berkenhead whose loyalty to his King won him the name, among friends, of 'Cratander', the hero of Cartwright's play.

Samuel Butler later observed that wit was an instrument that could be used to make things appear 'greater or lesse than they really are';[1] and the Laudians certainly endeavoured to fulfil its dual functions, for as well as contributing to a drama that was thinly veiled propaganda, they hastened to defend the Court (and their own vested interests) by attacking the enemy frontally. Indeed, they proved even more adept at denigration than at flattery. When William Prynne's *Histriomastix* appeared in 1633, Cartwright and Jaspar Mayne, another Laudian, rallied to the flag by denouncing it vigorously. Prynne's notorious book was ostensibly an attack on the sinfulness of plays, dances, and similar pastimes; but the writer boldly and emphatically criticized the Queen's participation in such 'debaucheries'. This was implicitly an attack both moral and political on the culture of the ruling élite. Inevitably the assumption on which Royalist counter-attacks were founded was that these opponents of the King were detesters of learning, wallowing in ignorance of sciences and the arts. The Court did not, however, neglect practical measures of retaliation, and set another Laudian, Heylin, to hound down the insolent Presbyterian. The Court culture, including its literary traditions, was, it seems, now a potentially explosive political issue.

Opposition to Puritanism was, of course, neither new nor exclusively Laudian: as early as 1615 Cambridge University entertained James I with a Latin play, *Ignoramus*, in which Puritan philistinism was pilloried.[2] But before the 1630s religious minorities were largely prevented from publicizing their views, and attacks on

---

[1] *Characters*, ed. A. R. Waller (1908), p. 336.
[2] See '*Ignoramus*' . . . *An Examination of its Sources and Literary Influence*, J. L. Van Gundy (Lancaster, Pa., U.S.A., 1906).

them had been comparatively few and restrained in tone. Once the zealots began to break free of restrictions on press and pulpit they inevitably assailed their more unbending and extreme oppressors— the Laudian Anglicans. Naturally it was the Laudians who retaliated in the most caustic and even vicious manner.[1] In the persons of Peter Heylin and John Berkenhead all the assumptions and practices involved in the controversy of the 1630s were carried over into *Aulicus* and the new wave of Court propaganda. Both men were nurtured in the academic and courtly tradition which had become an article of Royalist faith and an object of Puritan scorn. So their newsbook's presentation of Royalist commanders as brave, noble, and sensitive men conquering by generic right predictably continued the convention of heroism already well established. The image of the Rebels as corrupt ignoramuses similarly extended the equally venerable tradition of denunciation. This view of *Aulicus*'s ancestry is not merely modern hindsight: it is exactly what *Britanicus* saw when it linked *Aulicus* with the world of Inigo Jones and the masks,[2] and traced its descent from Beaumont and Fletcher, Shirley and Jonson.[3] In a general sense this was obviously apposite; it was for example, the Oxford academic poets of Cartwright's generation who in 1638 commemorated Jonson in the famous volume of verse, *Jonsonus Virbius*, edited by Brian Duppa, their patron. But it also went home to the personal preferences of Berkenhead, who enthused over Jonson and admired Fletcher at the expense of Shakespeare.[4]

How deeply *Britanicus* saw into the nature of Cavalier art—into how its cynicisms and idealisms exactly reflected the pressure of ascendant Royalist political thinking—is not apparent; for it did not enlarge on the subject. But the instinctive equation of literary taste with political allegiance is indisputable. It was of first consequence to the future of a political satire founded on what has been called the 'Conservative Myth'. The fact that a propagandist newsbook was attacked as a manifestation of a particular literary tradition marks an important stage in this process. Here are the sources of those assured responses to which Dryden, relying on a

[1] See above, pp. 19–20.   [2] No. 64 (30 Dec.–6 Jan. 1645), p. 504.
[3] No. 20 (4–11 Jan. 1644), p. 152.   [4] See below, 134–5.

stock of devices and terms, could confidently appeal some forty years later in *Absalom and Achitophel* to describe John Dolben, 'Him of the Western Dome', who had fought for the King at Marston Moor and York: he is an example to others of 'Learning and . . . Loyalty', and an occasion to assert that 'never Rebell was to Arts a friend'. Dryden's relation to the line of Cavalier satire is apparent, too, in the controlling assumption of *Absalom and Achitophel*, constantly communicated through the poem's metaphors, that Rebellion is the sum of everything anarchical, barren, and destructive in human personality and the body politic, while loyalty to the throne is the fertile seed of all creative activity.

Anyhow, *Britanicus* certainly seems to have understood that *Aulicus* was exploiting for political ends the potential of innuendo, indelicacy, and scurrility which English satire had but recently acquired from a new familiarity with Roman satirists notably Persius, Martial, and Juvenal.[1] What is especially interesting about *Aulicus*, however, is that it helps one to understand how and why English letters took a new turn in the 1640s. In the wordy combat that then reached its crescendo the spirit of English satire changed: soon there was no place, in public at least, for a dilettante wit like Sir John Suckling, the gentlemanly sceptic, distrustful of all enthusiasms.[2] Men like Berkenhead, professional polemicists ready to strike ruthlessly in defence of a commitment, brushed those of weaker nerve or more moderate temper aside. In their care, letters became more overtly propagandist and propaganda grew more literary. Often the end for which such propagandists used their talent may be suspect: wit was readily used to beat off new ideas, to bar serious discussion of suggested changes in religious and political codes. Yet by and large the satiric mode gained enormously from the industry of such committed men: its scope and resources were expanded; its concerns and its methods were progressively clarified; and, in good writers, its tone was refined so that the best propaganda was urgent, purposeful, and

---

[1] See John Peter, *Complaint and Satire in Early English Literature* (1956).

[2] Samuel Butler, of course, was similarly distrustful; but however much *Hudibras* owes to the inspiration of the 1640s it naturally won the heart of the Court of Charles II. If there was little of Suckling's temper in Charles I, there was plenty of it in his son.

yet urbane. Satire became the accepted and most effective way of
conducting personal and public disputes: by 1643 it was necessary,
as one journalist found, to echo Juvenal's observation that it was
'hard now not to write a Satyr'.[1]

The disruption of effective restrictions was, of course, vital. It
became possible to scandalize individuals without fear of recrimination—at least, as long as they were on the other side. The libera-
tion was psychological as well as physical. If a writer like John
Marston was uneasy about making personal attacks, Peter Heylin,
though a priest, felt no such qualms of conscience. The newsbook he
launched did much to encourage scandal-mongering as a national
pastime. Berkenhead was, of course, much better at this sport
than Heylin; and a short piece by him, published about 27 March
1643,[2] as part of a 'supplement' to *Aulicus*, ably abetted the newsbook's policy of slandering Parliament's leaders. The *Battaile on
Hopton Heath* consisted of a dispatch (used by the editors in preparing their account of the fight for their twelfth number) and a
preface and epilogue written in Oxford. The epilogue's style is
Heylin's; but the preface is very much in Berkenhead's manner. It
pokes fun at Sir John Gell and Sir William Brereton, two commanders frequently attacked by *Aulicus*, describing them as 'two
that (one would think) have conspired together to be beaten as
often as they unite their mutuall forces'. This sarcasm is practically identical with one *Aulicus* aimed at Brereton shortly after-
wards.[3] Another jibe—that Brereton was brave, 'if lying downe in
a ditch, standing behind a hay-ricke . . . may goe for valour'—
appeared in the newsbook, with modifications, at the end of 1643.[4]
Even then the Cavaliers were not done with Brereton: his behaviour at Hopton Heath was still a joke in 1648;[5] Berkenhead
remembered him unlovingly in 1653;[6] and he was buffeted by
Royalists, Butler among them, at the Restoration.[7]

[1] *Mercurius Urbanus*, no. 2 (9 Nov.), p. 9.
[2] For the two issues see Madan, nos. 1294 and 1295.
[3] See above p. 92.   [4] No. 51 (17–23 Dec.), p. 732.
[5] *A Case for the City-Spectacles* (6 Jan.), pp. 11–12.
[6] See *Two Centuries of Paul's Churchyard* (1653), item 173 (reprinted in *Harl. Misc.*
ix. 417).
[7] Butler, *Mercurius Mennipeus* (1682), reprinted in *Satires and Miscellanies*, ed.
R. Lamar (1928), p. 350; see also *The Mystery of the Good Old Cause* (1660) (Aunger-

Cavalier satire thus singled out its favourite Aunt Sallies, and discovered the standard Rebel gestures. Berkenhead's preface alludes to Gell's alleged desecration of monuments: he acted 'as if his business lay (like that devil's in the Gospels) among the Tombes and Sepulchres'. In 1645 John Cleaveland, who had recently joined the Oxford propagandists, picked up their habit of mocking Gell and Brereton, and turned the joke on Cromwell, implying that he was only good at fighting 'an old Monument'.[1] He may have been recalling the preface again in 1649, when he characterized a Sequestrator as one who 'like the demoniack in the gospel . . . lives among tombs'.[2] Directly indebted or not, this illustrates graphically how Royalist writers amassed a common stock of motifs and techniques. For nearly twenty years they maintained their attack on targets first located between 1643 and 1646. Even a slight piece, like Berkenhead's preface, because of its 'official' origin and wide circulation, helped define the scope and direction of political satire.

Between March and August of 1643 no identifiable prose piece—*Aulicus* apart—came from Berkenhead's pen. He did, however, write two poems in that interval; and though his verse was much less distinguished than his prose, they rate a brief mention. The first was a contribution to *Musarum Oxoniensium Epibateria*, a volume of verse published in July 1643 to celebrate the Queen's safe return to Oxford on Friday 14 July with some sorely needed military supplies.[3] A manuscript or printed copy of this volume may have been among the 'bookes of verses & gloves'[4] given to Henrietta Maria that evening by the University—breathless loyalty indeed, if that is the case. Berkenhead, by then established in Court and academic circles, naturally added his voice to the chorus of acclaim

vyle Soc. Reprints, 2nd Ser., 1883), p. 103. The spurious second part of Butler's *Hudibras* seems to be an extended attack on Brereton.

[1] *The Character of a London Diurnall*, reprinted in *Character Writings of the Seventeenth Century*, ed. H. Morley (1891), pp. 311–12.

[2] *The Character of a Countrey Committee-Man*, reprinted in *Character Writings of the Seventeenth Century*, p. 302.

[3] Madan, no. 1418, dates it about 26 July.

[4] Brian Twyne, *An Account of the Musterings of the University of Oxford*, printed as an appendix to *Chronicon . . . De Dunstaple*, ed. Thomas Hearne (1733), ii. 786. As only 150 copies were printed, it is just conceivable that the Oxford presses ran them off in time for the presentation.

with a piece ostensibly written on that day. It is certainly clumsy and obvious enough to have been rattled off in a hurry. He realizes some of the ironic potential of the octosyllabic couplet, but the effort is pretty ponderous. The most notable thing about it is an adaptation of *Aulicus*'s jeer at Fairfax's flight from Leeds.[1] This readiness to work satirical reflection into complimentary verses alone distinguishes the piece from the more conventional adulation of most of its companions.

His second poem appeared about 7 August in an anthology of *Verses on the Death of . . . Sr. Bevill Grenvill*,[2] killed at the Battle of Lansdowne on 5 July 1643. This was the first time that such a volume had been prepared for anyone outside the Royal family[3]— Grenville, as a man of valour, substance, and breeding, represented much that was dear to the Cavalier heart. This anthology is dominated, like the first, by men of the Cartwright circle. Berkenhead's poem, in solemn and ceremonious heroic couplets like all the others, is extremely mannered. Its baroque conceits, however fashionable, are tortuous and the language and sentiment are excessive. The comparison of Grenville, a prop to the Crown, with Samson is not, albeit well-meant, exactly felicitous in all its implications. Still, it is a reminder that the liking for Biblical allusion was not, even at this stage, monopolized by the other side. The propagandist's hand shows most in a tendency to use the couplet in a mock-heroic manner; but it is not very expertly done, and the flippancy only accentuates the surrounding pretentiousness. Again, the poem's only real claim on us is its manifest desire to score political points on a solemn public occasion. The boldness and opportunism are characteristic of Berkenhead. Though of little intrinsic merit, these two poems of 1643 show something of the new inclination of polite letters.[4]

If the stress of conflict was leaving its mark on ceremonial verse, in prose too it was at work; and the complex, leisurely mannerisms of the scholarly style were giving way to a brisker,

---

[1] No. 27 (2–8 July), p. 361.   [2] Madan, no. 1436.

[3] *Verses by the University of Oxford on the Death of . . . Sr. B. Grenville* (1684), A1r. The editor was Henry Berkenhead, mentioned on p. 144 below.

[4] These developments in poetry and prose have been described by C. V. Wedgwood in *Poetry and Politics Under the Stuarts* (1960).

more forthright air, and to a more dramatic method of argument. Newswriters and preachers, involved in the front line of public debate, gave a great impetus to this development. And the fact that greater directness and so-called plainness did not mean more crudity owes much to the entry of men like Berkenhead into the often despised trade of journalism. For largely through them popular writing gained a new distinction. At the same time they carried over into more sophisticated letters the lessons of clarity, directness, and accessibility. The new trend in prose, apparent in the differences already noted between the styles of Heylin and Berkenhead, is also seen in one of the finest pamphlets produced by the Oxford propagandists, *A Letter from Mercurius Civicus to Mercurius Rusticus*. This has been much speculated upon by historians, and one has recently, and quite independently suggested on stylistic grounds that Berkenhead wrote it.[1] That is strongly supported by circumstantial evidence and by specific parallels in *Aulicus*.

This well-informed pamphlet, tracing at length the origins of the Civil War, was first published in Oxford about 20 August 1643, and soon after that reprinted in London.[2] About 20 January 1644, part of it was again reprinted in London under a new title, *A Discoverie of London's Obstinacies and Miseries*;[3] and the writer of another pamphlet about the beginnings of the War, published in April 1644, was seemingly familiar with it.[4] Later still, Clarendon appears to have had it in mind when writing his account of the internal revolution in the City of December 1641. In some half dozen instances he echoes its ideas and phrases; for example, *A Letter* called the Earl of Warwick's house 'the common rendevous of all schysmaticall preachers'; in Clarendon this became 'the rendezvous of all the silenced ministers'.[5] Either the historian used *A Letter* as a source, or he was close to the writer and furnished

---

[1] Valerie Pearl, *London and the Outbreak of the Puritan Revolution* (1961), p. 133 n.

[2] Madan, no. 1441.

[3] This appeared as an appendix to *The Case of our Affaires* by John Spelman, see Madan, no. 1516, and Valerie Pearl, loc. cit.

[4] See *An Orderly and Plain Narration of the Beginnings and Causes of this Warre* which Madan, no. 1620, dates. Compare its account of the flight of the Five Members (p. 8) with that in *The Letter*, in the *S. Tracts*, iv. 590–1.

[5] *A Letter*, p. 584 and Clarendon, *History of the Great Rebellion*, ed. W. D. Macray (1888), ii. 544. Professor Trevor-Roper pointed out these parallels to me.

him with details and interpretations in the first place. It is interesting to note, in this connection, that Clarendon's accounts of the execution of Sir John Hotham, former Governor of Hull, and his son, contain similar parallels with *Aulicus*'s narrative.[1] This may throw some light on the nature of Clarendon's relationship to *A Letter*: though the doctrines *Aulicus* advocated were often far from sympathetic to Hyde, he may have been obliged occasionally to assist the editor. By the same token he could have given the writer of *A Letter* information, gathered at first hand, of events in London in 1641.

Undoubtedly the pamphlet was very close to *Aulicus*: its title and form indicate participation in the newsbook war; the writer begins by putting into *Civicus*'s mouth a confession of past sins and of *Aulicus*'s truthfulness; and his language, treatment of various individuals, and general themes have much in common with the newsbook.[2] The twenty-sixth week of *Aulicus* illustrates this:[3] its castigation of London as 'that prodigall and licentious City'[4] was the theme of the Royal Proclamation of 17 July 1643, prohibiting traffic between London and the rest of the kingdom,[5] and is the impetus behind *A Letter*, which was published by way of an apology for that Proclamation. Equally striking is the resemblance between newsbook and pamphlet accounts of the steps taken in London to silence all periodicals except *The Parliament Scout*. These are too lengthy for quotation but the reasoning and illustrations used are practically identical.[6] Such parallels cannot be fortuitous; and though it is arguable that an independent writer used *Aulicus*, this is far less convincing than the conclusion that the pamphlet

---

[1] Compare no. 102 (12–19 Jan. 1645), pp. 1342–4 with Clarendon's *History*, iii. 526–9. The latter seems to be closer to the newsbook in some respects than is the account in the *Clarendon State Papers* (1767–86), ii. 181 and 184–5. *M. Aul.* does simplify and exaggerate some features of the story.

[2] Compare, for example, no. 42 (15–21 Oct. 1643), p. 589 with *A Letter*, p. 586 (about Pym) and no. 18 (30 Apr.–6 May), p. 227 with *A Letter*, p. 581 (about Bulmore).

[3] This number (25 June–1 July writes, for example, of 'straines of Rhetoricke ... to bewitch the people' (p. 331); while *A Letter*, p. 583, writes of preachers being drawn by the 'bewitchments of gaine and popular applause'. For fnrther variations on this theme see below, p. 118.

[4] p. 331.

[5] See *M. Aul.*, no. 29 (16–22 July), pp. 388–90.

[6] Compare no. 26 (25 June–1 July), pp. 343–5, with *A Letter*, p. 581.

issued from the newsbook's editorial office. Differences in handling arguments and images in parallel passages are such as would naturally occur in rewriting. Strongest candidates for the authorship are, therefore, Heylin and Berkenhead. The first can confidently be eliminated on stylistic grounds alone, and echoes of *A Letter* in the numbers of *Aulicus* which he edited immediately after its publication are certainly borrowings from it.[1] Heylin, moreover, seemingly laid no claim to *A Letter*, as it was not attributed to him by either of his biographers, Vernon and Barnard, who both had access to his papers. In any case, he published his own observations on the Proclamation a little later.[2]

The final link in the chain of evidence leading to Berkenhead is the sequence of events connected with the publication of *A Letter*. Under Friday 21 July of the twenty-ninth week *Aulicus* noted the Proclamation of 17 July; and on the following day the editor substituted an apology for his usual commentary on the London newsbooks—'an occasion (which admits no excuse) hath forced us to end thus abruptly'.[3] It is known that in August and September Berkenhead temporarily relinquished his work on *Aulicus*,[4] leaving it solely to Heylin for some weeks. The arrangement was probably due, like Heylin's stint in 1644, to Berkenhead's absence from Oxford. The King left the city for Bristol on 1 August 1643, and Berkenhead probably went with him. This departure, however, does not account for the sudden disturbance at the end of the twenty-ninth week, nor for the fact that the thirtieth week, 23–29 July, is noticeably less lively than usual and seems not to be Berkenhead's. The most likely explanation is that the 'occasion' which upset *Aulicus*'s routine was a command to Berkenhead to undertake the special task of writing *A Letter*, and that this occupied him fully for the week from 22 July to the end of the month. A second snag, if Berkenhead did leave Oxford on 1 August, is

---

[1] Compare no. 30 (23–29 July), p. 397, with *A Letter*, pp. 597–8 (about the Petition presented to the Commons on 20 July), and no. 32 (6–12 Aug.), p. 438, with p. 581 of *A Letter* (the phrase used about sprinkling truth and lies). There are many more similarities.

[2] His tract is called *Lord Have Mercie Upon Us: Or, A Plain Discourse*. Madan, no. 1486, dates it about 2 Nov., but it was, in fact, advertised as published in *M. Aul.*, no. 36 (3–9 Sept.), p. 489, under the title of 'A plain discourse'.

[3] p. 391.   [4] *Hist. and Antiq.* ii. 461.

the date of 5 August appended to *A Letter*. This might seem to rule him out, but the date is almost certainly as spurious as the supposed identity of the writer and place of composition. Presumably it was chosen as allowing a reasonable time lapse between alleged composition in London and the publication in Oxford of the King's 21 July Proclamation. The 5th was late enough for a Londoner to have received a copy of that from Oxford and written his reply; for the journey to London currently took about seven days, and the writing actually seems to have occupied Berkenhead for about the same time. The subterfuge is neat and carefully executed: this juggling with dates is, in fact, very much of a piece with Berkenhead's concealment of *Aulicus*'s falterings and lapses. His claim to *A Letter* admittedly rests on circumstantial and inferential evidence, which is always open to alternative interpretations, but none so adequately answers all the requirements of the situation.

Happily, though *A Letter* purports to be written by *Mercurius Civicus*, it does not try to fake that newsbook's style: it simply masquerades as a sober admission by a supporter of Parliament of London's guilt in fostering Rebellion. Even so the more gullible may have been taken in by the forgery; undoubtedly the intention was to foment enemy dissension and unease. This was in line with *Aulicus*'s unremitting policy of 'divide and rule', and like its current numbers, *A Letter* maintains a careful balance between serious narrative and satirical interjections. It advances no new or unorthodox political arguments and, again like *Aulicus*, allows no whisper of conciliation to be heard. Putting all the blame on London, it explains how control of the Militia, through cunning manipulation of pulpit and Common Council, was wrested from the loyal Lord Mayor and Aldermen and handed to a fanatical minority. The flight of the Five Members is interpreted not as a legitimate reaction to a sudden and arbitrary attempt by the King to suppress opposition, but as a logical step towards open Rebellion through a deep-laid plot concerted by City and Parliament, a plot given doctrinal sanction by Dr. Downing's famous sermon justifying taking up arms against the sovereign. There is simplification in all this, as there is in the argument that war followed the King's flight from London, not because men rallied to his flag, but because the City was put into an unnecessary defensive posture. The writer observes doctrinal matters in a similar spirit: 'Puritan' sermons and prayers are denounced as mere 'blasphemies, prophanations, and absurdities', and their preachers as ignoramuses without 'art and eloquence'.[1] The uncompromising conviction that the 'Rebels' had cancelled all 'tyes of religion, nature, lawes'[2] is the bedrock of this pamphlet, as it was of *Aulicus*. Here is the same absolute refusal to recognize that the King's actions could be held responsible for misunderstanding and discord and the same affirmation that the 'Rebels' were perverse conspirators against the peace and happiness of England. In his insistence on the Prerogative's untouchability the writer ascribes too much foreknowledge to the enemy, finding long-term planning where none existed. Presbyterianism was not devised, as he implies, expressly and solely to promote Rebellion, though that assumption was unavoidable for anyone so set on condoning all the King's doings. In its extremism and exclusiveness *A Letter* is close to *Aulicus*.

However misconceived the writer's assumptions, he conducts a plausible, persuasive argument. *A Letter* was brilliant propaganda built on an impressive knowledge of facts and circumstances. Inside information about events in London is copious and detailed; there is much truth in the account of the manipulation of public opinion there; and, setting aside the apportioning of blame, the deterioration in the relationship between King, Parliament, and City is accurately traced through its various stages. There is some shrewd judgement too: events are correctly emphasized according to their relative importance; nor can the central thesis—that the ambitions of the City and all it stood for were one cause of the war —be denied. The flaw, to modern eyes, is the conviction that these ambitions were illegitimate. At the same time, this very conviction does lend the piece its air of confident authority and poise.

Assurance is the hallmark of his writing: it ranges easily from the oratorical to the colloquial, taking serious exposition and satirical reflection in its stride, while remaining splendidly free from mannerism and affectation. Above all, a direct dramatic force makes

---

[1] p. 595.   [2] p. 596.

A Letter an outstanding piece of political pamphleteering. It shows
admirably the strength and flexibility of good journalistic prose.
In downright ridicule, the uninhibited colloquialism of phrases like
'broke the ice', 'rule the rost', 'bunge up our mouthes', and 'you
may judge of the whole bunch by one',[1] puts teeth into the attack;
scornful denigration here bites sharply instead of merely mauling.
This is felt in the smartly observed image of the Dissenting ministers as 'the dryest and the dullest beasts that ever peep'd over a
pulpit'.[2] Even indelicacy is put across smoothly: in the description
of London women's fears at rumours of Royalist plots, the slick
timing and witty use of parentheses, both observable in some of
Berkenhead's best sallies in *Aulicus*, save the passage from mere
crudity. The wives, the writer remarks, '(who as Mr. Peters did
instruct them in the pulpit, have hugg'd their husbands into this
rebellion) provide hot water, (beside what they sprinkled for feare)
to throw on the cavaleers'.[3] Equally pungent are the caricatures of
the stock villains of Royalist mythology like Pym, Colonel Venn,
Henry Martin, and Isaac Pennington. There are even moments
when the satire achieves an imaginative force above inspired
raillery: the concord between Commons and City is compellingly
realized in this musical image:[4]

as two strings set to the same tune, though on two severall violls,
at a convenient distance, if you touch one, the other by consent
renders the same sound, so the house of commons, and the common
councell of this city, were now grown to such a sympathy, that the
motions and endeavours of one were the work of both.

Here a political insight has inspired a fresh and witty application
of a commonplace figure: apt illustration and shrewd argument
enliven each other. This is effective and memorable writing.

As the premises of *A Letter* were ideas commonly accepted by
the Court and University, so some of the expressions used were, or
became, almost clichés of Oxford propaganda. John Cleaveland was
criticized in 1645 for his habit of using 'religious Epithites' and
hanging them 'as Boyes doe Foxtailes, upon their backes, whom

---

[1] pp. 594, 593, 581, and 598, respectively.
[2] p. 595.   [3] p. 588.   [4] p. 592.

hee would laugh at'.[1] But the use of biblical imagery—a feature of political satire in the seventeenth century—was not peculiar to Cleaveland. *A Letter* exploited the device tellingly before he came to Oxford about February 1645: it ironically tricked out the usual sneer at preachers with the sort of jargon that they themselves used—'when people are disposed into a rebellion, small helpes will serve their turne; a ram's horne is as good as Shebah's trumpet'.[2] Royalist polemicists, for all their disdain, were quick to learn from the preachers the dramatic force of biblical and of commonplace illustrations to drive home an argument. But in their usage there was, too, an element of parody, calculated to rile.

Resemblances in Samuel Butler's work are more extensive and specific than those found in Cleaveland. *A Letter*[3] relates the story of

what a wise lord keeper once spake to a recorder of London, dyning with him, upon occasion of a wood-cock-pye brought to the table, with the heads looking out of the lid—Mr. Recorder, you are welcome to a common-councell.

Butler may have had this in mind when, in *Mercurius Mennipeus*, he suggested that 'The fittest Emblem of the Parliament House, is a Turky-pie, the Heads without will inform you what Birds are within'.[4] He also used the image of 'a Woodcock's Head stuck in the Lid of a Pye' in his 'character' of *An Hermetic Philosopher*.[5] It is hardly surprising that *A Letter* has been ascribed to him, or that *Mercurius Mennipeus* has been tentatively attributed to Berkenhead.[6] The existence of a common satirical idiom can make extremely hazardous the attribution of anonymous pamphlets, particularly in the absence of circumstantial indications. There may be little danger of mistaking someone like John Taylor for Berkenhead, but Butler and Berkenhead are a different proposition. Butler has been praised[7] for his mastery in fitting a 'low' style to 'low' themes, for his great sensitivity to the analogical uses of language, and for his

[1] *A Character of the New Oxford Libeller* (10 Feb. 1645), p. 2.
[2] p. 595.   [3] p. 589.
[4] *Satires and Miscellanies*, ed. R. Lamar (1928), p. 349.
[5] *Characters*, p. 100.
[6] *S. Tracts*, iv. 580 and vii. 66, respectively.
[7] Ian Jack, *Augustan Satire* (1952), p. 25.

success in illustrating abstractions with 'concrete' images. The few quotations already given from *A Letter* show that Berkenhead was adept in similar techniques. He shared Butler's taste for prosaic diction, for epigrammatic *sententiae* couched in colloquial terms, and for illustrations from common life; he also possessed something of Butler's sharpness in metaphysical argument. Indeed, though he did not have Butler's genius, he did anticipate many of his best effects and is not disgraced in the comparison.

It must be understood, of course, that in writing *A Letter* he was almost certainly furnished with materials by his superiors, and with images, phrases, and jokes by his fellow wits. Like *Aulicus*, this pamphlet shows how far the foundations of mature political satire were laid by the corporate activities of Court and University talents between 1643 and 1646. Later and greater writers assimilated this material and deployed its resources with larger humanity and insight. Nevertheless, *A Letter*, besides being a valuable historical document, witnesses how, in skilled hands, ephemeral journalism could be truly imaginative and creative.

This—the best of the works outside the newsbook in which Berkenhead had a hand at Oxford—was not the last addition to his weekly stint of journalism. About 14 November 1644[1] there was published a sermon, allegedly preached before Charles I in Christ Church Cathedral in Oxford on the third of that month, two days after the King's return from Cornwall. The title-page attributes it to Berkenhead, and it has consequently been assumed that he was ordained.[2] Wood rightly insisted that Berkenhead was not a cleric; and in later years he himself stated explicitly that he had never been in Holy Orders.[3] Wood concluded that there must have been another John Berkenhead, also a Fellow of All Souls.[4] There was not. The homily was actually composed by Thomas Morton, Bishop of Durham, and first published in Oxford, probably in February 1643, under the title *The Necessity of Christian Subjection*. This edition is correctly attributed.[5] It was reprinted in London (a counterfeit of the Oxford original), appearing twice in the same

---

[1] Madan, no. 1691.   [2] Ibid.
[3] Bodleian Library, MS. Rawl. D. 371, f. 12ᵛ.   [4] *Ath. Oxon.* iii. 1206.
[5] See Madan, no. 1258.

year;[1] and this 1644 version was a re-issue of sheets printed in London, together with fresh (and fraudulent) preliminaries printed at Oxford.[2] Berkenhead certainly did not, as the title-page claims, write the sermon; nor is it even likely that he, a layman, delivered it from the pulpit before the King on 3 November. In fact, it was probably not preached in Christ Church at all. Some connoisseurs of sermons thought more highly of good second-hand homilies than of 'half-roasted' new ones;[3] and it could, theoretically, be that Morton's treatment of a subject dear to Charles's heart—the necessity of obedience to the Crown, come what might—was given an encore. Royalists were certainly anxious to hear the sort of reassurances it offered. But there were flocks of fully fledged divines in Oxford eager to please with fresh offerings. Everything suggests that the title-page statements were fictitious, as were most of those in Berkenhead's dedication to Charles, Prince of Wales:

It hath pleas'd your Highnesse to command this Sermon to the Presse, and me to be your servant: what you have observ'd from either, that might incline you to so much grace & favour, I know not; unlesse it were my plaine dealing with the Times. This (indeed) your Highnesse mentioned with a deep sence and relish.

Even the claim to have supervised the printing of the text is demonstrably spurious. The one certainty is the intention to mislead; another is the remarkable long-term success of the exercise. If nothing else, it confirms that Berkenhead was quite capable of devising the stratagems used to cover *Aulicus*'s decline. His motives here are less immediately apparent: probably the main purpose was to use his name to sell off copies of an old sermon;

---

[1] Madan, nos. 1258* and 1421.

[2] Madan (no. 1691) noticed that the first two leaves of the 1644 version were printed at Oxford, but did not identify it with the Morton sermon. In the Bodleian copies of 1691, 1421, and 1258* the tenth ornament from the left in the row of ornaments across the top of p. (1) is identically misprinted in each case. As it is unlikely that a printer would have kept type standing from 14 Mar. 1643 until 31 July 1643, let alone November 1644, it seems that there was one printing of the text of *The Necessity* of which copies were released at intervals and in suitably altered guises.

[3] C. F. Richardson, *English Preachers and Preaching, 1640–1670* (1928), p. 115; the phrase is Thomas Fuller's. Richardson points out (pp. 115–17) that the practice of repeating old sermons was not, however, universally approved of.

simultaneously it gave him an opening for some self-advertisement at a time when *Aulicus* was often at a standstill, and a chance to tell everyone that the heir to the throne looked on him favourably. The deception might also have been justified as covering up for the real author, then virtually under house arrest in London, and for the press that had printed the London counterfeit edition in the first place. None the less it is hard to imagine that the layman's masquerade would have been wholly pleasing to the King whose views on clerical propriety and ecclesiastical good form were strict, not to say stiff.

Perhaps, as the preliminaries were presumably sent to London for publication and may never have circulated in Oxford, Berkenhead calculated that the King would hear nothing of the matter. Possibly the young Charles was in on Berkenhead's little joke and could be depended on to smooth over any awkwardnesses that might arise. The Dedication does prove favourable contact between Berkenhead and the Prince. Anyhow, the opportunist in Berkenhead seems to have decided that the risk of offence was worth taking when, among other things, it might increase his stock of credit with a future monarch. Necessarily one can only speculate about the oddity of the case and the precise nature of his motives, and fall back on the certainty of fraud and the propagandist's cool nerve. He was to display that aplomb notably in later crises of his life. One can be confident, too, that by the end of 1644 he was in some sense in control of the Oxford press. In the following year he licensed pamphlets, although he was not one of the licensers nominated in June 1644.[1] It was natural, and later became the practice in London, to employ the approved newsbook's editor as censor of propaganda publications.[2] It looks as though Berkenhead was moving towards that position in November 1644, and making the most of it. His boldness appears all the more emphatic because in the 1640s and 1650s it was, by and large, politic and customary for writers of newsbooks and pamphlets to conceal their identity— a circumstance which, incidentally, heightens the amusing irony that the only pamphlet Berkenhead put his name to before 1663 was not his at all.

[1] Madan, ii. 313–14.   [2] J. B. Williams, *History of English Journalism*, p. 59.

In suggesting that Berkenhead was largely responsible for a 1645 pamphlet published in three parts on 4, 11, and 18 August respectively,[1] under the title *Mercurius Anti-Britanicus*, one has again to rely on internal and circumstantial evidence. The work was a desperate bid to discredit *Britanicus*, currently making tremendous capital of letters captured in the King's cabinet at the Battle of Naseby on 14 June. These had betrayed the monarch's true and not very honourable intentions; and their publication,[2] together with the virtual collapse of Royalist forces, took the wind out of Cavalier sails. Determined to keep their campaign moving the Oxford propagandists struck out furiously. If the earlier numbers of *Aulicus*, like *A Letter*, calmly mixed sober reflection with humorous observation, *Mercurius Anti-Britanicus*, even more than the newsbook's later issues, swept along a course of whirling ribaldry.

The three parts of this serial pamphlet are loosely constructed: they simply pile up witty images, illustrations, and almost random arguments. Some attempt is made to defend the King's policy towards the Militia and the Catholics; but there is little to be gained from expatiating on the arguments, as the real energy of the writer is spent on blackening *Britanicus*'s reputation. The fantastic agglomeration of images reminds one of that less successful baroque architecture in which bristling ornamentation has got out of hand. 'Frippery' was the word *Britanicus* shrewdly used to describe it.[3] Setting aside the possibility of multiple authorship, the lack of shape was inevitable in a work which was really a running commentary on *Britanicus*'s criticisms of the King's letters. It follows the order of the Londoner's observations, not any thematic logic of its own. The remarkable volubility of the ridicule betrays the desperation with which Oxford tried to make the best of a bad case. The basic drift of the defence—that Parliament stood condemned in the dishonourable methods of its apologists—was specious. The writer was trying to maintain a position which, though tenable in 1643, was almost indefensible by 1645. This bespeaks an extraordinary tenacity, but one also recognizes something approaching

---

[1] Madan, no. 2064.
[2] They appeared under the title *The King's Cabinet Opened* about 9 July, 1645.
[3] No. 97 (8–15 Sept. 1645), p. 865.

light-headedness in the gay refusal to compromise even trivial prejudices, which are as zealously defended as matters of highest principle. Reckless abandon is shown in the way the writer seeks to answer defeat and disgrace with a bravura display of wit and smart debating tricks. *Mercurius Anti-Britanicus* was a fire-cracker, fabricated expressly to deafen and dazzle the reader.

It shared more with *Aulicus* than this desire to laugh in the face of disaster. The newsbook had fallen silent for many weeks after Naseby, but with the opening of the new propaganda offensive in August the editor brought out another number. Nominally for the week 13–20 July, it was actually published about 12 August. It referred the reader to a work dealing with the King's letters:[1] this may have been the second part of *Mercurius Anti-Britanicus* which, in turn, directed attention to the next number of *Aulicus* for 10–17 August.[2] The interrelationship was not merely temporal however, for there are some striking coincidences of phrasing and argument. *Aulicus*'s assertion under 14 August that 'none but Rebels of a barbarous presumption would offer to draw the Curtaine when Husband and Wife are private', parallels the complaint, in the third part of the pamphlet, that 'to prye into their Princes Curtaines, and to divulge what the Queen said to her Husband in his Armes, is a Crime certainly, next to his who saw a Goddesse naked'.[3] The same number of *Aulicus* observes: 'we need not quote Scripture when we say, Rebellion is as the sinne of Witchcraft',[4] while the pamphlet cites the 'saying of the Scripture . . . that Rebellion is as the sinne of Witchcraft'.[5] *Mercurius Anti-Britanicus* also reiterates points from earlier numbers of the newsbook: the accusation that the 'Rebels' had 'inchanted the People into their Disobedience'[6] matches the notion in *Aulicus*'s twenty-sixth week that they had used 'straines of Rhetoricke . . . to bewitch the people'.[7] As *Britanicus* descreetly put it, *Mercurius Anti-Britanicus* had borrowed 'a little language out of *Aulicus*'.[8]

[1] p. 1665.   [2] p. 19.
[3] pp. 1704 and 30, respectively.
[4] p. 1698. Butler was fond of this saying: see his *Characters*, pp. 302–3, and *Satires and Miscellanies*, p. 362.
[5] p. 5.   [6] Ibid.
[7] p. 331. Cf. also the phrase in *A Letter*, cited above, p. 108, n. 3.
[8] No. 97 (8–15 Sept. 1645), p. 865.

In fact, it borrowed from other Berkenhead pamphlets. The description of a preacher who could 'passe for a Britanicus in the Pulpit' touches *A Letter*'s observation that 'our new preachers entertain their auditories with newes'.[1] Berkenhead's Preface to *The Battaile on Hopton Heath* is similarly recalled by an allusion to Goths and Vandals 'who took Armes against Statues, and made warre upon the dead'.[2] The description of Lord Say as 'a Brother of the Circumcised ruffe, short haire, and large eares'[3] employs phrases used earlier in *Aulicus*, and is recalled by jibes at 'short hayre' and 'little ruffs' which Berkenhead shortly after this inserted into a pamphlet by John Taylor.[4] The image appeared again in *The Assembly Man*, whose 'own neck is palisadoed with a ruff'. Berkenhead pictured the Assembler as 'the states trumpet; for then he doth not preach, but is blown; proclaims news, very loud, the trumpet and his forehead being both of one metal';[5] this seems to have been inspired by *Mercurius Anti-Britanicus*'s dig at *Britanicus* as a 'brazen Head as often as they bid Him speak in defamation of the Kings side'.[6] Dryden's vignette of Corah as a figure of brass draws some of its associations from this tradition. It is a reminder, too, that many satirical images were public property; but the closeness and frequency of echoes in the pieces under discussion, together with circumstantial evidences of Berkenhead's connection in time and place with *Mercurius Anti-Britanicus*, justify the conclusion that he at least had a hand in it.

At the same time it certainly shows Cleaveland's influence and maybe his participation. Some months before this his famous *Character of a London Diurnall* had been published at Oxford,[7] and earned him the title of 'A whelp of the same litter with Aulicus . . . things halfe made up between Syllogisme and Sophistry'.[8] The proliferation of imagery in *Mercurius Anti-Britanicus*—few points

---

[1] p. 3 and p. 594, respectively   [2] p. 17; see above, p. 105.   [3] p. 9.

[4] For these phrases in the newsbook see no. 66 (31 Mar.–6 Apr. 1644), p. 926 and no. 113 (27 Apr.–4 May 1645), p. 1569. For the Taylor pamphlet see below, p. 124.

[5] *The Assembly Man* (1647), reprinted in *Harl. Misc.* v. 101 and 103 respectively.

[6] p. 4. Cf. Dryden in *The Medall*, ll. 162–3, which was published in the year of *The Assembly Man*'s reappearance.

[7] See Madan, no. 1708.

[8] *M. Brit.*, no. 70 (10–17 Feb. 1645), p. 549. Cleaveland shared Berkenhead's admiration for Laud: see his poem to the Archbishop in *The Works* (1687), pp. 63–4.

are made that do not carry their attendant simile or metaphor—is very much in his manner, as is the extensive range of illustrations, from Machiavelli, the Bible, and philosophy, down to the common street-cryer. The *Character of a London Diurnall* also inspired specific points in *Mercurius Anti-Britanicus*: Cleaveland's jest that 'the onely playhouse is at Westminster'[1] seems to be behind the observation that the stage had moved from Blackfriars to Westminster, and would return to its proper home only when the Londoners reverted to their 'old harmless profession of killing Men in Tragedies without Manslaughter'.[2]

The very comprehensiveness of *Mercurius Anti-Britanicus* well demonstrates the communal character of Royalist satire, something a Londoner put his finger on when he suggested that George Digby had lent Cleaveland 'two or three of his jests' for the *Character of a London Diurnall*, and that Oxford's wit was 'raked out of the dunghill of ruined stages'.[3] Many of the three-part pamphlet's motifs recur as stereotypes through the next twenty years and more. The joke about the stage, for example, subsequently recurred in various guises in Berkenhead's *The Assembly Man* and *Bibliotheca Parliamenti*, and in Butler's *Mercurius Mennipeus*.[4] A similar course could be plotted for many of its jeers at 'Rebel' ignorance and sexual immorality. But most interesting are the comments on eloquence and wit: the first article of faith is that Royalists have a sort of Divine Right to these things. The Speaker of the Commons is sneered at because his Latin is 'scarce Classicke', and there is lofty disdain for *Britanicus*'s Billingsgate language. True wit (and Dryden's strictures again come to mind) is defined as more than simply 'a Liberty of rayling at Great Men': to write thus was to 'defile and strumpet, one of the greatest ornaments God and Nature have bestowed upon us; And to make Wit, which was borne to rule, the Foole and Jester of the people'.[5] The writer did not mean that satirizing individuals was wrong in principle, though he undoubtedly regarded reflections on the King as improper: what is

---

[1] *Character Writings of the Seventeenth Century*, p. 308.   [2] p. 20.

[3] *A Character of the New Oxford Libeller*, pp. 3–4.

[4] See in, respectively, *Harl. Misc.* v. 103, ix. 418 (the work was first published in 1654) and *Satires and Miscellanies*, p. 363.

[5] pp. 12, 26, and 25 respectively.

really behind his remarks is a concern with decorum and 'good tone'. His complaint was that in two years there had been nothing 'well, or sharply ill said' by the London propagandists.[1] The point is taken if one looks at *Britanicus*, for its humour was broader, less easy, and less refined than that of *Aulicus*. *Mercurius Anti-Britanicus*'s basic notion, which rests on certain assumptions about class and education, is one that became an increasingly active force in Cavalier prose and poetry in the 1640s and 1650s. Social and political developments confirmed them in their contention that fine writing was the prerogative of men who respected Crown, Aristocracy, Church, and University.

Wit, in this context, was seen as the natural inheritance of men 'borne to rule', just as, for Dryden, the couplet appeared to be a princely instrument 'fit for the ends of government'.[2] That is why another Royalist described wit in a Roundhead as an anachronism.[3] This preoccupation with good breeding in men and letters is explicit in *Mercurius Anti-Britanicus*; and it is interesting to see that it informed even the most ephemeral propaganda. It is noteworthy, too, that even at this stage Royalist apologists usually scorned to flirt with unbelievers. As defeat loomed larger, in fact, extremists like Berkenhead became, if possible, more intransigent. The full weight of their defiance was exerted to widen differences by emphasizing supposedly immutable social and political distinctions. Berkenhead's next work, *A Discourse Discovering some Mysteries of our New State*, published in Oxford on 19 September 1645, reinforces the point.[4] It takes the form of a three-cornered conversation between a Protestant, a Puritan, and a Papist—a form which, with its logical divisions, and recapitulations, its casuistry and earnestness of tone, suggests that it originates in academic disputations, polemical dialogues, and the serious *débats* of Cavalier drama.[5]

The ascription to Berkenhead rests on resemblances to his known works and on biographical and stylistic evidence. First, the pamphlet's general theme, that the 'Rebels' though professing to

[1] p. 4.
[2] *A Defence of An Essay of Dramatic Poesy* (1668).
[3] *Britanicus Vapulans*, no. 1 (4 Nov. 1643), p. 3.
[4] Madan, no. 1816. He describes it as 'smartly written and worth reading'.
[5] See A. Harbage, *Cavalier Drama* (New York, 1936), pp. 35–6.

be Brownists were Jesuits at heart, occurs in *Aulicus* about this time.[1] Second, a reference to 'a mock-play at Guildhall'[2] and a sneer at the Londoners' bad Latin[3] are repetitions of points in *Mercurius Anti-Britanicus*.[4] It is also instructive to compare the two pamphlets' mockery of three speeches made in London about the King's letters,[5] and their attempts to defend the King's use of the Duke of Lorraine's troops.[6] Third, and most persuasive, are parallels in *A Letter from Mercurius Civicus*. *A Discourse* actually repeats that pamphlet's exposition of the internal revolution of 1641, borrowing phrases and arguments wholesale. The same quotation from Hooker occurs in both,[7] as does the description of Rebellion's chief supporters as broken Citizens.[8] But the following passages best illustrate the coincidences: *A Letter* describes how Rebellion was 'conceived (some say) neere Banbury, and shaped in Grays-Inne-Lane, where the undertakers for the Isle of Providence, did meet and plot it, yet you know it was put out to nurse to London'; while *A Discourse* explains how 'this Monster was whelped . . . neare Banbury, and moulded in Holborne (for as yet it did not see the way into Scotland) by the Islanders of Providence, and put to nurse in London'.[9] The specific echoes are substantial, and the device of the parenthetical aside also suggests Berkenhead's hand. Indeed, the whole character of the piece, with its blend of systematic argument and caustic interjection, relates it more closely to *A Letter* than to *Mercurius Anti-Britanicus*.

Berkenhead's penchant for satirizing his victims' humble origins appears notably in the treatment of Dr. John Bastwicke, who 'because he could not cut his cloath according to his mind, he ranne Byasse; some great Patient had kept him as quiet as when he kept his Fathers Tanne-pits, or waited upon his Father in Lawes Hawkes'.[10] Sarcasm like this is commonplace in *Aulicus*. As a Laudian, Berkenhead of course had a special motive for pitching into Bastwicke, Burton, and Prynne; and *A Discourse* specifically recalls

[1] *M. Aul.*, no. 117 (10–17 Aug. 1645), p. 1705; cf. *A Discourse*, p. 38.
[2] p. 26.   [3] p. 10.
[4] pp. 20 and 12 respectively (cited above, p. 120).
[5] pp. 37–8 and 28, respectively.   [6] pp. 37 and 14, respectively.
[7] *A Letter*, p. 584 and *A Discourse*, p. 7.   [8] pp. 584 and 7, respectively.
[9] pp. 582 and 7, respectively. More such parallels can be found.
[10] pp. 17–18.

Prynne's time at Oriel College, Oxford,[1] the details of which Berkenhead might naturally have been familiar with as a past member
of the College. The writer's reverent allusions to Laud are similarly
suggestive: he recalls his famous debate with the Jesuit Fisher, and
his treatment of Puritans in the Ecclesiastical Courts,[2] and he goes
into some detail about the Archbishop's conduct as President of
St. John's College, referring to things that happened 'to my knowledge'.[3] Altogether, the indications that Berkenhead wrote *A
Discourse* are strong.

The pamphlet purports to present a serious theological and
political discussion; in fact, the reasoning is so specious that no
uncommitted observer could take the arguments seriously. From
the start the outcome is a foregone conclusion; and there can never
have been more amenable proselytes than the Protestant's antagonists. Questions put to him as an Anglican representative are
framed so that he can state his case as persuasively as possible and
discredit deviationist arguments with the utmost of ease. To do
him justice, he has a glib tongue and runs us lightly through authorities like Bellarmine, Beza, Calvin, Hooker, and Featley; and—his
premises once accepted—his agile mind and lucid power of exposition are thoroughly winning. But his partiality is unmistakable
and interesting: for all the show of representing fairly Puritan
thinking, palpable injustice is done them; and there is barely a
pretence of treating the Papist with equal rigour. He is let off very
lightly in return for a promise of loyalty to the King and Irish
Catholic military aid.

Real impartiality is not, of course, to be expected; but purely as
propaganda *A Discourse* is, for all its affectation of confidence,
inferior to *A Letter*. Much of it, being a reworking of old material,
inevitably seems a little stale and more than a little beside the
point, except, perhaps, as an overture to the Catholics and a wan
attempt to placate English fear that Irish troops would turn the
country into a province of Rome. Its estimate of the state of the
war is absurdly unrealistic: the Protestant blithely observes that,

[1] p. 17.
[2] p. 17. See above, p. 25, for Berkenhead's interest in the Fisher debate. His Lambeth sojourn may have given him first-hand experience of the trials of Puritans.
[3] p. 13.

setting aside Horncastle, Marston Moor, and Naseby, Parliament has never been victorious.[1] That was cool, but it cannot have done much to convince supporters and potential allies that there was life in the cause yet.

A Discourse is an interesting document, nevertheless, because so obviously written by a man close to the King and Digby, who were still hopeful that Irish intervention would save the day. It faithfully mirrors their reliance on half-truths and cynical manœuvring. But for all his sincere loyalty and sleight of hand Berkenhead could not convincingly defend the whole of that policy in this pamphlet. As in *Aulicus*, he is betrayed into uncertainty when handling the delicate issue of Charles's Catholic flirtations. One of the abiding motifs of Royalist and Tory propaganda in the seventeenth century is the identification of Catholics and Presbyterians as tyrannicides.[2] It appears well before this time and Berkenhead himself was still canvassing it in 1663. But in *A Discourse* he has to compromise by insisting on a distinction between those Catholics fighting honourably and disinterestedly for the King and the calculating Jesuits. This focuses the dilemma in which Charles's toying with Catholicism had landed his apologists; it left even Berkenhead casting about fitfully for unconvincing excuses.

Oxford resistance was, in truth, fast running out; and Berkenhead's concluding foray into print while in Oxford, on 22 October 1645, was almost accidental. On 5 October he licensed John Taylor's pamphlet, *The Causes of the Diseases and Distempers of this Kingdome*, adding to the manuscript some notes of his own by way of parting jests.[3] So he ended his Oxford campaign as he had begun it, by interlacing another man's work with his own expressions. The five marginal notes in his hand are flippancies aimed at Knox, Henderson, Case, Prynne, and the Close Committee. But the chief interest of the pamphlet is the fact that Berkenhead licensed it: it seems that he was now virtually in full control of the Oxford press. As *Aulicus* had folded up and pamphlets were few and far between his duties cannot have been particularly onerous. He may, however,

---

[1] p. 30.   [2] See *A Discourse*, p. 3.
[3] Madan, no. 1820 dates the pamphlet about 15 Oct. 1645, but 22 Oct. is the date printed on its title-page. For the notes see Bodleian Library, MS. Add. c. 209.

have been acting as censor for some time, fulfilling by proxy, as it were, the ambition that Laud never achieved in his lifetime of establishing his imprimatur at Oxford.[1] And however brief Berkenhead's direct control of publications, it had long-term consequences: for at the Restoration he was to become, once more, official newsbook editor and Licenser to the Press. Such things contributed much to the continuity of Royalist propaganda, its attitudes and emotions.

By October 1645 Berkenhead, not yet 30, had come a long way, winning favour and some power. His name was a byword for Cavalier loyalty, tenacity, and wit. Yet ironically, his prospects were dim. There was little left for the King's spokesman to say: armed resistance was soon to collapse completely, and Charles had to try his luck with the Scots, leaving the Courtiers to fend for themselves. Berkenhead, like many others, had to work out his own 'salvation' in London. It was, and is, a moment for taking stock.

The uncompromising inflexibility of the King's outlook had encouraged the development of a tight-knit central group of loyal adherents who made it part of their business to establish a dominant control of the organs of public communication. The investigation of *Aulicus* showed Berkenhead's closeness to this group and his major role as publicist of its views. His other pamphlets issued by the Court sustain the earlier diagnosis. One observes particularly the way his propaganda is thoroughly informed by dominant Laudian attitudes; and one finds confirmed the earlier impression that beneath all momentary blandishments lay resolutely unaccommodating stances. One seeks in vain for hints of genuine compromise, for any serious wooing of moderate or popular opinion. Berkenhead's work—witness the open scorn for *Britanicus*'s common touch—is marked by a disdainful indifference towards the idea of conciliating the 'lower' orders of merchants, soldiers, yeoman, and apprentices. Such self-assurance was part of the gentleman-Courtier, a privileged, cultured, and superior being, defender of traditional values in literature and politics against the barbarism of the uncultivated herd. Naturally such a man drew on

---

[1] See F. B. Williams Jr., 'The Laudian Imprimatur', *The Library*, 5th Ser. xv (1960), 104.

the resources of that tradition to satisfy the needs of day-to-day political propaganda; and inevitably the Oxford wits, using common sources and working in close consort, rapidly evolved distinctive patterns of thought and image in their writing. The extent of Berkenhead's contribution between 1643 and 1646 justifies claiming for him a not inconsiderable role in the process whereby English political satire found an assured voice and a viable vocabulary. For he was a more dominant figure in the world of Oxford propaganda than has previously been understood.

Yet, as was remarked, the charmed circle of his life at Court was about to be broken, and the prospect of further promotion snatched from him. It might be imagined that the defeat of 1646 must irrevocably disturb the confident tenour of Cavalier satire, and shake the resolve and enterprise of a man like Berkenhead, maybe silence him altogether. But a diplomatic retreat into safe obscurity, even if it was open to him, did not suit his temperament. He was not the man lamely to abandon the fight or his own prospects now that his appetite had been whetted and part satisfied. There had to be changes of course: London was henceforth the base for Royalist propagandists, who had previously enjoyed the security of Oxford; and this shift of the scene of operations, together with the psychological impact of defeat, precipitated changes in the tone and attitudes of Berkenhead's writing. But he did survive to prolong the argument: indeed, events were destined to rouse him to activity again within a comparatively short space of time.

CHAPTER V

1646 to 1649
'Art and sophistry will compas nothing'

THOUGH Berkenhead had made a considerable name for himself
in the three years now ended, it would seem reasonable for Wood
to characterize the next phase of his life as one in which he scraped
a living from menial literary hack work.[1] Defeat and danger of
arrest might easily have muzzled him as they did Heylin and many
other Royalists. But Wood's picture of a man adrift is false. Berkenhead was certainly circumspect, but he did not lack courage
and grasped every opportunity of serving the King. Moreover,
although the Court ceased, substantially, to function, determined
Cavaliers continued to meet and sustain to a remarkable degree a
community of feeling and doing. Writers, acting in concert still,
carried ahead the development of agreed conventions. And though
Cartwright was dead, fashionable Cavalier society was still eager
to honour his memory and what he stood for, by making much of
Berkenhead as a survivor of his circle.[2] They respected his talent
and his critical judgement, and he became more intimately involved
in their literary (and musical) pursuits than has been realized.
Admittedly his verse has little intrinsic merit, but it is of some
interest because it reflected the general movement towards the
urbane, epigrammatic heroic couplet and because he so explicitly
appealed to political dogma to substantiate literary practice and
theory. This suggests some of the reasons why Royalists' literary
activities, far from being crushed in the Interregnum, were stimulated by the changed conditions. The *esprit de corps* built up in the
years of warfare was not dissipated by defeat but in some respects
consolidated. The unfamiliar hostile environment actually stiffened
the will to resist of the hard core of loyalists.

[1] *Ath. Oxon.* iii. 1203. [2] *Brief Lives*, i. 104.

Oxford propaganda had been, on the whole, strangely indifferent to pressures from outside the Court: it was, to put it perhaps rather baldly, out of touch with the feelings of society at
large. Those feelings were not exactly ignored, but even when
noted they were not absorbed as a real, substantial part of the
experience of the King and his spokesmen. Secure within city and
College walls, they were to some degree insulated from the tumults
without, and they had resolutely talked down to the rest of
the nation. A large measure of this aristocratic sense of inbred
superiority survived the military capitulation of 1646. The
'serious' verse they wrote was still uncompromisingly an upper-class
affair, imbued with the prejudices and discriminations of a social
and intellectual élite. Indeed, what they saw as the triumph of
anarchy and iconoclasm made them more than ever conscious of
their destiny as guardians of all things precious and noble in the
world of letters. There are many indications that they felt more
than ever besieged and that this increased sense of isolation and
exclusion fostered in men like Berkenhead an exalted sense of duty
and a greater feeling of mutual dependence. The outcome was a
closing of the ranks around established relationships and interests.

Nevertheless, the King's plight and the very different mode of
life at London forced even the most valiant loyalist to alter his
tactics, to do something to come to terms with a new experience.
For Berkenhead, at the age of 29, this was virtually the first
entrance upon a world where Court and University privilege did
not run supreme. His pamphleteering shows a new eagerness to
win sympathies previously disdained: one even catches him
flirting with Presbyterians and Levellers. But the most arresting
thing in the attempt of many Royalist apologists to appeal to
a wider audience is a noticeable, though not of course universal
shifting of emphasis towards a broader comedy of manners. One of
the best and most frequent solutions to the search for popularity
without vulgarity was burlesque. In this mode the Cavaliers set
out to amuse themselves and their readers with parodies of their
foes' language and thinking; and even the enemy must have been
diverted by the best of the imitations. At the same time burlesque
sorted well with the preoccupation of writers who, at another level,

were bent on cultivating ever greater purity and refinement of style. The parodying of vulgarity in their newsbooks and pamphlets was a discriminating revenge which, even as it entertained in a broadly accessible way, insisted on the writers' higher notions of social and literary decorum.

This tendency is marked in a number of interesting and, in some respects, influential pamphlets by Berkenhead, and in his contributions to the rather extraordinary Royalist newsbooks published during the second Civil War. These ephemeral pieces are, paradoxically, the most profitable outcome of his simultaneous involvement with serious letters. Here, in political caricature, is his best work. The publishing of prose and verse was not, however, the sum of his continuing partisan activity. He also undertook in these years new and more hazardous duties as a secret agent, travelling between England and the Continent in the service of the Crown. All that he did and wrote between 1646 and 1649 was a pledge of his stalwart faith. But while holding firm to his purposes he proved that he had the capacity to develop his talents and adapt his techniques; and that kept him in the front rank of Cavalier activists in this new phase of their struggle.

Berkenhead was launched into this more troubled passage of his life not at Oxford in 1648, as Wood and Aubrey both implied,[1] but at Wallingford in 1646. Late on the evening of 26 April Charles I took leave of his Council and slipped out of Oxford on the London road. Berkenhead, who had so far stuck as close to the throne as he could, presumably did not leave the University before that; but some time before the Parliamentary armies sat down before the city at the beginning of May, he too left the scene of his triumphs and disappointments. Somehow he made his way down river to Wallingford, and when the garrison capitulated on 27 July after a siege lasting sixty-five days among those who marched out on terms was 'Master Berkenhead (alias Mercurius Aulicus)'.[2] He carried a pass permitting him to report to the King at Newcastle,

---

[1] *Ath. Oxon.* iii. 1203 and *Brief Lives*, i. 105 both date Berkenhead's departure from Oxford from the Visitation of 1648.
[2] *The Weekly Account*, no. 32 (29 July–5 Aug. 1646), f. 212ᵛ.

but forbidding him to remain there. He had, in fact, five weeks in which to make himself scarce.[1]

What he did was to make himself useful—to the King. By the third week of October he was in London, acting as 'Iourney man to the Kingdomes Intelligencer'.[2] This was *The Kingdome's Weekly Intelligencer*, which carried an item by Berkenhead in its number for 13–20 October.[3] The fact that he was granted this space underlines current shifts of political allegiance. The weekly's editor, Richard Collings, like many Presbyterians felt personally loyal to the King and now that more extreme counsels seemed about to prevail in Parliament he feared for the Crown's safety and was willing to rally to its defence. Berkenhead, of course, was acting on the latest Royal policy of seeking moderate Presbyterian support. His brief contribution, arguing that a French invasion on Charles's behalf was imminent, was meant to persuade them that conciliation was best. Probably in going to London and intervening in the squabble about the disposal of the King's person Berkenhead was acting on orders.

The newsbook piece was only a testing shot: Berkenhead soon followed it up with heavier fire in two pamphlets. *An Answer to A Speech Without Doores* and *The Speech Without Doores Defended Without Reason*. The first was advertised by *The Kingdome's Weekly Intelligencer* on 15 November as already in print.[4] Possibly the editor had placed his press at Berkenhead's disposal. The ascription of the pamphlets to the latter, though not new, needs explanation: it is based on a note written by Thomas Barlow, President of the Queen's College, Oxford, on his copy of the first pamphlet.[5] This, coming from a close friend of Berkenhead, carries more authority than Thomas Audley's guess that the writer was Richard Little, editor of *Mercurius Academicus*.[6] The advertisement in *The King-*

---

[1] For the terms of capitulation and the length of the siege see Joshua Sprigge, *Anglia Rediviva* (1647) (reprinted 1854), pp. 292–6 and the table following p. 336. It is also the source of the information about the pass.

[2] *A Perfect Diurnall*, no. 169 (19–26 Oct. 1646), p. 1635.   [3] No. 170, p. 272.

[4] No. 174 (10–17 Nov.), p. 304. This stated that a warrant had been issued for the arrest of the author and printer. Thomason got his copy of *An Answer*, B.M., E. 362(9), on 16 Nov.   [5] This is in the Bodleian Library, C. 13. 16. Linc. (34).

[6] *Diutinus Britanicus*, no. 1 (25 Nov.–2 Dec. 1646), pp. 1–4, and *Mercurius Diutinus*, no. 3 (8–16 Dec.), pp. 17–21.

dome's Weekly Intelligencer clinches the argument. The second pamphlet, out by 5 December,[1] was a continuation of the first and obviously penned by the same man to refute criticisms published in the interim. The occasion of all this print was a Commons speech of 26 October by Thomas Chaloner, former opponent of Laud and one of Henry Martin's Republican allies. Chaloner argued against the Scots' demands for an equal say with Parliament in settling the King's future. The northern proposals had been canvassed in *Papers, Delivered in by the Commissioners of the Kingdom of Scotland*; so Chaloner's hostile reply was in turn published on 10 November as *An Answer to the Scotch Papers*.[2] As this contretemps suggests, there was a real chance that Scots and Parliament would fall out over their prize, who himself was not unaware of this and determined to exploit the differences between the claimants. Up to the end of November Charles toyed ostentatiously with schemes for establishing Presbyterianism in England for a limited period; and Berkenhead's pamphlets were designed to aid this strategy by stiffening English Presbyterian resistance to the alarming claim that Parliament had the sole rights to the King's person.

Berkenhead's tactic was to pose as a lover of Parliament, attacking not the policy of the House but Chaloner's heretical arguments. The gambit did not disarm men like Audley, who recognized behind the pose an orthodox Cavalier. None the less Berkenhead's insinuations showed an experienced hand at propaganda, trying, quite pertinently, to rouse moderates against extremists in the Commons and to alarm opinion at large. He questioned the authenticity of *An Answer to the Scotch Papers* by suggesting that Chaloner's printed speech was not word for word as delivered, and that various expressions against the King had been toned down.[3] Chaloner and his supporters were, he argued, nothing but ambitious and unscrupulous conspirators. In fact, the arguments against Scottish claims rested on a practical assessment of political realities. But Chaloner had tried to give his case a colouring of orthodoxy by appealing to legal and historical precedent. Here,

---

[1] B.M., E. 365 (4).
[2] *Perfect Occurrences*, no. 46 (13 Nov.), 2X3ᵛ.
[3] p. 2.

shrewdly, Berkenhead attacked, deploying considerable forensic skill and knowledge of precedent to expose the defects in Chaloner's logic.

Great store seems to have been set by Berkenhead's first pamphlet, no less than three editions of it being printed.[1] It provoked a strong reaction, too, in the shape of four replies, one, by Henry Martin himself, published in Edinburgh to counteract Berkenhead's influence on Scottish opinion. The gist of the replies was that the Cavalier had pedantically ignored the facts of power. Martin, more outspoken than the rest, put this with characteristic bluntness, 'all your art and sophistry will compas nothing'.[2] He was right: Berkenhead may have forced the enemy into the open; but matters had gone too far for theoretical arguments, however sound, to win the day. The issue, inevitably, was decided by the will to act of strenuous and determined men whose real appeal was to necessity, not theory. Indeed, Berkenhead's cleverness may even have rebounded on itself: by parading, however inadvertently, the King's continued hope of outwitting his enemies, he may have helped extremists like Martin to convince Parliament that Charles was fundamentally unprepared to make real concessions to the logic of circumstances.

On 28 November 1646 the Independents carried through the Commons a motion asserting that Parliament alone must dispose of the monarch. Undaunted, Berkenhead returned to the fray with his second pamphlet aimed at mobilizing opinion outside the House. This was again a technical *tour de force*: it would have won him high honours in the Schools at the University. Unfortunately, politics were not being conducted precisely by the rule-book, certainly not by the rules of theology and metaphysics which Berkenhead invoked. Nor, though it was undoubtedly what the King wanted, can this sort of propaganda have done anything to allay suspicion that Charles, through his apologist, was still

[1] These are represented in the Bodleian Library by the following copies: C. 13. 16. Linc. (34), Wood 610 (23), and Pamph. C. 38 (5).

[2] *A Corrector of the Answerer to the Speech out of Doores* (3 Dec.), p. 14. The other replies were *An Answer to Severall Objections* (23 Nov.), and *The Justification of a Safe and Well-grounded Answer* (27 Nov. 1646), both by Chaloner, and *A Reply to a Nameless Pamphlet* (23 Nov.).

fishing in troubled waters. Indeed, the vote of 28 November had made Berkenhead less cautious: he flung out some characteristic taunts like the sarcasm that he was 'no such Guifted Brother, as to draw from a Text, what is not in it'.[1] The conservatism of his position is openly displayed in the dogma that 'All changes of Government are mortiferous'.[2] Equally revealing is the general posture of disdainful condescension, inspired both by a conviction of the Divine Right of the cause and by confidence that he had an answer for anything that Chaloner could think up. This was hardly a diplomatic boast, since it implied that the argument was some sort of competition in cleverness.

Samuel Butler once wryly described such confidence as 'commonly a great Support to Wit', because partisans willing to break jests on the enemy inevitably pleased patrons and could not 'but be understood to have done very good Service'.[3] Doubtless some of Berkenhead's witticisms pleased the King, although he was in no position to reward his servant immediately. For both pamphlets are attractively spiced with humorous repartee, and even the first, examining the speech point by point in an intricate argument, is conducted with winning clarity and spirit. Such sophistical power made Berkenhead the natural exponent of Charles's current policy, which was to lie low and entangle the enemy in dialectic. This faithful mirroring of the Royal strategy, not least apparent in the dependence on forms of words and hair-splitting, is one of the most interesting features of these pamphlets. The old relationship between Berkenhead and the Crown had unquestionably survived the flight from Oxford.

That Berkenhead had not scuttled away was public knowledge: in December, when the King was still in Newcastle, Audley, keeping a wary eye on Cavaliers' doings, rumoured cryptically that 'Aulicus his Maske' had 'contracted a Company . . . to shew Gamballs at Court this Christmasse'.[4] Possibly he had nothing specific in mind, but it could be a reference to the publication that next brought Berkenhead's name before readers—the Folio edition

---

[1] pp. 1–2. There is a copy of this second pamphlet in the B.M., E 365 (4).
[2] p. 2.   [3] *Characters*, p. 14.
[4] *Diutinus Britanicus*, no. 2 (2–8 Dec. 1646), p. 9.

of Beaumont and Fletcher's works. Even as Audley was writing his remarks, this was in the press in London; and its frontispiece portrait of Fletcher carried nine lines of Latin verse by Berkenhead, who also contributed one of the many commendatory poems. Whether or not Audley had this in mind, his theatrical allusion is peculiarly pertinent to the Beaumont and Fletcher project. Their works, beloved of the Jacobean gentry,[1] were regarded by the Cavaliers as enshrining the noblest artistic and political ideals; and to some opponents, at least, the dramatists were *Aulicus*'s spiritual antecedents.[2] One reason for this was that, as Coleridge observed, their plays carried 'even *jure divino* principles . . . to excess'.[3] The folio was not, in other words, simply a commercial or aesthetic venture: it was also a morale-boosting gesture of defiance, a propagandist reassertion of the Stuart ethic at a crucial moment in the fortunes of the Court. This probably accounts for the haste with which it was produced by its loyal publisher, Humphrey Moseley.[4]

Berkenhead's commendatory verses[5] show him using the heroic couplet for satirical purposes, a habit he was to persevere in even when many Royalist writers had resorted to safer themes. Here he slips in a caustic allusion to the £200,000 paid to the Scots, as Cavaliers saw it, for selling the King to Parliament. This proves that the poem was not written before the first week of December, when the rumour of the sum agreed was circulating. But most interesting of all is Berkenhead's praise of Fletcher's *The Faithful Shepherdess* as a play too refined for 'the bold Heepe'; people who do not respect the Crown, he implies, cannot appreciate Fletcher's art. His fluent and decorous style is applauded as the proper vehicle for sound moral views rooted in respect for 'Lawes' and 'holy Page'. In so insisting on the ethical content of poetry Berkenhead was putting the standard case of the English Platonists, but giving it a political colouring and, like Cartwright, 'taking a step towards

---

[1] See L. B. Wallis, *Fletcher, Beaumont & Company Entertainers to the Jacobean Gentry* (New York, 1947).

[2] See above, p. 102.

[3] Quoted by Clifford Leach in *The Fletcher Plays* (1952), pp. 11–12.

[4] See R. C. Bald, 'Bibliographical Studies in the Beaumont & Fletcher Folio of 1647', *Transactions of the Bibliographical Society*, Supplement 13 (1938), p. 20.

[5] They are reprinted in *The Works of Beaumont and Fletcher*, ed. Arnold Glover and A. R. Waller (1905–12), vol. i.

Dryden, or one of several Drydens'.[1] He plainly exposes the class
and partisan assumption behind Cavalier reservations about Shakespeare by turning up his nose at his 'Trunk-hose-wit' and
diagnosing, in the unevenness of his style, the infection of writing
too much for the 'mob'. It is a reminder of how the Cavaliers'
collective sense of political and ethical order conditioned their
literary theory. It acted on the form as well as on the content
of their verse, by confirming their inclination towards the technical virtues of Classical poetry. The growing security and self-
sufficiency of the couplet, apparent in Berkenhead's usage, reflects
this mounting preoccupation with moral orthodoxy and regularity.
It naturally led Berkenhead not only to criticize Shakespeare, but
also to deplore 'Metaphysical' excesses and cherish the memory of
Ben Jonson. In short, Berkenhead's verses afford a glimpse into
the complex of pressures behind the aristocratic, neo-Classical
fashions then coming to the fore. The desire for rule, uniformity,
and 'decorum' was not motivated merely by some arbitrary
aesthetic theory: it images the centralizing and institutionalizing
tendencies of the aristocratic élite, tendencies only fortified by the
upheaval of 1646.

Berkenhead's ideal of patriotic humanism—he wished all letters
to be 'English borne or English made'—was also one that Dryden
would have understood. It was an heroic ideal; and Berkenhead
pictures Fletcher, appropriately, as a hero sustaining a noble
literature. In principle this view of poetry's destiny was much like
Milton's; but there was an important difference between the sort
of heroism orthodox Royalists revered and that pursued by
Puritans. This difference, due in no small measure to the influences
of political and religious codes, shows in the contrast between
Dryden's heroes, inspired by a sense of public propriety and con-
formism, and Milton's, fired by private and inward revelation. It
was the orthodox ideal here applauded by Berkenhead and the
other contributors (among whom Laudians were prominent) that
triumphed at the Restoration. Milton's great epic, like Cromwell's
Republic, was an isolated phenomenon.

[1] Douglas Bush, *English Literature in the Earlier Seventeenth Century* (Oxford, 1962
(1945)) p. 121.

It was an honour much sought after to have verses printed in this Beaumont and Fletcher Folio,[1] and a singular courtesy was extended to Berkenhead in printing his Latin lines on the frontispiece.[2] They were a fitting flourish before a great monument to the Cavalier spirit; and no one was fitter to herald the 1647 Folio than '*Aulicus*', whose loyalty and orthodoxy were almost proverbial. His 1647 verses, though more polished than those of 1643, are not distinguished; but they suggest he was in the fashionable literary swim. This is a side of his life that Wood and Aubrey left virtually uncharted. It calls for more than passing allusion, not least because Berkenhead's career touches those of so many Cavaliers and helps us to understand what was happening to polite letters in these hard times. It is worth suspending the strict march of events in his life in order to take a broad survey of this territory.

Like so much in his career, Berkenhead's acquaintanceship among literary folk grew out of his Oxford years. There he apparently first met Thomas Stanley (of whom more later); there he certainly was close to Cartwright; and it was probably because of this connection that he got to know Katherine Philips, the 'matchless Orinda', who was one of Cartwright's most youthful and enthusiastic admirers. She was only twelve when Cartwright died in 1643, and lived to achieve enough to be honoured by Dryden (to whom she was distantly related by marriage)[3]—and justly, as she was one of the writers who carried on the Cavalier tradition through the Commonwealth and handed it on, slightly changed, to the Court of Charles II.[4] She is remembered principally as patroness of a so-called 'circle' of writers. She did invent a Society of Friends, but its only known member was a woman, Anne Owen (Lucasia) to whom she was related by marriage. Men, it seems, were excluded from this fanciful cult. So there was no active *salon* of Platonists. But Orinda did have many literary friends and all of them Royalists, though

---

[1] See the commendatory poem by Richard Brome, reprinted in *The Works of Beaumont and Fletcher*, i, p. liv.

[2] I am indebted to Mr. J. G. Griffith, Senior Tutor of Jesus College, Oxford, for advice on these Latin verses.

[3] P. W. Souers, *The Matchless Orinda* (Harvard Univ. Press, 1931), p. 21. Dryden recalls her in his 'Ode to Anne Killigrew'.

[4] Ibid., p. 264. He mentions some of the possible connections between her works and Dryden's on pp. 60, 197, 252–3.

her family were Parliamentarians and close to the centre of power in the Commonwealth. To the nearest of them she gave pet Latin names:[1] and in 1651 together they helped launch an edition of Cartwright's works; in 1653 and 1655 their names came together again in the two volumes of *Ayres and Dialogues*, published by another of her friends, Henry Lawes.[2] So, though not a *salon*, there obviously was some sort of coherence and co-ordination of effort here. Berkenhead contributed to all the volumes mentioned, and the 1655 one included a poem by him addressed, significantly, to one 'Lucasia'. This was the name given to Anne Owen on her 'adoption' by Orinda on 28 December 1651. The likelihood that she is Berkenhead's 'Lucasia' is made virtual certainty by another poem, addressed by Orinda to 'Mr. J. B. the noble Cratander, upon a composition of his which he was not willing to own publickly'.[3] Cratander was the hero of Cartwright's 1636 play, *The Royal Slave*, whom Berkenhead singled out for special mention in his verses for the 1651 Cartwright volume, as he did Lucasia, heroine of another Cartwright drama.[4] The 1651 collection appeared in June, so it may be that Berkenhead's linking of the two names actually inspired Orinda's choice of pseudonym for Anne Owen, whom she first met in that year. The aptness of Cratander as a nickname for Berkenhead needs no stressing; one cannot be so certain about when Orinda so dubbed him, nor about his relationship with Anne Owen. He seems to have been a confirmed bachelor, more concerned with his career than with dalliance;[5] and as Lucasia was married (her husband died in 1655) their association was, presumably, properly Platonic. At least we can be sure that

[1] P. W. Souers, *The Matchless Orinda* pp. 39 ff. and 58.

[2] See W. McClung Evans, *Henry Lawes, Musician and Friend of Poets* (New York, 1941), p. 206. The coincidence of names is noted by P. W. Souers, op. cit., p. 59. The Lawes volume was dedicated to the wife of Sir Edward Dering, one of Orinda's close friends.

[3] The coincidences were pointed out by P. W. Souers in *The Matchless Orinda*, Souers (p. 61 n.) reprints Berkenhead's poem to Lucasia. Orinda's verses appeared in her *Poems* (1664), pp. 62-4. The version printed in later editions of her works is shortened.

[4] See G. B. Evans, *The Plays and Poems of William Cartwright* (Univ. of Wisconsin Press, 1951), p. 185 n., and P. W. Souers, op. cit., p. 259.

[5] In *C.S.P. Dom.*, 1666-7, p. 270, there is a reference to Berkenhead's son. This can be discounted: the key word in the original document, 'for' (P.R.O., S.P. 29/178/114), has been incorrectly transcribed as 'son'.

we have here to do with people who, remembering Cartwright's energetic advocacy of the 'Science of Platonic friendship', helped preserve the tradition of Cavalier gallantry and courtliness through uncongenial days.

The title of the work Berkenhead was so coy about is unknown; but Orinda's comments are interesting. Setting aside conventional flattery, there remains an unfeigned respect for Berkenhead's sharp tongue, critical acumen, and loyalty. She praises, too, his copious facility as a writer (handy for a journalist and remarked on by others) and his intense conservatism. To her he is a champion of 'Learning and Law'—understandably, if one thinks of the 1646 pamphlets' familiarity with legal and historical precedent. This aptitude, incidentally, must partly account for his intimacy both before and after the Restoration with various members of the Finch family, several of whom were famous lawyers. Anyhow, one of them, Francis, brother of Sir Heneage who died in 1631, was in Oxford with Berkenhead and like him contributed to the 1643 volume *Musarum Oxoniensium Epibateria*. They appeared together again in the Cartwright and Lawes volumes, and, it seems, in the company of Orinda, whose 'Palaemon' Finch was.[1] Berkenhead appears to have been on close, if not exactly equal, terms with him in 1656 when he did valuable service for him and his niece, Anne Conway, friend of Henry More, and poetess and philosopher in her own right. Later on, Anne's half-brother, Francis Finch junior, patronized Berkenhead so generously that one wonders whether his service to the family went beyond the one recorded instance. Henry More, after the Restoration, certainly referred to Berkenhead as if he, too, knew him quite well.[2]

Finch, however, was not the only 'Palaemon' in Orinda's experience: the name seems also to have been given to Jeremy Taylor in 1657 when he wrote a treatise on friendship for her.[3] Like Berkenhead, Taylor knew Henry More and the Conways, and the Egerton family (his patron's wife was Alice Egerton), and he had been a protégé of Laud and Fellow of All Souls. Oxford had

---

[1] See P. W. Souers, *The Matchless Orinda*, pp. 61 ff.
[2] For more on his connection with the Finch family see below, pp. 194–5.
[3] P. W. Souers, op. cit. pp. 64, 73, and 259.

brought Taylor and Berkenhead together, and they met at least once during the Interregnum, probably in London, which Taylor visited regularly from 1653 on. Anyhow, Taylor recorded the occasion in a letter to John Evelyn, where he relates with relish the story of Berkenhead's encounter with some Jesuits. This meeting took place in the presence of Taylor himself and Lord Lucas,[1] another Laudian and brother of Margaret Cavendish the eccentric Duchess of Newcastle, who helped Berkenhead during the Interregnum. The Jesuits, apparently, had talked sneeringly of the Anglican Church as a body without a head (as was their wont after the execution of Charles I) to which Berkenhead swiftly riposted that they could afford to lend the Anglicans one since they themselves had 'two and three at a time'.[2] Whatever enemies insinuated later, Berkenhead was obviously no more friend to Rome than his great patron had been. It was the witty champion of the Anglican Church that Taylor was confidently recommending to Evelyn's approbation. Little wonder, with such friends, that Orinda was a staunch Episcopalian by the Restoration. One should clearly not think of her as a patron with disciples: she may have been some sort of catalyst, or even, with her family connections, able to give Cavalier friends some sort of protection; but men like Berkenhead, Finch, and Taylor had common bonds before she came on the scene.

Still, Interregnum conditions undoubtedly did encourage the making of cliques among Royalists. One of the most exclusive was the 'Black Ribband', whose members looked to Thomas Stanley as their patron. There is no evidence that Berkenhead was *persona grata* in this alliance; possibly he was not quite socially acceptable at this level. That might also explain why he seems not to have been one of the 'Sealed Knot' of Cavalier agitators, although he was politically active during its lifetime. Probably some Royalists regarded him as an upstart. None the less there is proof of connection with Stanley: their names are first linked in 1640, when

[1] For him see Douglas Grant, *Margaret the First* (1957), p. 48; Alice Egerton's brother, Viscount Brackley, married in 1642 Elizabeth, daughter of the Earl (later Duke) of Newcastle. So Berkenhead's introduction to the Newcastles may have come through the Egertons, who were also linked with the Earls of Derby.

[2] *Diary and Correspondence of John Evelyn*, ed. William Bray (1906), p. 567. The letter was written in 1656, but the incident is not dated.

Berkenhead presented him for a degree at Oxford[1]—a fact retailed
to Wood by one of Stanley's closest friends, Edward Sherburne,[2]
who as Commissary General of the King's artillery must have
encountered Berkenhead at Oxford. Stanley, like Berkenhead,
contributed to the Beaumont and Fletcher Folio and to the two
Lawes volumes; and Berkenhead's translations of Anacreon's
verses in the 1655 volume reflect the influence of Stanley's justly
popular renderings of the Greek lyricist. Berkenhead may have
been imitating from a distance; but the 1640 connection makes
closer contact in poetic matters likely. The two certainly had a
number of mutual acquaintances. One was James Shirley, whose
career more than once touches Berkenhead's: he had enjoyed
Laud's patronage in the 1630s, and defended the Queen against
Prynne's *Histriomastix*;[3] in 1647 he, as editor, wrote the enthusiastic address prefaced to the Beaumont and Fletcher Folio, and
he later contributed to the Cartwright and Lawes volumes. More
important, he too was patronized by the Duchess of Newcastle: she
took an interest in Shirley both before the Civil War and during
the Interregnum;[4] while Berkenhead, besides knowing her brother,
received help from her when he was in France,[5] some time before
July 1648, when she left Paris for the Low Countries.[6] So some
acquaintance between the two men seems almost certain. Berkenhead made much of Shirley in a literary sense: his celebration of
Henry Lawes as 'A man to tune an Angel by' was cribbed from
Shirley's earlier description of the Duke of Buckingham as 'A man
to draw an Angel by'.[7] The good journalist, then as now, knows
how to adapt other men's inspirations. Speculation about Berkenhead and Shirley has a conclusion that reminds us of what, in
another way, these Cavalier writers shared. For Giles Jacob and

[1] See above, p. 24.

[2] See G. M. Crump, 'Thorn-Drury's Notes on Thomas Stanley', *Notes and
Queries*, N.S. v (1958), 101–3.

[3] A. Harbage, *Cavalier Drama*, p. 16.

[4] See the 'Life' in the *D.N.B.*

[5] *Brief Lives*, i. 105.

[6] The time of her departure is given by H. T. E. Perry, *The First Duchess of
Newcastle and her Husband as Figures in Literary History* (London, 1918), p. 127.

[7] Berkenhead's line occurs in his commendatory poem printed before *The Second
Book of Ayres and Dialogues* (1655); Shirley's will be found in his *Poems*, ed. R. L.
Armstrong (New York, 1941), p. 15.

William Winstanley, in their potted biographies,[1] both quoted this compliment to Berkenhead:

> Whilst Lawrel sprigs another's head shall Crown,
> Thou the whole Grove may'st challenge as thy Own.

They do not give their source; but it recalls Stanley's praise of Shirley:[2]

> Each line deserves a laurel, and thy praise
> Asks not a garland, but a grove of bays.

The praise of Berkenhead clearly came from someone who spoke what, for the sake of argument, may be called Stanley's language. He was, this suggests, more involved with this 'group' than has been realized.

Fortunately, his connection with another of Stanley's close friends, John Hall of Durham, confirms this. In 1648, when Berkenhead was editing a newsbook called *Mercurius Bellicus*, Hall produced a periodical against the Royalists. This drew some very tart remarks from most Cavalier editors; but Berkenhead's comment was mild and familiar. He called him 'Jack Hall' and conceded that 'because I know him to bee a man of parts sufficient, I will not divulge him'.[3] Hall, by virtue of his much admired precocious talents, occupied what seems at first sight to have been a curiously anomalous position—it is, in fact, a reminder of how complicated the pattern of relationship and dependence sometimes was in this period. Berkenhead may have got to know Hall through Stanley or through Hall's biographer, John Davies of Kidwelly. Davies was another associated with both Katherine Philips and Thomas Stanley,[4] who encouraged him in his work as a translator. Interestingly enough, Davies dedicated two of his translations to Berkenhead in 1665 and 1672 respectively. From the first we gather that he met Berkenhead at a time when the latter 'thought it dangerous

---

[1] In, respectively, *An Historical Account of the Lives and Writings of Our Most Considerable English Poets* (1720), p. 8 and *Lives of the Most Famous English poets* (1687), p. 181.

[2] *Thomas Stanley: His Original Lyrics*, ed. L. I. Guiney (1907), p. 19.

[3] *M. Bell.*, no. 19 (30 May–6 June 1648), A4ʳ.

[4] G. M. Crump, 'Thorn-Drury's Notes on Thomas Stanley', *Notes and Queries*, N.S.V. 101–3.

to know or be known to many'.[1] This cloak-and-dagger talk makes
it suitably hard to date their encounter; but Davies alludes to a
ballad written by Berkenhead in 1647[2] in a way that suggests they
may have met around 1648, when Berkenhead was travelling as a
Royalist agent. If Davies pinpoints necessary circumspection, he
also honours his literary activities in his second book, a rendering
of Rapin's influential *Observations on the Poems of Homer and Virgil*.
He recalls those 'recesses during the late unparallel'd Usurpations',
when Berkenhead at leisure dilated knowledgeably on the merits of
Homer and Virgil.[3] Davies may or may not be exaggerating
Berkenhead's perspicacity, but the 1672 Dedication witnesses to
some of the means whereby some sort of literary continuity was
achieved in the 1650s. Berkenhead, then, was apparently not one
of Stanley's very close friends,[4] but with so many mutual acquaintances and in conditions that threw devoted Royalists ever closer
together, the two could hardly have failed to meet.

It has, indeed, been postulated that Berkenhead and Davies were
intermediaries between the poetic circles of Philips and Stanley,
bringing them closer together than has been imagined;[5] and purely
for the convenience of presentation, the foregoing discussion has
dealt with the two circles separately. But one must insist that
the word 'circles' is potentially misleading. Stanley's friends and
Philips's intimates had interests in common, but there is no need
to look for an explanation of this in the mediation of one or two
particular men. To assume the existence of neatly enclosed poetic
groups at this date is anachronistic. Philips herself, of course,
offends in this way: she liked to think that the literary world
revolved around her 'Society'; but the affectation should not
deceive. Nor is Stanley blameless: he, too, rather self-consciously

---

[1] A2ᵛ of his translation of Savorsano's *La Picara*; the second work is a translation
of Rapin's *Observations on the Poems of Homer and Virgil*.

[2] *La Picara* A2ᵛ. Davies uses the phrase 'All Christians and Lay-Elders', which
occurs in the first line of Berkenhead's *The Four Legg'd Elder*, published in late
August 1647 (see below, p. 145).

[3] *Observations*, A4ᵛ.

[4] See J. M. Osborn, *Thomas Stanley's Lost 'Register of Friends'*, reprinted from
Yale Univ. Gazette xxxii (1958).

[5] G. M. Crump, 'Thorn-Drury's Notes on Thomas Stanley', *Notes and Queries*,
N.S. v. 101–3.

entertained the ideal of *amicitia*, and his retrospective 'Register of Friends' smacks of romantic whimsy.[1] These neo-Platonic 'conceits' should be regarded with the same reservation as are the writers' habitual overpraises of one another. That sort of mutual self-esteem was partly a survival, even an intensification, of the inward-looking habit of the Stuart court. It testifies to the resilience of the 'old' patterns of behaviour and relationship. By dispensing with the myth of the total collapse and dispersal of Cavalier society one comes closer to the truth, which is that the Cavaliers were a comparatively small group of people, united by political and cultural and, very often, by family ties, who naturally sought out each other's company during the Interregnum. The questions of where and when they foregathered cannot be precisely or fully answered at present: Lawes's London house was one meeting place, and Stanley certainly put his residence and library at Cumberlow at the disposal of his friends. There seems to be no evidence that Orinda entertained her friends in her Cardiganshire residence, but it is not impossible; Jeremy Taylor, after all, found in near-by Golden Grove a safe and refreshing retreat. Perhaps, too, the Egerton family, to which his patron's wife belonged, gave sanctuary in their Hampshire home to Cavaliers of kindred spirit. After all, they had a noble tradition of literary patronage and were very close to Henry Lawes, besides being related by marriage not only to the Carberys but also to the Stanley and Cavendish dynasties. Perhaps it was in some such setting that Berkenhead held forth on the great masters of epic, contributing his mite to the clarification and formulation of 'modern' literary standards. Whatever the precise details of all this, it seems reasonable to suggest that the Interregnum actually did something to renew (or prolong) the influence of aristocratic country-house patronage in English letters, and that the neo-Classicism of the second half of the seventeenth century did have those domestic roots that are still commonly denied it.

Be that as it may, Davies and Berkenhead do not so much bestride gaps between circles as demonstrate that no such gaps existed. An intricate web of friendship, patronage, and kinship

---

[1] For this 'Register' see above, p. 142, n. 4.

connected these Cavalier writers, and sometimes even linked them with political opponents. A typically complicated pattern is displayed in the case of Sir Justinian Isham, who corresponded regularly with Brian Duppa, was a friend of Jeremy Taylor, and an intimate of Thomas Stanley.[1] In reality, men like Henry Lawes, by culling songs from most of the Cavalier poets, and Humphrey Moseley, by publishing their works, were at least as instrumental as Stanley and Philips in stimulating Royalist letters. Some verses addressed to Moseley in 1651[2] underline this: they praise him for bringing the best wits to light, and urge him, among other things, to

> Give us all Berkenhead, whose soul can more
> In half an hour than others in four score.

That quickness seems to have impressed everyone; but the plea went unanswered, though Berkenhead did edit some fairly important works for Moseley.

As for Lawes, it was under his roof in the early 1650s that many Royalists foregathered to listen to music. His assemblies were attended by several noble families, and, inevitably, the most ambitious came too. Here the never-bashful Berkenhead must again have kissed the hand of the Duchess of Newcastle and rubbed shoulders with his old friend Henry Berkenhead, who remained close to him till the end of his life. Henry's sister, Mary Knight, was celebrated as a singer at these *musicales*.[3] She was also Orinda's close friend and wrote a commendatory poem for the 1655 Lawes volume. So the old relationships were maintained and new ones developed, even during the lean years. The mood of resistance, the sense of being protectors of sacred traditions, played its part in all this; and it had its triumphant outcome in the neo-Classicism of the Restoration. That was manifestly no sudden or surprising creation,

[1] See *The Duppa–Isham Correspondence, 1650–1660* (Northants Record Soc. xvii, 1951) and the 'Life' of Isham in the *D.N.B.*

[2] This couplet is from the poem by John Leigh, printed before the 1651 Cartwright volume, and reprinted by J. C. Reed, 'Humphrey Moseley, Publisher', *Oxford Bibl. Soc., Proceedings and Papers*, ii, Pt. II (1929), 66.

[3] For an account of those who attended these musical gatherings see W. McClung Evans, *Henry Lawes, Musician and Friend of Poets*. There is a brief biographical notice of Mary Knight in *The Diary of John Evelyn*, ed. E. S. de Beer (1955), iii. 203, n. 3. Dr. Henry Berkenhead witnessed John Berkenhead's will, 4 Dec. 1679.

nor a lock-stock-and-barrel import, but the fruit of a 'natural' evolution.

Such processes are often minute, and even minor figures like Berkenhead contribute to them. He was, in fact, more respected as a man of letters than has been thought; and in the light of what has been seen of his activities and connections, his part in the Beaumont and Fletcher Folio at last falls into place. His next work of that year of 1647 was a very different affair—an obscene broadside ballad, *The Four Legg'd Elder*, published at the end of August.[1] Its theme, an act of sodomy between a Presbyterian Elder's maid and his dog, was not new to Cavalier propaganda: Berkenhead, who had a nose for useful scandal, had inserted a similar item in *Aulicus* in 1643.[2] Nor, apparently did the joke get stale, for the ballad was reprinted in the 'Rump' collections of satirical verse at the Restoration, and appeared again as a broadside in 1677.[3] Even in the 1680s the Dog and the Maid were recalled in the second part of *Absalom and Achitophel*[4] and figured in an anti-Nonconformist cartoon.[5] Such was the durability of Conservative polemic in the period. The ballad's author remained decently anonymous; and the attribution to Berkenhead, long accepted, is based on three points: it was reprinted in 1653 in an edition of his *Bibliotheca Parliamenti*;[6] his later ballad, *The Four Legged Quaker*, described itself as being 'To the tune of the Dog and Elder's Maid'; and an attack on Berkenhead in 1666 unhesitatingly ascribed it to him.[7] He can safely be given the credit (dubious as it is) for popularizing one of those sadistic jokes with which seventeenth-century partisan satire teems. What he tried to get across was that the Maid's perversion was the Presbyterian equivalent of a Cavalier *amour*—witness the

---

[1] Thomason received his copy, B.M., 669 f. 11 (70) on 1 Sept.

[2] See above, p. 94.

[3] For details of all these reprints see the Bibliography. The piece is mentioned as typical of Cavalier balladry in *Bloody News from Chelmsford* (1660), reprinted in the *Bagford Ballads*, ed. J. W. Ebsworth (1876–8), ii. 736.

[4] ll. 437–40.

[5] M. D. George, *English Political Caricature to 1792*, Plate 14.

[6] This is described by W. C. Hazlitt in *Bibliographical Collections and Notes*, Third Series (1887), p. 18.

[7] This was an *Answer*, in verse, to a ballad written by Berkenhead in 1666; it exists only in manuscript and the references to copies extant are given below, p. 201, n. 6.

claim that the ballad is 'To the Tune of the Ladies fall; Or Gather your Rose Buds'. The burlesque intention shows also in his aping the mannerisms of 'graceless Ballads', notably the clumsy rhymes which are meant to be farcical. Technically there is something here in common with the low vein of grotesque comedy in *Hudibras*. Berkenhead obviously had one eye on the growing need to enter-tain (and influence) a popular audience; but as he was not whole-heartedly of Grub Street he signals to the sophisticated reader that he knows what he is doing is vulgar. Literary decorum is observed; but the ballad still reads rather like a joke in poor taste.

Its political feeling is interesting, however; in reviling Presby-terian instincts as corrupt, uncivilized, and unnatural, Berkenhead abandons the conciliatory attitude of 1646. By now Royalists were bitter at the failure of the Scots and Presbyterian M.P.s to stand up to the Independents and save the day for Charles. This disillusioned and somewhat aggressive temper also inspired Berkenhead's most substantial work of 1647, *The Assembly Man*. That summer and autumn a number of satires against the Assembly of Divines appeared. They attacked the Assembly's part in promoting the Visitation of Oxford University, begun in May; and spurred on by the Divines' publication of the new Catechism in October and November, assaulted it with undiminishing ferocity until the end of the year. *The Assembly Man* first circulated in manuscript,[1] and was not printed until 1663; but references in it to the Catechism, the plight of Oxford, and the subject of *A Four Legg'd Elder*[2] suggest that it was penned during the last two months of 1647. The 1663 edition carried a prefatory address signed 'J. B.'; and the second and third editions, of 1681 and 1682 respectively, gave the author's full name. Like the ballad this owed the new lease of life to continued religious discord and to the determination of a power-ful section of Royalist opinion to keep alive the memory of a hateful past. Even after the end of the century Tory apologists found it useful;[3] then it fell into the hands of cheap-jack editors of

---

[1] There is a copy in the B.M., MS. Harleian 3638, ff. 82–8.
[2] See the reprint in *Harl. Misc.* v. 99 and 100.
[3] It was reprinted by them in 1704 and appeared againi n 1730 in *A Collection of Tracts Written by the Author of the Snake in the Grass*.

Butler who were grabbing most of the successful prose satires of the Civil War.[1] It was more worthy than most of the honour of being associated with his name.

The Assembly Man is a 'character' sketch, and interesting partly because it shows how the form was developing in the field of political journalism. The mode's satirical potential was self-evident, not least in its fundamental Aristotelian assumption that virtue was a mean between extremes.[2] Even before the Civil War partisans had realised that the genre lent itself to the presentation of opponents as immoderate extremists; and the Royalists had simply to substitute their ideal of cultivated aristocratic behaviour for the old Aristotelian measure. True, it has been suggested that the 'character' was a poor weapon of war;[3] but in fact, by using it political satirists brought it into fresh contact with contemporary life and renewed the sense of purpose it had been in danger of losing.

Berkenhead's concern with the here and now is unmistakable; the Assembler was a newly created social type, and writing about him enforced frequent allusion to current events and contemporaries. Thumb-nail sketches of John Selden, the Earl of Pembroke, Stephen Marshall, Philip Nye, Oliver Cromwell, and Hugh Peter fell naturally into place. At the same time Berkenhead was aware of the formal tradition and used it to give shape, style, and moral weight to his propaganda. The recognized way of universalizing a 'character' was to employ 'witty Allegories, or Allusions, to things or terms in nature or art . . .'[4] and this technique shapes Cromwell's brief portrait. He is described as terrifying the Assembly because he had disposed of rivals before and was, they feared, 'like Milo, in the Olympicks, who, by practising on a calf, grew strong enough for a bull, and could with ease give a lift to an asse'.[5] The parallel makes the joke, points the political observation, and (if one may use the word here) elevates it imaginatively. With the same sort of urbane condescension the Assembler's dress, his cant, his demeanour in the

---

[1] See in Butler's *Satires and Miscellanies*, p. xiv.

[2] For the origins and development of the 'character' see E. N. S. Thompson *Literary Bypaths of the Renaissance* (Yale Univ. Press, 1924), pp. 1–26.

[3] G. S. Gordon, *English Literature and the Classics* (1912), p. 69.

[4] This rule, stated in 1665, is quoted by F. P. Wilson in *Seventeenth Century Prose* (Cambridge, 1960), p. 14.

[5] *Harl. Misc.* v. 100.

pulpit and at table, and his political opinions are mocked, not simply as bad habits of the moment but as new manifestations of the age-old sins of Vanity and Hypocrisy; and his alleged antagonism towards orthodox Law, Religion, and Learning is presented as an embodiment of archetypal Ignorance and Presumption. In European satirical tradition Faustus was the great type of such Presumption, and Berkenhead, defender of received *mores* and scholarship, identifies the Assembler's 'progressive' theories with this legend.[1] He draws further on Continental satiric traditions when he alludes to Don Quixote[2] and to a famous graphic caricature drawn by Hans Sachs at the time of the Reformation.[3] So the fashionable Cavalier preoccupation with European literature was exploited to give universality and the advantage of accumulated wisdom to their propaganda. Classical allusion served similarly; and one reference to Menander's *Thais*[4] is a fruit of the Courtiers' interest in the Greek Comedy of Manners, a genre not unakin in spirit to Restoration Comedy. These few instances show that Royalist propaganda was far from sub-literary; and, as will be seen shortly, even their newsbooks of late 1647 and 1648 are crammed with this sort of allusion to tradition.

The *Assembly Man* does not depart decisively from the conventions of its genre; but it moves tentatively in a new direction. Berkenhead may not wholly eschew the quibbles on words and meanings so dear to English character-writers; but his sentences occasionally break out of the predictable pattern of concise epigram and discover a more natural movement. Take his account[5] of the homilist:

He divides his text, as he did the kingdom, makes one part fight against another; or as Burges divides the dean of Paul's house, not into parts, but tenements; that is, so as it will yield most money.

The wit here snowballs as the narrative progresses, instead of blocking its movement. This is closer to Butler's manner in

---

[1] p. 100.   [2] pp. 102 and 103.
[3] His image (p. 100) of the Assembler clambering up into the Church through the window of sequestration should be compared with the caricature, which is reproduced by Thomas Wright in *A History of Caricature and Grotesque* (1875), p. 260.
[4] p. 103.   [5] p. 102.

Mercurius Mennipeus or *An Hypocritical Nonconformist*, which contain echoes of *The Assembly Man*, than to Cleaveland's more old-fashioned flippant and 'conceited' manner. In Berkenhead, as in Butler, metaphors have almost disappeared, making way for similes. Some of the homely touches too—as when Berkenhead writes that the preaching Assembler 'can glibly run over Nonsense, as an empty Cart trundles down a hill'[1]—also resemble Butler.

Both men, though acknowledging the outline of formal tradition, feel the pinch of its limitations.[2] Like an essayist shaking off restriction Berkenhead goes on until he feels he has exhausted his topic. Aware of exceeding his mandate, he even turns that to good account as he pulls himself up: 'But I forget, a Character should be brief, though tedious length be his best character . . .'.[3] Conventionally, the character-writer was expected to be what Berkenhead elsewhere described as 'a brief, elegant, smart Anatomist';[4] and *The Assembly Man* has smartness and elegance; but Berkenhead's journalistic instinct rightly led him towards flexibility and a wider scope.

He was also practical enough to acknowledge his work's short-comings, and observed in 1663 that 'better times have made it worse' because 'men and manners are changed: at least, they say so'.[5] The equivocation is characteristic, and he obviously did not believe that things had changed enough to make publication pointless. Old antipathies and quarrels die hard in men of his cast; and the idea of progress was not really in his bones. But in fact, old enmities had not withered overnight; the Restoration was not a blissful dawn for everyone; and Berkenhead was right to feel that *The Assembly Man*, though it may have lost some of its immediacy, was still not a little pertinent. It was also not a little partial, of course, in spite of its urbanity. Nothing is conceded to the Assembler, who is damned from top to toe—a strategy that throws some doubt on the writer's own reasonableness and

---

[1] p. 102.

[2] For Butler's treatment of the 'character' see F. P. Wilson, *Seventeenth Century Prose*, pp. 17–18.

[3] p. 104.

[4] This phrase is from his letter prefaced to John Raymond's *Itinerary*, published in 1648.

[5] pp. 99 and 98 respectively.

moderation. It is especially risky when it produces the accusation that Assemblers do not 'read, but weed authors, picking up cheap and refuse notes'.[1] The sarcasm comes oddly from one who parades a legion of references, learned and otherwise, especially as he borrowed the very phrase from Anthony Stafford's *A Just Apology*.[2]

The partiality is undisguised in the 1663 Preface to *The Assembly Man*, where Berkenhead gives free rein to his indignation against men 'whose hands were knuckle-deep in the blood of . . . archbishop Laud . . . that great martyr'.[3] The fervour here seems almost to be that of a man who has fused (or perhaps confused) the common Jacobean notion that it took a squint-eyed man to see the world straight[4] with the Restoration idea that the satirist rests his case on urbane, well-balanced commonsense. To be fair, the pamphlet is a little lacking in poise not simply because Berkenhead was no Dryden but also because pressures on Royalists in the late 1640s were particularly exasperating. It is not only in Berkenhead that we find a discrepancy between the profession of guarding rational values and an actual ferocity of manner. But it is still a weakness.[5] Technically proficient and informative as it is, and packed with much amusing wit, *The Assembly Man* cannot fully engage our sympathy. The heat of the moment warped it.

Since the Oxford periodical *Mercurius Academicus* foundered in March 1646, the Royalists had had no newsbook to represent them. This was remedied in September 1647, when four were launched to back up new military initiatives then in preparation. These four —*Mercurius Clericus, Melancholicus, Morbicus*, and *Pragmaticus*— were soon followed by two more, *Elencticus* and *Bellicus*. From then until the last survivor, *Pragmaticus*, went under in June 1650, the Cavaliers had some periodical afloat.[6] Because of governmental hostility they were all produced with considerable difficulty and in some secrecy, so it is not easy to identify editors. The situation is

---

[1] p. 103.   [2] MS. Queen's College, Oxford, 227. See above, p. 19.

[3] p. 98.

[4] Alvin Kernan, *The Cankered Muse* (Yale Univ. Press, 1959), p. 252.

[5] See Dryden's 'Discourse of Satire', prefaced to his translation of Juvenal in 1693, on the danger of manifesting the excess one is attacking.

[6] These are only the most prominent of the numerous newsbooks brought out by the Royalists in this period. For further details see J. B. Williams, *A History of English Journalism*, and J. Frank, *The Beginnings of the English Newspaper, 1620–1660*.

further complicated because when, as frequently happened, they were caught their work was taken over by other writers; and sometimes the newsbooks were compiled by 'Clubs' of consulting Cavaliers.[1] So news items, images, phrases, and attitudes were often shared; and all were commentators rather than reporters. Even the format of these periodicals was standardized: there was no systematic division of news under date headings, and title-pages of the single-sheet small quartos bore similarly worded titles and, usually, satirical verses. They were also in the habit of inserting satirical verses into the text proper. Well might one opponent grumble that it was impossible to distinguish between *Elencticus, Melancholicus,* and *Bellicus,*[2] and another that *Bellicus* was but 'three quarters of notes upon the Text of *Pragmaticus* and *Elencticus*'.[3]

It would be extraordinary if Berkenhead, celebrated by one enemy in July 1647 as an arch disturber of the nation's peace,[4] had no part in this activity. Contemporaries did not doubt his involvement: at the end of September 1647 a Royalist suggested as a fit prayer for the enemy, 'From Hopton's sword, and Berkenhead's pen, Libera nos';[5] and in November 'Berkenhead that Corah, Melancholicus that Dathan, and Pragmaticus that Abiram' were stigmatized as persistent murmurers against the government.[6] It was, apparently, common knowledge that he was at work again—and even before *Bellicus* had appeared.

His general influence on this new campaign is unmistakable: material was derived from the stock of Oxford journalism; and an opponent recognized this aptly when he reproached *Pragmaticus* first, for writing 'as if he had Berkenhead's patent to raile by', and secondly, for imitating *Aulicus*'s practice of retelling 'light skirmishes and triviall Victories, in as high Language as Homer the acts of Achilles'.[7]

[1] *Mercurius Britanicus Alive Again,* no. 1 (16 May 1648), B1ᵛ.

[2] *A Muzzle for Cerberus* (20 June 1648).

[3] *Mercurius Censorius,* no. 3 (8–20 June 1648), p. 21.

[4] *Looke about you, or the Fault-finder* (16 July 1647), p. 7.

[5] *The Parliaments Letanie* (30 Sept. 1647), p. 3.

[6] *Mercurius Anti-Pragmaticus,* no. 4 (4–11 Nov. 1647), p. 3. The first issue of *M. Bell.* was for 13–22 Nov.

[7] These two quotations are from *Mercurius Anti-Pragmaticus,* no. 1 (12–19 Oct. 1647), pp. 2 and 7 (misnumbered 5) respectively.

To identify his specific contribution is more difficult, but there are some suggestive coincidences worth noticing. An early number of *Pragmaticus* describes Thomas Chaloner as 'one that said not long since in Parl. that the best Scot in the world was not worth a whistling after'.[1] That may have been common gossip among Cavaliers; but directly or indirectly, the point derives from Berkenhead who, apparently, first made Chaloner's remark public in 1646.[2] Similarly, *Pragmaticus*'s jeer that the Londoners cried up 'the diana of this Reformation, with more furious uproares at London than ever their Predecessors did at Ephesus'[3] recalls Berkenhead's 'Privileges of parliament! Great is Diana of the Ephesians was never roared louder'.[4] Such resemblances also crop up in *Melancholicus* and *Elencticus*; and, though Berkenhead has not previously been connected with them, he may well have assisted in at least a desultory fashion.

Fortunately his responsibility for *Bellicus* can be more securely documented. Its editor, according to an uncomplimentary contemporary, had 'goggle eyes' and 'Durst neer see sword in wrath'.[5] That recalls Aubrey's description of Berkenhead's 'great goggli eies',[6] which, together with the fact that he was of middling height, is all we know about his appearance. And the point about cowardice is identical with an accusation against Berkenhead in 1666 that 'all ye World knows, he durst never fight'.[7] There may have been more than one goggle-eyed man alive in 1648, but it is less likely that there was more than one who was also a journalist, and allegedly a coward. Examination of the newsbook's text confirms that it was, in fact, Berkenhead. *Bellicus*'s observation that the Rebels had 'now pluckt of their vizards and unmask'd themselves'[8] appeared more than once in *Aulicus*, and was used in *The Assembly Man*.[9] If by 1648 this was a stock phrase in Cavalier satire, *Bellicus*'s portrayal of Philip Nye, the Independent, dividing his

---

[1] No. 2 (21–28 Sept. 1647), B2ᵛ.

[2] *An Answer to A Speech Without Doores*, p. 2.

[3] No. 15 (21–28 Dec. 1647), B3ʳ.   [4] *A Letter* (1643) in *S. Tracts*, iv. 590.

[5] *Mercurius Anti-Mercurius*, no. 1 (12–19 Sept. 1648), p. 3.

[6] See J. B. Williams, *A History of English Journalism*, p. 88; Aubrey uses the phrase in *Brief Lives*, i. 105.

[7] Bodleian Library, MS. Don. b. 8, p. 344.

[8] No. 21 (13–20 June 1648), A2ᵛ.   [9] *Harl. Misc.* v. 99.

text 'from London to Colchester'[1] seems to have been specifically modelled on the preacher in *The Assembly Man* who 'divides his text as he did the kingdom'.[2] Similar parallels occur in another Berkenhead pamphlet, *Newes from Pembroke and Mongomery*, published during *Bellicus*'s run. In this satire on Pembroke's leadership of the 1648 Visitation of Oxford University, the Earl thanks the University for giving him 'a gilded bible; you could not give me a better book . . . I can love it, though I cannot read it'.[3] *Bellicus*, denouncing the Visitation, played a variation on the point: the Earl 'became so far taken with the beauty of the varnish, that some think he will shortly learne to read English on purpose, to read the inside of that gilded coffer'.[4]

Bellicus affords an extraordinary number of such parallels. Its confidence and vivacity, too, particularly recall *Aulicus*. This is all the more apparent because the first two numbers of *Bellicus* have the accent common in this second generation of Cavalier periodicals; but it is not heard in the rest of its run. That common style could be described as old-fashioned, as it takes up one strain of Elizabethan and Jacobean satire by combining scourging attitudes with a stuttering manner.[5] *Bellicus*'s second week, for example, snarled at Rebels who 'slash out their Wherligig'd whimseyes out of their Factious Noddles'.[6] This sort of 'Satyricall language' a contemporary attributed to Nashe's influence.[7] It was not Nashe's only style, but it was commonly associated with his name, and in this case shrewdly, as the Cavaliers were trying hard to capture the sort of metropolitan bourgeois audience that once read Nashe. Anyhow, *Bellicus*'s third week is remarkable because it dropped that idiom, which the editor subsequently stigmatized as 'dirtie dialect';[8] he boasted of his 'streine that's new'.[9] Almost certainly there had been a change of editor; and the new, comparatively polished manner is closer to *Aulicus* than anything else in the Cavalier journalism of 1647–8.

[1] No. 22 (20–27 June 1648), A2^v.   [2] *Harl. Misc.* v. 102.
[3] *Harl. Misc.* v. 112.   [4] No. 14 (25 Apr.–2 May 1648), O4^v.
[5] Alvin Kernan, *The Cankered Muse*, p. 248.
[6] No. 2 (22–29 Nov. 1647), B1^v.
[7] *Mercurius Anti-Pragmaticus*, no. 1 (12–19 Oct. 1648), p. 2.
[8] No. 5 (22–29 Feb. 1648), E1^v.   [9] No. 6 (29 Feb.–7 Mar. 1648), F1^r.

Bellicus's political views are broadly identical with those of its associates. They can be summed up as hatred of Democracy, and respect for ordered traditions of Law and Learning, the Church and Monarch. Yet, if not unique, the ultra-Royalist image of the latter as 'the lively representative of the Government amongst the Angells'[1] is one that Berkenhead wholeheartedly underwrote. And Laud's memory is celebrated in terms that recall his sentiments in other texts.[2] Altogether there are sufficient grounds for believing that he edited *Bellicus* in 1648.

Discounting the first two numbers in 1647, he published twenty-one, covering the period from 8–14 February to 19–26 July 1648, and two supplementary pamphlets, of which only one has survived. He seemingly avoided arrest for these activities—probably, as John Davies suggested, he was living under an assumed name[3]— but the searchers' efforts to winkle out secret presses and subversive editors appear to have forced him to suspend publication of *Bellicus* on three occasions. If that assumption is correct, he repeated his Oxford strategy of falsifying signatures or issue numbers to conceal the gaps. One of the brief delays—that in publishing no. 23, for 27 June to 5 July—was possibly due to Berkenhead's temporary absence from England about that time.[4]

Despite such resemblance to *Aulicus*, however, *Bellicus* is a far less important newsbook: it was not even the most substantial Cavalier periodical of 1648, and contented itself with reinforcing arguments broached by the others. Obviously it did not enjoy *Aulicus*'s status or resources. The Royalists were in no position to organize an extensive intelligence network: so the dating and factual content of their newsbooks' reports are frequently imprecise; there is no inside information about Parliamentary debates; and events outside London are, on the whole, sketchily described. Developments within the City are more substantially covered, and there is a fair amount of information concerning Rebels' private

[1] *A Cittie Dog in a Saints Doublet* (19 July 1648), A2ʳ. This was by the editor of *Bellicus*: see below, App. IV.

[2] *M. Bell.*, no. 6 (29 Feb.–7 Mar. 1648), F2ʳ, describes Laud as a man 'martyred . . . for maintaining a decencie in God's worship'. Compare with this Berkenhead's phrase in the Preface to *The Assembly Man*, quoted above, p. 150, and in *Mercurius Publicus* (1660), quoted below, p. 217.   [3] See above, pp. 141–2.

[4] For further details see below, pp. 164–5 and App. IV.

lives.[1] In other words, there is little news in *Bellicus* which was not publicly accessible, either in the licensed newsbooks, or in other Cavalier periodicals, or in common gossip. Berkenhead's editorial duties were clearly nothing like as onerous as they had been in Oxford; and the newsbook was but one of many tasks he was currently busy with. The criticism unfairly levelled at *Aulicus*— that it was untruthful and rumour-mongering—can more justly be levelled at *Bellicus*. In matters of fact it is unreliable. But its political tactics and satirical habits are worth contemplating. They reveal some interesting changes from the Oxford pattern.

When Berkenhead restarted *Bellicus* in February 1648, events were moving fast towards a resumption of hostilities between Parliament and Royalists. The latter were busily casting around for potential allies, willing now to seek support in quarters they had previously disdained. That consideration dominated *Bellicus*'s policies. Burying his recent open animosity towards Presbyterians, Berkenhead, as in 1646, set about conciliating them. He emphasized everything that might increase their dissatisfaction with Parliament's handling of affairs. So he reminds his readers correctly that the Independents, backed by the army under Cromwell, are now the dominant power in England. Parliament's advances to Charles, he insists, are pure dissimulation; and he scoffs at proposals to settle Presbyterian Church government as 'a meere trick of our new States' designed to lull the Scots.[2] The latter are assured that the Independents really care nothing for 'the league between both Kingdomes',[3] and urged to stand on the letter of the Covenant and demand a personal treaty with the King.

Scots were not the only potential comrades in arms: Berkenhead also, for a time, expediently championed the cause of John Lilburne and the Levellers, with an eye to winning over the London citizenry. Foreign aid, too, was hoped for, and *Bellicus* recklessly boasted that the French clergy would finance the Queen's efforts to raise an army.[4] Apparently the editor cared nothing for the discrepancy between this and his constant lament over the plight

[1] For example, see the account of a mishap involving Richard Cromwell in Hyde Park, in no. 19 (30 May–6 June), A3v.

[2] No. 7 (7–14 Mar.), G1v.

[3] Ibid., G2r.

[4] No. 10 (28 Mar.–4 Apr.) K3r.

of the Protestants in Ireland. The inconsistency arose, of course, because current Cavalier concern for Ireland was inspired not so much by compassion for Protestant 'martyrs' as by a desire to see a substantial Parliamentary force shipped out of the country, leaving the coast clear for a military *coup*. Few, if any, can have been deceived about the true motivation. And by April 1648 Berkenhead gave up trying to conceal his hopes: he admitted that overtures to the Scots were meant to encourage an invasion which would put the Cavaliers once more 'in a defensive condition',[1] by which he meant, of course, an offensive condition. The most arresting of his manœuvres however, is the smart about-turn executed in May. From the third week of March *Bellicus* followed with mounting optimism the progress of the risings engineered by Langdale, Lucas, Dives, and Glemham. Concurrently, though toning down his early enthusiasm for the Covenant, he continued to write of Scottish intervention as essential to success. Then suddenly Berkenhead was carried away by premature hopes: he decided that the Scots were no longer necessary and exultantly sneered at the Covenant and the 'shapeless Presbyterie'.[2] It was the unexpected rising in Kent and mutiny in the fleet that inspired him to chance his arm like this; but his bid, like that of the insurgents, was ill-timed and went astray.

Even so, *Bellicus* insisted that the second Civil War was going well, but reversion to former tactics gave the lie to that. Once more he turned to the indispensable Scots: differences in Parliament between Presbyterians and Independents were underlined, and the new debate about propositions to be submitted to the King was discredited as yet another Independent stratagem to stay the northerners' advance. That was not totally inaccurate, nor, as events were soon to show, was *Bellicus*'s characterization of the Independent leaders as 'Regicides'.[3] But the determination to stake all on arms, born of a conviction that no serious negotiations were intended, was a forlorn hope. Many soon acknowledged this, but Berkenhead was not the man to confess defeat: he reproached the Cavaliers for being discouraged by set-backs,[4] and almost

[1] No. 10 (28 Mar.–4 Apr.), K2ʳ.   [2] No. 17 (15–23 May), R2ᵛ.
[3] No. 23 (27 June–5 July), A2ʳ.   [4] No. 21 (13–20 June), A2ᵛ.

his last words were the bold cry 'Now, now things begin to work'.[1]

So extremists like Berkenhead, even when most hard-pressed by facts, clung to their faith in Charles as 'the mightiest Monarch in Europe',[2] and to the old policy of *divide et impera*. The consistency of Berkenhead's real aim and the variety of means he was prepared to advocate to encompass it show him as a true Laudian still. *Bellicus* makes it plain, too, that the Cavaliers in England seriously miscalculated the strength and preparedness of their resources. This has long been recognized; what has, on the whole, been underemphasized is the fact that their own propaganda aided and abetted that miscalculation, and did so because it was still fundamentally dominated by the thinking that had led them to defeat in the first Civil War.

Changing political conditions nevertheless had some effect on the character of their satire, as *Bellicus* nicely demonstrates.[3] Two new major factors can be isolated: the need to attract popular support, and the dominance of Independency. In Royalist eyes the latter, even more than Presbytery, represented the negation of 'All ancient Orders Morall and Divine';[4] and it was accordingly described in debasing terms. This not only reflects the genuine opinion of men like Berkenhead, but was also meant to appeal to Presbyterians, whose religion was in essence as formal as Anglicanism, and to all those who shared the attachment to stable social order. *Bellicus* under Berkenhead may have eschewed the excesses of the 'old fashioned', stuttering, scourging style, but like its fellows it is dominated by satirical motifs derived from the popular European and native tradition of caricature. There is more picaresque detail, ribaldry, and coarse humour in *Bellicus* than in *Aulicus*.

German sixteenth-century satire was fond of indulging cruel practical jokes, and the habit appeared in English writing in the coney-catching pamphlets of Robert Greene. *Bellicus*'s sport with Sir William Masham, a prisoner of the Royalist troops, exhibits the same spirit: the editor describes with relish how Masham is kept

[1] No. 27 (19–26 July), A4ᵛ. [2] No. 23 (27 June–5 July), A4ᵛ.
[3] Of course, many of the following observations apply also to its fellow newsbooks.
[4] *A Cittie Dog*, A2ᵛ.

fasting in darkness and brought out occasionally by his captors who, for their amusement, hang a crust on a string and 'make him leap for a snap at it'.[1] In the Germanic tradition this sort of humour was commonly accompanied by a great deal of diabolical and animal imagery. Here, too, a major theme is the devilish inspiration of the leaders and followers of Parliament, descendants of all those who, in past ages, had been 'prompted by Lucifer, to assassinate Monarchy and to over-turne amiable order and discreet Discipline'.[2] The full range of *Bellicus*'s imagery is deployed about this central notion.

As it always had done, the concept inspired robust comedy appealing to obvious class distinctions and an elementary sense of established order.[3] The satirist plays for laughs by parading the indecorous, unrefined, and indecent behaviour of his victims. 'Parading' is the right word, for a major motif of the old tradition was the Row or Ship of Fools; and in a spirited lampoon *Bellicus* marches the Knaves of Parliament before the reader in a row, at their head the trimming Earl of Pembroke.[4] The grotesque physical detail of each figure embodies his particular intellectual and spiritual deformity. The intention is direct: adopting a 'low' style Berkenhead characterizes his foes as the 'basest of men',[5] or less than men. As befits the spawn of the Devil, whose 'eldest Son' Cromwell was,[6] the Rebels often take bestial shape: Philip Skippon struts 'like a crane'[7] and Stephen Marshall lifts up his nose to preach, like a porpoise.[8] The Devil traditionally took terrible as well as amusing shapes;[9] and *Bellicus* duly shudders at them as 'dreadful and ominous to behold'.[10]

To describe society in the grip of the powers of darkness the Cavaliers ransacked the literature of all ages, identifying contemporaries with the elves and goblins of Romance and the tyrants and

[1] No. 22 (20–27 June), A4^r.
[2] No. 14 (25 Apr.–2 May), O3^v.
[3] C. H. Herford, *Studies in the Literary Relations of England and Germany in the Sixteenth Century* (1886), p. 245.
[4] No. 26 (11–18 July), A1^v. The whole lampoon occupies six pages.
[5] *A Cittie Dog*, A4^v.
[6] No. 19 (30 May–6 June), A3^v.
[7] No. 23 (27 June–5 July), A3^r.
[8] No. 11 (4–11 Apr.), L2^r.   [9] C. H. Herford, op. cit., p. 241.
[10] No. 14 (25 Apr.–2 May), O2^v.

traitors of biblical, classical, and native dramatic tradition. They rivalled 'Lucullus in Luxurie, Domitian in cruelty, and Dioclesian in impiety',[1] besides recalling Marlowe's Tamburlaine or Jonson's Cataline.[2] Well might opponents have repeated the accusation of 1645 that Royalist wit was raked from the ruined stages.[3] It was more than ever true: for the old theme that 'the Rebels are resolved to bee the onely Tragedians'[4] and the standard association of Rebellion with witchcraft were being explored with a new concentration and inventiveness. The Row of Fools motif epitomizes this development: nothing like it was found in Oxford journalism. The new emphasis owes much to current interest in Continental letters and in Cabbalism; and in a sense the propagandists were defiantly flaunting their learning and literary preoccupations in the face of a regime determined, they believed, to eradicate such things. So their special interests fed into the main stream of propaganda and, paradoxically, gave it more of the common touch as the emphasis shifted from witty polemic towards more fundamental 'streins' of human comedy.

Wit and urbanity are not wholly lacking in *Bellicus*. *Aulicus*'s caricatures are recaptured by the observations that the removal of arms from the Tower had left it 'almost as naked as the Crowne of my Lord Says head';[5] and the slow progress of the personal treaty with the King is neatly likened to the 'celerity that the limping Generall hath from Regiment to Regiment'.[6] These represent the most attractive side of Berkenhead's satire. But hard as he tried to maintain a confident, relaxed tone *Bellicus* not infrequently yielded to the current vogue for more lurid effects. The editor cannot sustain an unruffled poise in the face of swiftly changing events, bitter frustrations, and excited hopes. Outbursts of almost hysterical ferocity and fear are the sad consequence. Such extravagances betray also the fickleness of the Cavaliers' professed willingness to be conciliatory and do the sensible thing. Their real thoughts were

[1] No. 22 (20–27 June), A1v.
[2] No. 21 (13–20 June), A1r, and no. 22, A2v.
[3] See above, p. 120.   [4] No. 4 (14–20 Feb.), D4r.
[5] No. 19 (30 May–6 June), A2r.
[6] No. 26 (11–18 July), A1r. The general is, of course, Fairfax, who had been afflicted with gout.

as melodramatic as some of their gestures in the newsbooks, and as
incautious. There is no mistaking the political misjudgement and
the overplayed hand.

For all that, this phase of Cavalier propaganda was not totally
futile. The proliferation of debasing imagery, the habit of burlesque,
and the curious blend of fantasy and realism has a kinship with
Hudibras, though obviously that work is immeasurably superior in
scope, execution, and greatness of spirit. Dryden too, in *Mac Flecknoe* and *The Medall*[1] recalls the terminology and something of the
spirit of this decade; even in his 'higher' style in *Absalom and
Achitophel* he looks back over his shoulder at this time when

> They led their wild desires to woods and caves,
> And thought that all but savages were slaves.

The way he parades the rout of lesser Rebels—

> In the first Rank of these did Zimri stand . . .
>
> .   .   .   .   .   .
>
> But he tho bad, is follow'd by a worse—

recalls the Row of Knaves.[2] That is a reminder of how his poem
keeps faith with the popular as well as with the 'noble' tradition.
Nor was the Restoration taste for licentious humour brand new: it
can be found in Shirley's plays before the Civil War; and at a time
when the stage was virtually silent, propagandists like Berkenhead,
using spirited indecency as a political weapon, consolidated the
habit in the Courtly mind. As a reportorial art,[3] too, Restoration
Comedy probably owes something to the techniques of observation and humour deployed so extensively in this period.

Newes from Pembroke and Mongomery, a pamphlet Berkenhead
wrote while editing *Bellicus*, illustrates the point. For if Restoration
Comedy was indebted to 'character' writing, it must also have
learned something from this sort of burlesque monologue. The

---

[1] *Mac Flecknoe*, in ll. 195–6 invokes the Grobian mythology (see p .163 below), and
The Medall exploits the animal metaphors to good effect, for example in ll. 304–5. It
also employs the metaphor of 'unmasking Rebellion', of which the Cavaliers were
particularly fond in the late 1640s.

[2] ll. 55–6 and 544–83.

[3] A. Harbage, *Cavalier Drama*, p. 83.

presentation and method in these travesties of speeches by contemporary notabilities are essentially dramatic; and because they are about individuals, not types, satire was drawn into more subtle psychological ways. The considerable refinement in the satirical treatment of human character which Sutherland[1] has attributed to the developing 'character' sketch must have been compounded by the burlesques; for they called for accurate observation and precise registration of the speech and thought-habits of particular men. Preoccupation with personal details is writ large in them and they are an interesting comic manifestation of the reportorial instinct of the age which was simultaneously leading towards more factual methods in straight biography.[2]

So the Earl of Pembroke, long the butt of Royalist wit, had been attacked by Berkenhead in 1645 and 1647,[3] but in 1648 he gave final affront to faith in *noblesse oblige* by leading the Visitation of Oxford University. The academics lambasted him and the Visitors mercilessly in verse and prose,[4] but Berkenhead, perhaps incensed by the irrevocable loss of his title of Reader in Moral Philosophy, bettered all their efforts.[5] Wood rightly admired *Newes from Pembroke*,[5] which is the best of the many caricatures of the Earl and one of Berkenhead's funniest pamphlets. It parodied Pembroke's address to the University, delivered in his capacity as Chancellor, on the occasion of the ejection of the loyal Heads of Houses on 12 April 1648; and it met with great success on publication. The first edition of 25 April 1648 was followed by another on 28 April, and on 30 April a pirated edition appeared—the surest index of popular acclaim. On 5 June *Mercurius Domesticus*, a Royalist periodical, recognized its triumph by delightedly quoting from it.[7]

Burlesque was gaining popularity with the Cavaliers, and Berkenhead began his leg-pulling in the title-page legend, 'Printed at Mongomery'. Ironically, this deceived a zealous Welsh

---

[1] *English Satire* (Cambridge Univ. Press, 1962 (1958)), p. 2.
[2] For these developments in biography see F. P. Wilson, *Seventeenth Century Prose*, pp. 60–1.
[3] *Mercurius Anti-Britanicus*, p. 27, and *The Assembly Man*, in the *Harl. Misc.* v. 99.
[4] See Madan, nos. 1977, 1985, 1987, 1988, 1989, 1993, 1994, 1997, and 1998.
[5] See above, p. 34, and p. 41, n. 1.
[6] *Ath. Oxon.* iii. 1204–5.
[7] No. 1 (5 June 1648), A3r.

bibliographer in the last century;[1] it was really just a flippant allusion
to the Earl's title. The humour is broad, but the Earl was a victim
whose mannerisms lent themselves to such treatment. Clarendon[2]
described him as brash and loud-mouthed, given to blurting out
tactless admissions of his and his colleagues' secret motives; his
speech was liberally seasoned with oaths; and, by supporting the
Presbyterians and Independents in turn, he had acquired a name for
trimming. Cavaliers joked that he held no opinions of his own, but
had his views and his speeches made for him by his secretary,
Michael Oldsworth. They judged him a dangerous fool; and
Berkenhead's pamphlet is still amusing, appropriately because it
exploited the 'simple' comedy of the dullard who unblushingly
displays his corruptness which, having confounded evil with good,
he thinks to be virtue. Berkenhead, for example, makes Pembroke
demonstrate inadvertently that the newly installed Fellows are
idiots: 'Gentlemen, love one another, for there's twenty-thousand
do hate you; they say you are all either dunces, knaves, or mad-
men: s'death they will say so of me, if they durst.'[3] That sort of
criticism would have seemed forced and extravagant if made in the
satirist's own person. But here the victim unwittingly betrays the
inner contradictions of his own position and stands self-convicted.
The farcical manner is in character; it functions as an index of the
speaker's corruption, not as a flaw in the satirist's temper. In fact,
the writer's assumption of a common-sense, temperate position is
all the while implicit. So both style and argument are proper to the
Earl as ignoramus: since they would be clearly inappropriate,
epigram and witty simile are avoided; but puns are allowed,
because they become a vulgar buffoon—'you must give me leave
to clinch for those that have no wit must be content with clinches'.[4]
Actually Berkenhead slips here, for Pembroke seems momentarily
apologetic about his ignorance, which he should at all times be
shown to exalt as true illumination, as for the most part he does.
On the whole the speech has some success in imaging the total

  [1] For this, and for the dating of the editions of Berkenhead's pamphlet, see Madan,
nos. 1982, 1983, and 1984.
  [2] *History of the Rebellion*, ed. W. D. Macray (1888), iii. 485.
  [3] *Newes from Pembroke and Montgomery*, reprinted in *Harl. Misc.* v. 114.
  [4] Ibid., p. 113.

inversion of values of the man who thinks his vandalism is creative and whose very affirmations are denials of life. This was the meaning—to academic Cavaliers—of the Visitation, which they saw not simply as an offence to their self-esteem, but, more ominously, as a ludicrous and near-blasphemous affront to civilized values.

Pembroke is a gigantic figure of fun and ill-omen, a Prince of Fools vested head to toe in militant grossness and triumphing in vulgarity as though it were a refined and delicate sensibility. He is, in fact, a Grobius—the type, in the European comic tradition, of corrupt manners, as Faustus was the type of corrupt intellect. The method of satire by inverted precept which Berkenhead employs also had a long Continental history and was closely associated with the figure of Grobius and with the Foolish Messenger, a regular passenger in the *Narrenschiff*, whose habit of being fatuously communicative Pembroke unmistakably recalls.[1] The method had been introduced into England around 1605, when there was comparatively little satire of manners here;[2] and the Order of Grobians had flourished (metaphorically) in Jonson's London and Selden's Oxford.[3] It was natural for Cavaliers, the tribe of Ben, to revive that inspiration at this latest crisis of their culture and society. And Pembroke's errand to their beloved Oxford was tailor-made for the treatment. The success of Berkenhead's initiative (an inspired stroke of propaganda) led others to follow suit. He himself was to use the method repeatedly and sometimes with notable effect, though, of course, with nothing like the genius which Dryden brought to bear on the tradition in *Mac Flecknoe*.

In 1648 the technique of travesty very much fitted the Cavalier mood, a mood compounded of indignation and amusement, not untinged with a sense of amazed horror. But if the new comic emphasis was natural it was also, probably, profitable, since it made for more broadly entertaining pamphlets and presumably better sales. Propagandists, after all, had livings to make as well as axes to grind. For a variety of reasons the comic impetus was gathering force.

---

[1] See C. H. Herford, *Studies in the Literary Relations of England and Germany in the Sixteenth Century*, p. 366 n.

[2] Ibid., p. 389.   [3] Ibid., p. 379.

Royalists might joke, but the Visitation went forward: on 4 May 1648 the Fellows of All Souls were summoned to appear before the Visitors.[1] All but one refused to submit and Berkenhead was duly deprived of his Fellowship on 2 October.[2] Meantime, he had again appeared in print as writer of a letter prefaced to a travel book by John Raymond, a young friend. This *Itinerary contayning a Voyage through Italy* was licensed on 28 June 1648,[3] entered in the Stationers' Register by Humphrey Moseley on 4 July,[4] and published by him about 2 November.[5] The licenser did not see Berkenhead's letter, written on 1 July:[6] if he had done, he would almost certainly have censored it. For with characteristic bravado Berkenhead remarked tartly on the still rankling Oxford Visitation, on Parliamentary Committees, and on the 'thorough Reformation' generally. His style is concise and elegant: it has the pace and tone of polite conversation; and, because it was so much an occasional piece, shows how far a fine manner (sometimes thought of as springing up 'fully armed' at the Restoration) was already habitual to men like Berkenhead. Equally intuitive was the preoccupation with literary standards, which here gives us a chance to see Berkenhead the critic in some sort of action. In response to Raymond's request for his opinion of the book he offers some rather back-handed compliments and, as if to confirm what John Davies wrote about his interests, sings Virgil's praises.[7] This is eye-catching in a letter written under pressure in the midst of business at Amiens, on the day Prince Charles arrived there with his entourage. Berkenhead had himself just reached the town to collect dispatches, after riding 'three dayes poast'. He had presumably crossed from England to one of the Channel ports; and, if his protestations of fatigue and haste are any guide, was to do the return journey almost immediately.[8]

[1] Wood, *Hist. and Antiq.* ii. 579. He quotes the final section of *Newes from Pembroke and Mongomery* on p. 580.

[2] *Hist. and Antiq.* ii. 605, and *The Register of the Visitors of the University of Oxford, 1647–1658* (Camden Soc. N.S. lxxix, 1881), p. 194.

[3] The licence is printed in the book.

[4] *The Registers of the Stationers Company, 1640–1708* (1913–14), i. 298.

[5] Thomason received his copy, E. 1128, on that day.

[6] It is dated 11 July, new style, which was ten days ahead of English reckoning at this time. [7] See above, p. 142.

[8] See App. IV for the effect of his temporary absence on *Mercurius Bellicus*.

Far from being bashful about his identity, whereabouts, and role, Berkenhead seems eager to boast his diligence. Probably he was not putting himself at risk as long as he could preserve his incognito at home. He seems, anyhow, to have been operating successfully as a Crown agent for over a year, as his name is in one of Sir Edward Nicholas's cyphers for May 1647;[1] and he continued serving Nicholas in this capacity for at least two years more. It is unlikely that Amiens was his first or his last trip abroad: sea images were, admittedly, commonplace in contemporary writing, but the number of them in *The Assembly Man*, in late 1647, suggests that he may have been reflecting recent experience of cross-Channel journeys.

Truly these were years of continuous activity for Berkenhead—activity in which writing and riding courier were equal parts of his loyalty. *Bellicus* continued to appear throughout June and July; and towards the end of the latter month he seems to have published *The Earl of Pembrokes Speech in the House of Peeres upon the Debate of the Cities Petition for a Personall Treaty*. The City's Petition was delivered to Parliament on 5 July, and debated on 20 July. This pamphlet must have appeared soon after that. It is another travesty, longer and more intricate than *Newes from Pembroke* and concerned with a more complex political problem. But in general conception, tone, and language it is very like the earlier piece. At the outset, for example, the Earl identifies himself as the Foolish Messenger, boasting that he is 'the states half penny boy' running errands for his masters, the Commons, to the Lords.[2] But the suggested attribution to Berkenhead is based on more precise parallels in *Newes from Pembroke* and *Mercurius Bellicus*. The Earl's protest—'I cannot speak good English'—echoes his earlier admission 'I cannot spell English';[3] and his remark on the Duke of Hamilton—'he is a duke; I cannot abide a duke, because I am not one myself'—repeats the jibe at Gilbert Sheldon, 'Is he not Clerk of the Closet? I love no Clerks of the Closet; I am not one myself'.[4] *Bellicus* does not afford such specific resemblances, though there are shared

---

[1] B.M., MS. Egerton 2550, f. 5ᵛ.
[2] *The Speech*, repr. *S. Tracts*, vii. 80.
[3] Ibid., p. 80 and *Newes from Pembroke*, in *Harl. Misc.* v. 114.
[4] *The Speech*, p. 83 and *Newes from Pembroke*, p. 114.

images[1] and their arguments are identical in substance and scope when they analyse the Commons' motives for insisting on these three propositions before negotiating with the King.[2] Such similarities, in the absence of circumstantial confirmation, can admittedly be treacherous: and Berkenhead's authorship cannot be proved absolutely. The case for him is nevertheless more convincing than the old guess that *The Speech* was by Butler or Sedley.[3]

The Speech was designed to stir up the City against Parliament and the army by persuading it that the men in power had no genuine desire for accommodation. The core of its argument is that the Houses were deliberately proposing impossible terms so as to prevent a personal treaty which would inevitably reduce that power. Parliament's policy is discredited by making the Earl defend it with his usual ludicrously disingenuous cynicism. *The Speech* ironically reveals his perversion of reason: the citizens 'bring not a word of reason that I can understand'.[4] For the reason he does follow is material self-interest, and that narrow logic leads him to conclude that, as the treaty would corrode the State's absolute control of Church and Militia, it is reasonable to propose things 'out of reason, on purpose to prevent treating'.[5] What he is unwittingly arguing is that reason is irrational and irrationality reasonable, or that nonsense is sense. So he 'reasons' Parliament into disrepute and himself into circles of dizzy contradiction.

For the reader, his case reveals that the claims of Republican absolutism are absolutely nonsensical. This treatment is certainly different from the handling of the same political question in Berkenhead's two 1646 pamphlets. They tried to engage in a serious argument: this offers a comic image of Folly. Cavaliers felt that

---

[1] For example, *The Speech*, p. 84 asks 'shall our heads be . . . set sunning these dog-days upon the top of the house here?' and *M. Bell.* no. 21, A1[r], remarks that if there was a treaty the leaders of Parliament would not 'long keep their wise heads from perching on London Bridge'. *The Speech*, p. 82 observes that the Counties want a Treaty but states that 'they shall snap short'. *M. Bell.*, no. 22, A4[r], uses, in a different context, the phrase 'snap at it'.

[2] Compare *The Speech*, pp. 84–5 and *M. Bell.*, no. 21, A1[r]–A2[r].

[3] For the attributions to these writers see Butler's *Satires and Miscellanies*, ed. R. Lamar, p. xii, and *The Poetical Works of Sir Charles Sedley*, ed. V. de S. Pinto (1928), ii. 235.

[4] p. 85.

[5] p. 84.

things had gone beyond debate: short of the use of force, they could foresee no hope of a sane issue to events. Berkenhead makes the Earl demand rhetorically where reason had got the King and his supporters;[1] and one must wonder whether the writer, baffled and frustrated, does not after all share some of this disillusionment with reason, momentarily at least. The doubt, if it is there, contradicts the assumptions of his comedy, of course. Perhaps it is sounder to suggest that it is in character for the Earl ignorantly to think that reason can be measured by results, that it is a matter of mere expediency, not of principle as it is to the true Cavalier. There is, anyhow, no mistaking Berkenhead's desire to portray what was happening as an aberration of nature. Only laughter at such a thing could encompass the intolerable stresses, maintain the 'fact' of sanity in the teeth of madness, and perhaps exorcize a nation 'possessed'.

Propaganda takes many forms even in such a crisis: ostensibly neutral publications can serve their turn in the right context. Such a book was *The Works* of Judge David Jenkins. It probably appeared about March 1648, but may have come out later, which is why consideration of it has been delayed till now. Jenkins, captured by Parliamentary troops in 1645, had since then been incarcerated in the Tower pending proceedings which were at last begun in 1648. On 14 February he came before the Bar of the Commons to answer a charge of treason: he resolutely denied Parliament's competence to try the charge, delighting Royalists by his courageous resistance. *Bellicus*'s editor celebrated his virtues in four consecutive numbers during February and March,[2] and by composing the six lines of bombastic heroic verse, engraved on the frontispiece portrait of Jenkins in *The Works*. These verses are all too like many then being printed in the Cavalier newsbooks: they display the use of the couplet for political argument and satirical reflection, but have little or no intrinsic merit. A further accidental interest attaches to them because two lines were left out, and Thomas Barlow, President of the Queen's College, Oxford, wrote into his copy of *The*

---

[1] *The Speech*, p. 84.
[2] No. 4 (14–20 Feb.), D2ᵛ, no. 5 (22–29 Feb.), E3ʳ–E4ʳ, no. 6 (6 Feb.–7 Mar.), F1ᵛ–F2ʳ, and no. 7 (7–14 Mar.), G3ᵛ.

Works an angry complaint against 'ye roguy Printer'.[1] Actually it was the engraver's fault, and it is hard, anyhow, to share Barlow's indignation. What matters biographically is that Barlow was close enough to Berkenhead to know what he originally wrote. Their association lasted many years and will be heard of again. Meanwhile, one must assume that Berkenhead somehow concealed his whereabouts from the authorities, who can hardly have approved of the sentiments he expressed. Apparently he knew when and how to be bold and when and where to lie low; for he evaded arrest throughout these years, despite all his activities.

One thing those verses stress for us is Berkenhead's determination to insist as publicly as possible on the principles and standards he had espoused. Here and in works on the lower level he insists explicitly and implicitly on the differences between vulgarity and refinement, between the folly of innovation and the wisdom of traditional values, between philistinism and the civilization of the Court. Here the concerns of propagandist and littérateur meet; for the insistence on defined standards of political and social behaviour was a major dynamic in the formulation and organization of critical precepts. Berkenhead's experience shows how in the midst of mounting confusion the making of distinctions was felt to be more than ever an imperative function. Discrimination and refinement were duties both to nature and to art.

The concern for propriety and decorum are therefore not to be seen as artificial or peripheral concerns. Preoccupation with them grew naturally out of the complex organic relationship between writers and their environment; and there were solid reasons in nature for the advance of Cavalier neo-classicism. Far from being the waste interlude of inactivity that they are often thought to have been, the 1640s and 1650s saw much important revival and experiment. The processes of evolution are never stilled; and the close scrutiny of their workings in this period only confirms that literary theories and fashions do not exist in a vacuum but through 'natural selection'. From this it follows that they are capable of

---

[1] Barlow's comments and the verses are printed in Wood, *Ath. Oxon.* iii. 645. The verses were reprinted in the edition of Jenkins's works published in 1681 and 1683.

considerable variation and are continually changing, however gradual the mutations may be, and one cannot fail to observe that there do exist variations upon what seem to be the dominant tendencies of Cavalier practice. Those dominant tendencies, however, are equally detectable; a large inclination to move in a discoverable direction existed.

Casting back to *The Speech* it is apparent that various pressures operated to shift Cavalier propaganda towards the comic. And there is much in their response to support Bergson's notion that comedy laughs at men obsessed by *idées fixes*, because they appear to behave in deference to the tyranny of some abnormal (and mechanical) compulsion, not according to reason and sense. There is certainly a warning, something of the magisterial and legislative, in Cavalier laughter. Equally, Freud might have found here much to confirm the hypothesis that laughter is an expression of fundamental aggressive drives, fears, and frustrations. But neither view seems wholly adequate; for they both stress, tacitly or otherwise, laughter as a way of saying 'No'. Its function for the Royalists, however, seems to have been more complex and positive than that. Obviously, they were responding to alien experiences; but the existence and power of the abnormal is not denied. It is, ironically, celebrated; but simultaneously the truth and survival of normative behaviour is asserted. In other words, rather than saying 'No', comedy says 'It is, but it is not'. The recognition and revelation of the victim as a man who is dangerous because he has taken Evil as his God, but ultimately impotent because he is therefore divided against himself, is at the heart of their comedy. Laughter here is a gesture that recognizes the victim's inner contradictions and affirms that he cannot stand. He can even be treated with condescension and pity, because he is seen to be self-destroying.

This kind of analysis emphasizes that comedy is a complex mode of perception, and one whereby the possibility of wholeness and coherence is confirmed in the face of incoherence. It does not follow, of course, that Cavalier burlesque pamphlets are necessarily great comedy, though they may help us to understand how that works, for naturally they achieve varying degrees of subtlety and insight; but it is to be insisted that comedy in the late 1640s was inevitable, and profoundly necessary to the Cavaliers; necessary, that is, if they were to adjust to changing circumstances and survive in some way more than mere brute survival. They had to sustain a sense of identity, a self-respect, and a belief in human society as they understood it, in a hostile, unaccommodating, and deteriorating environment. Paradoxically, it was in the 'discovery' of the enemy's total depravity (which they themselves stressed in the recurrent image of stripping the mask from the face of Rebellion) that the Cavaliers found a way of living with the undeniable fact of Rebel ascendancy. The laughing Cavalier was not only a joke: he was a man adapting himself (sometimes desperately and hysterically) to his new environment.

More simply, perhaps, their comedy is a reminder that the idiom and attitudes of Restoration literature did not spring up overnight. The satiric comedy of manners in the late 1640s assumes the gentlemanly norm as readily as does its later manifestation. Yet the Cavalier gentleman's laughter was, in one sense, premature. For though they could see neither rhyme nor reason in Parliament's doings, many still felt that the King's intransigence was the most truly absurd and dangerous factor in the situation. It was Charles's unnatural execution that finally brought substantial numbers to feel that Royalist reasoning had not been so misguided after all. Ultimately, many outside the Cavalier party were to join in the chorus of mockery that ushered out the Rump Parliament in 1659 and 1660. That mockery was remarkably close in spirit and execution to the satire of this time. The ten years between, however, were fraught with hardships for Cavaliers; some were persecuted; some had to make all sorts of compromises to survive. Berkenhead, who had consolidated his reputation and extended the range of his satire by 1649, came through considerable difficulties as will be seen, unscathed by persecution and remarkably true to form.

CHAPTER VI

1649 to 1659

'No man must print or write Books'

WITH the collapse of their second war effort it soon became
impossible for the Cavaliers to produce any newsbook; and from
the demise of *Bellicus* until 1660 Berkenhead was not involved with
periodicals. It became harder, too, to publish single pamphlets. As
Cromwell took firmer hold of affairs, the press felt the pinch: the
'Licence' of which Milton and others had complained, was at last
rebated. Berkenhead, after 1655, published nothing at all until
1659; but even in the early 1650s conditions drove his propaganda
into more desultory and oblique modes.

The burlesque habit still enlivened his prose pieces; they were,
indeed, more than ever designed for a popular market. According
to Aubrey, Berkenhead made 'many a fourty shillings . . . by
pamphletts',[1] and possibly he had to make his work more than
ever competitive and saleable in order to keep his head above
water. This would certainly account for their catch-penny character. The need to earn a living with his pen (up to 1647, at least, his
pamphlets had been subsidized or underwritten by the resources
of the Court and its supporters) may also help explain Berkenhead's
interest in major Cavalier literary projects, and his editing of other
men's works in the early 1650s.

Typically Berkenhead still introduced Cavalier protest into
practically everything he wrote. His tenacity was rewarded with
recognition from the King's Court in exile. But there were no places
or cash to spare; and it was friendship with the Finch family that
carried Berkenhead through years of enforced silence that might
have ruined him. The romantic notion that, like many Cavaliers,

---

[1] *Brief Lives*, i. 105.

he scraped through the Interregnum suffering many imprisonments and indignities is erroneous. While some really were crippled by debt, Berkenhead managed by 1656, when his pen could gain him nothing more, to find a patron willing to protect and sustain him.

The decade opened with the terrible fulfilment of worst fears: Charles I was brought to trial and executed. The deed stunned the nation and gave the Cavaliers the one martyr they really needed. The voices of lamentation and recrimination were raised, Berkenhead's among them. His name is associated with two publications directed to this grave situation: the first is a brilliant prose pamphlet *King Charles's Case Truly Stated*; the second is a long elegiac poem, *Loyalties Tears*. The pamphlet, ascribed to him on stylistic grounds in the last century, was not his but Butler's.[1] He probably did write the poem: it was first published about 25 June 1649, anonymously; but the second edition, issued about 30 January 1650, ascribes the verses to 'J. B.'.[2] It was suggested a century ago that the initials stand for John Berkenhead;[3] and the poem gives this identification some support. It is steeped in the imagery of the Cavalier newsbooks, and there is one close echo of an image in Berkenhead's then unpublished *The Assembly Man*: the poet's mention of 'Pulpit garrisons' recalls the preacher who spoke 'If his Pulpit be large . . . as from a garrison'.[4] Altogether, Berkenhead is the most likely candidate.

The King's conduct during imprisonment and trial, and on the scaffold, sanctified Cavalier heroism. Memories of past errors and defeats were overwhelmed in the piety and stoicism of the Martyr: so, in the poem, the stigma of 'fatall Nasebies plunder' (the King's letters) is healed by the thought of the immaculate *Eikon Basilike*. The enormity of his murder (for such it was to Cavaliers and many others) seemed out of all proportion to his shortcomings; and the poem, in common with many publications, seized this psychological moment to recall his reign as a 'sweet tyrranie'. The image may

[1] The attribution was suggested by the editor of the *S. Tracts*, v. 237; but see Butler's *Satires and Miscellanies*, p. ix.

[2] The second of these is not listed in the Index to G. K. Fortescue's *Catalogue of the Thomason Tracts, 1640–1661*, but will be found under that date.

[3] W. C. Hazlitt, *Hand-Book to Early English Literature*, p. 40.

[4] *Harl. Misc.* v. 101.

have touched many hearts and consciences, still shaken by the thrill of guilt and remorse that ran through the nation.

Amazement and bitter resentment dominate *Loyalties Tears*: it is, as the writer confessed, far from being 'A generous and time-defying Strein'. The writer lashes out angrily at treacherous Scots and 'Independent spawn'; and the overthrow of orderly Nature, savagely manifested in the King's death, is contemplated with grim irony. There is little or no sense of personal grief, tenderness of regret, little warmth of feeling: the oratory is instead coldly ferocious. Berkenhead's was an aggressive rather than a reflective temperament; and his elegy turns into a somewhat melodramatic and monotonous attempt to whip up zeal for revenge.

If he meant to remind the new King of his loyalty (and he was never backward in canvassing his claims) he succeeded however. On 22 August 1649 he obtained a grant of arms from Sir Edward Walker, Garter in Chief at the Court of St. Germain in France.[1] This was gratification indeed for one so ambitious to rise in the social hierarchy. It placed him in the rank of gentlemen who ascended by government service, not agricultural dexterity. In the long run it was the prelude to profitable office and even higher status. For now, it appears to have fed the conceit of the *arriviste*, and he snobbishly flaunts his new-found dignity in verses of 1651 and 1655.

The Court was not, of course, in the habit of granting such honours just for a few verses; and Berkenhead's main claim to reward was his current service as a Crown agent. 1 September 1649 found him still in France, scribbling a note acknowledging receipt from Robert Long, Secretary of State, of nine letters of £500 a piece, 'to be delivered and disposed in England'.[2] Obviously he was trusted by Royalist leaders abroad, but not all Cavaliers regarded him so favourably. On 10 May 1649 John Evelyn had referred to a rumour that Berkenhead was one of Parliament's paid

---

[1] *Grantees of Arms . . . to the end of the Seventeenth Century* (Harleian Soc. lxvi, 1915), p. 24. The description of his coat of arms (in B.M., MS. Harleian 1172, f. 72ᵛ) is as follows: '3 Bay leaves proper in a field or and in a field gules 3 Crownes Or: crest an arme naked out of a Crowne holding 3 Arrowes gules headed and plumed or.' The symbolism is self-explanatory.

[2] Bodleian Library, MS. Clarendon 38, f. 1.

spies at Court. He doubted it strongly, but recorded it for what it was worth.[1] It looks as though the grant of arms in August was in part reassurance to Berkenhead that the Court did not suspect him.

In December 1649, however, Lord Hatton, less sceptical of rumours than Evelyn, complained bitterly to Sir Edward Nicholas that Berkenhead had got himself in bad odour at home. Apparently Berkenhead had some sort of responsibility for Royalist publicity in England, since Hatton grumbled that the printers had recently refused to trust Berkenhead in the matter of printing the King's Declaration from Jersey. It was published rather late, on 23 October 1649 and Hatton blamed Berkenhead for this delay.[2] He again wrote to Nicholas in January 1650 to accuse Berkenhead of revealing to John Ashburnham everything he knew 'or that Mr. Long or Oudart write unto him', so that many loyalists had not 'dared to stirr or appeare'.[3] But Ashburnham was, in fact, unjustly suspected of treachery in the events leading to the capture of Charles I in 1647. His actual innocence and Hatton's unreliability— he was a vindictive trouble-maker—sufficiently exonerate Berkenhead from blame. He still figured in Nicholas's cyphers in April 1650,[4] so the charges against him cannot have been taken seriously. In Nicholas he had a powerful friend, and one whose faith in him remained unshaken. It brought Berkenhead considerable advancement later.

It may be true, none the less, that he had offended the printers, perhaps by getting them to print something of his own on the pretext that it was a Royal Command. His later conduct shows that he was quite capable of such high-handedness. He was willing, too, to gossip about things he had been asked to keep to himself; and though not a traitor like his brother, he may have

---

[1] *Diary and Correspondence of John Evelyn*, p. 558. The letter written by a John Berkenhead to a Mr. Woolley in Whitehall about this time (*C.S.P. Dom.*, 1648–9, p. 435), which looks suspicious, is not his, as the handwriting of the original (P.R.O., S.P/520/140) shows.

[2] *The Nicholas Papers*, vol. i, 1641–1652 (Camden Soc. N.S. xl, 1886), p. 158.

[3] Ibid., p. 164. Hatton does not actually give the Christian name of Berkenhead, so it is just possible that he was referring to John's brother Isaac (see above, pp. 10–12). But as John's connection with propaganda was so close, and since his name appears in Nicholas's cyphers, the present identification is not really in much doubt.

[4] B.M., MS. Egerton 2550, f. 9ᵛ.

committed venial indiscretions. Political principles or patrons were sacrosanct; but he could intrigue ruthlessly when his ᵨersonal welfare was at stake. A little calculated careless talk might have been his way of reminding superiors of the importance of keeping him sweet. Be that as it may, he survived the storm in a teacup and all other hazards of the Interregnum without losing face at Court or running into trouble with the English authorities.

Albeit busy spying, Berkenhead still found time to write: on 23 January 1650 the Earl of Pembroke died, and about 19 February yet another parody, *The Earl of Pembrokes Last Speech*, appeared. Aubrey stated that Berkenhead composed 'The Last Will and Testament of Philip, Earle of Pembroke';[1] and though there are two earlier publications to which this might at first sight refer,[2] the style of the February squib is closest to Berkenhead's. Moreover, when reprinted in 1680, it used the very title Aubrey gives: so Berkenhead can confidently be credited with it.[3]

The mock testament was yet another old-established form in European and English satire revived now burlesque was in the air. Berkenhead's 'testament' masquerades as a legal document, comprising a brief meditation on approaching death, an 'Imprimis' and sixteen 'Items' drawn up in proper form. The method is exemplified by the bequest of nothing to Lord Say, 'which legacy I give him because I know he will bestow it on the poor'.[4] The 'Will' is simply a handy frame for a miscellany of sarcasms directed at deserving but random targets. They are not even confined to politics, for Berkenhead scoffs at a very coarse lampoon which had offended his sense of propriety.[5]

The 'Will' is an adroitly designed piece of merchandise: Pembroke's death was not of sufficient political importance to merit the lengthier, more scabrous treatment it received at other hands.

[1] *Brief Lives*, i. 105.

[2] These are *The First Part of the Last Wil and Testament of Philip, Earl of Pembroke* (11 May 1649), and *The Last Will and Testament of Philip Herbert* (23 Jan. 1650).

[3] This 1680 edition had added to it the 'Codicill' from the 'testament' of 23 Jan. 1650, and it is in this form that it is reprinted in the *S. Tracts*, vii. 89–92. It has been variously attributed to Butler (see *Satires and Miscellanies*, p. xiii) and Sir Charles Sedley (see *The Poetical And Dramatic Works*, ii. 235).

[4] *S. Tracts*, vii. 90.

[5] Ibid., p. 91. The pamphlet was *News from the New Exchange*.

Berkenhead's pamphlet was both more appropriate and easier to write, print, and read. There was a good market for jest-books and he shrewdly catered for it. He used the method again, and with overwhelming success, in the next year.

On 26 February 1650 Parliament passed an Act banishing Papists and Delinquents from London. The Cavaliers were given until 20 March to make themselves scarce; and on that day thousands of them left the City. Berkenhead was not among them, though he was in London: defying the Act he lingered in hiding, for a while at least, to keep an appointment, presumably with a fellow agent. The latter failed the rendezvous, and Berkenhead seems to have passed the time by writing a poem about it all.[1] Anyhow, he evaded detection; nor did the new restrictions stop him giving work to the press.

Among the publications he was concerned with in 1651 are two that show his involvement in fashionable letters. The first is *Amoris Effigies*, a neo-Platonic tract in Latin written by Robert Waring, another survivor of the Cartwright clique.[2] He had lost his Fellowship in 1648 and retired to the country, giving Berkenhead a manuscript of the treatise with a request that he should get it printed for him.[3] The actual date of publication is a matter of some dispute: 1649 and 1657 have been suggested,[4] but 1657 seems too late, in view of the close control of the press then; and 1649 is probably too early, as the printer, Roger Daniel, who had his patent as printer to Cambridge University cancelled on 1 June 1650,[5] does not use his official style on the title-page. 1651 seems the most likely date, since publication then would have been a fitting accompaniment to the appearance of Cartwright's works in June.

Berkenhead's initiative in preparing the tract for the press was praised by *Amoris Effigies*'s second editor, William Griffith, in 1661. He paid tribute to Berkenhead's accurate editing and to his

[1] See below, p. 186.

[2] David Lloyd, *Memoires* (1668), p. 425, note *b*.

[3] *Ath. Oxon.* iii. 453.

[4] Ibid. iii. 1205 and the Bodleian Catalogue respectively. Wood was similarly mistaken about the date of Berkenhead's *Paul's Church-Yard* (see below, p. 180).

[5] H. R. Plomer, *A Dictionary of the Booksellers and Printers in England, Scotland and Ireland from 1641 to 1667* (1907), p. 62.

honesty in not claiming the text as his own.[1] This was only tactful since Berkenhead had lent him the original manuscript and he had emended his text. Griffith, however, went beyond mere tact and described Berkenhead as the greatest of the old Oxford Wits, suggesting that if he published his own works people would be astounded—favourably, of course. Fulsome compliments were common enough; and this one was doubtless inspired by the fact that in 1661 Berkenhead had control of the press and not a little influence at Court.

Yet it does suggest that he enjoyed some special literary prestige as a survivor of the Cartwright group; and Davies of Kidwelly, Katherine Philips, and John Leigh, as well as Griffith, all suggest that his serious output was more considerable than his surviving publications indicate. If they were being more than conventionally complimentary, it obviously confirms that Berkenhead's solid ambitions were political, not literary. Even after the Restoration and in spite of Griffith's appeal, the only work he bothered to republish was *The Assembly Man*, and there were good political reasons for that.

Berkenhead, however, knew his duty as an academic and understood the advantages of being in the swim. His second excursion into fashionable letters in 1651 was the contribution of the longest of the commendatory verses prefixed to Cartwright's *Comedies, Tragicomedies, with Other Poems*, published about 23 June. Like the Beaumont and Fletcher Folio, this volume was implicitly a reaffirmation of Cavalier ideals and a gesture of defiance against the society which had repudiated them. Berkenhead's verses are especially bold in their equation of prevailing political and literary decadence. Inferior wits, he writes, scorn serious verse as they do bishops and kings; while Cartwright's technical propriety images the correctness of his beliefs. Good verse is composed of 'Great Sense, rich words, full Numbers'; and by 'Sense' he means political and religious orthodoxy. In the name of this concept of social order he

---

[1] Griffith flatters Berkenhead not only in his dedication of the book to him, but also in the address to the reader. I am grateful to the Librarian of Norwich Public Libraries for information concerning the 1661 edition, of which they possess the only copy. The dedication and address occur also in the later editions of 1664, 1668, and 1671.

advocates neo-classical principles of regularity and propriety. Taking his verse as a whole, Berkenhead certainly 'afforded more in precept than in example';[1] but the precepts of the Cartwright verse are particularly arresting because his attempt to 'define Lawes' attracted Bishop Sprat's attention and approval,[2] and was known to Dryden. He cited his 'worthy friend' Berkenhead in the *Defence of An Essay of Dramatick Poesy* in 1668 where he quoted, as a summing-up of their poetic credo, Berkenhead's dictum (from the Cartwright verses) 'the Great Wit's great work is to Refuse'.[3] This, it has been remarked, 'expressed what they were all trying to learn . . .'.[4] Of course, Berkenhead was not alone in advocating such ideas of restraint and selection: he derived them very largely from Cowley's ode, 'Of Wit', which he tried in these 1651 lines to clarify and codify by turning it into epigram. But clearly his advocacy, if only by virtue of being representative, did have some direct influence on Restoration critical theory. He was a believer in rule and regulations in all walks of life—an inclination which, together with a smart turn of phrase and ready critical dogmatism, made him an effective spokesman in 1651 for those who wished to rationalize poetry and make it the voice of civic virtue. When he sat with Dryden and Sprat on the Royal Society Committee appointed to consider the reform of the English language,[5] he must have had opportunity to canvass further his ideas on style. A number of his 1651 points—the demand for the labour of rejection, the concern for smooth ease, the tender regard for maidenly modesty, and the antagonism to strong lines and Metaphysical excesses generally—were the commonplaces of Restoration criticism.

What is especially interesting is that these ideas, although not exactly original, were advanced in this way and in this place in 1651. Assumptions and standards were being established, which Dryden inherited and out of which he was to evolve a viable

[1] G. Williamson, *The Senecan Amble* (1951), p. 340.

[2] He quoted Berkenhead in a letter to Sir Christopher Wren, reprinted in James Elmes's *Life of Sir C. Wren* (1823), p. 122.

[3] See *Dryden and Howard, 1644–1668*, ed. D. D. Arundell (1929), p. 109. The line was also quoted by Walter Harte in 'The Courtier and Prince' in *The Amaranth* (1767), p. 126.

[4] G. Williamson, loc. cit.

[5] See below, p. 233.

poetic theory, profoundly relevant to the nature and needs of his society. The Cavaliers' insistence on including politics in their poetry marks their refusal to acquiesce (at any level) in the ortho-doxies prevailing against them; and this was one means by which the received aristocratic culture of the Court, which had once drifted dangerously into escapist fantasy, was brought back into vivifying contact with reality—a reality which included philis-tinism, ignorance, opposition, and barbarity.[1] The Interregnum stimulated the rationalization of poetic theory, the formulation of general standards, and the emergence of a corporate criticism.

It is the shared consciousness of the need for serious commitment in the writer that leads Berkenhead to slate 'would-be Atheists' ready to scribble for any side for money, and to denounce as mercenary those poets who find their inspiration in alcohol. Cart-wright, he reminds them, was 'As far 'bove Tavern Flash as Ribaldry'. Certainly Berkenhead himself wrote ribald ballads; but however low the style that he and others like him adopted for propagandist purposes, they carefully avoided debasing the coinage of higher poetry. Popular ballads and serious verse were seen as distinct kinds, and decorum was observed in both. So in the Cartwright verses Berkenhead introduces nothing that might disturb the tone of urbane common sense which they were striving for. It is important to understand that there was this dividing line between tavern poets like Brome and Bold and the academic and Court wits: Berkenhead's poem gives the lie to the fallacy that in defeat the Cavaliers, disorientated and decadent, became universally addicted to irresponsible light-heartedness, and eagerly drowned their sorrows in drink.[2] On the contrary, theirs was the conviction, reiterated by Dryden,[3] that poetry is as seriously concerned with truth and right conduct as is moral philosophy. The recent sug-gestion that the antecedents of Restoration heroic and satiric verse are all to be found in hurried war-time balladry cannot be sustained.[4]

---

[1] Cf. Dryden in the *Essay of Dramatick Poesie* alluding to a 'barbarous race of men, enemies of all good learning'.

[2] This notion has been rather too heavily emphasized by C. V. Wedgwood in *Poetry & Politics under the Stuarts* (1960), pp. 105–9.

[3] *Defence of An Essay of Dramatick Poesy* (1668).

[4] C. V. Wedgwood, op. cit., p. 74.

Whatever his involvement in literary debate, Berkenhead could not neglect his propagandist obligations. Ironically speculating that 'since no man must print or write Books, we may print the names of Books that never were written',[1] he again struck out, in July 1651. He strung together a number of unrelated witticisms about 'Rebels', in the manner of his Pembroke 'testament'. This time he marshalled them as groups of mock book titles, Acts of Parliament, Queries, Orders, and Cases of Conscience. Assembling these in three 'centuries', he made up three mock catalogues each with the title *Paul's Church-Yard*. Wood's ascription to Berkenhead[2] is confirmed by the reappearance in them of many of his earlier jokes. But Wood wrongly dated publication to 1649: the first 'century' actually appeared about 24 July 1651, the second in February 1652, and the third about 20 September 1652.[3] Their bibliographical history is complex, but variations in the character and setting of the type enable one to distinguish three editions of the first 'century' and four of the second; only one edition of the third has survived.[4] However, one of the editions of the first and second centuries was not published until July 1659, so it is not certain that all the others came out in 1651 and 1652. In addition to these separate 'centuries', a composite version of the first two was published in 1653 as *Two Centuries of Paul's Church-Yard*. This also contained another, and similar, pamphlet by Berkenhead, *Bibliotheca Parliamenti*. It, too, was originally printed in separate parts: the first 'Classis'—they are not centuries—appeared about 3 May 1653, and the second about 23 June 1653.[5] The version in *Two Centuries*, however, was virtually a third 'Classis', for, though it incorporates items from the first part, it contains much new material. Possibly, as it does not borrow from the second part, it was published between 3 May and 23 June 1653.

---

[1] *Two Centuries of Paul's Church-Yard*, item 74 (see the reprint in *Harl. Misc.* ix. 412). *Two Centuries* was a combined reprint, published in 1653, of the first two 'centuries'.

[2] *Ath. Oxon.* iii. 1205.

[3] See under these dates in G. K. Fortescue's *Catalogue of the Thomason Tracts, 1640–1661*. The first 'century' is not mentioned in his Index.

[4] For further details of identification see App. V.

[5] The second 'Classis' is reprinted in the *S. Tracts*, vii. 92–7. The dates are from Thomason.

The character of the pamphlets can best be described by quoting
a few random items:

Tot quot, The unlawfulness of holding two Benefices and the
lawfulness of holding four, by the assembly of Divines.[1]

Whether Cromwell be not an absolute hater of images, since he hath
defaced God's in his own countenance.[2]

Ordered, That all seamens widows be sent to Obadiah Sedgewick
for due benevolence: and this Ordinance to last both now and anon
too.[3]

An Act for admitting Jews into England with a short Proviso for
banishing the Cavaliers.[4]

The first item recalls *Aulicus*'s closing comment on the Assemblers:
'tis unlawfull for a man to hold Two Benefices, unlesse he hold
foure'.[5] If Berkenhead had a way of repeating his own jokes[6] (and
few caricaturists lack some such signature) he was also prepared
to borrow; for the second item is a crib of Cleaveland's comment
that Cromwell was 'so perfect a hater of images, that he hath
defaced God's in his own countenance'.[7] Similarly the query
'Whether Venter and Neuter be not as true an Anagram as Atkins,
a stink?'[8] comes from a 1648 newsbook reference to 'Alderman
Atkins (the anagram of whose name is A Stink)'.[9] This, like
many other jests, turned up again among the host of 'Queries'
printed in 1660: 'Whether Atkins be the anagram of a stink, or a
stink of Atkins'.[10] The wretched Alderman was not allowed to
forget the lamentable occasion on which he broke wind publicly.

This reiteration of motifs was signally abetted by this series of
pamphlets by Berkenhead. Like the popular jest-books, they
renewed from decade to decade a pattern of humour; unlike

---

[1] *Two Centuries*, item 10, p. 409.
[2] *Bibliotheca Parliamenti*, Classis 2, 'Cases of Conscience', item 21, p. 97.
[3] *Bibliotheca Parliamenti* (in *Two Centuries*), 'Acts and Orders', item 14, p. 420.
[4] *Two Centuries*, item 125, p. 414.
[5] No. 118 (31 Aug.–7 Sept. 1645), p. 1736.
[6] For further examples see App. V.
[7] *The Character of a London Diurnall*, reprinted in *Character Writings of the Seventeenth Century*, p. 311.
[8] *Bibliotheca Parliamenti* (in *Two Centuries*), 'Cases of Conscience', item 10, p. 420.
[9] *The Parliament Kite*, no. 4 (1–8 June 1648), p. 16.
[10] *Free Parliament Queries* (10 Apr. 1660), p. 5, no. 30.

them, they are not unified by the association of all the jokes with some famous jester, nor do they contain any of the extended tales of earlier tradition. Brevity here is the soul of wit with a vengeance. Robert Chamberlain's *Conceits, Flashes and Whimsies* of 1639 had already shown the drift towards jests that were 'pointed, sudden and brief';[1] and some of Berkenhead's items were slotted neatly into *The Tales and Jests of Mr. Hugh Peters* in 1660.[2] Berkenhead cannot be credited with inventing the mode he uses,[3] any more than with thinking up all the jokes he retails. But it seems to have been his idea to work up a combination of mock resolves, acts, queries, and book titles into one collection with a burlesque framework. That little touch of originality—a canny piece of journalism—proved enormously successful. The proliferation of editions and the imitations show that: *Mercurius Democritus*, published about 8 April 1652, contained numerous satirical queries; and *Mercurius Zeteticus*—of about 22 April—was a 'century' of sarcasms against Presbyterians. The writer promised another 'century' each week, but nothing survives to prove he kept his word. The form enjoyed its greatest popularity in 1659 and 1660, when mocking queries and satirical catalogues showered on the Rump Parliament.[4] It is impossible to tell in which of them, if any, Berkenhead had a hand; but it was certainly his effort of the early 1650s which established the effectiveness of this sort of ephemeral pamphlet.

Commentators have been united in praise of *Paul's Church-Yard* and *Bibliotheca Parliamenti*: one even described their 'spirited humour' as 'worthy the pen of a Butler'.[5] In a sense they were

[1] F. P. Wilson, *The English Jestbooks of the Sixteenth and Early Seventeenth Centuries*, reprinted from the *Huntington Library Quarterly*, ii (1939), 131.

[2] Compare, for example, that collection's story about Peters telling George Wither that 'he was a pittifull Prophet, and a pitiful poet, otherwise he had not wrote such predictions for a pittiful Parliament' (in the 1807 reprint, p. 44), with Berkenhead's book title: '*Pseudo Propheta*, or the Pittifull Parliament, by George Withers, the pittifull Poet'. The latter is in *Bibliotheca Parliamenti*, Classis 2, 'Books', item 11, p. 93.   [3] See App. V for some earlier examples.

[4] These can easily be picked out of G. K. Fortescue's *Catalogue of the Thomason Tracts, 1640–1661*. It is worth drawing attention here to *Bibliotheca Fanatica* (1660), reprinted in *Harl. Misc.* viii. 71–3, and to *Bibliotheca Militum* (1659), reprinted in *Harl. Misc.* vii. 334–5; for these are obviously modelled on Berkenhead's *Bibliotheca Parliamenti*.

[5] This comment is quoted by the editor of *Harl. Misc.* ix. 408. He also quotes

worthy the pens of all the wits whose jokes were borrowed for the occasion, and are, among other things, a tribute to Berkenhead's exceptional memory.[1] He distilled the essence of Cavalier badinage: classical allusion and contemporary gossip jostle together unself-consciously; and the man of letters and the reader with no more than a lively interest in scandal may both have found diversion here. Some of the jokes are crude, some savage, some rely on more subtle and ironic analogy; and some fall flat today unless the reader is well briefed. But there is no mistaking even now the vivacity and sense of spontaneous fun; and only the solemn would fail to be amused.

Berkenhead by no means confined himself to immediately current affairs. He fed ancient hostility towards Prynne with a jibe at his notorious annotations to Laud's *Diary*;[2] he also recalled the scandal of the Elder's Maid,[3] and the Visitation of Oxford University, showing himself notably tender to his old college, All Souls, and to Laud's college, St. John's.[4] Recapitulation is particularly marked in the first two pamphlets; in the later parts there is more attention to immediate problems, like the rule of Major-Generals and the maritime ambitions of the Protectorate.

Among the up-to-the-minute references are jokes about the current price of coal in London,[5] obviously designed to stir up popular discontent. That is a reminder that the original jest-books and these their descendants were essentially popular reading, appealing strongly to the bourgeoisie;[6] and Berkenhead wanted to entertain not only Cavalier sophisticates, but also the Inns of Court men, the country gentry, the London citizens, and even the

Zachary Grey, the eighteenth-century editor of Butler's *Hudibras*, who made great use of Berkenhead's pamphlets. Sir Egerton Brydges passed some enthusiastic remarks in *Censura Literaria* (1815), vi. 287; and William Beloe reprinted a number of items from the first 'century' of *Paul's Church-Yard* in *Anecdotes of Literature* (1812), vi. 352–9. For a modern appreciation see the remarks of Don M. Wolfe in the *Complete Prose Works of John Milton*, vol. iv, 1650–5 (Yale Univ. Press, 1966), pp. 207–9.

[1] Aubrey, *Brief Lives*, i. 106.
[2] *Two Centuries*, item 150, p. 416.
[3] Ibid., item 13, p. 409. [4] Ibid., items 53 and 54 respectively, p. 411.
[5] *Bibliotheca Parliamenti* in (*Two Centuries*), 'Acts and Orders', item 11, p. 420.
[6] C. H. Herford, *Studies in the Literary Relations of England and Germany in the Sixteenth Century*, p. 242.

army officers.[1] Anything that might raise a laugh was grist to his mill: he even commented wryly on the current Cavalier fashion for translating Continental authors.[2] This readiness to joke about fellow Cavaliers is intriguing; Berkenhead inevitably jested about Cromwell's nose, but he could not resist combining this with a dig at Davenant's notorious facial disfigurement.[3] The comic spirit could not resist any deviation from normality. Impropriety, of course, was not to be forgiven even in sympathizers: Berkenhead, reaffirming his stand in the Cartwright poem, attacked tipplers and sarcastically suggested that drinking was not the whole duty of a loyal subject.[4] Here was one Cavalier who did not easily succumb to despair, whose determination to preserve standards was almost Puritanical in its sternness and zeal. His pride, his sturdy instinct for self-preservation, and his toughness in a tight corner—all these qualities must have helped sustain his morale.

He may have compiled the squibs because he needed the money, but he was also doing his best to rally Cavalier spirits, and remind them of their duties and destiny. He also had one very personal motive for 'inventing' his mock catalogues: his own library, as he mentions in *Paul's Church-Yard*, had been confiscated;[5] and this was an ironical revenge on the regime which had stolen his books. Where they were when requisitioned is unknown, as is the size of his collection. Possibly they had been left in his rooms in All Souls and were simply acquired by his successor. There may be a connection between the loss of his books and a petition which the ejected Fellows—Berkenhead presumably included—put before the Warden in 1652. It was ordered to be read at a special College meeting, but unfortunately no record of its contents survives.[6] It may have been a joint protest about the sequestration of books.[7]

[1] This was the audience singled out by one of the imitators of these pamphlets, *Mercurius Zeteticus* (22 Apr. 1652), B3ʳ.

[2] *Two Centuries*, item 98, p. 413.

[3] *Bibliotheca Parliamenti* (in *Two Centuries*), 'Cases of Conscience', item 1, p. 420.

[4] *Two Centuries*, item 192, p. 417.

[5] Item 100, p. 413, and item 199, p. 417.

[6] I am indebted to Professor E. F. Jacob, Librarian of All Souls College, for information about this petition.

[7] G. Williamson, *Seventeenth Century Contexts* (1960), p. 191, writing about Richard Whitlock's *Zootomia*, suggests that the author, also a Fellow of All Souls, had had his library sequestered.

The tone of Berkenhead's remarks certainly suggests a recent loss and if he was one of several sufferers he could refer to the matter without fear of identifying himself.

He either managed to salvage some of his collection or acquired new volumes fairly speedily, for between 1653 and 1660 he presented several manuscripts and one printed book to the Bodleian Library,[1] of which his friend, Thomas Barlow, was Librarian from 1652 to 1660. The book and one of the manuscripts were donated on 28 July 1653; another manuscript was given in December 1653, two more on 13 November 1656, and the fifth and last manuscript some time between 1655 and 1660. All these volumes show the stamp of Laud's training in some way: two are copies of the Statutes of other Universities, and the rest are concerned with scholarly theological and ecclesiastical matters. One is worth singling out further: it is *A Relation of the State of Religion* written by Sir Edwyn Sandys in 1599, and contains a passage that could have inspired some of Berkenhead's ideas about news and propaganda. He certainly acted on the Jesuit assumption, described by Sandys, that favourable intelligence, even if later proved inaccurate, has a strong hold on popular imagination because men are naturally reluctant to relinquish first impressions.[2] But perhaps the donations are most interesting as evidence of Berkenhead's friendship with Barlow during the Interregnum: it raises the possibility that he spent some of the time in Oxford.

He next appears, however, in gayer company in Henry Lawes's *Ayres and Dialogues* in 1653. His three lyrics in this collection, together with others in Lawes's *Second Book* of 1655, were presumably what Wood was thinking of when he remarked that Berkenhead eked out a living during the Interregnum by writing poems

---

[1] The printed book is mentioned by W. D. Macray in his *Annals of the Bodleian Library* (1890), p. 427. Its shelf-mark is 4° A. 11. Jur. BS. For the manuscripts see the 'Index of Owners' in the *Summary Catalogue of Western Manuscripts in the Bodleian Library*, vol. vii, ed. P. D. Record (1953). It was probably in this period that Berkenhead gave Barlow the manuscript of Anthony Stafford's tract (see above pp. 19–20). He also gave a manuscript to his friend William Creed, expelled from his Fellowship in 1648 and made Regius Professor of Divinity at Oxford after the Restoration. They must have met during the Civil War, when Creed was University Proctor, but the gift is undated and may have been made in the early 1660s. It is described in H. O. Coxe's *Catalogue of College MSS.* (1852) under MS. Balliol 328.

[2] Bodleian Library, MS. e. Musaeo 211, f. 27.

for young men in love.[1] They may not have been written for cash
at all, but for the gratification of appearing in yet another of the
major Cavalier literary enterprises of the period—this one inspired
by the wish to emulate the Greek art of uniting verse and music.
Berkenhead's lyrics show he was not very good at the light
fantastic touch: he replaces delicacy of sentiment with a rather
disconcertingly aggressive note. His translation of Anacreon's ode
The Lute, which compares unfavourably with Thomas Stanley's
version,[2] characteristically includes an exhortation to 'all true
Trojan Cavaliers'.[3] Nor is one ravished by the contrived sentimen-
tality of his poem written for festivities at the tenth wedding anniversary of the Earl and Countess of Bridgewater on 22 July 1652.
This is interesting chiefly as an indication that Berkenhead was cultivating aristocratic friends: he may have assisted at the 1652 celebrations, presumably held at the Egerton family home at Ashbridge
in Hertfordshire. His introduction to the Egertons may have come
through Jeremy Taylor, Stanley, the Duchess of Newcastle, or Lawes
himself, who was long and intimately associated with the family.

Berkenhead's third poem was the best he gave to Lawes. It was
written in 1650 when the Act for banishing Cavaliers from London
had been put into effect. He stayed in London to meet a friend who
failed to appear at the appointed hour, and he seems to have
passed the time of waiting by writing these verses. They communicate incisively his exasperation and depression (both personal
and political) and establish a sense of the danger of hiding from
'these Seekers', as he waits for darkness to make his getaway.
Spare and matter-of-fact, it is a neat enough piece of reportage and
a more authentic experience than the other poems. Presumably the
lapse of three years between the event and the publication were
sufficient protection for the writer; but in view of its strong
Royalist feeling it could fairly be described, as all these poems by
Berkenhead have been, as 'bravely printed in 1653'.[4] Perhaps a

[1] *Ath. Oxon.* 1203. The picture Wood draws of Berkenhead's life at this time is
altogether too sordid.

[2] See *Anacreon, Translated by Thomas Stanley*, ed. A. H. Bullen (1906), p. 1.

[3] For details of the reprint of this and many of the other lyrics see the Bibliography. Manuscript copies are also listed there.

[4] W. McClung Evans, *Henry Lawes, Musician and Friend of Poets*, p. 201.

song-book was the last place a suspicious licenser would look for Royalist propaganda.

Lawes's *Second Book of Ayres and Dialogues* in 1655 included five lyrics and a commendatory poem by Berkenhead. Other commendatory poems were contributed by Katherine Philips, her friend Mary Knight (Henry Berkenhead's sister), and two Doctors of Music, John Wilson and John Coleman. Berkenhead's effort surpasses the others in length, if nothing else. In fact, it does contain some interesting details about Lawes's life which suggest that Berkenhead knew him quite well.[1] Almost certainly he was a regular attender, and possibly a performer, at Lawes's gatherings; and his commendatory poem advances the fashionable Cavalier view of the musician's art as loftier than poetry, at least in Lawes's hands. The familiarity with musical techniques and terminology is also noticeable. Berkenhead once owned a copy of John Dowland's book on the art of singing, *Andreas Ornithoparcus*, which he gave some time after 1660 to Henry Aldrich, famous Dean of Christ Church in Oxford, and a skilled musician.[2] It seems likely that Berkenhead himself had some musical talent.

As an attempt to define the principles and qualities of Lawes's art the poem, inevitably, has much in common with the 1651 verses about Cartwright. Indeed, though both pieces contain strictures about borrowing from other artists, Berkenhead here filches at least one image from Cartwright.[3] He also adapts a line by Shirley[4] and recapitulates a number of ideas from earlier works of his own.[5] The role Berkenhead assigns himself is the same as that of 1651— to be a spokesman, legislating general standards and urging conformity to them. We are aware of a man speaking the language of group consensus.

[1] W. McClung Evans, *Henry Lawes, Musician and Friend of Poets*, p. 210.

[2] This is now in the Library of Christ Church. Aldrich, who did not graduate until 1666, collected a large musical library (see the 'Life' in the *D.N.B.*).

[3] For Cartwright's expression see his poem addressed to Beaumont and Fletcher in *The Works*, vol. i, p. xxxvii.

[4] See above, p. 140.

[5] He recalls the phrase describing England as a 'floating Island' used in his letter of 1648 to John Raymond; and he echoes his Latin verses to Fletcher in the notion that Lawes, after his brother's death, continued his work and made their joint art 'one Pyramid' (see the verses in *The Works of Beaumont and Fletcher*, vol. i, p. iv).

Some of his key sentiments are worth looking at: he praises Lawes's originality, his Englishness and independence of 'foreign Aid', and his direct reliance on Greek inspiration. Lawes was actually influenced by Italian Renaissance imitation of the Ancients;[1] but Berkenhead's inaccuracy displays a typical Cavalier zeal for the cause of patriotic humanism. To him Lawes is the type of civilized Renaissance hero in whom 'Art and Life are Unison'd'. The pursuit of 'Sense', the smooth matching of 'Ayre and Words', and the 'Symmetry' that results are all praised. What Berkenhead sees in Lawes is a classical order and harmony, which he approves in the name of the Cavalier gentleman. Even his political protest is veiled in classical allusion, but there is no mistaking Cromwell in the Roman dictator Sylla who 'Taught but two Arts, Speacking [*sic*] and Cutting Throats', and 'Whose Fire and Blood met in his copper-face'. The tone of these and other reflections on the Protectorate is, if anything, more patronizingly indignant than ever.[2] Proud of his coat of arms but frustrated in his ambitions, Berkenhead likens the state of England to the time

> When Rome thought Britain so despis'd a Clod,
> No Gentleman but scorn'd to be its God.

Here is the fusion in Cavalier minds of political, social, and literary criteria. The classical standard is invoked not as a distant ideal nor as some merely aesthetic fashion, but as a complete measure of contemporary life. It is felt as directly and intensely apposite to the current crisis. Berkenhead, however pedestrian in his verse, provides an especially explicit account of this preoccupation and its relationship to Cavalier resilience and endeavour. The lyrics themselves were not so offensive politically, though Berkenhead in one specifically indicated his preferences. They are, however, not irreproachable. The first, a conventional persuasive to an unwilling mistress, is distastefully melodramatic, and exhibits the masochistic self-pity of the Platonic lover at its worst. One is not sorry when 'Charons boat' heaves in sight to carry off the expiring swain to the accompaniment of an execrable refrain.

---

[1] W. McClung Evans, *Henry Lawes, Musician and Friend of Poets*, p. 162 n.
[2] Possibly the Licenser did not see the commendatory verses.

The poem's greatest interest is that it is addressed to 'Lucasia', presumably Orinda's friend, Anne Owen.

The second piece is an angry denunciation of the fickle lover, designed to satisfy Lawes's liking for complex metrics.[1] Its scorn and disappointment are, interestingly, as much political as amorous in origin: the falsehood of 'the new Court' and the docile subservience of London are deeply resented. The reflection that 'He that can dwell with none, must out of door' speaks ostensibly of the lover's dejection but principally of the insecurity of men excluded from accustomed power.

The third and fourth poems are translations from Anacreon. The third is strangely unmusical;[2] and in the fourth, a lament for old age, Berkenhead strikes a scornful rather than a whimsical note. Anacreon's hedonism has here been transformed into a stoical resolve to face death not with a sigh, 'but with a jest'.[3] The sardonic toughness and call for wit *in extremis* is Cavalier rather than Greek.

Berkenhead's last contribution, a rendering of Orpheus' 'Hymn to God', contrives, like inferior baroque, to be simultaneously ponderous and fussy. The sentiments are, of course, stoutly Anglican, and it seems to have been well enough liked; for Samuel Pepys, before setting out for church on Sunday, 4 March 1660, prepared his mood by taking up his lute and singing it.[4]

Lawes set one other lyric by Berkenhead which, though not written till after the Restoration, is best dispatched here. 'An Old Knight, to a Young Lady', printed in *Select Ayres and Dialogues* in 1669,[5] shows Berkenhead fumbling at courtly gallantry. But there is something irascible beneath the forced gaiety: he was not exactly light-hearted, although witty, and one senses an impatience with digression. By 1669 he was of course no longer young and very busy as politician and bureaucrat. The exercise of office and the

[1] See W. McClung Evans, *Henry Lawes, Musician and Friend of Poets*, pp. 164–5.

[2] This piece, 'Among Rose buds slept a Bee', compares unfavourably with Stanley's version: see *Anacreon, Translated by Thomas Stanley*, p. 46.

[3] Compare Stanley's version, op. cit., p. 16.

[4] See Macdonald Emslie, 'Pepys' Songs and Songbooks in the Diary Period', *The Library*, 5th Ser. xii (1957), 248.

[5] This poem is identified as Berkenhead's by C. L. Day and E. B. Murrie in *English Song-Books, 1651–1702, A Bibliography* (1940).

pursuit of power were his real preoccupations. His verse is wooden except when fired with what can best be described as political emotions; and then some sort of individuality, brisk and argumentative, comes into play. Altogether the Lawes songs show how much better he functions as a pamphleteer and how eager he was to give courtly verse the immediate reference of partisan journalism.

Between the two Lawes song-books Berkenhead wrote another ballad called *A Jolt.*[1] In July 1654 Cromwell, driving his coach in Hyde Park, was thrown from the box; the incident amused Royalists and produced a number of jeering ballads. Like most of them Berkenhead's was not printed until 1660, presumably circulating in manuscript meantime. It then appeared in *The Rump*, a collection of songs and ballads where the editor gave it honourable mention.[2] *A Jolt* is a burlesque, a low sort of mock-heroic poem aping the sturdy tradition of ballad–panegyric: witness the comparison of Cromwell with Hector and Phaeton, and the *Hudibras*-like farcical rhymes. The retailing of commonplace reactions to the incident was also standard ballad practice; and items like the suggestion that Cromwell was carrying a pistol in his pocket when he fell were frequently remarked on by Cavaliers in private and public.[3] *A Jolt* summed up their reactions effectively enough.

At the other end of the literary scale Berkenhead was doing some editing for the industrious Moseley, presumably to make some money. The first of his undertakings was Richard Whitlock's *Zootomia*, a book of great and various interest to anyone concerned with seventeenth-century prose, and one of considerable importance to the Interregnum debate about learning and science.[4] This compilation of characters and essays, with its pronounced

---

[1] Wood, *Ath. Oxon.* iii. 1205, attributes it to Berkenhead.

[2] For details about reprints of the ballad see the Bibliography. See also App. VI, where it is suggested that the editor of *The Rump* may have been Berkenhead himself.

[3] For an account of the accident and of Royalist reactions to it see D. L. Hobman, *Cromwell's Master-Spy. A Study of John Thurloe* (1961), pp. 51–3. There are allusions to it in *Fourty Four Queries to the Life of Queen Dick* (15 June 1659), p. 6; *A Copie of Queries* (22 June 1659), p. 7, and *Several Resolves Prepared by the Commanding Junto* (14 June 1659), p. 6.

[4] The present account is heavily indebted to George Williamson's essay in *Seventeenth Century Contexts*.

medico-scientific slant, is especially interesting for the light it throws on the intellectual concerns of the All Souls Fellows of the period and on their continued reading and thinking in this decade. It is, indeed, one of the works which conclusively prove that England in these years was the scene of considerable scientific and literary ferment.

That John Berkenhead was instrumental in bringing such a book into print at this juncture is to his credit. Yet all is not completely straightforward, for Whitlock, unlike him, was apparently a trimmer and something of a radical.[1] This is initially perplexing; but at least the attribution to Berkenhead of 'The Publisher to the Reader', which first appeared in the second issue of 1654 and was signed 'J. B.' (the first issue came out about 24 January)[2], is safe. It rests on a note in one copy of the second issue[3] and is confirmed by the style and sentiments of the urbane Preface: 'The Author did not (as the Fashion is) first write Bookes, and then fall to study.' That recalls comments made elsewhere by Berkenhead.[4] Nor, on closer inspection, is his association with Whitlock altogether surprising: both were Fellows of All Souls, of course, Whitlock being elected two years before Berkenhead in 1638; both were friendly with Henry Berkenhead and with Jaspar Mayne who contributed a prose encomium to *Zootomia*; and Whitlock, in fact, expresses anti-Puritan, anti-philistine sentiments Berkenhead must have sympathized with. Both men objected to quibbles passing for wit and themselves wrote relaxed, running prose of the Senecan rather than the Ciceronian school. They shared, too, displeasure at the Sequestration of Colleges and Libraries: it seems they both had unhappy personal experience of this. Berkenhead can have felt nothing but enthusiasm for Whitlock's celebration of the Church of England as the most effective opponent of Rome, and for his defence of music, painting, and poetry, particularly his emphasis on the public role of the latter. Whitlock's

---

[1] Wood, *Ath. Oxon.* iii. 985.

[2] The date is from Thomason's copy of the first issue. The work was reprinted in 1664 and 1679.

[3] There is a copy in the Guildhall Library of the Corporation of the City of London. Williamson's *Seventeenth Century Contexts* reprints the meat of the preface.

[4] See p. 193 below.

central general premiss that 'Rebellion against Knowledge, is but
Allegiance to the Prince of Darknesse' is, after all, couched in the
very idiom of militant Cavalier propaganda and could be read as
conveying an inference highly acceptable to Loyalists. It was at
least possible for Berkenhead to make good Cavalier sense of such
things. To this extent Whitlock, far from representing Puritan
utilitarian antagonism to the Universities, appears in the role of a
traditionalist defending things dear to his friends and Fellows of
All Souls. Even his 'moral earnestness', which George Williamson
in *Seventeenth Century Contexts* described as untypical of a Cavalier,
would have appealed to Berkenhead.

Nevertheless, there is much in *Zootomia* that one would hesitate
to identify Berkenhead with: his attitude on other occasions
suggests that he was hardly a protagonist of the progressive
rationalism that Whitlock espouses; and it is unlikely that he would
have gone along with his scientific scepticism or his disillusion
with the study of Theology and Civil Law. Nor can one envisage
him agreeing with Whitlock's genuine, impartial distrust of political and moral absolutes. In fact, the tone of the Preface is far from
radical: it is, rather, magisterial and legislative and the substance
of his remarks is of a very general nature (concerning Whitlock's
Wit and knowledge of Arts and Languages). Characteristically
Berkenhead closes by underlining Whitlock's 'discovering the now
Rayning Vanities (or Ignorance in Fashion)' and lamenting that
'Truth, and Wit begin to grow deare'. All of this suggests that he
is bent on enlisting the book on his side; and his editing it has to be
explained not in terms of a close philosophical rapport with his
author, but of a personal friendship, an association with Moseley,
and a need for employment, to say nothing of propagandist opportunism, and a genuine concern to appear as a leading light in the
world of letters. And after all, however mixed his motives, Berkenhead did perform that world a real service by editing *Zootomia*.

It may also help to explain how he later came to be a founder
member of the Royal Society, the cautious rationalism of which
Whitlock in so many respects anticipated. Coincidentally, his next
known piece of work for Moseley related to another Royal Society
man, Sir John Denham. His poem *Cooper's Hill* was first published

in 1642; and no doubt because it epitomized some central aspects of the neo-classical ideal it was decided to produce a new edition in 1655. This corrected edition carried an address to the reader signed, like that in *Zootomia*, 'J. B.'; and the present contention is that this was Berkenhead.[1] He opens with a playful witticism and closes with a familiar sort of sarcasm:[2]

You may know this by that excellent Allegory of the Royall Stag (which among others was lop't off by the Transcriber) skilfully maintain'd without dragging or haling in Words and Metaphors, as the fashion now is with some that cannot write, and cannot but write.

It is like Berkenhead to insinuate such criticism and to make play with the royal image. More specifically, the final phrase recalls his query, in *Paul's Church-Yard*, 'Whether ever there was so much and so little written as now?'.[3] The editor's comment on the 'false Transcript' that 'stole into Print' and his impatience at seeing 'so Noble a Peece so Savagely handled' similarly resemble expressions in the 1663 Preface to *The Assembly Man*.[4] He probably met Denham at Oxford during the Civil War and later they were both Royalist agents. The friendship lasted until Denham's death in 1669, when he appointed Berkenhead and William Ashburnham, 'my faithfull friends', as overseers of his will.[5] Berkenhead would almost certainly have had that access to 'the Author's owne papers' which the editor claims. Altogether this edition of *Cooper's Hill* can reasonably be regarded as another item in Berkenhead's association with Moseley.

Between this and 1659, when the press temporarily regained its freedom, Berkenhead published nothing. These four years have always seemed a blank in Berkenhead's life, apart from his

---

[1] For a notice of this and earlier editions of *Cooper's Hill* see Madan, no. 1570. The 'Preface' is reprinted by J. C. Reed in his article 'Humphrey Moseley, Publisher', *Oxford Bibl. Soc., Proceedings and Papers*, ii, Pt. II (1929), 111.

[2] Cf. the remark in the *Zootomia* Preface cited above, p. 191.

[3] Item 90 (*Harl. Misc.* ix. 413).

[4] The phrases used there are 'made false transcripts', 'crept to the press', and 'mangled and reformed' (*Harl. Misc.* v. 98).

[5] *Wills from Doctors Commons, 1495–1695*, ed. J. G. Nichols and John Bruce (Camden Soc., lxxxiii (1863), pp. 122–3.

incorporation at Cambridge University on 8 July 1657.[1] His sponsors are unknown: his friends Davies of Kidwelly, Taylor, and
Stanley were all Cambridge men, and Stanley could have been
returning the compliment of 1640. There may, however, be a clue
in a later encounter with the Cambridge philosopher Henry More.
In 1671 More attended the installation of the Duke of Buckingham
as Chancellor of Cambridge University. After the ceremony he
fell into conversation with Berkenhead, who praised to the skies
the Vice-Chancellor's oration. More, who agreed, subsequently
recommended the speech to his friends on Berkenhead's authority,
only to find when he met the latter a day or two later at Charing
Cross that he had changed his mind. Berkenhead kept him 'at
least half an hour drawling' and heartily abused the speech. More,
despite this, continued to rate it highly for having initially won
the approbation of 'so peevish a critick' as Berkenhead was known
to be.[2] Obviously he was an exacting, opinionated man, and this
seems to be the sort of behaviour behind Aubrey's judgement that
he would 'lye damnabley'.[3] He was clearly not above shifts and
intrigues, however unflinching in large loyalties. The 1671 exchange, anyhow, was probably not the first of the two men's
acquaintance: early in June 1656 Viscount Conway, husband of
More's great friend, Anne Conway, was arrested by the Dutch at
Ostend while on his way to join his wife in Paris. On 7 August
Anne's uncle, Francis Finch the elder (one of Orinda's 'circle')
petitioned the Council of State requesting that a messenger be
allowed to travel to Ostend to solicit Conway's release. A pass was
immediately granted for a man to go to Flanders, dispatch the
business, and return to England. The messenger, whose mission
was successful, was 'John Birkhead'[4]—a common alternative
form of Berkenhead or Birkenhead. He appears abroad again

---

[1] Only the year is given in Venn's *Alumni Cantabrigienses* (1922), i. 157; and I am
grateful to Miss H. E. Peek, Keeper of the Archives at Cambridge University, for
informing me of the precise date given in *Liber Gratiarum H, 1645–1668* (MSS.
Univ. Cantab. Arch.), p. 159. The identity of Berkenhead's sponsors is, unfortunately, not known.

[2] See his letter to Anne Conway in the *Conway Letters*, ed. M. H. Nicolson (New
York, 1930), pp. 335–6.   [3] *Brief Lives*, i. 105.

[4] The episode is described by M. H. Nicolson in the *Conway Letters*, pp. 118 and
147 n.

in 1658, carrying gifts from the Duke of Florence to Anne Conway.[1]

His known association with Finch, together with the later familiarity with More, suggest that the journalist was the man in question. He was certainly accustomed to foreign travel and may even have been known to the authorities at Ostend through previous excursions; and his powers of persuasion—to say nothing of his guile—fitted him for the delicate task. Once again it is chance evidence from the 1670s that clinches the identification. In 1676 Berkenhead instituted proceedings to establish his possession of some seven acres of land, known as Fickett's Fields, near Lincoln's Inn in London. In his Bill of Complaint to the Attorney General[2] he states that the property was sold on 3 May 1657 to Francis Finch the younger (Anne Conway's stepbrother) in trust for himself. His claim to the land had been disputed in October 1659 when he decided to build on it; and because of his known loyalty he had been unable at that time to fight the case. Risk to liberty, life, and property had, he claims, made him hold his peace, and cost him several thousand pounds in lost profit. Despite his efforts the case dragged on after his death, and its outcome is of no consequence here. But Berkenhead was indisputably very close to the Finch family: unless he had somehow accumulated enough money to finance the initial purchase it looks as if Francis the younger was a truly generous patron. Maybe the land and the incorporation were rewards for his good offices of 1656. Undoubtedly all this lays the ghost of a poor Berkenhead weathering out the Interregnum in hardship and hard work. Even his own boast about living in danger may be exaggerated: one can hardly believe that changing his name to Birkhead was enough to conceal his identity from Cromwell's very efficient secret service. More likely he was by 1656 considered harmless. His apparent non-involvement in the Royalist plots of the late 1650s suggests that he had by then decided on discretion and patience.

So he was far from destitute when the Restoration came to carry him to office; and it is particularly interesting to see that patronage

[1] *Conway Letters*, p. 147.
[2] P.R.O. (Chancery Proceedings), C6/62/13.

could be instrumental in ensuring the survival and continued loyalty of chosen Cavaliers. The system of aristocratic clienteles did not, it seems, collapse utterly during the Interregnum: some men whose abilities and services were valued could still seek its protection. Berkenhead's attachment to a moneyed family of prosperous lawyers certainly paid off in terms of property and power. For after the Restoration, though he apparently had never attended the Inns of Court, he swiftly obtained a D.C.L. from Oxford and was appointed to posts involving him in legal work.

Before embarking on events which swept the monarchy back, it is well to pause and reflect briefly on the decade drawing to a close. It brought to the Cavaliers profoundly disturbing experiences; and the altered circumstances left their mark on the quantity and character of Berkenhead's work. As pamphleteer he became more emphatically popular in his approach; as versifier and editor he was more busy and more in the van of fashion than has been recognized. Above all, his career in these ten years exposes the falsity of thinking that the Cavalier spirit was universally depressed. Berkenhead was outspoken among those who retained their self-respect and sense of community and purpose. In the name of that community he boldly denounced, at every opportunity, the corruptness of the new rulers and the cowardice of faint-hearts who abandoned their principles. Whatever one may think of his political views, there is no doubting their strength and sincerity. It was the deep commitment and resilience of such men that enabled hard-core Royalism to sustain so remarkably its traditional interests and attitudes. For all his necessary circumspection after 1655—and he did set about reorganizing his life with astute practicality—Berkenhead remained true to his Laudian convictions. We see in him how the diehards of that party, far from accepting defeat, closed their ranks, and at the Restoration were in a condition to emerge triumphant and shape the course of the Settlement.[1]

[1] See R. S. Bosher, *The Making of the Restoration Settlement, 1649–1662* (1951).

CHAPTER VII

1659 to 1679

'Commented upon by Sir Jo. Berkenhead'

BERKENHEAD had settled down to find what felicity he could and was managing quite nicely when events took a sudden turn in 1658. On 3 September Cromwell died and was succeeded as Protector by his son Richard. He soon earned his nickname of 'Tumble-down Dick' when the fabric of his father's Republic crumbled about his ears. All around him dissatisfaction, held in check by Oliver's masterful hand, began to erupt. Royalists and others roused themselves with alacrity to hound their doomed enemy, and pamphleteers snapped hungrily at his heels.

Writers and printers enjoyed a field-day, better than anything they had experienced before or were to know for many years to come. And in the joyous pack of propagandists Berkenhead gave tongue as loud as any. His place in the van of the rush to agitate confusion and discontent is not established by pamphlets already known to be his, but it is substantiated by fresh attributions suggested here. The outburst of 1659 and 1660, a relief of pent-up pressures, not unnaturally caught up the themes and moods of ten years before: men who had smarted under prohibitions hastened to pay off old scores. Looking back it may seem that pamphleteers blew the Republic flat in a gale of laughter; but in reality its collapse was, for some time, not inevitable. The rather wild way in which Berkenhead hit out at first suggests that indiscriminate revenge rather than a defined political objective was Royalist propaganda's initial purpose. Any target, regardless of its importance, was smothered in rhetorical grape-shot. But in early 1660 Berkenhead's mood changed: his propaganda grew more purposeful and precisely directed as the return of the monarchy became increasingly likely. For now public opinion and events had to be carefully moved in the right direction. By reminding Londoners generally and Presbyterians in particular of specific grievances he, like many others, tried to push them into calling for the King once more.

The combination of Monke's troops and indecision among staunch Republicans with propaganda against the Rump Parliament from many quarters produced the longed-for outcome. Charles II came into his own again, and Berkenhead entered on the most prosperous phase of his life. His career between 1660 and 1663 was, indeed, a personal restoration to something like his position in Oxford from 1643 to 1646: working closely with the Secretary of State, Sir Edward Nicholas, he took control of the official newsbook and acted as Licenser to the press. After 1663 circumstances virtually put an end to his career in propaganda; but as office-holder, Member of Parliament, and man of affairs (he obtained a knighthood and was elected Fellow of the Royal Society) he continued to advocate the views for which his name had become something of a byword. He was one of the ultra-Royalist administrators and legislators who worked hard to make the Restoration as conservative as possible. His rapid promotion, in fact, was symptomatic of the spirit in which the re-established Court was to deal with its major problem, the treatment of Dissenters. For, as the policy of his newsbook shows, he worked for the fulfilment of policies Laud might have approved, doing everything in his power to discredit and block schemes for toleration. He was, in short, prominent among those who carried into the 1660s and 1670s the attitudes of 1641. This process had a major influence on the course of political debate and of satire in the second half of the seventeenth century. The 'Conservative mythology', with its stock of shared consciousness and standard terms and devices on which a writer could draw was among the most treasured inheritances of the restored Court.

Berkenhead's first publication after four years' silence, *The Last Words of Thomas Lord Pride*, appeared in January 1659.[1] It was

---

[1] The date 'January: 1658' is written on Wood's copy in the Bodleian Library, Wood 609 (44). This can only mean 1659 (in 'old style' reckoning the year began on 25 Mar.).

another of those pieces that Tory propagandists still found worth printing in the 1680s.[1] Aubrey observed that Berkenhead wrote a satire on Colonel Pride;[2] internal evidence suggests that this is it. Some points of his attack on the Colonel in *Paul's Church-Yard* are taken up here in a suggestive way. The earlier statement that 'Col. Pride (alias Bride) was Founder of St. Bride's Church, and not found in the Porch, because the Porch was built before the Church; that is, not behind it'[3] is paralleled by this later complaint —'How have they dragged my poor name, and set me back from P. to B. to make me born in Bride's church-porch?'[4] Similarly, Pride recalls *The Four Legg'd Elder* when he remarks 'how Swash, the abominable mastive took a dispensation with an elders maid'.[5] Oblique resemblances like this, coinciding with Aubrey's statement, make it safe to conclude that this is Berkenhead's work.

Colonel Pride, notorious for his 1648 Purge of Parliament, subsequently distinguished himself as High Sheriff of Surrey by closing the bear-garden in 1656. Later he was made a peer; but he took little active part in politics up to his death on 23 October 1658.[6] The pamphlet, therefore, is not closely related to any recent event. It is a conglomeration of all the old Royalist jokes about the Colonel, worked up into a narrative and embellished with scathing remarks on a variety of topics, among them the Major-Generals' rule, the wars in the Indies, the Danish threat, the army generally and the new peerage. In raking over old grievances the writer even harks back to the treatment of Strafford and Laud; and, eager to belittle all the Rebels' achievements, he dismissively attributes their victories of Marston Moor and Naseby to luck and Royalist faintheartedness.[7] The pamphlet's whole aim is the general one of boosting morale ready for some hoped-for crisis.

There is one significant omission: Pride's Purge is not mentioned; and Berkenhead slightingly makes the 'great action'[8] of Pride's life the killing of the bears, which he ironically equates

---

[1] It was reprinted in 1680 under the title *The Last Speech and Dying-Words of Thomas (Lord, alias Colonel) Pride*.

[2] *Brief Lives*, i. 105.   [3] Item 5 (*Harl. Misc.* ix. 409).

[4] See the reprint of the 1680 edition in *Harl. Misc.* iii. 139.

[5] *The Last Words*, p. 136.   [6] See the 'Life' in the *D.N.B.*

[7] *The Last Words*, pp. 137–8.   [8] Ibid., p. 140.

with slaying 'the best Cavalier among them all'.[1] Berkenhead,
recalling the 1640s with some bitterness, was out to represent
Pride (and the Protectorate) as altogether brutal and thuggish; but
for all the implicit resentment, the tone of the piece is strongly
farcical: Pride was certainly not as ineffectual and muddled as he
appears here.

The Colonel is made out to be another thorough-paced philis-
tine, a Grobian rampant. Pembroke, in the 'travesties' which this
pamphlet naturally brings to mind, was a buffoon whose logic was
cynically perverse: Pride appears as a mundane self-seeker lacking
even the affectation of principles. His is the money-ethic of
the small-time tradesman, who reckons that running a nation is
the same as running a business.[2] He rejects anything outside the
narrow scope of his utilitarian ethic, scorning Greek and Latin
because they cannot make a man honest, and jeering at spelling
because 'a man may speak true without true spelling'.[3] He is a
deliberate rule-breaker, making his ignorance a virtue, the seventeenth century's 'plain, blunt man and proud of it' whose stunted
notion of human behaviour and capacities shows itself in his absurd dislocation of language. His rambling and inconsequential
speech comically enacts the disorder and displacement of his
personality. Were he a writer one could happily name him one of
MacFlecknoe's dynasty.

In this miniature comedy of manners Berkenhead's norm is that
of gentlemanly conduct; and his burden is not so much the political
villainy as the social and intellectual ineptitude of Republicanism.
Matters political are reflected on, of course, but the emphasis falls
principally on simpler things. As Pride had been for so long politically unimportant this was very proper; and it served the purpose
of much satire at this time, which was to enlist broad sympathies
against the Republic. *The Last Words* in fact verges on pure slap-
stick, and its most obvious defect is that the writer attempted to
squeeze too many jokes in. He is clearly not disciplined by the need
to address himself to precise political problems. But his implicit
recognition that the choices to be made were not merely theoretical
but involved basic questions of human conduct was most pertinent.

---

[1] *The Last Words*, p. 138.   [2] Ibid.   [3] Ibid., p. 139.

For it was as much the inhumanity of executing Charles I (which Berkenhead forcibly underlines) as any theoretical constitutional considerations that eventually led men to welcome back the monarchy.

Berkenhead's highlighting of past errors carries with it the implication that reparation is necessary and possible, and that there is a way out of the mess. Indeed, the appealing vitality and bubbling inventiveness of *The Last Words* suggest the relief that Royalists experienced in 1659, in common with many who were far from subscribing to all the articles of their faith. A sense of release from an exacting and thorough-going regime was in the air, and Berkenhead tried to foster this by representing the Protectorate as a barbarous, ignorant, laughable tyranny.

Queries, both mock and serious, were now flying thick and fast; and he had written a number of sarcastic questions into *The Last Words*.[1] He followed this up by republishing the first two 'centuries' of *Paul's Church-Yard* on 9 July 1659. He again reverted to the tactics of the late 1640s in his ballad, *The Four-Legg'd Quaker. To the Tune of the Dog and Elder's Maid.* This appeared as a broadside some time in 1659,[2] presumably before November when it was included in a collection of ballads.[3] It subsequently figured in two other collections of Rump songs and was reprinted in Tory anthologies in 1682 and 1731.[4] Like his 1647 ballad, it also found its way into a cartoon of the 1680s.[5] Wood's attribution to Berkenhead is supported by an offended contemporary writing in 1666,[6]

---

[1] pp. 140–1.

[2] The broadside is dated 1664 in Wing, *Short-Title Catalogue . . . 1641–1700* (New York, 1945–51). But this appears to be based on a misinterpretation of a remark written by Wood on his copy of the ballad, Bodleian Library, Wood 416 (70). 1659 is the year assigned to it by Wood in *Ath. Oxon.* iii. 1205.

[3] This was *Ratts Rhimed to Death*, of which Thomason received his copy, E. 1761(2), in November. This version, like the broadside, omits one stanza found in the later editions.

[4] For details of the reprints see the Bibliography. See also App. VI for the possibility that Berkenhead edited one of the volumes of Rump songs.

[5] M. D. George, *English Political Caricature to 1792* (1959), Plate 14.

[6] For the Wood reference see n. 2 above. The attack on Berkenhead took the form of a ballad *Answer* to two ballads written by the latter in 1666. There are copies in the Bodleian Library: MS. Don. b. 8., pp. 344–5, MS. Firth c. 18., ff. 4–5, and Wood 416 (112). The latter ascribed the *Answer* to one 'Porter' but according to a copy in the British Museum, MS. Add. 18220, f. 27ᵛ, it was Doctor Robert Wilde, the Presbyterian, who wrote it.

by the title itself, and by the resemblance of the first line to that of
Berkenhead's poem to Lawes.[1]

It is a typical Cavalier ballad of the coarse kind; but for all its
popularity[2] it is inferior to the 1647 model. The obvious and
vulgar ribaldry is a natural corollary of the extravagant assumption
that Quakers were promiscuous and politically menacing. They
did not really threaten to overwhelm Presbyterians and Independents, as Berkenhead asserts; but the chance to make scandal and
spread alarm was too good to miss at a critical juncture in affairs.
Nor was it objectionable to Berkenhead to have to do this: his
subsequent Parliamentary utterances reveal the rooted, almost
compulsive fear of conventicles which Laud had grounded him in.

Later in 1659 appeared a pamphlet—*The Exaltation of Christmas
Pye*—burlesquing the Nonconformist preacher. Its special aim
was to discredit Puritan antipathy towards religious festivals,
notably Christmas; so it may have been published about then. It
certainly post-dates the ballad, which is recalled by the comparison
'as when an Elders maid lyes with a Mastiff or as when a Quaker
buggereth a Mare'.[3] This raises the possibility of a link with
Berkenhead, which is strengthened by a number of parallels in his
earlier works. The sermon's text, 'And they did eat their Plum-
pies and rejoyced exceedingly',[4] focuses the anti-Christmas
theme, as had Berkenhead's recently republished query 'Whether
Master Peters did justly preach against Christmas-Pyes the same
day he eat two Mince-pyes to his dinner?'[5] When the preacher
gets down to his task he handles his text in the manner of *The
Assembly Man*, who butchered it 'into many dead parts, breaking
the sense and words all to pieces'.[6] And when he wanders from his
point he pulls himself up: 'Truly I had almost forgotten my text,

---

[1] The first line of the ballad is 'All that have two or but one Eare'; that of the
Lawes poem is 'All you that have, or ought to have, no Ears'.

[2] It is singled out as typical of Cavalier ballads in *Bloody News from Chelmsford*
(1660), reprinted in the *Bagford Ballads*, ed. J. W. Ebsworth, (1876–8), ii. 736.

[3] p. 4. There has not been a modern reprint, and references are to the first
edition of 1659. It is rare, but there is a copy in the Bodleian Library, Wood 613 (13).
It was reprinted in 1728, but copies of that edition appear to be just as scarce. The
latter is in any case a shortened and emended version of the text.

[4] p. 3.   [5] *Paul's Church-Yard*, item 175 (*Harl. Misc.* ix. 417).
[6] *Harl. Misc.* v. 102.

but my beloved 'tis the same thing; for so a man keep talking, you know, 'tis no great matter what he talks of.'[1] This recalls Berkenhead's observation on *The Assembly Man*, that 'it is easier to make stones speak, than him to hold his peace' for 'his invention consists in finding a way to speak nothing upon any thing'.[2] Last and best, the 1647 'character' described the preacher in action: 'when he first enters his prayer before sermon, he winks and gasps, and gasps and winks as if he prepared to preach in another world'.[3] In *The Exaltation* the homilist pictures St. James of Compostela 'at prayers, gasping and winking, as our brother Case used to doe'.[4] Such coincidences of conception and phrasing, though not conclusive, point quite strongly to Berkenhead as the author.

The Exaltation may have been directed against Hugh Peter himself, whose attack on 'Christmas-Pyes' had already inspired the accusation that he was guilty of a hypocrisy exactly like that the sermon portrays. The preacher's verbal facility, too, touches a feature of Peter's pulpit manner often acknowledged. He was certainly one of Berkenhead's *bêtes noires*, attacked by him in *Aulicus*, *The Assembly Man*, and the official newsbook of 1660.[5] *The Exaltation* reopened other old scores by jeering at Henderson, Colonel Pride, and Sir William Brereton.[6] The last was currently featured in Royalist propaganda as a notorious glutton, and here fleshes out the comic image of Grobian Gluttony. The writer aims at no specific event, endeavouring through parody to substantiate the broad notion that grossness and hypocrisy typify the Nonconformist Republican.

The sermon opens with a suggestive analysis of the grammatical 'Conjunction Copulative'—an old joke; but it is the Dissenter's appetite for food, not his licentiousness, that is dwelt on. The 'congregation' is treated to a lengthy, lip-smacking harangue on the origin, nature, variety, virtue, composition, and ways of eating plum-pies. The preacher is an unashamed gourmand, scandalized by brethren who 'had persecuted these pyes so furiously in their

---

[1] p. 4.
[2] p. 103.
[3] p. 101.
[4] p. 9.
[5] See below, p. 216.
[6] The preacher's text is attributed to 'Brewerton'. For Berkenhead's earlier skirmishes with Sir William see above, p. 104.

pulpits: for can they undergo a worse persecution then to be eaten'?[1] The laws of appetite are his criteria, and he defends them to his own obvious satisfaction. His god is his belly, and his smattering of learning—he cites Lipsius, Cicero, and various theologians—is paraded in Pecksniffian defence of self-indulgence. The full-flavoured language and the sometimes hilarious formal analysis of the text both make mock of the current Nonconformist pulpit technique, and make this in some respects the most success- ful burlesque with which Berkenhead's name can be associated. It is shrewdly observant and neatly constructed, and the pedantic preacher, full of cant and mannerisms, is a type that has survived the passage of time. Following the continuing trend of 1659 towards social comedy, this appeals sympathetically to the natural human inclination to mock professional piety.

As a squib lobbed into the mêlée, *The Exaltation* was wisely projected: at the close of 1659 there was no knowing what form of government would emerge from the threatening conflagration; and for men like Berkenhead the most important thing was to see that questions, doubts, disagreements, and grievances were kept smouldering. The last thing they wanted was public calm or inertia. This may explain why Berkenhead attended the meetings of James Harrington's 'Rota' in November and December of that year.[2] Harrington's proposed solution to the crisis, a Republic on a moderate aristocratic basis, was embodied in his book, *The Rota*, published in early January 1660. His ideas had been discussed and hammered out, however, at the previous meetings of his 'club' of wits, who continued to foregather at the Turk's Head in New Palace Yard until the end of the third week in February 1660. Not all who attended were members of the inner circle, or necessa- rily enthusiastic about Harrington's plans. Every night listeners crowded into the upstairs room simply to enjoy the excellent con- versation, and Berkenhead was among these. It is hard to imagine that he liked all he heard: among the participants was William Petty, mathematician and inventor, whom he had derided in the

---

[1] p. 6.
[2] For facts about the 'Rota' generally see the 'Life' of Harrington in the *D.N.B.* Aubrey, *Brief Lives*, i. 290 is the authority for Berkenhead's attendance.

past;[1] and Berkenhead's antagonism towards Hobbes's ideas[2] suggests that Harrington's Hobbesian principles and proposals would not have won his approval. One can safely assume that his presence at the 'club' was not a gesture of sympathy for progressive thinking. He was, more likely, interested in anything that kept questions of government open. Or perhaps he was simply being circumspect, keeping in with a group who might emerge with some sort of power or influence. Or yet again, he may have attended the meetings to keep his ear to the ground and report back to the Royalist leaders abroad, for there is some suspicion that he was once more acting as an agent for Nicholas. His name occurs in several of the cyphers used by the Secretary of State after 1646: many of these are unfortunately undated,[3] but it is possible that Berkenhead was the writer of an interesting series of intelligence letters sent to Nicholas from England in 1659 and early 1660.[4] This is very speculative and must be regarded with the utmost caution, but his swift promotion at the Restoration and close association then with Nicholas suggests that he had kept in the Secretary's sight in the late 1650s.

Anyhow, the anonymous correspondent made one statement very relevant to the activities of propagandists like Berkenhead. He assured Nicholas that if people attended to unlicensed pamphlets pouring from the presses they would inevitably see the light;[5] but he observed anxiously that the Londoners seemed to have no stomach for throwing off an irksome tyranny.[6] To arouse that spirit and spur the City into action was Berkenhead's endeavour in his next pamphlet, *The Apology of Robert Tichborn and John Ireton*, published about 12 March 1660.[7] This was a 'travesty' much like the Pride pamphlet, repeating and developing themes first mooted some years before. The attribution to Berkenhead

---

[1] He sneered at him as an empiric in 1648, when Parliament granted him a patent for a method of double-writing: see *M. Bell.*, no. 8 (14–21 Mar.), H2^v–H3^r.

[2] See below, p. 211.

[3] The cyphers are in the B.M., MS. Egerton 2550; Berkenhead's name occurs on ff. 9^v, 30^v, 53^r, and 63^r.

[4] See App. VII.

[5] *Nicholas Papers*, vol. iv, 1657–1660, p. 152.

[6] Ibid., p. 123.

[7] This is the date on which Thomason received his copy, E. 1017 (3).

depends on general and specific resemblances to other works of his.

It shares with *Bibliotheca Parliamenti* a commonplace joke about Tichbourne's book of 1649, *A Cluster of Canaans Grapes*;[1] but more striking is Tichbourne's recalling the time when 'because I had not so much money then, as I have now, I even contented my self with my Lord of Pembrokes old Cloaths . . .' and became a 'living Monument' to the dead Earl.[2] For this appears to adapt the idea and wording of another of Berkenhead's mock book titles, '*Post-huma Pembrochiana.* The late Earl of Pembroke's old cloaths worn by Alderman Titchbourn: first, because he bought them; secondly, because they fit him'.[3] Tichbourne's words, moreover, seem to fuse with this a memory of Pembroke's bequest in the mock testament Berkenhead drew up: 'My will is, that I have no monument, for then I must have epitaphs and verses; but all my life long I have had too much of them'.[4] There are sufficient grounds for suspecting that Berkenhead wrote *The Apology.*

It shows, however, one important change from the Pride pamphlet: it deals with two living men and aims specifically to turn London opinion against them. John Ireton, brother of Cromwell's close colleague Henry Ireton, was elected Lord Mayor in 1658. His origins, like Tichbourne's, were humble; but his rise was less spectacular. For Tichbourne, who had sat in judgement on the King in 1649 and been Lord Mayor during the Protectorate, was elected to the House of Lords in 1657 and nominated as one of the twenty-one conservators of liberty appointed by the army to save the Republic in December 1659. Both were regarded as pillars of the Good Old Cause in the City, and as such were well-chosen targets at this precarious moment.[5]

The pamphlet rightly concentrates on Tichbourne, underlining his extreme political and religious attitudes and accusing him of feathering his nest during the Interregnum. The absence of any

---

[1] p. 5 and second 'Classis', 'Books', item 9 (*S. Tracts*, vii. 93) respectively.
[2] p. 5.
[3] *Two Centuries*, item 107 (*Harl. Misc.* ix. 414).
[4] *The Last Will and Testament*, in the *S. Tracts*, vii. 90. Such adaptations can be more persuasive than verbatim parallels.
[5] See the 'Lives' in the *D.N.B.*

reference to his regicidal role is intriguing: the writer evidently decided that this was no moment for Royalists to demand revenge for that. Instead he emphasizes what was offensive to London Presbyterians, making Tichbourne flaunt his Independency and boast of his service as a spy who foisted Cromwell's designs on the City and snooped on his 'Fellow Gown-men'.[1] His motive, he unrepentantly confesses, was money; he put his debt to Cromwell before his duties to the Citizens, at whose Charter he openly jeers.[2]

Barefaced effrontery is his essence: his self-righteousness is monumental and, even after reciting past misdeeds, he remains convinced that reasonable men will be satisfied of his innocence. For his 'reason' is self-interest, and his morality the cynicism of the petty crook of politics. The time-server whose life of deception has issued in the grossest self-deceit is convincingly and amusingly caricatured in this *Apology* which is no apology. It is only towards the end, when Tichbourne asserts that all but those 'as unreasonable as ourselves' will forgive him, and prophesies his own death on the scaffold,[3] that the writer's control of the characterization falters. Here he contradicts the premise of his comedy, which is that Tichbourne has utterly confounded folly and reason. Self-knowledge is the last thing such a figure should be permitted. The propagandist in a hurry has succumbed to the temptation to 'overkill'. He would, doubtless, have happily borne with the fault when on 20 April 1660 events fell out as he wished, and a warrant was issued for Tichbourne's arrest.

The pressure of political expediency was not, however, always or simply an impediment. The pamphlet demonstrates how close address to particular men and situations also inspired careful registration of idiosyncracies of speech. The same concentration shows itself in the selection of material: little is made, for instance, of Tichbourne's humble origins, because to emphasize that was not the best way to turn London Presbyterian opinion against him. The boisterous farce of the Pride pamphlet is disciplined here; comedy of manners is tempered by precise political considerations and cuts more dangerously. Tichbourne and Pride, and Berkenhead's other victims, all have some things in common, however. All of

[1] pp. 6–7.   [2] p. 7.   [3] p. 8.

them talk, to use Bergson's terminology,[1] like men in a dream; they are all in the grip of obsessions and betray the professional callousness of men dwelling in small enclosed societies, floating on the surface of society proper, so that we see in them a divisive fragmentation of man's social experience and personality. This, *pace* Bergson, is not necessarily comic, however;[2] it becomes so because the victims themselves mistake their apartness for integration, and confound their dream with reality. Division, both from one's fellow men and, more importantly, against oneself is at the heart of this sort of comedy at least; and it is no accident that an era when English society was so deeply and openly divided against itself produced so much of this laughter.

To the Cavaliers, the Rebel is the type of low-born foolish man on the make, ambitious and avaricious, and altogether distorted by the pressures of the expansionist and divisive forces he embodies— forces often remarked on subsequently as characteristic of modern capitalist society.[3] For all its manifest partisanship Cavalier satire was no mere trifling with social or political etiquette, but an expression of a major anxiety of the middle seventeenth century. It was a reflex in which, whatever the immediate rights and wrongs of the argument, a deep sense of coherence and continuity confronts the anarchic and disruptive. It is the general rightness of opposing coherence to incoherence and meaningfulness to Babylonish jargons, and not the local accuracy of criticisms made, that our instinctive laughter acknowledges.

Each victim's self-contained (and self-taught) system of speech establishes his isolation, his failure to make meaningful contact with the normal community. He is apart, trapped in a sterile and repetitive routine of living by rote. That, perhaps is the chief significance of the recurrent motifs of Cavalier satire. They indicate not lazy duplication but an instinct for what is essentially comic.

---

[1] See his essay, *Laughter* (1900), translated by C. Brereton and F. Rothwell, 1935.

[2] It is at this point that his account of the mechanism of comedy seems rather oversimplified.

[3] D. Bush, *English Literature in the Earlier Seventeenth Century* (Oxford, 1962 (1945)), detects in Puritan debates about education 'the gritty voice of Mr. Gradgrind and his numerous modern descendants'. The allusion to Dickens' tragi-comic characterization is apposite: the Cavaliers, too, heard the voice of utilitarianism and, according to their capacities, responded to it in a not wholly dissimilar way.

Rebel egomania is presented as a denial of that sense of knowing oneself and belonging to one's place in society which Royalists felt so strongly (and the question of their motives for doing so are another matter of no immediate relevance). Cavalier comedy, like Cavalier neo-classicism, is fundamentally a preoccupation with being properly related to other members of a community in which an ordered hierarchy of traditional *mores* and institutions can express and preserve shared values.

Berkenhead had a good reporter's eye for detail, an ear for gossip, and a more than ordinary talent for mimicry; and his satire benefited from his closeness to the centre of contemporary experience. His is a notable contribution to this comedy of the abnormal which, in the propaganda of 1659 and 1660, exultantly gathered up the mockery of some twenty years and ushered the Republicans and radicals out of their places.

He was rewarded shortly after Charles II's return in May 1660. On 17 August he was restored to his Oxford Fellowship;[1] but academic life had never been for him more than a means to an end, and he resigned from All Souls in the next year.[2] He may have tendered his resignation around the time he received an honorary D.C.L. from the University on the King's recommendation—on 6 April 1661.[3] Meanwhile, he landed the sort of official appointment he had always coveted: on 2 November 1660 he was granted Letters Patent by the Archbishop of Canterbury to act as Master of the Faculties.[4] The Master was responsible for appointing public notaries, granting dispensations for Pluralities, Commendams, and ordination of men under age or of illegitimate birth, and for dispensing Marriage Licences and Lambeth Degrees.[5] It was largely routine work and not especially arduous; but it was an apt post for one who had worked under Laud, and it carried some useful fees.

[1] *The Restoration Visitation of the University of Oxford* (Camden Soc., 3rd Ser. lxxix (1948), no. 3, p. 33.
[2] *Catalogue of the Archives . . . of All Souls College* (1877), p. 381.
[3] Congregation Register, 1659–1669, MS. Univ. Oxon. Arch. Q.b. 18, f. 181ʳ. Wood (*Fasti Oxon.* ii. 254) states that the King took a hand in this.
[4] *Ath. Oxon.* iii. 1204 n.
[5] The duties of this office are explained in the typescript 'Guide to the Records of the Faculty Office', drawn up by M. B. Parkes in 1958. There is a copy of this in the Bodleian Library, R. 14. 407 e/i.

The honorary D.C.L. was presumably bestowed to fit him formally for the office.

On 29 October 1660, four days before he became Master of the Faculties, Berkenhead took up another more important task. That day he began a three-year stint as press Licenser by passing for publication an account of the trial of twenty-nine regicides, written by Heneage Finch, the Solicitor-General. Berkenhead's name last appears in the *Stationers' Register* on 24 October 1663. In those three years he vetted a number of periodicals and popular books, among them Butler's *Hudibras* and his own piece, *The Assembly Man*.[1] After October 1663, his duties were taken over by Roger L'Estrange, who had by then fought his way to the post of Surveyor of the press.[2]

Berkenhead's appointment as Licenser was a first step taken by the restored Court to control the press. Its measures culminated in the Printing Act, passed on 14 August 1662; this was makeshift legislation, little more than a repetition of the Star Chamber decree of 1637.[3] It aimed at controlling the press through the Stationers' Company monopoly and the old system of licensing. Unfortunately, though Berkenhead insisted that he could maintain efficient censorship by these means,[4] illicit publications still appeared in fair numbers. L'Estrange, therefore, launched a vigorous campaign to have power taken from the Stationers' Company and vested in his own hands. The absorbing struggle for power between Berkenhead and L'Estrange will be scrutinized shortly; for now, suffice it to remark that it was really part of a battle being waged between two more exalted courtiers, Sir Edward Nicholas and Henry Benet, later Lord Arlington. Besides the privilege of licensing, it involved the valuable control of the official newsbook. The fact that Berkenhead relinquished the latter and appears to have ceased licensing in 1663 seems to suggest that

---

[1] See the *Stationers' Register, 1640–1708*, printed in three volumes (1913–14). Berkenhead licensed *Hudibras* on 11 Nov. 1662, and his own *The Assembly Man* on 10 Feb. 1663.

[2] J. G. Muddiman, *The King's Journalist, 1659–1689* (1923), p. 151.

[3] Ibid. p. 149.

[4] See his letter dated 6 Jan. 1662, to Joseph Williamson, Secretary to Sir Henry Benet (P.R.O., S.P. 29/49/19). This is summarized in *C.S.P. Dom.*, 1661–2, p. 237, but the point is not there clear.

L'Estrange overcame him. In fact, the next Act for Printing in 1665 was little more than a renewal of the 1662 measure and a victory for the methods of Berkenhead as Chairman of the Committee that framed it.[1] He was apparently still Chairman of the 'Committee for the Printers' in January 1667, when he is recorded attempting to present its report to the Commons.[2] The survival of the Star Chamber decree as the basis of regulating publications, and the fact that cynicism and suspicion, rather than open rigour, remained the order of the day in press supervision was, in some measure, due to Berkenhead's determined adherence to methods he had learnt as a young man.

Moreover, though Berkenhead's name does not appear in the *Stationers' Register* after 1663, he retained some power of censorship into the 1670s, probably by virtue of his position as Master of the Faculties, on the analogy of the old jurisdiction of Star Chamber.[3] Anyhow, in 1670, much to Thomas Hobbes's annoyance, he refused to license the philosopher's letter concerning Daniel Scargill's recantation of a Hobbist sermon preached at Cambridge in 1669. Berkenhead's motive for refusal was, according to Aubrey, that he wished 'to collogue and flatter the bishops'.[4] With typical high-handedness he declined to return Hobbes's original manuscript and even refused him a copy of it.[5] In 1672 Berkenhead was still busy with books; Walter Slingsby, wishing to publish his brother's narrative of Stafford's trial, submitted it to the scrutiny of 'three special persons both for friendship and judgement . . .'.[6] They were Sir Charles Scarborough, Roger L'Estrange, and Sir John Berkenhead. In the same year Andrew Marvell referred sarcastically to L'Estrange and Berkenhead as 'the publick-tooth drawers' of the press.[7] The latter had by no means relinquished

---

[1] Thomas Hearne, *Collections*, vol. iii (1710–12) (Oxford Hist. Soc., xiii, 1888), p. 214, and C. H. Timperley, *Encyclopaedia of Literary and Typographical Anecdotes* (1842), p. 145.

[2] *Diary of John Milward*, ed. Caroline Robbins (Cambridge, 1938), p. 70.

[3] J. B. Williams, *A History of English Journalism*, p. 181, suggests this.

[4] *Brief Lives*, i. 360–2. The quotation is from p. 361. Wood also records this episode (*Ath. Oxon.* iii. 1215). For Scargill see the 'Life' in the *D.N.B.*

[5] Loc. cit., *Brief Lives*.   [6] H.M.C., *6th Report*, p. 340 *a*.

[7] *The Rehearsal Transpros'd* (1672–3), in the *Complete Works*, ed. A. B. Grosart (1872–5), iii. 8. Marvell simply refers to 'B.' and 'L.' but there is little doubt whom he meant.

all his interest and influence. The extent of his powers in these affairs has previously been underestimated: as legislator and administrator he played a substantial part in directing the fortunes of the English press at an important stage in its development. And if his aims were not exactly enlightened, his methods were less interfering and oppressive than some of those advocated by L'Estrange.

If this involvement with the press was a fulfilment of work begun at Lambeth and Oxford, Berkenhead brought the wheel full circle by acting as supervising editor of the official Court newsbook, which he conducted until the end of August 1663. This actually began its run before the Restoration, in December 1659, under the editorship of Henry Muddiman and Giles Dury, who used it to support General Monke. Two editions a week were published, one on Monday and the other on Thursday—a step made possible by the increase in the number of posts. The editions were entitled, respectively, *The Parliamentary Intelligencer* and *Mercurius Publicus*; each normally contained sixteen pages and cost twopence. The second title was unchanged throughout the run, up to August 1663; *The Parliamentary Intelligencer* became *The Kingdomes Intelligencer* in the first week of 1661 and kept that title to the end. In all, some 190 numbers of each edition were published. At the start they were opposed by several other newsbooks, but in April 1660 Muddiman and Dury were granted a monopoly of news; and from October 1660 their newsbook was wholly unopposed. The fortunes of this periodical, in fact, reflect the fortunes of the Court party.

It is not quite accurate, however, to refer to it as their news book: it was really the responsibility of the Secretary of State and compiled under the supervision of higher officials. According to J. B. Williams, Muddiman and Dury were responsible to Joseph Williamson, Nicholas's Latin secretary,[1] just as Nedham had been formally responsible to Milton during the Protectorate. But in several modern accounts Berkenhead is named as supervisory editor from 1661 to 1663.[2] Williams disputed this, arguing that

---

[1] *A History of English Journalism*, p. 183.

[2] H. R. Fox Bourne, *English Newspapers* (1887), i. 29; David Masson, *Life of John Milton* (1871–94), vi. 325–6; also the *Supplement* to the *British Museum Catalogue of Printed Books*, and George Kitchen, *Sir Roger L'Estrange* (1913), pp. 129–30, n. 4.

Berkenhead only licensed the newsbook.[1] There is, however, a letter from Berkenhead to Nicholas, dated 22 October 1662, which undermines his case: in it Berkenhead writes of the King's displeasure that the newsbook had ignored the appointment of Henry Benet as successor to Nicholas. Fearing that Charles was angry with him, Berkenhead begs permission to rectify the oversight.[2] It is hard to see why the King should blame Berkenhead if he was merely licensing the periodical; and the letter actually makes it quite plain that he was in a real sense editor, by informing Nicholas that friends had defended him to the King on the ground that 'without notice of you I would have no Hint to introduce Sr. H. Benet'. He then dictated a notice for the next number repairing the neglect, and this in turn makes nonsense of Williams's statement that the newsbook contains nothing approaching Berkenhead's style.[3] As he himself referred to Berkenhead's notes to Nicholas, one is forced to conclude that he was determined to represent Muddiman, for whom he had a great partiality,[4] as the driving force in Restoration journalism. In fact, nothing could have been more natural than for Nicholas to pitch on his old ally, the most experienced and successful Cavalier journalist, to assume responsibility for Restoration propaganda.

Contemporaries certainly understood that Berkenhead had resumed his old office. On 8 August 1662 the Privy Council ordered him to 'take care that this Advertisement be printed in the next weekly News Book';[5] and about that time Henry Bold thanked him in verse for printing a list of Presbyterian prisoners in the Gatehouse gaol.[6] The best witness, however, is John Collins, uncle to Monke's secretary, Sir William Clarke. In 1674, apropos of two tracts against Monke published abroad in the 1660s, he wrote that

there was soon after interposed in the London printed weekly intelligence near a full leaf of encomiums . . . which I observing and

[1] 'The Newsbooks and News-Letters of the Restoration', *Eng. Hist. Review*, iii (1908), 259 n. [2] B.M., MS. Egerton 2538, f. 186.
[3] Ibid., f. 189 is the notice. For Williams's remarks see n. 1 above.
[4] J. B. Williams's real name was J. G. Muddiman (see the Bodleian Library Catalogue, pre-1920).
[5] White Kennet, *A Register and Chronicle Ecclesiastical and Civil* (1728), i. 740.
[6] *Latine Songs* (1685), p. 117. The list is in *M. Publ.*, no. 2 (10–17 Jan. 1661), pp. 22–3.

asking Sir John Birkenhead who then wrote or put forth these intelligences about it, he told me that Sir Thomas Clarges brought to him that part ready written.[1]

The phrase 'wrote or put forth' suggests Collins was not sure whether Berkenhead actually penned all or even most of the newsbook's copy. But manifestly he was acting as editor in 1662 when the 'encomiums' appeared.[2]

Oddly, even those who have accepted that Berkenhead edited the Restoration newsbook have only linked his name with *The Kingdomes Intelligencer* from 1661 to 1663. There are two misunderstandings here. First, their distinction between that and *Mercurius Publicus* is purely arbitrary, since the two were compiled from identical materials and printed identical accounts and lists; and by taking one of them the reader could obtain all the official news available. He presumably took the two (they overlapped) if he did not want some of his news to be rather stale. Second, *The Kingdomes Intelligencer* was not a new periodical started in 1661, but simply *The Parliamentary Intelligencer* continued under a new title. As Berkenhead began licensing books in October 1660, he had probably taken full control of propaganda, including the newsbook, by then. In fact, his editorial supervision probably antedates that.

'Editorial supervision' is the definition of his functions to be insisted on: his duties were like those of a modern newspaper editor and rather unlike his work in Oxford. He was responsible for directing policies, and only wrote copy himself on special occasions. In other respects, too, the Restoration periodical differs from *Aulicus*. On the whole, it is little more than a Gazette, listing government appointments, printing Royal Proclamations, and describing official ceremonies, the trials of regicides, and executions. It is also technically inferior to *Aulicus*, being comparatively slapdash about giving dates and often untidy and haphazard in layout. An unpretentious news-sheet would, in fact, have been better suited to the task, but Berkenhead continued to pay lip-service to the tradition of consecutive narrative. He pads this with a deal of foreign intelligence; and there is comparatively little

---

[1] H.M.C., *Leyborne Popham* (1889), p. 231.
[2] *M. Publ.*, no. 5 (30 Jan.–6 Feb. 1662), pp. 65–8.

solid home news in it. Parliamentary Acts and Bills are merely listed; the actual debates are ignored. Most of the items are conveyed in a sort of colourless officialese, very different from *Aulicus*'s smart style. It is largely a typical product of the bureaucratic machine, reassuring the faithful, calming the restless, and denouncing waverers and all who step out of line. The intention is not to inform and entertain, but to buttress a *status quo*. Indeed, its responses are as predictable, because automatic and inflexible, as those which Cavaliers when excluded from power had found so laughable in their usurpers. The gaiety and high spirits which enliven propaganda just before the Restoration are repressed. The dominant mood is subdued and grimly purposeful; and the image offered is that of an administration calmly, efficiently, and tranquilly setting about putting the nation's house in order. Public excitement was the last thing the Court wanted now: it needed to cultivate a calm, a mood of solemn repentance and rededication; and hilarity would have jarred on that as much as *Aulicus*'s jests in the 1640s had grated on Parliament's solemn and anxious resolves.

There are, none the less, exceptions to the general deadness which led, or rather misled, J. B. Williams to conclude that the newsbook's contents are worthless.[1] A racy tone occasionally suggests that Berkenhead was writing or inspiring passages himself; and though government policy is never discussed, he did use the periodical to advocate his own views. As early as May 1660, only a month after Muddiman and Dury had been granted their monopoly, a report appeared seemingly from Berkenhead's pen. Dealing with an abortive attempt by Fifth Monarchists to steal horses in preparation for a rising, the editor writes that if they had 'got on horseback, they might have fulfilled the proverb: in the meanwhile they have minded us of another, to shut the stable-door'.[2] The terse sarcasm is very much in Berkenhead's manner. Similarly, in July 1660 Samuel Moyer is attacked for his conduct at Haberdasher's Hall 'where he filled the Chair and his own Purse'; and Thomas Scot, the regicide, is mocked as 'a person not to be

---

[1] *A History of English Journalism*, p. 182.
[2] *M. Publ.*, no. 20 (10–17 May), p. 310.

match'd in Scotland, nor any where else but where he now is',[1] which was in prison. In September 1660 the long account of the arrest of Berkenhead's old foe, Hugh Peter, also contains some astringencies that distinguish it from the surrounding workaday reports.[2]

In 1661 a dig at John Durant, 'that hath made more good Washbals than sermons, though a Wrestless Preacher', actually revives *Aulicus*'s sneer at the man.[3] The attack on James Guthrie, a Scottish minister who with 'his fellow Pulpit-Trumpeters sounded all for Battaile', echoes the phraseology of *The Assembly Man*.[4] The reflection that if all the clergy would use the Book of Common Prayer 'we should have more Devotion and less News' resembles another observation of Berkenhead's—this time in his 1648 letter to John Raymond.[5] This is especially interesting because in a passage he is known to have dictated for the newsbook Berkenhead used another phrase, 'floods of business', which he employed in that letter.[6] Obviously his memory and his habit of reiteration were as strong as ever. The parallels observed might in themselves be rather inconclusive: in the light of other evidence it is reasonable to isolate them as proof that he sometimes wrote or revised copy.

Bearing in mind Berkenhead's confident opportunism, it would be strange to discover that he tamely took no advantage of his position; and behind the official front one can, in fact, detect the pressure of conflicting opinions and policies at Court. Those who hoped that the Restoration Settlement would be moderate must have been dismayed to find the official mouthpiece so uncompromising an advocate of the interests of Laudian bishops and

---

[1] *M.Publ.*, no. 29 (12–19 July), p. 451.

[2] No. 36 (30 Aug.–6 Sept.), pp. 574–6.

[3] *M. Publ.*, No. 2 (10–17 Jan.), p. 31; compare *M. Aul.* no. 51 (17–23 Dec. 1643), p. 721 and no. 52 (24–30 Dec.), p. 735.

[4] No. 7 (14–21 Feb. 1661), p. 100; compare the phrase quoted above, p. 119.

[5] No. 8 (21–28 Feb. 1661), p. 128.

[6] The passage he dictated is in *M. Publ.*, no. 42 (16–23 Oct. 1662), pp. 693–4, and is reprinted by Donald Nicholas in *Mr. Secretary Nicholas (1593–1669)*, pp. 307–8. The phrase in the 1648 letter was 'a floud of businesse'. Such proof of his habit of repetition, incidentally, underwrites the propriety of attributing works to him on the basis of such parallels when there is circumstantial support.

conservative lawyers. Berkenhead, of course, had a personal as well as party motive for flattering the judiciary. His panegyric on Sir Heneage Finch in August 1661[1] was both a gesture of gratitude to a family that had helped him, a 'puff' for the profession he was involved with as Master of the Faculties, and a flourish of praise for the rigidly conventional Royalist interpretation of the Law that Finch represented. To the end of his life Berkenhead had much resort among legal men, and his speeches in Parliament, to which he was elected in 1661, show a marked attachment to strict legality and the force of precedent.

The Laudians were still determined to impose the outward aspect of conformity on the nation, even where they knew the spirit was running counter to their doctrine. The newsbook's sympathy with them is pronounced in favourable comments on prominent clerics like Brian Duppa and Robert Sanderson;[2] and in November 1661 the editor recalls, as if he remembered it personally, the conduct of Dr. John Oliver when 'Domestick Chaplain' to Archbishop Laud.[3] Later, the Archbishop is enthusiastically praised, in terms highly reminiscent of *Bellicus*, as the 'Renowned Martyr . . . for endeavouring to prevent those confusions which we have all since sufficiently tasted'.[4] Nor are his enemies forgotten, let alone forgiven: the Presbyterian, Calamy, is bitterly assailed for disobeying the Act of Uniformity;[5] and in July 1661 special prominence is given to attacks in the House of Commons on William Prynne. This was almost the only occasion on which proceedings in Parliament were reported in detail, and to rub salt in Prynne's wounds Berkenhead had the account printed in two successive numbers of *Publicus*.[6] He had a special motive, over and above old scores, for this nastiness: he and Prynne, who both loved to cite endless precedent in their speeches, were constantly clashing in Commons debates.[7] So Prynne's indiscretion in criticizing the

[1] *M. Publ.*, no. 33 (15–22 Aug.), pp. 513–17.
[2] No. 40 (27 Sept.–4 Oct. 1660), p. 625 and no. 5 (29 Jan.–5 Feb. 1663), p. 72.
[3] No. 45 (31 Oct.–7 Nov. 1661), p. 701.
[4] No. 49 (29 Nov.–6 Dec. 1660), p. 790. Cf. *M. Bell.*, above, p. 154, n. 2.
[5] No. 1 (1–8 Jan. 1663), pp. 14–16.
[6] No. 28 (11–18 July 1661), pp. 447–8 and no. 29 (18–25 July), pp. 449–51.
[7] *Brief Lives*, ii. 173. See *Diary of John Milward*, pp. 69–70 for an example.

Corporations Bill in 1661 came as a welcome chance for Berkenhead to triumph over his ancient enemy.[1]

The editor's gratitude shows most notably towards Sir Edward Nicholas, who had always trusted and favoured him. In November 1660 the newsbook flattered Nicholas's brother, the Dean of St. Paul's;[2] and in October 1662, as has been seen, Berkenhead did his best for the Secretary in his moment of defeat by temporarily suppressing the news of his removal from office. When forced to publish the notice of 'retirement' he penned an eloquent and dignified tribute, reminding the reader that for virtue, modesty, and industry he had 'not known a more worthy servant to the Crown of England'.[3]

Probably Nicholas had been instrumental in getting the Faculty Office for Berkenhead; he must have chosen him for editor; and he seems, also, to have secured his entry into the House of Commons, which was the main scene of Berkenhead's activities in the last eighteen years of his life. During this period he sat for Wilton in Wiltshire, the home county of the Nicholas family. In fact, the Secretary's son, Sir John Nicholas, was initially chosen to represent Wilton borough in 1660; and it was when he subsequently chose to serve for Ripon instead that the vacancy was earmarked for Berkenhead, who was returned on 20 June 1661.[4] All this advancement was the reward for which Berkenhead had striven so long; and it is to his credit that he stood by his benefactor in an hour of need.

The soundness of Nicholas's choice, from his own point of view, was corroborated by the newsbook's handling of the Religious Settlement. In 1660 and 1661 Quakers and Fifth Monarchists were its main targets, and everything was done to conciliate Presbyterian opinion. The newsbook, which from 1661 on was reprinted at Edinburgh[5] (a passing sign of the determination of the central

---

[1] Prynne had published a tract against this Bill, which Parliament voted scandalous and seditious (see the 'Life' in the *D.N.B.*).

[2] *M. Publ.*, no. 45 (1–8 Nov. 1660), p. 706.

[3] No. 42 (16–23 Oct.), pp. 693–4, reprinted by Donald Nicholas in *Mr. Secretary Nicholas (1593–1669)*, pp. 307–8.

[4] 'A List of the Representatives in Parliament from 1295–1832 for the County and Burroughs of Wiltshire', *Wiltshire Arch. & Nat. Hist. Magazine*, xlvii (1935–7), 223.

[5] W. J. Couper, *The Edinburgh Periodical Press* (1908), i. 185–6, states that *The Kingdomes Intelligencer* was reproduced there.

authority to assert and extend its control), repeatedly asserted that the Scots ministers were submitting amicably to orthodox discipline.[1] Excepting attacks on the lunatic fringe of Dissent, the emphasis was firmly on reconciliation. By late 1661, however, the honeymoon was over. On 3 July Berkenhead was appointed to the Committee formed to draw up the Act of Uniformity;[2] and as the time for its implementation approached, his newsbook became increasingly sour about Presbyterian deviationism.[3]

In the newsbook's determination to justify the Act and secure its rigorous enforcement it was voicing the sentiments of the old guard, Nicholas and Clarendon. They feared that the King was not truly devoted to establishing an Anglican monopoly; and in moments of decision this loyalty to the Established Church was stronger than loyalty to the monarch.[4] So in August 1662 Berkenhead actually tried to put pressure on Charles by repeatedly dismissing the rumour that he might waive the Act of Uniformity for some Nonconformists.[5] The deliberate silence about Nicholas's 'retirement' was another manœuvre in this campaign to undermine the King's moderate position. Nicholas's successor, Benet, was inclined towards toleration, and by saying nothing about his appointment Berkenhead, as the King himself feared,[6] encouraged the *canard* that he had been brought in by a Popish faction at Court. Faced with Charles's high displeasure, Berkenhead had to draw back. On 22 December 1662 the King, having thus overcome opposition, published the Declaration of Indulgence, composed by Benet. Again Berkenhead, jibbing at the idea of toleration, completely ignored it in *Mercurius Publicus* for 25 December 1662 to 1 January 1663. In the next number, making an excuse for the 'oversight', he was forced to acknowledge its existence, but did so with manifest reluctance.[7]

---

[1] *M. Publ.*, no. 31 (26 July–2 Aug. 1660), p. 483.

[2] *Commons' Journals*, viii. 288.

[3] For examples see *M. Publ.*, no. 51 (12–19 Dec. 1661), p. 791; no. 25 (19–26 June 1662), pp. 385–6; and no. 33 (14–21 Aug. 1662), pp. 551–3.

[4] D. T. Witcombe, *Charles II and the Cavalier House of Commons, 1663–1674* (Manchester Univ. Press, 1966), p. 173.

[5] For example, *M. Publ.*, no. 34 (21–28 Aug. 1662), p. 578.

[6] B.M., MS. Egerton 2538, f. 186.

[7] *M. Publ.*, no. 1 (1–8 Jan. 1663), p. 4.

Immediately he set about making toleration unworkable, by assailing Edmund Calamy as an epitome of Presbyterian ingratitude for the King's 'high Clemency'.[1] He studiously recapitulated Calamy's actions of the early 1640s. So throughout January and February of 1663 this offensive against 'the Presbyterian fals-Government' and 'Independent no-Government'[2] was sustained. In April the newsbook gave prominence to the Address to the King, prepared by Berkenhead and others under the chairmanship of Sir Heneage Finch.[3] It urged Charles to change his mind about Indulgence; and it was this opposition from the lawyers and bishops, encouraged by Nicholas and Clarendon and publicized by Nicholas's man, Berkenhead, that eventually frustrated the suspension of the Act of Uniformity.

The official newsbook was, in short, used with no little success by Berkenhead. For all its apparent anonymity he made it an instrument of policy and used it to block any genuine moves towards a generous accommodation of the nation's differences. He had lost none of his bold opportunism, skill, or prejudices; and he diligently canvassed the views of the old guard. He must be rated as not the least influential of those who did all they could to carry the fears and aspirations of the 1640s over into the second half of the seventeenth century. It was done not simply in a spirit of cynicism, but, as the risks he took prove, out of a dedicated (if misplaced) idealism. He must have regarded his work of the early 1660s with no little satisfaction as the crowning achievement of his life; for as publicist and Parliamentarian he was able to play a real part in shaping opinion and legislation along lines of a Laudian inclination. It was his consummation to join in making the Restoration Settlement not unsatisfactory to the rearguard of that party.[4]

Berkenhead supported his newsbook campaign with two forceful pamphlets published in the spring of 1663. The first of these,

---

[1] *M. Publ.*, no. 1 (1–8 Jan. 1663), pp. 14–16.

[2] No. 5 (29 Jan.–5 Feb. 1663), p. 72.

[3] No. 13 (26 Mar.–2 Apr. 1663), p. 200. For the constitution of the committee see *Commons' Journals*, viii. 441.

[4] See the study by R. S. Bosher, *The Making of the Restoration Settlement, 1649–1662* (1951).

The Assembly Man, was originally written in 1647. Its publication now—probably in February, 1663[1]—was calculated to revive bitter memories: not only was it scathingly anti-Presbyterian, but Berkenhead also added a new and outspokenly Laudian Preface. The second pamphlet, apparently the last that Berkenhead wrote, was new. Its title—appropriately long—was *Cabala, or an Impartial Account of the Non-Conformists Private Designs, Actings and Ways, from August 24, 1662 to December 25 in the Same Year*. Neither of the two surviving editions can be exactly dated, but a reference[2] to 6 April 1663 suggests that it may have been published in that month. The ascription to Berkenhead, which is not new, rests on a note in a contemporary hand on one copy of the first edition.[3] It is confirmed by resemblances between the pamphlet's arguments about Pluralities and those advanced by Berkenhead in a Commons speech in March 1663.[4] There are also general affinities between *Cabala*'s treatment of Presbyterian manipulation of the London press and pulpits and the handling of that theme in *A Letter from Mercurius Civicus*.

The influence of the burlesque fashion is still apparent: the pamphlet takes the form of a parody of the minute-book of the close committee of London Presbyterian ministers; it contains a take-off of the Presbyterian Petition for Toleration, presented to Charles on 25 August 1662;[5] and, throughout, the Nonconformists' pious cant is caustically imitated. Nevertheless, farce is decidedly played down: the ministers are not droll buffoons, but cunning seditionists plotting to overthrow the Anglican Church and the State. Substantially *Cabala* reverts to the tone and manner of Berkenhead's earliest pamphlets, proffering a serious analysis of a practical political problem, spiced with satiric wit.

His main aim was, of course, to justify the rigours of the Uniformity Act and discredit Toleration. Much of *Cabala* is devoted to

---

1 It was entered in the *Stationers' Register* on 10 Feb.
2 See the reprint in the *S. Tracts*, vii. 586.
3 This copy is Bodleian Library, Pamph. C. 119 (2).
4 See the notes he drew up for this speech in the B.M., MS. Lansdowne 958, ff. 17–25. He argued there that the Presbyterians and Papists were against Pluralities because, if they were abolished, learning and the Anglican Church would be destroyed. Compare this with *Cabala*, pp. 572 and 585.
5 pp. 572–3.

examining suggested ways round the Act: methods of infiltrating
into the Church and Parliament are closely considered; attention is
drawn to loop-holes in the Common Law, which, for example, left
ejected ministers free to teach in Church schools under pretence
of being wardens;[1] and various stratagems which enabled faithful
Presbyterians to maintain correspondence, continue secret meetings,[2] and print old and new pamphlets proclaiming the Good Old
Cause[3] are explained in some detail. Obviously, when such precise
analysis is the aim, buffoonery and drollery would be inappropriate, even distracting. *Cabala* is astutely designed as a serious
exposé of potential subversion.

The key to Berkenhead's attitude lies in the remark, put into a
Presbyterian mouth, that 'as soon as we understand the method of
the law, we may understand the method of affronting the law'.[4]
As in his approach to supervision of the press, he is implicitly
advocating an avoidance of open repression: government, he feels,
is most securely based on the powerful and secret operations of
ecclesiastical law along Star Chamber lines. Prospective and actual
offenders are found to left and right of the orthodox Anglican
position: he snipes at Prynne again and deplores the presence at
Court of Presbyterian sympathizers;[5] he even criticizes the King's
reliance on forms of supply like chimney tax[6] which, he thinks,
puts the State at the mercy of Presbyterian-dominated business
and financial interests. Catholics he treats with equal rigour,
representing them, as Cavalier satire had long done, as allies of
subversive Nonconformity. Berkenhead even asserts that it was
dabbling with Papists that destroyed Charles I [7]—a point obviously
made for the son's benefit, and indicative of true-blue suspicions.
Cabala confirms that Berkenhead was still an unwavering Laudian:
far from deterring him the experience of twenty years had fortified
his preoccupation with the *status quo* of pre-1641 days. Old policies
had not, in his estimation, failed but been betrayed by half-hearted
application. Terrified that another Stuart might repeat old mistakes,
men like Berkenhead set their faces against the accommodation

[1] p. 583.   [2] p. 582.
[3] p. 573.   [4] p. 580.
[5] pp. 568–9. He refers to Prynne as 'Mr. P.'.
[6] p. 581.   [7] p. 579.

Charles personally desired. Even marginal concessions to Non-conformity were regarded as signs of dangerous weakness: at all costs a recurrence of 1641 was to be prevented.

Cabala champions the *revanchistes'* cause[1] and in doing so exposes not only their determination but also their arrogance and nervousness. *A Mystery of Godliness, and No Cabala*, in reply, not unjustly called it 'a bitter and malitious Paper'.[2] The writer complained that *Cabala* wanted to spread fear of things not yet done—which was fair criticism, as Berkenhead undoubtedly distorts the views and aims of responsible Presbyterians and greatly exaggerates the efficiency of their organization. He was, as the replier put it, one of many 'crafty and subtle men'[3] on both sides who hoped by inflaming animosities to advance their own interests. Unquestionably the efficiency with which men like Berkenhead pushed through uncompromising policies did drive even well-intentioned Presbyterians into more embattled positions than they wished initially to occupy. Fear in politics is self-defeating; it strengthens the very thing it dreads. Well might *Cabala* rouse the anxiety of the authentically moderate.

It was not written simply for the advantage of a faction: Berkenhead also had a very personal motive. To understand this it is necessary to go back to 1662 and the rivalry between Nicholas and Benet where it affected press control. If, as Berkenhead wrote privately to Nicholas, the King never bothered to read the newsbook,[4] others did not neglect its demonstrable usefulness. The skilful publicizing of certain policies and playing down of others had not escaped Benet's notice. But Berkenhead was too inclined to act independently and too staunch a Laudian to serve his turn; so Benet sought out Roger L'Estrange, a man amenable to his ideas, and encouraged his attempts to oust Berkenhead as editor and censor. L'Estrange's campaign to discredit his rival's handling of subversive publications met its first success on 24 February 1662, when he was granted a warrant to search for and seize all seditious books and their contrivers.[5] Berkenhead continued to

---

[1] *Diary of John Milward*, pp. 218–19, shows how highly some Royalists valued his advocacy generally.   [2] p. 1.
[3] p. 21.   [4] B.M., MS. Egerton 2538, f. 186.
[5] J. B. Williams, *A History of English Journalism*, p. 187.

insist that his methods of control were adequate, and when a scandal blew up over the illicit publication of the farewell sermons of the London Presbyterian ministers he defended himself in the newsbook against the charge of slackness. He claimed that the presses responsible had been seized and that nothing subversive had appeared since.[1] L'Estrange continued complaining and began licensing books towards the end of 1662; but he had not as yet unseated Berkenhead. In fact, though Nicholas's dismissal deprived the latter of a powerful protector, he was strongly entrenched in favour on his own account, for on 14 November 1662 he received the honour of knighthood from the King.[2]

L'Estrange, undeterred, maintained his offensive; and on 31 March 1663 Berkenhead retaliated by denouncing him before the Committee for Indigent Officers as the writer of a book against the King.[3] This has been interpreted as a manœuvre to protect Muddiman from L'Estrange;[4] but clearly Berkenhead was guarding his own interest. His digs at Catholicism and the explicit defence in *Cabala* of his own record as a licenser were similarly part of this running fight with the Benet faction.[5] He was eager to shift blame for the continued appearance of seditious books onto the Stationers, but equally careful to argue against L'Estrange's demand for harsher regulations, reasoning that these would defeat their own purpose by inhibiting the publication of orthodox books as well.

[1] *M. Publ.*, no. 40 (2–9 Oct. 1662), pp. 660–1.

[2] Wm. A. Shaw, *The Knights of England* (1905), ii. 237. This invalidates the assertion by George Kitchen (*Sir Roger L'Estrange*, p. 91) that Berkenhead is attacked as 'Sir John B—' in L'Estrange's *The Relapsed Apostate*, published on 14 November 1661. In any case, despite the rivalry between the two men and Berkenhead's later charge against L'Estrange, the drift of *The Relapsed Apostate*, and the details about 'Sir John B—' do not suggest that Berkenhead, who was as violently anti-Presbyterian as L'Estrange, was the man in question. A more likely candidate is Sir John Baber, physician to King Charles II, knighted on 19 March 1661. He was frequently made use of by Charles in his negotiations with the Presbyterians and was a close friend of Dr. Thomas Manton, the divine, who held the living of St. Paul's, Covent Garden (mentioned here by L'Estrange). Manton was attacked by L'Estrange in *Truth and Loyalty Vindicated* (1662).

[3] *C.S.P. Dom.*, 1663–4, p. 92.

[4] J. B. Williams, 'The Newsbooks and News-Letters of the Restoration', *Eng. Hist. Review*, xxiii (1908), 262.

[5] He was still taking stands against them in 1673, when he defended the Speaker against attacks from the Arlington faction (see D. T. Witcombe, *Charles II and the Cavalier House of Commons, 1663–1674* p. 145).

This opposition to infringing the traditional privileges of the Stationers' Company (while retaining the right to grumble at them) conceals Berkenhead's real anxiety lest control should be taken from him and vested in L'Estrange. His private interest is scarcely disguised in the complaint, loaded with an implicit threat, that the King had lost many friends by neglect. Of course, he was not forgotten: and L'Estrange's subsequent policy of excising from Anglican tracts all anti-Catholic sentiments[1] proves that his concern was not, from one point of view, wholly mistaken.

Despite his efforts and despite his knighthood the tide was momentarily running against Berkenhead. In June 1663 L'Estrange, confident that his backers would see him through, assailed him in his *Considerations and Proposals in order to the Regulation of the Press*. Stung by the accusation that he had written against the King, he asserted that Sir John had whispered private tales against him in Chancellor Hyde's ear,[2] and that when confronted with it he had had the nerve to deny the charge of rumour-mongering in open Committee. For good measure L'Estrange hinted broadly that Berkenhead's 'Familiar Discourses' about the King and Commons were far from complimentary. Albeit L'Estrange was an unscrupulous intriguer and self-seeker, this account of his rival's bare-faced mendacity agrees with Aubrey's and Marvell's evidence.[3] Sometimes even close friends found they could not trust him with confidences.[4] On this occasion L'Estrange can be believed. His campaign bore fruit too, for at the end of August Berkenhead was relieved of his editorial duties and, at last, replaced by L'Estrange.

As men they were both ruthless and ambitious; but as journalists they were very different and Berkenhead was, in many ways, the finer editor. His successor's propaganda methods were comparatively brutal and heavy-handed, and he did not have Berkenhead's

[1] See the 'Life' in the *D.N.B.*
[2] He did not name Berkenhead in this pamphlet, which was a strenuous attack on the existing system of licensing, but Wood noted on his copy, Wood 608 (44), that it was Berkenhead L'Estrange was getting at.
[3] In, respectively, *Brief Lives*, i. 105 and the ballad 'The Chequer Inn', in the *Complete Works*, ed. A. B. Grosart (1872–5), i. 463. There is also a letter, in *C.S.P. Dom.*, 1671, p. 200, which suggests that Berkenhead was not exactly a man of his word. Compare also *The Diary of Samuel Pepys*, ed. H. B. Wheatley (1893–9), ii. 45.
[4] See below, p. 234.

polished way of insinuating biased views. A contemporary observed that he seemed to think that the nation should be governed by newsbooks.[1] This meant not that L'Estrange gave the reader more news than his predecessor, but less: his first action on taking over was to cut the newsbook to half its former size and make the two editions consecutive. In future the readers had to buy both to get all the news. This may have been commercially shrewd but in other respects it suggests a lowering of professional standards, which is literally visible in the poorer quality of printing under his supervision. Altogether, one can only endorse the contemporary judgement that L'Estrange was not 'so cliver . . . as his predecessor was'.[2] He may have increased the profitability of the official newsbook: he certainly brought it closer to Grub Street.

Berkenhead had lost one battle with L'Estrange, but not the war: the 1665 Printing Act, as has been seen, was something of a rebuff for the new man's more extreme ambitions. Nor, though loss of the newsbook may have been a financial setback,[3] was Berkenhead sunk: in January 1664 he became Master of Requests in succession to Sir Richard Fanshaw, who had taken another appointment. Formerly a judicial office, the Court of Requests no longer functioned and the Master's work consisted of entertaining personal petitions to the King.[4] The post brought Berkenhead £100 a year[5] plus perquisites,[6] and, it would seem, closer to the monarch than before. Indeed, in retrospect it appears that Berkenhead was the real winner of the tussle; for L'Estrange later coveted the office he had moved on to.[7]

The struggle displays Berkenhead's great capacity not just for survival but for actually turning crisis to advantage. By publishing *The Assembly Man* and writing *Cabala* he had, with very neat timing, reminded the Court of his past services and staked a strong claim

[1] *Lauderdale Papers*, vol. i, 1639–1667 (Camden Soc. N.S. xxxiv, 1884), pp. 185–6.

[2] Ibid., p. 183.

[3] See J. G. Muddiman, *The King's Journalist, 1659–1689*, p. 125.

[4] W. S. Holdsworth, *A History of English Law*, ed. A. L. Goodhart and H. G. Hanbury (1956), i. 416.

[5] There are entries concerning these payments in the *Calendars of Treasury Books* for the period 1660 to 1679.

[6] For an example, see the Bodleian Library, MS. Rawl. D. 395, f. 221.

[7] See below, p. 235.

to recognition. These public gestures he had backed up with strenuous private lobbying and diligent denigration of his foe. One may not admire his methods, but he was unquestionably a dangerous man in a tight corner and one the Court party could scarce afford to alienate. It is a tribute to his cool nerve and resourcefulness, not to say guile, that he survived at Court for another fifteen years.

On only one other occasion, as far as can be discovered, was he to exercise his talent for propaganda. This was in 1666 during the Dutch Wars. They stimulated a deal of satire both in England and abroad, most of it not very amusing or penetrating; and the two ballads Berkenhead wrote at the King's command to celebrate the English naval success of St. James's Day, 1666, are no exception.[1] Wood's ascription to Berkenhead[2] is confirmed by a contemporary *Answer* to them[3] which laments the decline of Berkenheads' powers, comparing the ballads unfavourably with those of 1647 and 1659. Their crude tub-thumping bellicosity justifies this verdict. The only feature of the first ballad, jingoism aside, is its reportorial accumulation of detail and a sneer at the Dutchmen's 'Impudent Gazette', both of which suggest the journalist. The second, which refers to the King's request, also affords a wealth of detail, gleefully totting up the plunder of rope and pitch—an unfortunate reflection on the state of the English navy. There is no element of burlesque in all this. Berkenhead styles them ballads 'of the old Fashion'. It looks as if he was trying to ape the popular style of writers like Taylor the Water Poet. But clumsiness and crude sentiments are the result, lamentably in a writer who had been capable of something better. It is hard to imagine that at fifty Berkenhead was in his dotage: more likely he had little time or energy to spare. Probably the touchiness of the Court, desperate to make the most of even a limited success, also had something to do with it. Berkenhead in the same year had had to defend Arlington in Parliament against charges of mismanaging the war. He was presumably called on to oblige poetically for similar reasons. His effort does not carry conviction.

---

[1] These were entitled *A New Ballad of a Famous German Prince* and *The Second Part of the Late and Terrible Fight*. See the Bibliography for reprints.

[2] *Ath. Oxon.* iii. 1205; he actually mentioned only the first.

[3] There is a copy in the Bodleian Library, MS. Don. b. 8, pp. 344–5.

Anyhow, as Master of Requests he was kept busy by the 'crowd of petitioners' that daily sought the King's favours;[1] and he was an industrious House of Commons man with a heavy work-load. In his eighteen years as representative for Wilton he established himself as one of the most active Members, sitting on over five hundred committees and speaking on over one hundred occasions.[2] His record in office, in fact, bore out Nicholas's judgement of his potentiality, for it is one of indefatigable and eloquent advocacy of Cavalier ideals. As a zealous member of the Court party, representing it on the Committees that drew up the Uniformity, Corporations, Conventicle, and Five Mile Acts, he doubtless contributed to the harshness of the Clarendon Code.

The Earl of Danby's lists of King's servants and government speakers prove him among the dependable hard-core Members who toed the line in Parliament.[3] In the difficult years after 1671 he was one of the few reliable Court speakers, even if he had lost the sparkle of *Aulicus* days; and after 1673 he was unmistakably a leading spokesman. In fact, if his speeches, for all their plausibility, were often badly received in these later years it may be due as much to the Commons' increased antagonism to the King as to any personal deficiency.[4] He was certainly very closely associated with the Crown and spoke with dutiful zeal on its behalf.[5] With regard to Catholicism, for example, he became, notwithstanding his sentiments in *Cabala*, tender of the Royal family's interests[6] and to his credit refused to be panicked by the wave of anti-Popery that swept through the country in the 1670s.[7] Similarly, in 1672 he rebutted criticism of the King's players by remarking that they had been of great service to Charles—an observation that led Sir John

[1] Bodleian Library, MS. Rawl. C. 421, f. 144ʳ.
[2] B. D. Henning, *The Representation of Wiltshire in the Long Parliament of Charles II*, Yale Ph.D. Thesis (1937); there is a microfilm copy of this in the possession of the History of Parliament Trust in London.
[3] See these in Andrew Browning's *Thomas Osborne Earl of Danby . . . 1632–1712* (1944–51), vol. iii.
[4] See D. T. Witcombe, *Charles II and the Cavalier House of Commons, 1663–1674*, pp. ix, 83 n. 1, and 197.
[5] See the sometimes detailed accounts of his speeches in Milward, Witcombe, and Grey.
[6] Anchitell Grey, *Debates 1667–1694* (1769), vi. 243–4.
[7] Ibid. ii. 153.

Coventry to enquire, indiscreetly, whether the King had been better served by the men or women players.[1] For this witty flash he was waylaid and assaulted. Six years later, as one of the 'unanimous Club of Voters' in Parliament, Berkenhead was instrumental in rallying support for Lauderdale, then under attack for misadvising Charles. At a critical point in the debate Sir John left the House and brought back '3 members from the Taverne, with himselfe, to vote'.[2] The contemporary historian Burnet poured contempt on such 'mercenary work';[3] but it was a necessary adjunct of party government and Berkenhead's action suggests nothing more sinister than that he would have been a good Party Whip today.

On 19 December 1678 Berkenhead was among the first to rally to Danby's side when Montague, former ambassador in France, produced in the Commons incriminating letters, apparently proving that the Earl had acted treasonably in negotiating a secret treaty with France. Quick as ever to carry the attack to the enemy, Berkenhead boldly pointed out that if Danby was guilty of treason Montague was guilty of misprision of treason in keeping silent about the letters for so long. It was a sound technical point, but the House was in no mood to heed it and his attempt to sidetrack the debate failed.[4]

Besides his conscientiousness and smartfootedness one is struck by Berkenhead's formidable use of precedents. His memory served him well here, for precedent carried great weight in Parliament's deliberations at this period.[5] The past was very much alive in Berkenhead's mind and he recurred with special frequency and feeling to the recent past of the Civil War and Interregnum. When the Dissolution was proposed in October 1675, for example,

---

[1] The story of this episode was recounted by Andrew Marvell: see his letter in *Marvell's Poems and Letters*, ed. H. M. Margoliouth (Oxford, 1952), ii. 307.

[2] *Lauderdale Papers*, vol. iii, 1673–1679, pp. 141–2.

[3] *Burnet's History of My Own Times*, ii. 80.

[4] Berkenhead's remark is reported in Grey, *Debates*, vi. 35. Andrew Browning comments on it in *Thomas Osborne Earl of Danby . . . 1632–1712*, i. 306.

[5] *Burnet's History of My Own Times*, ii. 92. Burnet was speaking of Henry Powle's expertise in matters of precedent; Berkenhead occasionally clashed with Powle in debates. Examples of Berkenhead's attachment to the letter of the law can be found in Grey, *Debates*, iv. 103, 378 and *Diary of John Milward*, p. 270.

he voiced the hope that he would never see a Rump again, for which sentiment he was, justifiably, laughed at.[1] But three years later he again reminded the House, glancing fearfully over his shoulder, that 'This very 7th. day of May the Rump Parliament was revived'.[2] In his attitude towards Dissent the same remembrance of things past appears almost compulsively.

The Laudians had always hated Presbyterians far more than Papists; and Berkenhead after the Restoration, while permitting latitude to the Catholics, constantly demanded that Dissenters be hounded down with utmost rigour. Simultaneously he defended Laud's memory against the common accusation that he had been a Papist at heart.[3] Yet, like a true Laudian, he was fundamentally not preoccupied with doctrinal issues. He opposed the suggestion that office-holders should be required to abjure the doctrine of transubstantiation,[4] though accepting that some tests be applied to discover Papists.[5] And he fulminated against a proposal to leave out some of the Thirty-Nine Articles precisely because that would, as he put it, leave nothing but doctrine.[6] For him the received Articles of the Church of England were a sufficient and definitive body of rules, so drawn up that all reasonable parties could subscribe to them. The important thing was that the King should not allow different customs of ceremony or worship within the Church because it was latitude on that very point that destroyed his father.[7] So he praised the uncompromising attitude of Queen Elizabeth and James I towards Papists and Dissenters;[8] but he showed which of those groups he was most troubled by when he spoke violently against repealing the clause in the Act of Uniformity that demanded abjuration of the Covenant.[9] Even after the House had decided to consider a Bill for ease of tender consciences Berkenhead rose to deliver himself of a speech against the

[1] Grey, *Debates*, iii. 341–2.
[2] Ibid. v. 355.
[3] Ibid. i. 161.
[4] *The Parliamentary Diary of Sir Edward Dering, 1670–1673*, ed. B. D. Henning (Yale Univ. Press, 1940), p. 137.   [5] Ibid., p. 149.
[6] Grey, op. cit. ii. 135.
[7] Ibid. i. 113–14; cf. *Diary of John Milward*, pp. 218–19.
[8] Grey, op. cit., i. 104–5.
[9] *The Parliamentary Diary of Sir Edward Dering, 1670–1673*, p. 125.

proposal.[1] What he wanted throughout was submission to the political forms of the Anglican Establishment. He saw the Church as an
arm of State government; and a preoccupation with legality and
political conformity is the foundation of all his utterances. To him
it was Parliament, not revelation or the Holy Ghost, that validated
a religion.[2]

The radical Dissenters consequently bore the brunt of his
repressive dogmatism; for they were the proven revolutionaries.
His harshness towards them never abated, and this obsession with
the past got the better of him, nearly with disastrous results, on
2 December 1678. On that day he rashly compared the Representation of the State of the Nation, addressed by the Commons to the
King, with the Remonstrance of 1641. A storm of protest immediately broke about his head: he was accused of being 'a favourer
of Popery' and Sir Thomas Clarges lamented that such dangerous
sentiments had come from one so near to the Crown. Only the
intervention of the Speaker and Secretary Coventry saved Berkenhead from being called to the Bar of the House.[3] Clearly his position, however sincerely held (and a trimmer would hardly have
committed such a gaffe), was becoming increasingly untenable.
His hatred of a conventicle had made him a byword in the House
for ultra-conservative views;[4] and this close call shows how his
refusal to move with the times was fast becoming a liability. His
political ideas had ossified: he was by the end of his life a prisoner
of memories and of his own success. He had lived through the
apparent defeat and ultimate triumph of Cavalier conservatism,
emerging with his party to enjoy the rewards of loyal endeavour;
and that must have seemed to him proof of the rightness of his
stand of forty years. Such dedication to the system to which one
has given and owes everything is neither unusual nor incompre-
hensible. If it is easy to denounce his obscurantism it is well, too,
to remember that in such stiffness there is a sort of courage,
albeit a lesser courage than that which faces squarely problems of
adjustment and reappraisal. And one might regard with some

[1] *The Parliamentary Diary of Sir Edward Dering, 1670–1673*, pp. 122–3.
[2] Grey, *Debates*, ii. 38.
[3] Ibid. vi. 309–10.   [4] Ibid. v. 252.

compassion the fate of a man whose once brave tenacity at last left him looking, to use his own word, 'superannuated'.[1]

Inexorably time and change overhauled him until they threw him down. For the elections of 1679 he set out for Wilton to present himself to the voters: he had got to Salisbury when news reached him that 'he was scorned and mocked' in his borough. He at last gave in to the unpalatable truth and returned to London, soon to die. He took the rebuff so to heart, according to Aubrey, that 'he insensibly decayed and pined away';[2] and he must have been bitterly hurt that the Wilton voters rejected him for that very loyalty to the Crown he prided himself upon. Yet for one 'exceedingly bold, confident, witty' to capitulate and pine like that seems odd. He was probably a sick man before he set out: his life had always been extremely demanding, and government officials, who since the Restoration had carried a mounting load of toil, were grossly overworked by 1678.[3] But Aubrey, as so often, shows imaginative perception: Berkenhead's day was done. But there is more to be said about his extra-Parliamentary interests after the Restoration.

Surprisingly little is known of his private life in this period. He appears to have remained on friendly terms with the Finch family: on 7 November 1665, he assisted Sir Heneage Finch and others to carry the thanks of the House to the Convocation of Oxford University for its stand against the Covenant in 1647;[4] and on 17 August 1666 Sir Heneage wrote his son a letter, enclosing a copy of a ballad by Lacy, the comedian, 'commented upon by Sir Jo. Berkenhead'.[5] It looks as though Finch, like Henry More, respected his critical acumen. Berkenhead was also familiar with the Bramstons, another legal family. John Bramston wrote of him in terms suggesting personal acquaintance;[6] and his brother, Francis Bramston, was one of the 'two noble frends' named in Berkenhead's will as executors. The second friend, Sir Richard Mason, was also

---

[1] In his song in Lawe's *Select Ayres and Dialogues* (1669).
[2] *Brief Lives*, i. 105, tells of this setback.
[3] Andrew Browning, *Thomas Osborne Earl of Danby . . . 1632–1712*, i. 310–11.
[4] Wood, *Fasti Oxon.* ii. 286.
[5] H.M.C., *Finch I* (1913), p. 433. The copy of the ballad cannot be found
[6] *The Autobiography of Sir John Bramston*, (Camden Soc. xxxii, 1845), p. 360.

a lawyer; and yet another barrister, a 'deare freind dr. Raines', was
a legatee under the will.[1] These are the few surviving memorials
of what appears to have been an extensive, and sometimes intimate
acquaintance among men of law.

Outside legal circles, as a founder member of the Royal Society,
of which he was elected Fellow on 22 June 1663,[2] he must have
known many of the learned and eminent of his day. Nor was he
just a name in a Register: on 30 March 1664 he was appointed to
the Committee 'To consider and improve all mechanical inventions',
and in the following December he joined Cowley, Dryden, Denham, Evelyn, Sprat, Stanley, Waller, and other literary men in
their deliberations about the English language.[3] It is known that
'three or fowre meetings were begun at Gray's Inn', but Cowley's
death and the plague, among other things, ended that project.[4]
Berkenhead's qualifications to sit on this Committee are obvious
enough, but his eligibility for the first one is more dubious. True,
he had promoted Whitlock's *Zootomia*, but little else in his career
suggests real sympathy for the New Learning. On the contrary,
everything points to devotion to the traditional academic disciplines: he had actually shown distrust of empirics by poking fun
at an invention of Sir William Petty,[5] best known as the founder of
the science of political economy. Perhaps he was nominated, like
some prestige figures, primarily because he could contribute to
expenses and pass a layman's opinion on the enthusiasts' investigations.[6] He demonstrated his serviceability, too, in August
1663, when he publicized Petty's invention of a double-bottomed
boat in the official newsbook.[7] That apparent volte-face makes
one doubt the genuineness of his scientific interests; scepticism is

[1] P.C.C. Wills, Bath, f. 15.

[2] *The Record of the Royal Society of London*, revised edition (1912), pp. 16 and 311.
Berkenhead's signature does not appear in *The Signatures in the First Journal-Book and
the Charter-Book of the Royal Society*, facsimile reprint (1912); but this is not a complete record of the founder-members (see its Preface, p. viii).

[3] Thomas Birch, *The History of the Royal Society* (1756–7), i. 406 and 500.

[4] John Evelyn, in *Critical Essays of the Seventeenth Century*, ed. J. E. Spingarn (1908–
9), ii. 329.

[5] *M. Bell.*, no. 8 (14–21 Mar. 1648), H3ʳ.

[6] Thomas Sprat, *The History of the Royal Society*, 4th edn. (1734), pp. 72–3,
pointed out that there was room for such members.

[7] *M. Publ.*, no. 32 (6–13 Aug.), pp. 501–3.

increased by two letters written in 1674 by Berkenhead's old friend, Thomas Barlow. It has already been suggested that Berkenhead spent some time in his company during the Interregnum; and their paths probably crossed again in 1660, when Barlow was one of the Commissioners who restored the Fellows of All Souls to their posts.[1] They must have met once more in 1665 when the Court removed to Oxford to escape the Great Plague. There is in the circumstances little doubt that 'Sir J. B.', to whom Barlow addressed himself as 'Your Affectionate Friend and Servant',[2] was Berkenhead. The subject of the letters is a lecture, of which 'Sir J. B.' had sent Barlow a copy.[3] It had been delivered to the Royal Society on 26 November 1674, by Petty; and Barlow writes sourly deploring his 'metaphysical Non-sense'. The mathematician's notions are portentously dismissed as impious if not downright atheistical. In his second letter Barlow remarks tartly that Berkenhead has related to a third party everything he had written in the first, despite having been asked to keep the matter to himself. Such was Sir John's way with some confidences. Undeterred by the indiscretion, however, Barlow now writes even more strongly: he is convinced that pursuit of scientific knowledge is a Jesuit plot, designed to infect the Universities with 'novel Whimsies' and divert the students from 'the severer studies of the old Philosophy and Scholastick Divinity'. One gets the impression that the two men were on the same wavelength in this respect and that Berkenhead sent the lecture initially so as to share his feelings of outrage. This puts his Royal Society Fellowship in its place; and on reflection his academic orthodoxy is no surprise, in view of the close Puritan connection with the movement away from conventional scholasticism and towards more practical education. This commitment, after all, was one element in their antipathy to the Anglican tradition. It is as defenders of Anglican uniformity and its scholastic premises that Barlow and Berkenhead eye the New Learning askance.

There is an odd tailpiece to their friendship: in 1680 a book

---

[1] See the 'Life' in the *D.N.B.*

[2] The letters were printed in *The Genuine Remains of . . . Dr. Thomas Barlow* (1693), pp. 151–6 and 157–9.

[3] It was '*The Discourse . . . concerning the Use of Duplicate Proportion*'.

appeared defending the right of bishops to judge in capital cases in Parliament.[1] Wood for a time believed that Barlow and Berkenhead had written this together; but the real author seems to have been Thomas Turner, a lawyer.[2] Berkenhead's involvement in the same question in 1662 possibly accounts for the misunderstanding.[3] Another work, published after Berkenhead's death and wrongly attributed to him, was the long satirical poem printed in 1681 as *Sir John Berkenhead Reviv'd*. This was compiled from verses first published in *Mercurius Pragmaticus*, the Royalist newsbook of the Second Civil War. It had actually been published before in 1661 as *A Short History of the English Rebellion* by Marchamont Nedham. There is nothing to suggest that Berkenhead ever disputed that ascription or that he had anything to do with the poem.[4] The 1681 edition was clearly an attempt to cash in posthumously on his reputation.

It shows, none the less, that in the 1680s he was remembered, as he would doubtless have wished, as a champion of the monarchy in its darkest hours. Yet when he died there was apparently no gesture of public or party grief; indeed some people were relieved. In November 1679, during his illness, Francis North wrote to the Archbishop of Canterbury staking a friend's claim to Berkenhead's post of Master of the Faculties. From what he wrote, Berkenhead's death on 6 December 1679 cannot have been exactly unwelcome to the Archbishop: 'I have heard yr Grace complain yt Sr John Berkenhead carried himselfe so as if he were independent, & would not consult yr Grace, for Rules to walke by.'[5] Nor was Roger L'Estrange brokenhearted: on 8 December he sent a letter to Archbishop Sancroft, reminding him of his own suitability for the vacant post.[6] Berkenhead's private possessions also attracted the acquisitive: his London property became the subject of extended

---

[1] It was entitled *The Right of the Bishops to Judge in Capital Cases in Parliament Cleared*.

[2] Wood linked Barlow and Berkenhead on the flyleaf of his copy of the tract, Wood 574 (3), now in the Bodleian Library. He identified Turner as the author in *Ath. Oxon.* iii. 1269 and iv. 337.

[3] White Kennett, *A Register and Chronicle Ecclesiastical and Civil* i. 620.

[4] This is not absolutely certain because, as was seen, the editing of *Pragmaticus* and other newsbooks of the time was sometimes shared among the Cavaliers.

[5] Bodleian Library, MS. Tanner letters 38, f. 97.   [6] Ibid., f. 106.

litigation;[1] his library was purchased by a lawyer, Sir Richard
Atkins, for £200; and his manuscripts, chiefly copies of records,
fetched £900. Among the printed books were copies of *Mercurius
Aulicus* and other of his own pamphlets;[2] and among the manuscripts were his transcripts of Parliamentary Rolls—possibly of
his own copying[3]—described by Edward Stillingfleet, in a letter to
Sancroft, as 'the best copies extant'. He urged the Archbishop to
obtain them for the Church, to which Berkenhead had apparently
wished them to go, and warned him that 'some great Persons' were
exerting all their influence to get hold of them.[4]

It is fitting that at the close of Berkenhead's life the points
which contemporaries drew attention to were penmanship, loyal
Anglicanism, and self-confidence. From the first interlacing of his
own remarks in *Aulicus* he had shown himself capable of independent, even arrogant, initiative. He was, in truth, far more than a
faceless bureaucrat, not least in his elderly blimpishness. It might
seem satisfying, too, to observe that his wheel had come full
circle, particularly when one thinks of his will with its dying
thoughts of the school that first set him on his course to Oxford
and the fateful encounter with Laud. But the metaphor distorts the
shape of his career, which had advanced from modest obscurity
through sudden fame to public rank and power.

From his modest beginnings in Northwich to his death sixty-two
years later in Whitehall Berkenhead conducted himself with circumspection and steadfastness. His whole career might be described
as, in a sense, a tribute of gratitude and devotion to the ideals
of his great patron, Laud. Certainly it has much to tell us of the
role of Laudianism in the prolonged crisis of the seventeenth
century—both of its inclination to ride rough-shod over genuine
dissent, and of its power to inspire dedicated service; for if

---

[1] *The Autobiography of Sir John Bramston*, pp. 359–63; and the *Records of the Society
of Lincoln's Inn, Black Books*, iii, 1660–1775 (1897–9), pp. 461–4.

[2] Aubrey, *Brief Lives*, i. 104 and 106 gives these details about Berkenhead's
library. According to him (op. cit. i. 361) Dr. Henry Berkenhead had the job of
sorting out the 'bookes and papers'.

[3] Extensive enquiries have failed to locate them.

[4] Bodleian Library, MS. Tanner letters 38, f. 107. According to Aubrey, *Brief
Lives*, i. 104, Berkenhead's executors were ordered by the King himself to give his
pamphlets to the Archbishop of Canterbury's Library.

Berkenhead first embraced it hopefully as likely to satisfy his ambition, he undeniably cleaved to it bravely even in its greatest discomforture. Though 1679 brought a last moment of truth for him and his *parti pris*, when he found in the cathedral town of Salisbury that he become a political irrelevancy, Laudianism gave him, through most of his adult years, a sense of belonging to a *corps élite* that was a source of strength and a spur to continuing endeavour. Some measure of what is best and worst in Laudianism can be taken from Berkenhead, who must be reckoned one of its most notable disciples.

No man, however, can be accounted for solely in terms of party affiliation. If Berkenhead played a not inconsiderable part in events (both literary and political), his fitness for that role owed as much to personal talent as to theoretical qualifications. Aubrey described him as "scholar enongh, and a poet,"[1] and we can agree that he was, if not inspired, a competent man of letters with a more than commonly shrewd critical instinct and a knack of hitting off the consensus of opinion. That won him the respect of the Cavalier literati and rewards our attention still. But it was in prose propaganda that he showed some sort of genius: in his methods he was inventive and enterprising; he had an eye for an opening and his sense of timing was acute; he argued smoothly and persuasively, and his quick repartee and witty caricature often went to the heart of the matter. His work is among the most sophisticated, informative, and amusing of a remarkable era of satirical journalism.

Berkenhead's then, is a distinctive and lively voice and in it we catch the authentic accents of Cavalier toughness and poise. Perhaps he was, in Aubrey's phrase, "not of a sweet aspect"[2]— he certainly looked antediluvian to the sceptical Wilton voters. But others cherished the memory of his wit and loyalty, and for us today he still touches the quick of Royalist experience in the Rebellion and after. When an opponent confessed that in his writing Berkenhead emerges "handsomly, like an Artist"[3] he left an enduring epitaph on the man and his society.

[1] *Brief Lives*, i. 104.   [2] Ibid.
[3] *Good News from All Quarters of the Kingdome*, (13 Sept. 1643), A3ᵛ.

APPENDIX I

Delays in the publication of *Mercurius Aulicus*

EVIDENCE of delays in the publication of *Aulicus* comes principally from two sources: the London newsbook, *Mercurius Britanicus*, which reviewed each number of *Aulicus* from late 1643 on, and the Oxford newsbook itself. It is dangerous to be too dogmatic in calculations of this sort, but it seems reasonable to assume that, as the first item below suggests, during the period when there were delays a book normally took seven days to reach London from Oxford (Madan, *Oxford Books*, vol. ii, p. xiii), so that there was usually a gap of about ten days between the publication of *Aulicus* in Oxford and the terminal date of the number of *Britanicus* which reviewed it. A gap of over ten days, therefore, commonly indicates a delayed appearance of *Aulicus*; but it sometimes could signify simply a hold-up in transit from Oxford to London.

Luckily the editor of *Aulicus* or his printers quite often give the game away themselves. More than once the compiler used reports which did not arrive in Oxford until after the terminal date of the week under which they appear. Similarly, confusion in date-headings in the body of the newsbook arises significantly at times when publication was lagging behind schedule. On the basis of this rather complex evidence one can reconstruct something of *Aulicus*'s pattern of publication. Since tabulation might suggest otherwise, it should be stressed that the following list has no claim to infallibility; there are too many variables for that. The evidence is, however, best presented in this form, with due caution. The actual dates of publication suggested are those for Oxford, not London.

No. 41 (*8–14 October* 1643)

Actual date: about 16 Oct.?

Evidence: *M. Brit.*, no. 9 (17–26 Oct.), stated that *M. Aul.* had not got to London until 23 Oct. in an attempt to avoid being criticized in its pages. For this reason *M. Brit.* delayed its own publication, which would normally have been on 24 Oct.

No. 50 (10–16 *December*)

Actual date: Wednesday, 20 Dec.

Evidence: One of the Parliamentary scouts of Sir Samuel Luke reported
that *M. Aul.* had been delayed till then because of the editor's
illness (*Journal of Sir Samuel Luke* (Oxon. Record Soc., xxix,
xxxi, xxxiii (1947–53), pp. 221–2).

Nos. 51 (17–23 *December*) *to* 53 (31 *December–6 January* 1644)

Actual dates: all these were running about four days late, or were sluggish
in their progress to London, witness the timing of *M. Brit.*'s
reviews.

No. 54 (7–13 *January*)

Actual date: about 20 Jan.?

Evidence: *The Spie*, no. 1 (23–30 Jan.) stated that *M. Aul.* had recently
been silent and then reviewed this number. It seems that the
Oxford editor had been unable to make up the time he had lost
by his illness.

No. 55 (14–20 *January*)

Actual date: about 26 Jan.?

Evidence: reviewed by *M. Brit.*, no. 21 (29 Jan.–5 Feb.)

Nos. 56 (21–27 *January*) *to* 58 (4–10 *February*)

Actual dates: all running about six days late, witness the timing of *M. Brit.*'s
reviews.

No. 59 (11–17 *February*)

Actual date: about 25 Feb.

Evidence: reviewed by *M. Brit.*, no. 25 (26 Feb.–6 Mar.) The latter
appeared on Tuesday instead of Monday as was normal; and
Thomason noted on his copy of this number of *M. Aul.* that it
did not appear in London until after *M. Brit.*'s usual time of
publication (see B.M., E. 36). *M. Aul.* used the date-heading
'Saturday Feb. 10' (p. 834), which suggests that the composi-
tors were beginning to get confused by having to work retro-
spectively.

No. 60 (17–24 *February*)

Actual date: about 2 Mar.

Evidence: reviewed by *M. Brit.*, no. 26 (5–12 Mar.).

Nos. 61 (25 *February–2 March*) *to* 72 (12–18 *May*)

Actual dates: all these were running about six days late, witness the timing of *M. Brit.*'s reviews.

No. 73 (19–25 *May*)

Actual date: apparently more than six days late.

Evidence: There was no *M. Brit.* for 3–10 June; *M. Brit.*, no. 39 (10–17 June), suggested that *M. Aul.* was routed.

No. 74 (26 *May–1 June*)

Actual date: about 8 June; but see the next item.

Evidence: not reviewed by *M. Brit.*, no. 39 (10–17 June).

No. 75 (2–8 *June*)

Actual date: about 14 June.

Evidence: reviewed by *M. Brit.*, no. 40 (17–24 June). The editor of *M. Aul.* stated this week that he had got many notes for 'these two last Weeks' from a dispatch brought into Oxford on Friday, 7 June (p. 1017). This could mean that nos. 74 and 75 were written concurrently and published together.

Nos. 76 (9–15 *June*) *to* 81 (14–20 *July*)

Actual dates: all these were running about six days late, witness the timing of *M. Brit.*'s reviews.

No. 79 (30 *June–6 July*)

Actual date: Saturday, 13 July.

Evidence: Letter of Sir Samuel Luke, dated 24 Aug. 1644 (letter 21 in *The Letter Books 1644–45 of Sir Samuel Luke*, ed. H. G. Tibbutt (1963)), states that since York *Aulicus* had taken 'a weekly consideration of what he writ the week before' and not appeared until the Saturday following the normal Sunday. So it seems that from no. 79 (which reported Marston Moor) onwards *M. Aul.* was consistently published at least a week later than its terminal date suggested.

No. 82 (21–27 *July*)

Actual date: about 9 Aug.

Evidence: *M. Brit.* suspended publication for a week; then no. 47 (12–19 Aug.), reviewed no. 82. The latter kept a running-head from the previous week (p. 1102).

Nos. 83 (28 *July*–3 *August*) *to* 86 (18–24 *August*)

Actual dates: all these were running about thirteen days late, witness the
timing of *M. Brit.*'s reviews.

No. 85 (11–17 *August*)

Actual date: some time after 24 Aug., possibly 31 Aug.?

Evidence: Luke (see on no. 79 above) remarks on Saturday, 24 Aug. on
Aulicus's non-appearance. Presumably no. 86 was similarly
behindhand.

No. 87 (25–31 *August*)

Actual date: about 15 Sept.? But see the next item.

Evidence: *M. Aul.* referred, under 31 Aug. (p. 1142), to an event that
took place on 1 Sept., and which appears to have been reported
in Oxford on 13 Sept., under which date *M. Aul.* reported it
fully.

No. 88 (1–7 *September*)

Actual date: about 20 Sept.?

Evidence: reviewed by *M. Brit.*, no. 51 (23–30 Sept.), which also dealt
with no. 87. No. 88, under 6 Sept., told readers that it would in
the next week describe the siege of Basing Castle, which had
been relieved. The party which achieved this did not leave
Oxford until 9 Sept., reached Basing on 11 Sept., and got back
to Oxford on the 13th.

Nos. 89 (8–14 *September*) *to* 93 (6–12 *October*)

Actual dates: all these were running about thirteen days late?

Evidence: the timing of *M. Brit.*'s reviews; and *M. Aul.*, no. 91 (22–28
Sept.) has running heads from no. 90 (on p. 1181) and from
no. 89 (on p. 1182).

No. 94 (13–19 *October*)

Actual date: about 1 Nov.?

Evidence: reviewed by *M. Brit.*, no. 57 (4–11 Nov.). *M. Aul.* kept a
running-head from no. 93 (on p. 1218); and in the body of the
text it headed the report for Saturday, 19 Oct., with 'Saturday.
October 12' (p. 1217). It also referred the reader to material
printed under 25 Oct.

No. 95 (20–26 *October*)

Actual date: about 8 Nov.?

Evidence: reviewed by *M. Brit.*, no. 58 (11–18 Nov.). It kept running-heads from no. 94 (on pp. 1227, 1228, 1229, and 1230), and had a date-heading in the text from that week (p. 1227). *M. Brit.* observed that *M. Aul.* was now often at a standstill.

No. 96 (27 *October*–2 *November*)

Actual date: about 18 Nov.?

Evidence: *M. Brit.*, no. 59 (18–25 Nov.), stated that *M. Aul.* was so slow in getting to London that it almost despaired of its arrival that week.

Nos. 97 (3–9 *November*) *to* 99 (17–23 *November*)

Actual dates: all these appeared about 13 Dec.

Evidence: *M. Brit.*, no. 60 (2–9 Dec.), observed that *M. Aul.* was not to be seen, and no. 61 (9–16 Dec.) repeated the point. No. 62 (16–23 Dec.) then stated explicitly that these three numbers of *M. Aul.* had arrived in London together. Even then, it will be noticed, the Oxford newsbook had been unable to avoid falling another week behind schedule. It was at this point that the editor was for the first time forced to leave gaps in the issue.

No. 100 (29 *December*–5 *January* 1645)

Actual date: about 17 Jan.?

Evidence: reviewed by *M. Brit.*, no. 67 (20–27 Jan.). *M. Aul.* had managed to catch up somewhat on events only by leaving out a number of weeks.

Nos. 101 (5–12 *January*) *to* 105 (9–16 *February*)

Actual dates: all these were running about twelve days late, witness the timing of *M. Brit.*'s reviews. *M. Aul.*, no. 104 (2–9 Feb.) referred to two dispatches that did not arrive in Oxford until 13 and 15 Feb. respectively, as its own reports show.

No. 106 (21 *February*–2 *March*)

Actual date: about 8 Mar.

Evidence: reviewed by *M. Brit.*, no. 74 (10–17 Mar.). But *M. Aul.* referred under 1 Mar. to an express that arrived while it was being written. This was from Newark and got to Oxford on 8 Mar., according to *M. Aul.* itself. The latter had, nevertheless, made up a lot of ground this week.

Nos. 107 (2–9 *March*) *to* 112 (20–27 *April*)

Actual dates: all these were running about five days late, judging by the timing of *M. Brit.*'s reviews.

No. 113 (27 *April*–4 *May*)

Actual date: about 16 May?

Evidence: reviewed by *M. Brit.*, no. 84 (19–26 May). *M. Aul.* referred to news of Montrose, which was printed in the next week under 10 May, when the express bringing it arrived. The Oxford newsbook had been unable to keep up its pace again.

No. 114 (4–11 *May*)

Actual date: about 23 May?

Evidence: reviewed by *M. Brit.*, no. 85 (26 May–2 June).

No. 115 (25 *May*–8 *June*)

Actual date: about 13 June?

Evidence: reviewed by *M. Brit.*, no. 87 (16–23 June). This was two weeks in one, so *M. Aul.* caught up a week again. Luke (letter 736, op. cit. under no. 79 above) remarks on 15 June 1645 that *Aulicus* has revived.

No. 116 (13–20 *July*)

Actual date: about 12 Aug.?

Evidence: reviewed by *M. Brit.*, no. 93 (11–18 Aug.). *M. Aul.* stated under 19 July that it would give certain news in the next week; this news was not received at Oxford until 12 Aug. under which date the newsbook reported it fully. The extremely late date of this week of *M. Aul.* means that only one number appeared in the whole of June and July; and where Madan's collation reveals two gaps of five and three weeks there was really one interval of nine weeks. Luke (letter 760, op. cit. under no. 79 above) remarks on 25 June 1645 that *Aulicus* has ceased publication since Naseby, 14 June.

No. 117 (10–17 *August*)

Actual date: about 22 Aug.?

Evidence: reviewed by *M. Brit.*, no. 95 (25 Aug.–1 Sept.), which stated that *M. Aul.* had only got to London just in time to be criticized. Even so, it had made up much ground.

No. 118 (31 *August–7 September*)

Actual date: about 12 Sept.?

Evidence: reviewed by *M. Brit.*, no. 98 (15–22 Sept.). This was the last number of *M. Aul.* The narrowing of the gap at this stage had been simply a final fling.

APPENDIX II

Mercurius Aulicus: 'Supplements'

THIS list is not exhaustive: it aims only to give a substantial sample of those pamphlets in which there are interesting resemblances to *Aulicus*. In most of this sample there are verbal parallels with the newsbook, sometimes extensive ones. The list at least shows that 1643 was a particularly busy time for Oxford apologists, that in 1644 they were far less active, and that they launched a last vigorous offensive in early 1645. It also establishes that *Aulicus* covered the ground remarkably well when at its best, and that it was the spearhead of the Royalist propaganda campaign. Berkenhead may have had a hand in composing some of these pamphlets, and he probably helped prepare them for the press. The dates are derived from Madan's *Oxford Books*, vol. ii, and the pamphlets are arranged in chronological order:

A True and Briefe Relation of the Great Victory Obtained by Sir Ralph Hopton, neare Bodmin, about 27 January 1643.

This, by Heylin, was a supplement in the strict bibliographical sense. Wood 375 (30).

A Second, but More Perfect Relation of the Great Victory, early February 1643.

This is a condensed rewriting of the first, also by Heylin, with material relating to subsequent events added. See *Aulicus*, no. 4. (22–28 Jan.), pp. 47–8 and no. 5 (29 Jan.–4 Feb.), pp. 59–60 for factual and stylistic resemblances. Bodleian Library, Antiq. e. E. 1642/75.

A Particular Relation of the Action before Cyrencester, about 11 February 1643.

This is far more detailed than *Aulicus*'s account, but compare the remarks about Captain Buck on p. 4 with no. 5 (29 Jan.–4 Feb.), p. 63. Wood 375 (33).

A Briefe Relation of the Remarkable Occurrences in the Northerne Parts, about 7 March 1643.

This, by Heylin, criticizes London newsbooks and implies that it is intended to supplement the account in 'the weekly Mercury' (p. 1). Compare pp. 3, 6, and 11 with no. 9 (26 Feb.–4 Mar.), pp. 109 and 115.

A View of the Proceedings of the Western Counties for the Pacification, about 21 March 1643.

Compare pp. 7 and 10 with no. 11 (12–18 Mar.), pp. 132–3 and no. 12 (19–25 Mar.), p. 145. The newsbook (p. 133) referred the reader to this 'larger and more full Relation'.

The Battaile on Hopton-Heath, about 27 March 1643.

The Preface and Conclusion of this seem to be by Berkenhead and Heylin respectively, and no. 13 (26 Mar.–2 Apr.), p. 160 referred the reader to this account. Compare also no. 12 (19–25 Mar.), pp. 147–8, which is clearly based on the dispatch printed verbatim in the pamphlet.

Theeves, Theeves, about 26 April 1643.

This was by Heylin, and its attack on the Rebel methods of raising money was in line with the tactics of *Aulicus,* no. 17 (23–29 Apr.), p. 218 and no. 18 (30 Apr.–6 May), pp. 225–6.

A Letter to a Gentleman of Leicestershire, 13 May 1643.

This, by Heylin, sets out to prove that all advances about peace had been made by the King. Compare the phrase used on p. 9 to describe the 'Preamble' of Parliament's Proposition of 1 Feb. 1643, with that in no. 5 (29 Jan.–4 Feb.), p. 61. The language of both owes something to the King's Message of 12 Apr. 1643.

The Round-Heads Remembrancer, about 2 June 1643.

This deals with Sir Ralph Hopton's victory at Stratton on 16 May, reported in no. 20 (14–20 May), pp. 262–3. Compare also the remarks on the Queen's having been voted guilty of High Treason on pp. 2–3 with no. 21 (21–27 May), p. 280.

An Express Relation of the Passages and Proceedings of His Majesties Armies under the Command of . . . the Earle of Newcastle, about 10 July 1643.

Compare the narratives in no. 27 (2–8 July), pp. 349–50, 357–8, and 361. It is interesting to note that the newsbook in this case alters casualty figures. Bodleian Library, 4°. L. 72. Art.

A Letter Written out of Bedfordshire unto the Earle of Manchester, about 20 July 1643.

Compare the account of the Battle of Roundway Down in no. 28 (9–15 July), pp. 371–2. B.M., 669. f. 8 (13).

A True and Impartiall Relation of the Battaile . . . neare Newbury, about 25 September 1643.

This account by Lord George Digby was clearly used as the source for *Aulicus*'s narrative of the battle: compare, for example, p. 7 with no. 38 (17–23 Sept.), p. 528.

Lord Have Mercie upon Us, about 2 November 1643.

This, by Heylin, echoes the newsbook's arguments about London's responsibility for the Rebellion. Compare also the wording of p. 38 with no. 31 (30 July–5 Aug.), p. 416.

The Copy of a Letter from Collonell Francis Anderson to Sir Thomas Glemham, about 1 February 1644.

This includes 'The Copy of a Letter from the Marques of Argyle . . . to Sir Thomas Glemham', and Glemham's letter in reply to this. This reply is printed verbatim in no. 57 (28 Jan.–3 Feb.), pp. 808–11.

A Description of the Siege of Basing Castle, late January 1645.

This appears to be an eyewitness account, but it is quite possible that it was really compiled at Oxford from dispatches. There are numerous parallels with accounts scattered through *Aulicus:* compare, for example, p. 9 with no. 85 (11–17 Aug. 1644), p. 1123, and p. 19 with no. 98 (10–16 Nov.), pp. 1257–8. No. 100 (29 Dec.–5 Jan. 1645), p. 1328 referred to this pamphlet as being ready for publication, but as the newsbook was being issued late, this is not an indication that Madan's dating is far out.

A True Relation of the Happy Successe of His Majesties Forces in Scotland, late January 1645.

This is clearly compiled from the various dispatches which *Aulicus* had used as the source of its accounts of Montrose's actions. No. 100 (29 Dec.–5 Jan.), p. 1328, referred readers to it. The same point about dating applies as for the *Siege of Basing Castle,* above.

A True Copy of Certain Passages of the Lord Arch-Bishop of Canterbury his Speech, early February 1645.

This is identical with the verbatim version of Laud's speech printed in no. 101 (5–12 Jan.).

A Briefe Relation of the Death and Sufferings of . . . the L. Archbishop of Canterbury, about 6 February 1645.

This was by Heylin, and it echoes *Aulicus*: compare pp. 2, 8, 11, and 27 with no. 101 (5–12 Jan.), pp. 1332–3. It is interesting to note that Heylin, in *The Life of William Lord Archbishop of Canterbury* (1668), p. 528, referred to *Aulicus*'s account. A contemporary, *The Kingdomes Weekly Intelligencer*, no. 96 (15–22 Apr. 1645), p. 774, noted that *Aulicus* had stated that the sun shone on Laud's face until the moment of his death. This in fact was not in the newsbook, but on p. 26 of the present pamphlet. This shows how closely these pamphlets were associated with the newsbook in the public imagination.

A True Copy of Colonel Sr Gamaliel Dudley's Letter to . . . Prince Rupert, about 15 March 1645.

The whole of this dispatch was printed in no. 107 (2–9 Mar.), pp. 1401–7. Bodleian Library, C. 14. 5. Linc.

Alter Britanniae Heros: or the Life of . . . Sir Henry Gage, 18 September 1645.

This was by Edward Walsingham. The section on p. 12 dealing with Gage's actions around Basing was clearly based on the practically identical passages in no. 89 (8–14 Sept. 1644), p. 1160.

Associated Pamphlets and Periodicals

Anti-Royalist Periodicals

MOST of the newsbooks published in London during *Aulicus*'s run were designed to counter it in one way or another. This list is confined to those which either introduced themselves as direct opponents of the Oxford newsbook or, though not announcing their intentions in this way, frequently criticized its narratives. The editors' names are taken from J. B. Williams, *A History of English Journalism* (1908), and Joseph Frank, *The Beginnings of the English Newspaper, 1620–1660* (Cambridge, Mass., 1961): these are also the source of most of the dates given, but they have been checked against G. K. Fortescue's *Catalogue of the Thomason Tracts* (1908), and the *British Union-Catalogue of Periodicals* (1955–58).

The number of opponents shows how extensive *Aulicus*'s influence was and suggests that opposition to it was commercially profitable as well as politically necessary:

A Continuation of Certain Speciall and Remarkable Passages,
  by Samuel Pecke (15–19 Aug. 1642 to 17 Sept. 1647).

An Antidote against the Malignant Influence of Mercurius (surnamed) Aulicus.
  Only one number survives, for 2 Sept. 1643. Copy in Yale Univ. Library.

The Kingdomes Weekly Intelligencer,
  by Richard Collings (27 Dec.–3 Jan. 1643 to 9 Oct. 1649).

Certaine Informations,
  by William Ingler (16–23 Jan. 1643 to 21 Feb. 1644).

Mercurius Civicus,
  by Richard Collings (4–11 May 1643 to 10 Dec. 1646). This proclaimed itself an opponent of *Aulicus* in its first number.

The Parliament Scout,

by John Dillingham (20–27 June 1643 to 30 Jan. 1645).

A Perfect Diurnall of Some Passages in Parliament,

by Samuel Pecke (26 June–3 July 1643 to 8 Oct. 1649). The first number stated that countering *Aulicus*'s reports was among its aims; thereafter the editor simply presented news without alluding to the Oxford newsbook.

Mercurius Britanicus,

by Thomas Audley and Marchamont Nedham (23–29 Aug. 1643 to 18 May 1646). Criticism of *Aulicus* was the main function of this newsbook; and it seems to have been, in consequence, the most popular of the London periodicals up to 1646. It boasted of being, and was recognized as, *Aulicus*'s arch enemy.

The Weekly Account,

by Daniel Border (from 1 Sept. 1643 to 29 Apr. 1645, when it changed its title, continuing until 28 June 1647). The first number offered, for the satisfaction of the reader, six reasons against *Aulicus.*

The Scotch Mercury,

by George Smith; one number only appeared, dated 5 Oct. 1643. It tried to get into *Britanicus*'s profitable act, by making observations on the quarrel between that newsbook and *Aulicus*. After this initial move the editor changed his title, and his periodical appeared as the next item.

The Scotch Intelligencer

(13–17 Oct. 1643 to 25 Oct. 1643). The second number, for 19–25 Oct., warned readers against *Aulicus* and, inspired by commercial ambition rather than political loyalty, advised *Britanicus* that it had done enough! Meanwhile Smith brought out the next periodical, which succeeded in establishing itself.

The Scotish Dove

(13–20 Oct. 1643, to 25 Dec. 1646). The title-page of earlier numbers carries the legend, 'an Antidote against . . . Mercurius Aulicus'. It is mentioned, together with *Mercurius Civicus, The Parliament Scout,* and *Mercurius Britanicus,* as a principal opponent of *Aulicus* by John Taylor, *No Mercurius Aulicus* (about 15 June 1644).

The Welch Mercurie

(from 21–28 Oct. 1643 to 11 Nov. 1643, when it changed its title to the next listed). The Londoners were now competing with one another for the title of *Aulicus*'s most effective enemy; and no. 2 (28 Oct.–3 Nov.) of the present periodical passed nasty remarks about *The Scotish Dove*.

Mercurius Cambro-Britannus.

This carried on from the last with no. 4 (11–20 Nov. 1643). It is not certain how long it lasted, but there is extant a no. 8 (17–24 Jan. 1644).

Informator Rusticus,

probably by Henry Walker; one number, for 27 Oct.–3 Nov. 1643, has survived. After some rude comments on *Aulicus* the editor observed that *Britanicus* has sufficiently revealed its fallacies, and proceeds to retail news.

The Kingdomes Weekly Post,

probably by John Rushworth (9 Nov. 1643 to 8 Dec. 1645). No. 5 (28 Nov.–6 Dec.), passed some remarks about *Aulicus*, and then decided to 'leave him to *Mercurius Britanicus*' (p. 34).

Mercurius Anglicus

(31 Jan.–7 Feb. 1644 to 20 Feb. 1644). The first number referred sarcastically to *Aulicus*, but explicitly stated that it would not concentrate exclusively on it, for fear of becoming too satirical and trying the readers' patience.

The Spie,

by Durant Hotham (23–30 Jan. 1644 to 25 June 1644). This set about *Aulicus* from the start, in the same dedicated way as *Britanicus*; in the second week (for 30 Jan.–5 Feb.), in fact, the editor stated that he aimed to do the same as the latter, but with a better grace. It did, indeed, achieve a better standard of style and humour than *Britanicus*. There was open rivalry between these two Londoners: *Britanicus* accused *The Spie* of being a subversive ally of *Aulicus*, see no. 24 (19–26 Feb. 1644); and *The Spie* boasted of beating *Britanicus* to the punch with criticizing *Aulicus*, see no. 5 (20–27 Feb. 1644).

Anti-Aulicus.

Only two numbers survive, dated 6 and 13 Feb. 1644 respectively.

The Military Scribe,

possibly by Sir John Wray (20–27 Feb. 1644 to 2 Apr. 1644); see *M. Aul.,* no. 61 (25 Feb.–2 Mar. 1644), p. 861; he was a zealous Presbyterian.

A Counterfeit *Mercurius Britanicus*

(12–18 Mar. to 1 Apr. 1644). The three numbers of this ran parallel to numbers 27, 28, and 29 of the genuine *Britanicus* and copied its typography, lay-out, and style. This practical attempt to cut out the genuine *Britanicus* aroused the latter's wrath, and the editor was forced to change his title to that next listed.

Mercurius Aulico Mastix.

Only one number survives, dated 12 Apr. 1644. Presumably, without the attraction of the name *Britanicus* on the title-page, the project failed.

Britaines Remembrancer

(12–19 Mar. 1644 to 2 Apr. 1644). The first number called itself another of *Aulicus*'s 'enemies in print' (p. 1).

Perfect Occurrences of Parliament,

by Henry Walker from late 1644 on (24–31 May 1644 to 5 Mar. 1646).

Le Mercure Anglois,

by John Cotgrave (7 June 1644, to 4 Mar. 1649). This was in French and designed for circulation abroad. It makes a number of remarks against *Aulicus.*

The Court Mercurie,

by John Cotgrave (22 June–2 July 1644 to 16 Oct. 1644). The title suggests that this had designs on *Aulicus,* and it is, in fact, rich in interesting comments on the latter.

A Letter from a Minister in His Excellencies Army,

by E. B. (20 Apr. 1643). This was a serial rather than a periodical, growing, without premeditation, out of what was meant to be a single pamphlet in the first place. It was an account of the siege of Reading and claimed to be 'By way of prevention to Mercurius Aulicus'. It was followed by *The Second Intelligence from Reading* (24 Apr.), *The Third Intelligence* (26 Apr.), which called itself 'Mercurius Bellicus' (C2ʳ), and *The Last Joyfull Intelligence* (27 Apr.). See H. M. Weber, 'The *Mercurius Bellicus* of 1643', *Notes and Queries,* clxv (1933), 345–6.

Anti-Royalist pamphlets

The dating of most of these is that suggested by Madan, *Oxford Books*, vol. ii.

A Copy of a Letter Written by Mr. Stephen Marshall

(about 17 May 1643). This was directed against *A Letter of Spirituall Advice*, published in Oxford at the end of March 1643; but it also complains bitterly about rumours spread by the newsbook.

A True Relation of the Great and Glorious Victory Obtained by Sir William Waller

(14 July 1643). This was published to refute *Aulicus's* version of events. Wood 376 (20).

(*Good Newes from All Quarters of the Kingdome, particularly from Gloucester*), *Oxfords Latin Rimes*

(13 Sept. 1643).

A Counterfeit *Mercurius Aulicus*.

This was a spurious edition of no. 40 (1–7 Oct. 1643). It differed in content from the real number, and insinuated Parliamentarian views.

An Answer to Mercurius Aulicus: or his Communicated Intelligence from the Court

(about 15 Dec. 1643). This refutes in detail no. 49 (3–9 Dec.).

Mercurius Coelicus,

by John Booker (25 Jan. 1644). This was aimed mainly against George Wharton, the Royalist astrologer, but also sneered at 'Mercurius Aulicus his abominable lying Legend' (A1ᵛ).

The Recantation of Mercurius Aulicus, or Berkinhead's Complaint

(14 Mar. 1644). B.M., E 37 (17.).

Aulicus his Dream,

by Francis Cheynell (15 May 1644).

Ruperts Sumpter and Private Cabinet Rifled

(about 19 July 1644). This takes the form of a dialogue between *Aulicus* and *Britanicus*. B.M., E. 2 (24).

No Mercurius Aquaticus,

> by John Booker (19 July 1644). This was aimed mainly at John Taylor, but also hits at *Aulicus*. B.M., E. 2 (22).

A Rope Treble-twisted for John Taylor,

> by John Booker (27 Sept. 1644). This is concerned with *Aulicus* to the same degree as the last item.

The Devill's White Boyes,

> by Richard Brathwaite (26 Oct. 1644). B.M., E. 14 (11).

The Arraignment of Mercurius Aulicus

> (about 4 Feb. 1645). The title-page of this carries a woodcut of a man, presumably meant to be Berkenhead, in a pillory. It is the usual crude sort of representation, and no guide to Berkenhead's actual appearance.

Newes from Smith the Oxford Jaylor. With the Arraignment of Mercurius Aulicus . . .

> (about 4 Feb. 1645). This carries the same woodcut as the last. See *Catalogue of Prints in the British Museum*, Div. I, Satires (1870), i. 306–7. B.M., E. 27 (13).

The Great Azzizes Holden in Parnassus

> (11 Feb. 1645). This is a mock trial at which most of the contemporary newsbooks are arraigned. *Aulicus* is one of the principal defendants.

A Whip for an Ape: or Aulicus his Whelp Worm'd

> (about 28 Aug. 1645). B.M., E. 298 (18).

The True Character of Mercurius Aulicus.

> Beyond the year, 1645, nothing is known of the date at which this was published. This is the best and most informative of the pamphlets attacking *Aulicus*. B.M., Burney 20 (1).

A Character of the New Oxford Libeller

> (10 Feb. 1645). This was a reply to John Cleaveland's *Character of a London Diurnall*, but also got in some blows at *Aulicus*.

A Full Answer to a Scandalous Pamphlet

> (about 9 Apr. 1645). Another reply to Cleaveland, which had some things to say about *Aulicus*.

The Oxford Character of the London Diurnall Examined

(30 Mar. 1645). Of the three replies to Cleaveland this has the most to say about *Aulicus*. B.M., E. 274 (32).

Periodicals in support of Aulicus

Mercurius Rusticus,

by Bruno Ryves (20 May 1643 to 16 Mar. 1644). This, a kind of supplement to *Aulicus,* consisted largely of accounts of sieges and of desecration of churches by the Rebels. The events it described were by no means of immediately recent occurrence: for example the first four numbers deal with events of the summer of 1642. Many of its twenty-one numbers were reprinted at Shrewsbury, often several weeks after the publication in Oxford; but as it was in any case retrospective this did not deprive it of all value. It was also reprinted in July 1646.

Mercurius Academicus,

by Richard Little (15 Dec. 1645 to 21 Mar. 1646). This began after *Aulicus* ended, but it represented an attempt to restart the Oxford periodical under another title. It was more preoccupied with London newsbooks than *Aulicus* was.

Britanicus Vapulans,

by Daniel Featley (4 Nov. 1643). This was the first number of a serial, of which the second appeared under the next title.

Mercurius Urbanus

(9 Nov. 1643).

Pamphlets in support of Aulicus

A New Diurnall of Passages

(May 1643). This caricatures various weekly London newsbooks, especially *A Perfect Diurnall.* Bodleian Library, Bliss B. 49.

A Preter-Pluperfect, Spick and Span New Nocturnal,

by John Taylor (about 6 Aug. 1643). This is a humorous imitation of the London newsbooks that were trying to copy *Aulicus.* B.M., E. 65 (1).

A Letter from Mercurius Civicus to Mercurius Rusticus,

by John Berkenhead (about 20 Aug. 1643). It, incidentally, attacks London newsbooks.

The Gentle Lash,

by Daniel Featley (2 Jan. 1644). This was primarily a defence of the writer's reputation; but, as it attacked London newsbooks, it did assist *Aulicus.*

Mercurius Aquaticus,

by John Taylor (about 13 Jan. 1644). This was a detailed criticism of *M. Brit.*, no. 16 (7–14 Dec. 1643). B.M., E. 29 (11).

No Mercurius Aulicus,

by John Taylor (about 15 June 1644). This was primarily aimed against John Booker; but it also attacks various London newsbooks and defends 'our true and exact *Mercurius Aulicus*' (p. 3).

Sacra Nemesis . . ., or, Mercurius Britan-Civicus Disciplin'd,

by Daniel Featley (1 Aug. 1644). The author had been accused of acting as intelligencer to *Aulicus,* and in this hit back at the London newsbooks.

The Character of a London Diurnall,

by John Cleaveland (late January 1645). This was primarily directed against *Britanicus* and *A Perfect Diurnall,* but also mentioned *Mercurius Civicus* and *Mercurius Scoticus.* It was an attempt to sustain *Aulicus*'s faltering reputation by satirizing the London opposition.

The Rebells Anathematized,

by John Taylor (about 18 May 1645). This was an attack on various London newsbooks.

Mercurius Anti-Britanicus,

by John Berkenhead; in three parts, dated 4, 11, and 18 Aug. 1645. This contains useful information about the editors of the London newsbook. For the second part see B.M., E. 296 (9).

Aulicus his Hue and Cry Sent forth after Britanicus,

possibly by Francis Cheynell (about 12 Aug. 1645). It was in reply to *M. Brit.*, no. 92 (28 July–4 Aug. 1645), and triumphed that Nedham, *Britanicus*'s editor, had been imprisoned for his indiscreet attacks on the King. J. Frank, *The Beginnings of the English Newspaper, 1620–1660,* p. 99, describes it as almost certainly by Berkenhead. In fact, its style does not suggest him.

APPENDIX IV

Mercurius Bellicus

THE collation of all the extant copies reveals three gaps in the series (nos. 9, 15, and 20 below) and the missing numbers were probably never printed. In the case of no. 9, for example, the preceding and succeeding number both comment on the activities of the searchers. The editor presumably had to lie low for a week, and it was probably similar considerations that kept him quiet in the fifteenth and twentieth weeks. If so, he must have adopted, in the first two cases, *Aulicus*'s trick of adjusting page signatures to disguise the lapse.

There is no twenty-fifth number of the newsbook, but the apparent gap in the sequence is filled by a supplementary pamphlet, advertised in no. 24 and received by Thomason on 19 July. It must have been published concurrently with no. 26. The second supplementary pamphlet, at the end of the list, was also advertised in *Bellicus*, no. 27. It is not extant and may not have been printed.

1.	13–22 Nov. 1647,	Sun.–Mon.,	A⁴,	pp. 1–8.
2.	22–29 Nov.	Mon.–Mon.,	B⁴,	pp. 9–16.
3.	8–14 Feb. 1648,	Tues.–Tues.,	C⁴,	pp. 1–8.
4.	14–20 Feb.	,, ,,	D⁴,	,, ,,
5.	22–29 Feb.	,, ,,	E⁴,	,, ,,
6.	29 Feb.–7 Mar.	,, ,,	F⁴,	,, ,,
7.	7–14 Mar.	,, ,,	G⁴,	,, ,,
8.	14–21 Mar.	,, ,,	H⁴,	,, ,,
9.	No issue.			
10.	28 Mar.–4 Apr.	Tues.–Tues.,	K⁴,	pp. 1–8.
11.	4–11 Apr.	,, ,,	L⁴,	,, ,,
12.	11–18 Apr.	,, ,,	M⁴,	,, ,,
13.	18–25 Apr.	,, ,,	N⁴,	,, ,,
14.	25 Apr.–2 May	,, ,,	O⁴,	,, ,,
15.	No issue.			
16.	9–16 May	Tues.–Tues.,	Q⁴,	pp. 1–8.
17.	16–23 May	,, ,,	R⁴,	,, ,,
18.	23–30 May	,, ,,	A⁴,	,, ,,
19.	30 May–6 June	,, ,,	A⁴,	,, ,,
20.	No issue.			

21.	13–20 June	Tues.–Tues.,	A⁴,	pp. 1–8.
22.	20–27 June	„ „	A⁴,	„ „
23.	27 June–5 July	„ Wed.,	A⁴,	„ „
24.	4–11 July	„ Tues.,	A⁴,	„ „

A Cittie Dog in a Saints Doublet (19 July), four leaves, unpaged and unsigned.

26.	11–18 July	Tues.–Tues.,	A⁴,	pp. 1–8.
27.	19–26 July	Wed.–Wed.,	A⁴,	unpaged.

A Scotch Broom with an English handle, not extant.

APPENDIX V

Paul's Church-Yard and Bibliotheca Parliamenti

THE editions of *Paul's Church-Yard* are identical in format and cannot be distinguished by variations in the contents; they are therefore identified by differences in the type-setting. In the case of two of the editions of the second 'century', E. 652 (14) and Wood C. 26 (16ᵇ), the variations cited are the only ones detectable; in the others the variations listed are merely samples; and E. 989 (7), for example, can also be distinguished as the only copy of the second 'century' which does not have red type in the title-heading. Similarly, among the editions of the first 'century', G. Pamph. 1780 (27) has in its title-heading '(*una cum* Templo) prostant venales', whereas E. 989 (7) has '(una cum Templo) prostant venales'. The present method of identification has, however, been adopted as the most consistent and clear for purposes of tabulation.

The G. Pamph. and Wood copies are in the Bodleian Library; the others are in the Thomason Collection in the British Museum. Thomason acquired E. 637 (15) on 24 July 1651, E. 652 (14) in February 1652, and the E. 989 (7) copies on 6 July 1659. It is impossible to date the G. Pamph. copies from this, though it seems likely that they antedated Thomason's editions. The Wood copy of the second 'century' appears to have been a reprint of E. 652 (14) and probably appeared, like it, in 1652. The third 'century', E. 675 (12) reached Thomason on 20 September 1652.

The contents of the various editions of each 'Classis' of *Bibliotheca Parliamenti* are also identical; but simpler methods of identification are adequate. Again, the dating of the editions not in the Thomason Collection is uncertain. He received E. 693 (19) on 3 May 1653 and E. 702 (8) on 23 June 1653.

Identification of editions:

Paul's Church-Yard (first Centuria)

G. Pamph. 1780 (27),	A1ʳ, item 4,	Scripture, / taken out
	A1ʳ, item 6,	12 per Cent. By / Dr.
E. 989 (7),	A1ʳ, item 4,	Scripture / taken out
	A1ʳ, item 6,	12 per Cent. / by Dr.
E. 637 (15) and Wood C. 26 (16ᵃ)	A1ʳ, item 4,	Scripture, taken / out

Paul's Church-Yard (second Centuria)

G. Pamph. 1780 (27),	B1ʳ, item 103,	bet–/ter than Kings
E. 989 (7),	„ „	better than / Kings
E. 652 (14),	„ „	better / than Kings
	B1ʳ, item 107,	Penbrochiana
	B4ᵛ, item 195,	Defence
Wood C. 26 (16ᵇ)	B1ʳ, item 103,	better / than Kings
	B1ʳ, item 107,	Pembrochiana
	B4ᵛ, item 195,	defence

Paul's Church-Yard (third Centuria)

E. 675 (12), the only copy.

Bibliotheca Parliamenti (first Classis)

E. 693 (19),	sm. 4°,	this has on the title-page a woodcut representing Mercury in a chariot.
Bodleian Library, 70b. 63,	sm. 4°,	this has no woodcut.

Bibliotheca Parliamenti (second Classis)

E. 702 (8),	sm. 4°,
B.M., 103. h. 8 (2),	12°.

Some parallels with 'Paul's Church-Yard' and 'Bibliotheca Parliamenti' found in other works by Berkenhead:

1. *The Assembly Man*

The Assembler curses the King in the pulpit, 'though heaven strike him dumb in the very Act, as it did Hill at Cambridge, who while he prayed, "Depose him, O Lord, who would depose us", was made the dumb devil'. [*Harl. Misc.* v. 101.]

Compare:

'Whether Doctor Hill were a King when he prayed, O Lord do thou depose Him, who would depose Us?' [*Two Centuries*, item 169 (*Harl. Misc.* ix. 416).]

'Whether the said Doctor Hill (being then strook spechlesse) had the spirit of Utterance or the Dumb Devill?' [*Two Centuries*, item 170, ibid.]

2. *The Assembly Man*

'When Rous stood forth for his tryal, Robin Wisdom was found the better Poet.' [P. 102.]

Compare:

'Whether Mr. Rous or Robbin Wisdome be the better Poet?' [*Two Centuries*, item 87, p. 413.]

3. *Mercurius Bellicus*, no. 16 (9–16 May 1648)

'That it shall be high Treason, for any whatsoever to touch the Nose of Leiutenant Generall Cromwell, either with Pincers, Snuffers, or Fingers.' [Q4ʳ.]

Compare:

'Whether Cromwell's nose, though (as yet) the great light of our New England, be not likely, ere long, to go out in a snuff?' [*Bibl. Parl.*, in *Two Centuries*, 'Cases of Conscience', item 25 (*Harl. Misc.* ix. 421).]

4. *Newes from Pembroke and Mongomery*

'Mr. Palmer, I have made you Head of All-Souls, and have turned out Sheldon; I hope you love me, for you are a Physician, and never any Physician was Head of All-Souls: they say their statutes do keep you out; hang their statutes, I'll keep you in: you are a member of the House of Commons, and, a Member of Parliament may be Head of any house.' [*Harl. Misc.* v. 113.]

Compare:

'A Declaration from All-Souls College in Oxford, that since they were deprived of their Warden Doctor Sheldon, they have not been an hour out of the Physicians hands: most members of that College being strangely taken away; and a Member of Parliament set over the rest.' [*Two Centuries*, item 53, p. 411.]

5. *The Speech in the House of Peeres upon the Debate of the Cities Petition*

'I hate surplices too ever since Mr. Henderson preached it up for the whore of Babylon's smock. It seems he had taken it up often, for he had many a bout with her (as Mr. Sedgwick sayes) now and anon too.' [*S. Tracts*, vii. 85.]

Compare:

'Ordered, That all seamens widows be sent to Obadiah Sedgewick for due benevolence: and this Ordinance to last both now and anon too.' [*Bibl. Parl.*, in *Two Centuries*, 'Acts and Orders', item 14, p. 420.]

6. *The Last Will and Testament of the Earl of Pembroke*

'Item, Because I threatened Sir Henry Mildmay, but did not beat him, I give fifty pounds to the footman that cudgelled him.' [*S. Tracts*, vii. 90.]

Compare:

'Whether Balaam's beating his owne ass were a sufficient warrant for the footman's cudgelling Sir Harry Mildmay?' [*Bibl. Parl.*, 'Cases of Conscience', item 1 (*S. Tracts*, vii. 96).]

Compare:

Mildmay 'was soundly cudgelled the other day, and kickt (most soundly kickt in sooth la) by a resolute Footman of my Lord Dukes'. [*M. Bell.*, no. 22 (20–27 June 1648), A4v.]

7. *The Last Will and Testament of the Earl of Pembroke*

'Item, my will is, that the said Sir Harry shall not meddle with my jewels. I knew him when he served the Duke of Buckingham; and since how he handled the state jewels.' [*S. Tracts*, vii. 90.]

Compare:

'*Chiromantia*, The baudy Language of the Hand and Fingers, invented and found out by Sir Harry Mildmay, whilst he was Pimp to the Duke of Buckingham.' [*Bibl. Parl.*, second Classis, 'Books', item 14 (*S. Tracts*, vii. 93).]

Some earlier examples of mock resolves, edicts, etc.:

A Wife now the Widdow of Sir Thomas Overburye, 1615.
This includes some mock resolves.

New and Choice Characters, 1615.
This includes 'Certain Edicts from a Parliament in Eutopia'.

The Resolution of the Round-Heads, 1641.
This includes some mock resolves and orders.

A Pleasant Purge . . . consisting of a Century of Polemical Epigrams, 1641.
By William Prynne.

New Orders, New, 1642.

Certain Propositions Offered to the . . . Houses of Parliament, 1642.

A New Mercury, Called Mercurius Problematicus, 1644.

A Character of a London Diurnall, 1645.
By John Cleaveland. This includes some mock resolves.

The Editor of Rump Songs

THE two chief collections of Rump Songs were *The Rump, or A Collection of Songs and Ballads*, published about 21 June 1660, and *Rump: or An Exact Collection*, published in 1662. A full account of the second volume and details of later reprints of the Songs is obtainable in H. F. Brooks's 'Rump Songs, An Index with Notes', *Oxford Bibl. Soc. Proceedings and Papers*, v (1936–9), 281–93.

In both collections there were three poems by Berkenhead: *The Four-Legg'd Elder*, *The Four-Legg'd Quaker*, and *A Jolt*, and the editor, 'I. B. Esq', intriguingly draws special attention to them in his address to the reader. There is, therefore, reason to suggest that the modest editor was John Berkenhead, who was certainly never averse to self-advertisement. Moreover, the style and sentiments of his address lend some weight to the suggestion. 'I. B.' rejoices that 'we have liv'd to see that day, that there is no Cavalier, because there is nothing else . . .', and that 'those that wrote against the King do now write for Him, and those who wrote for Him, need now write no more'. He defends his selection of ballads with almost cock-sure confidence: 'We confess wee refused some Ballads (and we know why wee did so) which perhaps you will have from some other officious hand. But you'll grant we have made you ample satisfaction . . .' It is at this point that he mentions the ballads by Berkenhead. The address is, in short, moderately witty, urbane, and inclined to be magisterial, as Berkenhead was wont to be. It is interesting, too, to find the editor reminding the reader that 'If thou read these Ballads (and not sing them) the poor Ballads are undone': this was the very point that Berkenhead made about his own ballad of 1666, *A New Ballad of a Famous German Prince*, 'not to bee said, but sung'. These are grounds sufficient for suspecting that Berkenhead edited *The Rump*.

APPENDIX VII

Nicholas's Unknown Agent

PROMINENT among the letters of intelligence that Sir Edward
Nicholas received from England in 1659 and 1660 are an interesting
and lively series from an unidentified agent who used a number of
different pseudonyms. The original letters are, with one exception,
now in the British Museum, MSS. Egerton 2533–62; they are reprinted in the *Nicholas Papers*, vol. iv, 1657–1660 (Camden Soc. 3rd
Ser. xxxi, 1920). They range from March to August 1659, with the
exception of one letter dated 16 March 1660, which is printed in
C.S.P. Dom., 1659–60, pp. 393–4.

Nicholas, on receiving the letters, endorsed all of them with the
name 'Miles' or 'Milles'; but the editor of the *Nicholas Papers*, G. F.
Warner, suggested that this too was a pseudonym.[1] As one refers to
'your friend Miles' being in town, and as in another the agent signs
himself 'W. Miles',[2] that assumption seems reasonable. In drawing
attention to some features of the letters which suggest that 'Milles'
may have been Berkenhead, it must be emphasized that the evidence
is not conclusive, but is sufficient to justify a cautious speculation.

It is known that Berkenhead was an agent for Nicholas in the late
1640s and early 1650s; and in one of Nicholas's cyphers, unfortunately undated but probably scrapped before 1659, his pseudonym was,
in fact, 'Mills'.[3] It is not impossible that in the easier conditions of 1659
he resumed his old *nom de plume*. Against this it must be recognized
that the writing in the letters is not like Berkenhead's normal hand;
but it was not unusual for agents to disguise their hand and Berkenhead as an accomplished scribe would have found no difficulty in
doing so.

It would have been harder for him to suppress his habitual expressions; and the occurrence of satirical motifs and turns of phrase
also found in Berkenhead's writing is worth looking into. The
raciness is kin to Berkenhead's: phrases like 'The Parliament sitt
very close and doe as little',[4] or the army officers 'seeke God for

---

[1] p. 88 n.
[3] B.M., MS. Egerton 2550, f. 32.

[2] pp. 147 and 157 respectively.
[4] p. 101.

councell and act there owne way',[1] follow a familiar pattern of sarcasm. Much of Miles's colourful imagery indicates that he was versed in the techniques of Cavalier satire. The language of the late 1640s newsbooks is frequently rehearsed: Miles writes ironically that 'The old foe, that grand enemy the Cavee, must be reviled and blowen upp into a formidable Hobgoblin',[2] and remarks that the Londoners are sensible of their grievances but are ignorant 'howe to unhorse' the soldiers who oppress them.[3] 'The citty beast', he sneers, 'is as tame as a tyred jade that cannott soe much as kicke'.[4] This echoes Berkenhead in *Mercurius Bellicus*, telling the citizens that they were 'foundred Mules' and that their masters had 'ridden you like jades off your legs'.[5] And in 1660, in his pamphlet about Robert Tichbourne, Berkenhead again used this idea: 'Therefore when the Protector went first about to ride the great City he made use of us, as of two Bitts to rein his High-metal'd Steed.'[6] He also likened the House of Lords, where Tichbourne had sat, to Hell, to which he was going, and made him describe Hell as a place 'heated with perpetual fires even like a Glass-house'.[7] He also used the motif in his attack on Colonel Pride, where he compared the 'heats' in the Lords to the 'great heats' in Pride's old brewhouse.[8] Miles exploits the same image of the weather growing as 'hott as the members, and a moneth hence it may be thought convenient to adjourne ye hott Howse till a milder season'.[9] Again Miles's comment on the rehabilitation of the ejected members of the Long Parliament is like a jest in Berkenhead's *Paul's Church-Yard*, which had been reprinted in July 1659. Miles wrote: 'They entred the howse from the Paynted Chamber, as the beasts did the arke, in couples';[10] and Berkenhead had suggested 'That the Army ought to march but two abreast, since all creatures at Noah's Ark went by couples'.[11] Such resemblances are suggestive, but in the absence of further circumstantial evidence they must be treated warily. They could be just stock phrases. However, it is perfectly safe to state that Miles was a writer of more than ordinary satiric flair, and steeped in the idiom of Royalist propaganda. He was a skilled reporter with an eye for illuminating detail, though somewhat

---

[1] p. 122.
[2] p. 101.
[3] p. 171.
[4] p. 123.
[5] In nos. 13 (18–25 Apr. 1648), N3ʳ and 3 (8–14 Feb. 1648), C1ᵛ respectively.
[6] *The Apology of Robert Tichborn*, p. 5.
[7] Ibid.
[8] *The Last Words of Thomas Lord Pride* (1659), reprinted in *Harl. Misc.* iii. 141.
[9] p. 91.
[10] p. 134.
[11] *Two Centuries*, item 46 (*Harl. Misc.* ix. 411).

optimistic in his interpretation of the 'facts', and a mite over-confident of his own cleverness.[1] He also made it his business to keep a weather eye on the pamphlets pouring from the press;[2] and at one point he informed Nicholas that if only the people would attend to the unlicensed pamphlets, they would soon see the light.[3] There spoke a convinced propagandist.

Miles's ostensible reason for writing to Nicholas was to report on the progress of a lawsuit in Chancery. This was almost certainly mere camouflage, but it was a colouring that might easily have recommended itself to Berkenhead, allied as he was with the Finch family. Miles's anxiety to have his services brought to the King's attention[4] would also be in character for Berkenhead. If he was serving Nicholas as correspondent it would help explain how he came to the fore so rapidly at the Restoration. Still, as matters stand it can only be argued that there is nothing to exclude the possibility that Berkenhead was Nicholas's unknown informant, and not a little to sustain it.

[1] p. 162.
[2] pp. 102, 139, 154, 157, 167–8, 171, 177, and *C.S.P. Dom.*, 1659–60, pp. 393–4.
[3] p. 152.
[4] See the reply from Nicholas in Jan. 1660 (*C.S.P. Dom.*, 1659–60, pp. 304–5). He assured 'Milles' that the King had been informed of his diligence and was greatly pleased with it. The tone of his remarks suggests that 'Milles' had asked Nicholas to speak to the King about him.

BIBLIOGRAPHY

WHEREVER possible modern reprints of Berkenhead's works have been consulted and will be found listed in this Bibliography in addition to all the extant contemporary editions. Where no reprints exist, pressmarks of original copies of his pamphlets are given, unless they are available in both the British Museum and the Bodleian Library. This rule has been followed for important pamphlets by other writers too. In the case of newsbooks, the location of complete sets of those by Berkenhead is indicated; but that of other newsbooks has not been listed. In most instances the sets in the Bodleian are incomplete, and it has usually been necessary to consult the copies in the Thomason Collection. Pressmarks for these are readily accessible in G. R. Fortescue's *Catalogue of the Thomason Tracts*.

BERKENHEAD'S WORKS[1]

NEWSBOOKS

Mercurius Aulicus. Oxford, pr. by Henry Hall for W. Webb, 1643–5, 4°, repr. London, by Richard Royston? Complete sets in the Library of Corpus Christi College, Oxford, and in the Thomason Collection in the B.M.

Mercurius Bellicus. London, 1648, 4°. B.M., E. 427–9, 431–7, 443–4, 446–9, 451–4.

*Mercurius Publicus. London, pr. by John Macock, Thomas Newcombe, D. Maxwell, etc., 1660–1663, 4°. Bodleian Library, Wood 393–4, 520–1; from no. 15 (1660 on), B.M., Burney 54–61.

*Parliamentary Intelligencer, The. Pr. as *Mercurius Publicus*; from January 1661 called *The Kingdomes Intelligencer*, and repr. in Edinburgh.

PAMPHLETS

Answer to a Speech Without Doores, An. London, 1646, 4°, 8 pp.
Another edn., 1646, 4°, 8 pp.
Another edn., 1646, 4°, 8 pp.

*Apology of Robert Tichborn and John Ireton, The. London, 1660, 4°, 8 pp.

Assembly Man, The. London, pr. for Richard Marriot, 1663, 4°, 22 pp.
Another edn., for Walter Davis, London, 1681, 4°, 16 pp.
Another edn., for Walter Davis, London, 1682 (in *Wit and Loyalty Reviv'd*).
Another edn., London, 1704, 4°.
Another edn., 1730 (in *A Collection of Tracts*).
Another edn., *Harl. Misc.* v. 98–104.

---

[1] Works newly attributed to Berkenhead are marked with *.

Another edn., *S. Tracts*, v. 487–93.

B.M., MS. Harleian 3638, ff. 82–8.

Bibliotheca Parliamenti. London, 1653.
 First 'Classis', 4°, 8 pp.
 Another edn., 4°, 8 pp.
 Second 'Classis', 4°, 8 pp.
 Another edn., 12°, 12 pp.
 Another edn., *S. Tracts*, vii. 92–7.
 Another 'Classis' (including items from the first) in *Two Centuries of Paul's Church-Yard*, 1653, 8°.

Cabala, or An Impartial Account. London, 1663, 4°, 40 pp.
 Second edn., corr., London, 1663, 4°, 40 pp.
 Another edn., *S. Tracts*, vii. 567–86.

★*Cittie Dog in a Saints Doublet, A*. London, 1648, 4°, 8 pp. B.M., E. 543 (24).

★*Discourse Discovering some Mysteries of our New State, A*. Oxford, pr. by L. Lichfield, 1645, 4°, 44 pp.

★*Earle of Pembrokes Last Speech, The*. London, 1650, 4°, 8 pp.
 Another edn., London, 1680, s.sh., 4 pp.
 Another edn., *S. Tracts*, vii. 89–92.

★*Earle of Pembrokes Speech in the House of Peeres, Upon the Debate of the Cities Petition, The*. London, 1648, 4°, 16 pp.
 Another edn., *S. Tracts*, vii. 79–86.

★*Exaltation of Christmas Pye, The*. London, 1659, 4°, 12 pp. Bodleian Library, Wood 613 (13).
 Another edn., London, for J. Roberts, 1728, 16 pp. B.M., 1480 aaa13.

★*Last Words of Thomas Lord Pride, The*. London, 1659, 4°, 8 pp.
 Another edn., London, for C. W., 1680, 12 pp.
 Another edn., *Harl. Misc.* iii. 136–41.

★*Letter from Mercurius Civicus to Mercurius Rusticus, A*. Oxford, pr. by L. Lichfield, 1643, 4°, 36 pp.
 Another edn., *S. Tracts*, iv. 580–98.

★*Mercurius Anti-Britanicus*. Oxford, pr. by L. Lichfield, 1645, 4°, 32 pp. In three parts: the first titled as above; the second titled *Mercurius Anti-Britannicus; or, Part of the King's Cabinet Vindicated;* and the third titled *Mercurius Anti-Britanicus; or, The Second Part of the Kings Cabinet Vindicated*. Second part of the Bodleian Library set is defective; a perfect copy of that is B.M., E. 296 (9).

Newes from Pembroke and Montgomery. London, 1648, 4°, 8 pp.
 Another edn., London, 1648, 4°, 8 pp.
 Another edn., London, 1648, 4°, 8 pp.
 Another edn., *Harl. Misc.* v. 112–14.

Paul's Church-Yard. London, 1651 and 1652, 4°.
   First 'Centuria', 1651, 8 pp.
   Another edn., 1651?, 8 pp.
   Another edn., 1659, 8 pp.
   Second 'Centuria', 1652, 8 pp.
   Another edn., 1652?, 8 pp.
   Another edn., 1652?, 8 pp.
   Another edn., 1659, 8 pp.
   Another edn., of both, entitled *Two Centuries* (see below).
   Third 'Centuria', 1652, 8 pp. B.M., E. 675 (12).

Speech Without Doores Defended Without Reason, The. London, 1646, 4°, 12 pp.
   B.M., E. 365 (14).

Two Centuries of Paul's Church-Yard. London, 1653, 8°, 64 pp. This includes the
   first and second parts of *Paul's Church-Yard* and another edn. of *Bibliotheca Parliamenti.*
   Another edn., *Harl. Misc.* ix. 408–21.

PREFACES BY BERKENHEAD

★*Battaile on Hopton Heath, The.* Oxford, pr. by H. Hall, 1643, 4°. On A2ʳ.

★*Cooper's Hill,* by Sir John Denham. Sixth edn., corr., London, pr. for Humphrey Moseley, 1655, 4°. The Preface is repr. by J. C. Reed in 'Humphrey
   Moseley, Publisher', *Oxford Bibl. Soc. Proceedings and Papers,* ii (1927), 111.

Itinerary Contayning a Voyage through Italy, An, by John Raymond. London,
   pr. for Humphrey Moseley, 1648, 12°. Berkenhead's Letter occupies
   A6ʳ–A9ᵛ.

*Sermon Preached before His Majestie at Christ-Church in Oxford, on the 3 Novemb.
   1644, A,* by Thomas Morton. Berkenhead's Dedication occupies π2ʳ⁻ᵛ of
   this sermon, printed by Henry Hall at Oxford, 1644, 4°.

Zootomia; or, Observations on the Present Manners of the English, by Richard
   Whitlock. London, pr. for Humphrey Moseley, 1654, 8°. Berkenhead's
   Preface first appears in the second issue (copy in London Guildhall Lib-
   rary) and occupies A5ʳ⁻ᵛ. The work was repr. in 1664 and 1679. An
   extract of the Preface is repr. in George Williamson, *Seventeenth Century
   Contexts* (1960).

VERSES

These are listed by first lines; titles, where they exist, are given in italics.

The following abbreviations have been used in listing reprints:

The Rump	*The Rump, or A Collection of Songs and Ballads,* London, pr. for H. Brome and H. Marsh, 1660.
Rump: or	*Rump: or An Exact Collection of Songs and Ballads,* London, pr. for H. Brome and H. Marsh, 1662; repr. 1874.

A. & D.   Henry Lawes's *Ayres and Dialogues*, London, pr. by T. H. for John Playford, 1653.

Sec. A. & D.   Henry Lawes's *Second Book of Ayres and Dialogues*, London, pr. by T. H. for John Playford, 1655. There is a copy of this in the B.M.

Sel. A. & D.   Henry Lawes's *Select Ayres and Dialogues*, London, pr. by W. Godbid for John Playford, 1669.

W. & M.   *Wit and Mirth*. This title was given to a number of song-books in the later seventeenth century. The editions are identified by date in the list below.

All Christians and Lay-Elders too. 156 ll. *The Four Legg'd Elder*. Brs., London, 1647; repr. London, 1677, for D. Mallet; *Bibliotheca Parliamenti*, 1653; *The Rump*, pp. 1–5; *Rump: or*, i. 350–4; *W. & M*., 1682, pp. 76 ff.; 1707, iii. 9–12; 1712, iii. 9–12; 1719, v. 1–4; *Songs Compleat, Pleasant and Divertive*, 1719, v. 1–4; *A Collection of Loyal Songs*, 1731, ii. 14–19.

All that have two or but one eare. 180 or 192 ll. *The Four-Legg'd Quaker*. Brs., London, 1659; *Ratts Rhimed to Death*, 1659, pp. 73–8; *The Rump*, pp. 9–14; *Rump: or*, i. 358–62; *W. & M*., 1682, pp. 81 ff.; *A Collection of Loyal Songs*, 1731, i. 235–42.

All you that have, or ought to have, no eares. 120 ll. *To the Great Master of his Art my Honoured F. Mr. Henry Lawes on his Book of Ayres*. Sec. *A. & D*., b3ʳ–b4ʳ.

Among rose buds slept a bee. 16 ll. *Sec. A. & D*., p. 36.

As the great world, built in a week, shall lye. 240 ll. *In Memory of Mr. William Cartwright*. Cartwright's *Comedies, Tragi-comedies, with Other Poems*, London, pr. for Humphrey Moseley, 1651, *8ʳ–[*11]ʳ.

Away, away, Anacreon. 12 ll. *Anacreons Ode Englished*. Sec. *A. & D*., p. 40.

Blood! and a Kings! and such a Kings! and that. 240 ll. *Loyalties Tears*. London, 1649, 8°. B.M., E. 561 (15). Another edn., London, 1650, 4°. B.M., E. 1244 (3).

Day's return'd, and so are we to pay, The. 32 ll. *An Anniversary on the Nuptials of John Earle of Bridgewater*. *A. & D*., p. 33; repr. by W. McClung Evans, *Henry Lawes, Musician and Friend of Poets* (New York, 1941), pp. 192–3; Bodleian Library, MS. Rawl. Poet. 147, p. 155.

Felicis aevi ac praesulis natus. 8 ll. Latin verses pr. on the frontispiece of Beaumont and Fletcher, *Comedies and Tragedies*, London, pr. for Humphrey Moseley, 1647; repr. in Beaumont and Fletcher, *Fifty Comedies and Tragedies*, London, for J. Macock, etc., 1679; and in *The Works*, ed. Arnold Glover and A. R. Waller (1905–12), vol. i, p. iv.

Fletcher arise, usurpers share thy bayes. 122 ll. *On the Happy Collection of Master Fletcher's Works, never before Printed*. Beaumont and Fletcher, *Comedies and Tragedies*, London, pr. for Humphrey Moseley, 1647, E1ᵛ–E2ᵛ; repr. in Beaumont and Fletcher, *Fifty Comedies and Tragedies*, London, for

J. Macock etc., 1679, A3^v; and in *The Works*, ed. Arnold Glover and A. R. Waller (1905–12), vol. i, pp. xli–xliv.

Here Jenkyns stands, who thundering from the Tower. 6 ll. *The Works of . . . Judge David Jenkins*, London, pr. for J. Gyles, 1648, on the frontispiece portrait; repr. in the 1681 and 1683 edns. of *The Works*, and in Wood, *Ath. Oxon.* iii. 645, where there are two extra lines omitted by the engraver in 1648.

I long to sing the seidge of Troy. 14 ll. *Anacreon's Ode, call'd The Lute, Englished. A. & D.*, p. 27; repr. E. F. Rimbault, *The Ancient Vocal Music of England*, no. 5 (1847). Bodleian Library, MSS. Mus. Sch. c. 71, p. 81, and Rawl. Poet. 147, p. 156.

It fell on a day. 72 ll. *A Jolt on Michaelmas Day*, 1654, *The Rump*, pp. 15–18; *Rump: or*, i. 363–6; *A Collection of Loyal Songs* (1731), ii. 20–23; W. Walker Wilkins, *Political Ballads of the Seventeenth and Eighteenth Centuries* (1860), i. 121–4.

Madam, your beauty (I confess). 18 ll. *An Old Knight, to a Young Lady. Sel. A. & D.*, p. 88; *W. & M.* (1714), p. 348; (1719), p. 352; *Songs Compleat, Pleasant and Divertive* (1719), p. 352.

Now let them vote, declare, contrive. 48 ll. *Musarum Oxoniensium Epibateria*, Oxford, pr. by L. Lichfield, 1643, 2A^{r-v}.

Now, Lucatia, now make haste. 24 ll. *No Reprieve. Sec. A. & D.*, pp. 3–4; *Sel. A. & D.*, pp. 3–4; Bodleian Library, MS. Mus. Sch. F. 572, ff. 86–7. Repr. by P. W. Souers, *The Matchless Orinda* (Harvard Univ. Press, 1931), p. 61 n.

O how I hate thee now, and my selfe too. 20 ll. *Sec. A. & D.*, p. 14; *Sel. A. & D.*, p. 16.

O King of Heav'n and Hell, of Sea and Earth. 14 ll. *Orpheus Hymn to God. Sec. A. & D.*, pp. 47–8; *Sel. A. & D.*, pp. 46–7.

Second part, I here indite, A. 144 ll. *The Second Part of the Late and Terrible Fight on St. James's Day, One Thousand 666.* Brs., London, 1666; repr. *Naval Songs and Ballads*, ed. C. H. Firth (1908), pp. 76–9.

There happen'd of late a terrible fray. 144 ll. *A New Ballad of a Famous German Prince and a Renowned English Duke.* Brs., London, 1666; repr. Edinburgh, 1666; repr. *Naval Songs and Ballads*, ed. C. H. Firth (1908), pp. 72–5. Bodleian Library, MS. Don. b. 8, pp. 341–4.

Two hundred minutes have run down. 24 ll. *Staying in London after the Act for Banishment, and going to meet a Friend who fail'd the hour appoynted. A. & D.*, p. 34; Bodleian Library, MS. Rawl. Poet. 147, p. 156.

Villaines now are ripe, let's pay our vow, The. 58 ll. *Verses on the Death of the Right Valiant Sr Bevill Grenvill*, Oxford, pr. by L. Lichfield, 1643, pp. 15–17; repr. in *Verses by the University of Oxford on the Death of . . . Sr B. Grenville* (London, 1684), pp. 12–13.

PRIMARY SOURCES

MANUSCRIPTS

Bodleian Library

MS. Add. C. 209, autograph works by John Taylor, the Water-Poet.

MS. Clarendon, manuscripts of the first Earl of Clarendon, being State Papers relating to the Civil War, Commonwealth, and Restoration periods.

MS. Don. b. 8., Sir William Haward's Collection, mostly relating to the reign of Charles II to 1681.

MSS. Rawlinson, including papers formerly belonging to Archbishop Sancroft.

MSS. Tanner, including papers formerly belonging to Archbishop Sancroft.

MSS. Univ. Oxon. Arch., Registers etc. of the University of Oxford.

All Souls College

Admission Book.

Benefactors' Register.

Warden of All Souls College MS. 51, an eighteenth-century history of the Fellows.

British Museum

MSS. Egerton, including papers formerly belonging to Sir Edward Nicholas.

MSS. Harleian, including miscellaneous historical papers.

MSS. Lansdowne, including papers relating to English ecclesiastical history formerly belonging to White Kennett.

Public Record Office

State Papers, Domestic, 1648–9, 1661–2, and 1666–7.

Institution Books (Sec. B.), 1660–1721, vol. i.

Chancery Proceedings, 1676.

Somerset House

P.C.C. Wills, 1655 and 1679.

Cheshire Record Office, Chester

Wills and Inventories of the family of Berkenhead of Northwich and Witton, Cheshire, 1636, 1661, 1674, and 1678.

List of Feoffees of Witton School, up to 1722.

Church of St. Helens, Northwich

Witton Chapel Register, 1561–1678.

CONTEMPORARY PERIODICALS AND SERIALS

Anti-Aulicus, 1643.

Antidote against the Malignant Influence of Mercurius (surnamed) Aulicus, An, 1643. Copy in Yale Univ. Library.

Britaines Remembrancer, 1644.

Britanicus Vapulans, 1643; continued as *Mercurius Urbanus.*

Certaine Informations, 1643–4.

Court Mercurie, The, 1644.

Diutinus Britanicus, 1646; continued as *Mercurius Diutinus.*

Kingdomes Weekly Intelligencer, The, 1643–9.

Letter from a Minister in His Excellencies Army, A, 1643; continued as *The Second Intelligencer from Reading, The Third Intelligencer,* and *The Last Joyfull Intelligencer.*

London Post, The, 1644–5.

Mercurius Anti-Mercurius, 1648.

Mercurius Anti-Pragmaticus, 1647–8.

Mercurius Britanicus, 1643–6.

Mercurius Britanicus (a counterfeit), 1644; continued as *Mercurius Aulico-Mastix.*

Mercurius Britannicus, 1648.

Mercurius Civicus, 1643–6.

Mercurius Elencticus, 1647–9.

Mercurius Melancholicus, 1647–9.

Mercurius Pragmaticus, 1647–50.

Scotish Dove, The, 1643–6.

Spie, The, 1644.

True Informer, The, 1643–5.

Welch Mercurie, The, 1643–4.

CONTEMPORARY PAMPHLETS

Answer to Mercurius Aulicus, An, 1643. B.M., E. 79 (14).

Arraignment of Mercurius Aulicus, The, 1645. See *Newes from Smith.*

Booker, John, *No Mercurius Aquaticus,* 1644. B.M., E. 2 (22).

Chaloner, Thomas, *An Answer to the Scotch Papers,* 1646.

Cleaveland, John, *The Character of a London Diurnall,* 1645; reprinted in *Character Writings of the Seventeenth Century,* ed. H. Morley, 1891.

Devills White Boyes, The, 1644. B.M., E. 14 (11).

Featley, Daniel, *The Gentle Lash,* Oxford, 1644.

—— *Sacra Nemesis,* Oxford, 1644.

Full Answer to a Scandalous Pamphlet, A, 1645.

L'Estrange, Roger, *Considerations and Proposals in order to the Regulation of the Press,* 1663.

Lilburne, John, *England's Birthright,* 1645. B.M., E. 304 (17).

Looke about you, or the Fault-finder, 1647. B.M., E. 398 (25).

Marshall, Stephen, *A Copy of a Letter Written by Mr. Stephen Marshall,* 1643.

Martin, Henry, *A Corrector of the Answerer to the Speech out of Doores,* Edinburgh, 1646.

Marvell, Andrew, *A Seasonable Argument,* Amsterdam, 1677; reprinted in *Hansard's Parliamentary History,* vol. iv, 1660–1688, App. III.

Milton, John, *Areopagitica,* 1644.

Muzzle for Cerberus, A, 1648. B.M., E. 449 (3).

Newes from Smith . . . with the Arraignment of Mercurius Aulicus, 1645. B.M., E. 27 (13).

Oxford Character of the London Diurnall Examined, The, 1645. B.M., E. 274 (32).

Parliament Letanie, The, 1647. B.M., E. 409 (17).

Prynne, William, *Canterburies Doom,* 1646.

—— *A Checke to Brittanicus,* 1644. B.M., E. 253 (1).

—— *A Fresh Discovery,* 1645.

Recantation of Mercurius Aulicus, or Berkinheads Complaint, The, 1644. B.M., E. 37 (17).

Robinson, Henry, *Liberty of Conscience, or the Sole Means,* 1644. B.M., E. 39 (1).

Ruperts Sumpter, 1644. B.M., E. 2 (24).

True Character of Mercurius Aulicus, The, 1645. B.M., Burney 20 (1).

True Relation of the Great and Glorious Victory . . . Obtained by Sir William Waller, A, 1643. Bodleian Library, Wood 376 (20).

Whip for an Ape, A, 1645. B.M., E. 298 (18).

Other periodicals that have been of some use in the present study will be found listed, together with many of those above, in App. III.

PRINTED BOOKS

Aubrey, John, *Brief Lives,* ed. Andrew Clark, 2 vols. (1898).

Autobiography of Sir John Bramston, The (Camden Soc. xxxii, 1845).

Barnard, George, *Theologo-Historicus, or the True Life of Peter Heylin* (1683), repr. in vol. i of Heylin's *History of the Reformation,* ed. J. C. Robertson, for the Eccl. Hist. Soc. (1849).

Barwick, Peter, *The Life of Dr. John Barwick,* ed. G. F. Barwick (1903).

Beaumont, Francis, and Fletcher, John, *Comedies and Tragedies* (1647); see *The Works,* ed. Arnold Glover and A. R. Waller, ten vols. (1905–12).

Bold, Henry, *Latine Poems* (1685).

Burnet, Gilbert, *History of My Own Times,* ed. O. Airy, 2 vols. (1897–1900).

Butler, Samuel, *Characters,* ed. A. R. Waller (1908).

—— *Satires and Miscellanies,* ed. R. Lamar (1928).

Calendar of the Committee for Advance of Money, Domestic, 1642–56.

Calendar of the Committee for Compounding, Domestic, 1643–60.

C.S.P. Dom., 1636–78.

C.S.P. Ven., 1642–52.

Carte, Thomas, *A Collection of Original Letters and Papers*, 2 vols. (1739).

Cartwright, William, *Comedies, Tragi-comedies, with Other Poems*, (1651).

Clarendon State Papers, 3 vols. (1767–86).

Commons' Journals, 1640–87.

Conway Letters, ed. M. H. Nicholson (Yale Univ. Press, 1930).

Davies, John of Kidwelly, Savorsano's *La Picara* (1665), Rapin's *Observations on the Poems of Homer and Virgil* (1672).

Diary of John Milward, The, ed. Caroline Robbins (Cambridge, 1938).

Dryden, John, *Defence of an Essay of Dramatick Poesy* (1668).

—— 'Discourse of Satire', prefaced to his translation of Juvenal (1693).

Dugdale's Visitation of Lancashire, Part II (Chetham Soc. lxxxviii, 1873).

Elmes, James, *Memoirs of the Life of Sir Christopher Wren* (1823).

Evelyn, John, *Diary and Correspondence*, ed. William Bray (1906).

Genuine Remains of . . . Thomas Barlow (1693).

Grey, Anchitell, *Debates of the House of Commons, 1667–94*, 10 vols. (1769).

Heylin, Peter, 'Diary', publ. with his *Memorial of Bishop Waynflete* (Caxton Soc., 1851).

H.M.C., *5th Report* (1876).

H.M.C., *6th Report* (1877).

H.M.C., *7th Report* (1879).

H.M.C., *Finch* I (1913).

H.M.C., *Leyborne Popham* (1889).

H.M.C., *Ormonde*, N.S.I. (1902).

Hyde, Edward, Earl of Clarendon, *History of the Rebellion*, ed. W. D. Macray, 6 vols. (1888).

—— *Life of Edward Earl of Clarendon*, 2 vols., 1817.

Journal of Sir Samuel Luke (Oxon. Record Soc. xxix, xxxi, and xxxiii, 1947–53).

Kennett, White, *A Register and Chronicle Ecclesiastical and Civil* (1728).

Lancashire and Cheshire Wills and Inventories (Chetham Soc. N.S. iii, 1884).

Lancashire Funeral Certificates (Chetham Soc. lxxv, 1869).

Laud, William, *The History of the Troubles and Tryal of William Laud*, ed. H. Wharton (1695), vol. i of the 'Remains'.

—— *The Second Volume of the Remains of William Laud*, ed. E. Wharton (1700). See Laud's *Works*, ed. James Bliss, 7 vols. (1847–60), part of the Library of Anglo-Catholic Theology.

Lauderdale Papers, 1639–79, 3 vols. (Camden Soc. N.S. xxxiv, xxxvi, and xxxviii, 1884–5).

Lawes, Henry, *Ayres and Dialogue* (1653).

—— *The Second Book of Ayres and Dialogues* (1655).

Letter Books 1644–45 of Sir Samuel Luke, The, ed. H. G. Tibbutt for H.M.C. (1963).

Lloyd, David, *Memoires* (1668).

Lords' Journals, 1643–5.

Marvell, Andrew, *Poems and Letters*, ed. H. M. Margoliouth, 2 vols. (Oxford, 1952).

—— *The Rehearsal Transposed* (1672–3), repr. in the *Complete Works*, ed. A. B. Grosart, 4 vols. (1872–5).

—— *The Chequer Inn*, a ballad, repr. ibid.

Musarum Oxoniensium Epibateria (Oxford, 1643).

Nicholas Papers, 1641–60, 4 vols. (Camden Soc. N.S. xl, 1, lvii, and 3rd Ser. xxxi, 1886–1920).

Ottley, Papers, The, Part I (Trans. Shropshire Soc. 2nd Ser. vi, 1894).

Oxford Protestation Returns, 1641–2 (Oxford Record Soc. xxxvi, 1955).

Parliamentary Diary of Sir Edward Dering, The, ed. B. D. Henning, (Yale Univ. Press, 1940).

Philips, Katherine, *Poems* (1664).

Register of the Visitors of the University of Oxford, 1647–58, (Camden Soc. N.S. xxix, 1881).

Registers of the Stationers' Company, 1640–1708, 3 vols. (1913–14).

Registrum Orielense, ed. C. L. Shadwell, 2 vols. (1893–1902).

Restoration Visitation of the University of Oxford and its Colleges (Camden Soc. 3rd Ser. lxxix, no. 3, 1948).

Rump, or a Collection of Songs and Ballads, The (1660).

Stanley Papers, The, 5 vols. (Chetham Soc. xxix, xxxi, lxvi, lxvii, and lxx, 1853–67).

Vernon, George, *The Life of . . . Dr. Peter Heylyn* (1682).

Verses on the Death of the Right Valiant Sr. Bevill Grenvill (Oxford, 1643); second edn., 1684.

Wills from Doctors' Commons, 1495–1695, ed. J. G. Nicholson and J. Bruce (Camden Soc. lxxxiii, 1863).

Wood, Anthony, *Athenae Oxonienses*, ed. Philip Bliss, 4 vols. (1813–20).

—— *Fasti Oxonienses*, ed. Philip Bliss, 2 parts (1815–20).

—— *The History and Antiquities of the University of Oxford*, ed. John Gutch, 3 vols. (1792–6).

SECONDARY SOURCES

BOOKS

Bergson, Henri, *Laughter* (1900), translated by C. Brereton and F. Rothwell (1935).

Bosher, R. S., *The Making of the Restoration Settlement, 1649–1662* (1951).

Bourne, H. R. Fox, *English Newspapers*, 2 vols. (1887).

Browning, Andrew, *Thomas Osborne . . . Earl of Danby, 1632–1712*, 3 vols. (1944–51).

Bush, Douglas, *English Literature in the Earlier Seventeenth Century* (Oxford, 1962).

Calendar of the Clarendon State Papers, 1523–1660, ed. W. D. Macray and F. J. Routledge, 4 vols. (1869–1932).

Cibber, Theophilus, *Lives of the Poets*, 5 vols. (1753).

Collins, D. C., *A Handlist of News Pamphlets, 1590–1610* (1943).

Couper, W. J., *The Edinburgh Periodical Press*, 2 vols. (1908).

Coxe, H. O., *Catalogus Codd. MSS. in Collegiis Aulisque Oxon.*, 2 vols. (1852).

Dahl, Folke, *A Bibliography of English Corantos and Periodical Newsbooks, 1620–1642* (Bibliographical Soc., 1952).

Day, C. L., and E. B. Murrie, *English Song-Books, 1651–1702, A Bibliography* (1940).

Dictionary of National Biography, 22 vols. (1921–2).

Emden, C. S., *Oriel Papers* (1948).

Evans, G. B., *The Plays and Poems of William Cartwright* (Univ. of Wisconsin Press, 1951).

Evans, W. McClung, *Henry Lawes, Musician and Friend of Poets* (New York, 1941).

Fortescue, G. K., *Catalogue of the Thomason Tracts, 1640–1661*, 2 vols. (1908).

Foster, Joseph, *Alumni Oxonienses, 1500–1714*, 4 vols. (1891–2).

Frank, Joseph, *The Beginnings of the English Newspaper* (Cambridge, Mass., 1961).

—— *The Levellers* (Harvard Univ. Press, 1935).

Gardiner, S. R., *History of the Commonwealth and Protectorate, 1649–1660*, 3 vols. (1894–1901).

—— *History of the Great Civil War, 1642–1649*, 3 vols. (1886–1891).

George, M. D., *English Political Caricature to 1792* (1959).

Gordon, G. S., *English Literature and the Classics* (1912).

Grantees of Arms . . . to the End of the Seventeenth Century (Harleian Soc. lxvi, 1915).

Harbage, Alfred, *Cavalier Drama* (New York, 1936).

Hazlitt, W. C., *Bibliographical Collections and Notes*, 3rd Ser. (1887).

—— *Hand-Book to Early English Literature* (1867).

Hearne, Thomas, *Collections*, vol. iii, 1710–12 (Oxford Hist. Soc. xiii, 1888).

Henning, B. D., *The Representation of Wiltshire in the Long Parliament of Charles II*, Yale Ph.D. thesis (1937). There is a microfilm copy of this in the keeping of the History of Parliament Trust in London.

Herford, C. H., *Studies in the Literary Relations of England and Germany in the Sixteenth Century* (1886).

Hill, J. E. C., *The Century of Revolution, 1603–1714* (1961).

Jack, Ian, *Augustan Satire* (1952).

Kernan, Alvin, *The Cankered Muse* (Yale Univ. Press, 1959).

Kitchen, George, *Sir Roger L'Estrange* (1913).

Leach, Clifford, *The Fletcher Plays* (1962).

Madan, Falconer, *Oxford Books*, vol. ii, 1641–1650 (1912).

Mallet, C. E., *A History of the University of Oxford*, vol. ii, 'The Sixteenth & Seventeenth Centuries' (1924).

Milford, R. T., and Sutherland, D. M., *A Catalogue of English Newspapers in the Bodleian Library, 1622–1800* (1936).

Muddiman, J. G., *The King's Journalist, 1659–1689* (1923). See also Williams, J. B. (pseud.).

Narrative of the Indictment of the Traitors of Whalley and Cartmell, 1536–7, The (Chetham Soc. N.S. xc, 1931).

Nicholas, Donald, *Mr. Secretary Nicholas (1593–1669)* (1955).

Ormerod, G., *History of Cheshire*, ed. T. Helsby, 3 vols. (1882).

Pearl, Valerie, *London and the Outbreak of the Puritan Revolution* (1961).

Peter, John, *Complaint and Satire in Early English Literature* (1956).

Pinto, V. de S., *The Poetical and Dramatic Works of Sir Charles Sedley*, 2 vols. (1928).

Previte-Orton, C. W., *Political Satire in English Poetry* (1910).

Records of the Royal Society of London, revised ed. (1912).

Richards, E. A., *Hudibras in the Burlesque Tradition* (New York, 1937).

Shaw, Wm. A., *The Knights of England*, 2 vols. (1905).

Souers, P. W., *The Matchless Orinda* (Harvard Univ. Press, 1931).

South Lancashire in the Reign of Edward II (Chetham Soc. 3rd Ser. i, 1949).

Summary Catalogue of Western Manuscripts in the Bodleian Library, 7 vols. (1895–1953).

Thompson, E. N. S., *Literary Bypaths of the Renaissance* (Yale Univ. Press, 1924).

Trevor-Roper, H. R., *Archbishop Laud, 1573–1645* (1940).

Van Gundy, J. L., *'Ignoramus' . . . An Examination Of Its Sources and Literary Influence* (Lancaster, Pa., 1906).

Varley, F. J., *The Siege of Oxford* (1932).

Venn, John, and Venn, J. A., *Alumni Cantabrigienses (Part I to 1751)*, 4 vols. (1922–7).

Wallis, L. B., *Fletcher, Beaumont & Company, Entertainers to the Jacobean Gentry* (New York, 1947).

Wedgwood, C. V., *Poetry and Politics under the Stuarts* (1960).

Weston, J., *Historical Notes and Records of the Parish Church, Northwich* (1908).

Williams, J. B., *A History of English Journalism* (1908). See also Muddiman, J. G.

Williamson, George, *Seventeenth Century Contexts* (1960).

Wilson, F. P., *Seventeenth Century Prose* (1960).

Wing, Donald, *Short-Title Catalogue . . . 1641–1700*, 3 vols. (Colombia Univ. Press, New York, 1945–51).

Winstanley, William, *Lives of the Most Famous English Poets* (1687).

Witcombe, D. T., *Charles II and the Cavalier House of Commons, 1663–1674*, (Manchester Univ. Press, 1966).

ARTICLES

'A List of the Representatives in Parliament from 1295–1832 from the County and Burroughs of Wiltshire', *Wiltshire Arch. and Nat. Hist. Magazine*, xlvii, 1935–7.

Beaumont, H., 'Arthur, Lord Capel, The King's Lieutenant-General for Shropshire, 1643', *Trans. Shropshire Soc.* x (1939–40).

Brooks, H. F., 'Rump Songs, An Index With Notes', *Oxford Bibl. Soc. Proceedings and Papers* v (1936–9).

Clyde, Wm. M., 'Parliament and the Press, 1643–7', *The Library*, 4th Ser. xiii (1932–3).

—— 'Parliament and the Press, II', *The Library*, 4th Ser. xiv (1933–4).

Crump, G. M., 'Thorn-Drury's Notes on Thomas Stanley', *Notes and Queries*, N.S. v (1958).

Emslie, Macdonald, 'Pepys's Songs and Songbooks in the Diary Period', *The Library*, 5th Ser. xii (1957).

Firth, C. H., 'Thomas Scot's Account of his Actions as Intelligencer during the Commonwealth', *Eng. Hist. Review*, xii (1897).

Hanson, L., 'The King's Printer at York and Shrewsbury, 1642–3', *The Library*, 4th Ser. xxiii (1943).

Lloyd, L. C., 'The Book Trade in Shropshire', *Trans. Shropshire Soc.* xlviii (1934–5).

'Pedigree of Middleton or Myddleton of Chirk Castle', *Miscellanea Genealogica et Heraldica*, 3rd Ser. ii (1896–7).

Philip, I. G., 'River Navigation at Oxford during the Civil War and Commonwealth', *Oxoniensia*, ii (1937).

Pritchard, J. E., 'The Earliest Bristol Printed Books', *Trans. Bristol and Gloucestershire Arch. Soc.* lvi (1934).

Reed, J. C., 'Humphrey Moseley, Publisher', *Oxford Bibl. Soc. Proceedings and Papers*, ii (1927–30).

Smith, G. C. Moore, 'Anthony Stafford', *Notes and Queries*, clii (1927).

Trevor-Roper, H. R., 'William Dell', *Eng. Hist. Review*, lxii (1947).

—— 'The Gentry, 1540–1640', *Econ. Hist. Review Supplements*, no. 1 (1953).

Williams, F. B., 'The Laudian Imprimatur', *The Library*, 5th Ser. xl (1960).

Williams, J. B., 'The Newsbooks and News-Letters of the Restoration', *Eng. Hist. Review*, xxiii (1908).

Wilson, F. P., 'The English Jestbooks of the Sixteenth and Early Seventeenth Centuries', repr. from *Huntington Library Quarterly*, ii (1939).

—— 'English Proverbs and Dictionaries of Proverbs', *The Library*, 4th Ser. xxvi (1945–6).

Parkes, M. B., Guide to the Records of the Faculty Office, typescript (1958).

INDEX

U

Index

same; *Mercurius Britanicus, see* Nedham; *Mercurius Britanicus* (counterfeit), 38 and n., 40, 89, 252; *Mercurius Britanicus* (1648), *see* Hall, John; *Mercurius Civicus, see* Collings; *Mercurius Clericus,* 150; *Mercurius Democritus,* 182; *Mercurius Domesticus,* 161; *Mercurius Elencticus,* 52, 150–2; *Mercurius Melancholicus,* 150–2; *Mercurius Morbicus,* 150; *Mercurius Politicus,* 10–11, 63–4; *Mercurius Pragmaticus,* and B.'s hand in, 150–2, 235 and n.; *Mercurius Publicus, see* Berkenhead, Sir John, *and* Muddiman; *Mercurius Rusticus, see* Ryves; *Mercurius Scoticus, see* Clarke; *Mercurius Zeteticus,* imitates Berkenhead, 182, 184 n.; *Military Scribe, The, see* Wray; *Parliament Scout, The, see* Dillingham; *Parliamentary Intelligencer, The, see* Muddiman; *Perfect Diurnall, A, see* Pecke; *Perfect Diurnall, A* (1649), *see* Rushworth; *Perfect Occurrences, The, see* Walker, Henry; *Publick Intelligencer, The, see Mercurius Politicus; Scotish Dove, The, see* Smith; *Spie, The,* quoted and cited, 30, 40, 42, 44, 87; *see also* Hotham, Durant; *Weekly Account, The,* quoted and cited, 46, 47, 129; *see also* Border.

Nicholas, Sir Edward, Secretary of State: recruits Heylin, 32; sponsors *Aulicus,* 42–3, 50, 59 and n., 76–7; employs B. as secret agent, 165, 174, 205, 264–6; sponsors *Publicus* and B., 64, 198, 212, 218, 228; who champions him against Benet, 210, 213, 218–20, 223–4.

— Sir John, his son, 218.

— Matthew, Dean of St. Paul's (Sir Edward's brother), 218.

Nonsense, satirically observed in the pulpit, 111, 149, 202–4; and other places, 162, 166–7, 207–8, 234. *See also* Fools *and* Ignoramuses.

North, Francis, Lord Guilford, 235.

Northwich, Cheshire: B.'s birth and upbringing there, 3–9, 236.

Nye, Philip, Independent preacher, satirized, 147, 152–3.

Oldsworth, Michael, the Earl of Pembroke's secretary, 93, 162.

Oliver, Dr. John, Laud's chaplain, 217.

Opportunism, *see under* Propaganda.

Ordination: a problem resolved, 18–19, 30 n., 114; a point of grievance, 85.

Ormonde, Marquis of, *see* Butler, James.

Osborne, Thomas, Earl of Danby, supported by B., 228–9.

Ostend, B. at, 194.

Ottley, Sir Francis, Governor of Shrewsbury, 50–1.

Oudart, Nicholas, Latin secretary to Charles II, 174.

Owen, Anne, Orinda's friend, 136–7, 189.

Oxford, City of: as Royalist headquarters and garrison, 21, 26, 28; printing at, 20–1, 28, 48–50, 116, 124–5; carriage of goods and information to, 45, 53–5; coverage in *Aulicus,* 70, 72; the Oxford Parliament, 78; siege and surrender, 129; Court at, in 1665, 234; mentioned, 99, 236.

Oxford University: B.'s matriculation, studies, degrees, and appointments at, 3, 8, 12–19, 34, 41 and n., 161, 209; the 'History' of, 23–4; B. takes Protestation, 25; 'the choicest Oxford Wits' sustain the Court, 26, 28, 99–102, 105–6; studies disrupted, 28; Fellows and 'giddy youth' help *Aulicus,* 29, 37, 39, 58; 1648 Visitation, 129 n., 185 n.; and B.'s response, 146, 153, 161–4 *passim,* 183; Parliament's thanks to, 232. **Bodleian Library**: B.'s gifts to, 185. **Colleges:** *All Souls,* B. a Fellow of, 16, 17–18; Nedham at, 17; B.'s gift of books to, 25 and n.; a manuscript history of the Fellows, 41 n.; the 1648 Visitation, 164, 183; the Fellows' Petition, 184; their continued interests in the Interregnum, 191; B. restored and resigns, 209, 234; B. on the 1648 ejections, 261. *Christ Church,* B.'s links with, 8, 14, 187 and n. *Oriel,* B. a servitor at, 13–14; and commoner, 17; ? his editorial office at, 38; Prynne at, 122–3. *The Queen's College,* 13, 130, 167–8. *St. John's,* and Laud, 22 n., 24, 123, 183.

Palmer, Dr. John, Warden of All Souls, 261.

Papers, Delivered in by the Commissioners of . . . Scotland, 131.

PRINTED IN GREAT BRITAIN
AT THE UNIVERSITY PRESS, OXFORD
BY VIVIAN RIDLER
PRINTER TO THE UNIVERSITY